LAW, SOCIETY, AND AUTHORITY IN LATE ANTIQUITY

Law, Society, and Authority in Late Antiquity

Edited by

RALPH W. MATHISEN

OXFORD
UNIVERSITY PRESS

OXFORD
UNIVERSITY PRESS

Great Clarendon Street, Oxford OX2 6DP

Oxford University Press is a department of the University of Oxford.
It furthers the University's objective of excellence in research, scholarship,
and education by publishing worldwide in

Oxford New York

Athens Auckland Bangkok Bogotá Buenos Aires Calcutta
Cape Town Chennai Dar es Salaam Delhi Florence Hong Kong Istanbul
Karachi Kuala Lumpur Madrid Melbourne Mexico City Mumbai
Nairobi Paris São Paulo Shanghai Singapore Taipei Tokyo Toronto Warsaw

and associated companies in Berlin Ibadan

Oxford is a registered trade mark of Oxford University Press
in the UK and certain other countries

Published in the United States
by Oxford University Press Inc., New York

First published 2001

British Library Cataloguing in Publication Data
Data available

Library of Congress Cataloging in Publication Data
Data applied for

ISBN 0-19-924032-9

1 3 5 7 9 10 8 6 4 2

Typeset by Graphicraft Limited, Hong Kong
Printed in Great Britain on acid-free paper
by Biddles Ltd., Guildford & King's Lynn

For daedala D.

Ruricius nostris facibus dulcique veneno
tactus votivum suspirat corde dolorem.
esset si praesens aetas, impenderet illi
Lemnias imperium, Cressa stamen labyrinthi,
Alceste vitam, Circe herbas, poma Calypso,
Scylla comas, Atalanta pedes, Medea furores,
Hippodame ceras, cygno Iove nata coronam,
huic Dido in ferrum, simul in suspendia Phyllis,
Evadne in flammas et Sestias isset in undas . . .

Sidonius Apollinaris, *Carmina* 11. 63–71

Preface

The sixteen studies presented below are the culmination of the work of participants at the second biannual 'Shifting Frontiers in Late Antiquity' conference, held at the University of South Carolina in March, 1997. All but one, that of the volume's editor, were presented orally at the conference, and all have undergone further extensive restyling and revision, not only as a result of discussions at the conference but also so as to fit the theme of this volume.

Both the conference and this collection could not have been produced without the lavish assistance of both individuals and institutions. The conference was generously funded by The College of Liberal Arts, The Office of the Provost, and the Departments of History, English, Philosophy, Religious Studies, and French and Classics, all of the University of South Carolina. Dr Peter Becker, Chair of the Department of History at the time, was especially forthcoming with both financial and moral support. Additional thanks are due to the USC Late Antiquity graduate student corps of Timothy Cox, Allen Jones, Tracy Keefer (who also served as Administrative Assistant), Walter Roberts, and Wendell Tate, for doing yeoman service ranging from registration work to chauffeuring duties. The production of this volume itself benefited at an early stage from the editorial advice of Gillian Clark, Jill Harries, and Hagith Sivan; and particular thanks are due to Gillian for her coordination across the water with Oxford University Press. Thanks are also extended to the two anonymous referees for the press whose criticisms and encouragement resulted in a much finer final product. It also goes without saying that without the unflagging encouragement, cogent advice, and genuine interest of Hilary O'Shea, Classics Editor for Oxford University Press, this book never could have been produced. And finally, profound thanks and appreciation are extended to the authors, whose commitment to creating studies of high scholarly merit (while at the same time putting up with my pestering, badgering, and occasional alteration of their deathless prose) is most truly appreciated.

Columbia, SC
22 July 1999

Contents

PART II. The Impact of Law on Society

List of Contributors

ANTTI ARJAVA, Institutum Classicum, University of Helsinki
GILLIAN CLARK, Department of Classics and Ancient History, University of Bristol
LESLIE DOSSEY, Department of History, Loyola University
VICTORIA ERHART, Catholic University of America
GEOFFREY GREATREX, Department of History, Dalhousie University
JUDITH EVANS GRUBBS, Department of Classical Studies, Sweet Briar College
JILL D. HARRIES, Department of Ancient History, St. Salvator's College, University of St. Andrews
MICHAEL E. JONES, Department of History, Bates College
NOEL E. LENSKI, Department of Classics, University of Colorado-Boulder
RALPH W. MATHISEN, Dept. of History, University of South Carolina-Columbia
JOHN F. MATTHEWS, Department of Classics, Yale University
KATHY F. PEARSON, Department of History, Old Dominion University
CATHERINE R. PEYROUX, Department of History, Duke University
BOUDEWIJN SIRKS, J. W. Goethe-Universität
HAGITH S. SIVAN, Department of History, University of Kansas
DENNIS E. TROUT, Department of Classics, University of Missouri-Columbia

Abbreviations

AASS	*Acta sanctorum*
ACO	E. Schwartz (ed.), *Acta conciliorum oecumenicorum* (Berlin, 1965 ff.)
CCL	*Corpus Christianorum, series Latina*
CJ	*Codex Justinianus*: P. Krüger (ed.), *Corpus juris civilis*, ii, *Codex Justinianus* (Berlin, 1954)
Collat. Mos.	M. Hyamson, *Mosaicarum et Romanarum legum collatio* (London, 1913).
Consult.	*Consultatio veteris cujusdam jurisconsulti*: A. Vargas Valencia (ed.), *Consulta de un jurisconsulto antiguo* (Mexico City, 1991).
Corp. leg.	G. F. Hänel (ed.), *Corpus legum ab imperatoribus romanis ante Iustinianum latarum, quae extra constitutionum codices supersunt. Accedunt res ab imperatoribus gestae, quibus romani iuris historia et imperii status illustratur* (Leipzig, 1857–60; repr. Aalen, 1965)
CSCO	*Corpus scriptorum Christianorum orientalium*
CSEL	*Corpus scriptorum ecclesiasticorum Latinorum*
CTh	*Codex Theodosianus*: T. Mommsen, P. M. Meyer, P. Krüger (eds.), *Theodosiani libri XVI cum constitutionibus sirmondianis et leges novellae ad Theodosianum pertinentes* (3 vols.) (Berlin, 1905; repr. 1970–1)

Epist. imp.	O. Guenther (ed.), *Epistulae imperatorum pontificum aliorum inde ab a. CCCLXVII usque ad a. DLIII datae avellana quae dicitur collectio*, *CSEL* 35. 1–2 (Vienna, 1895–8).
FIRA	S. Riccobono, J. Baviera, C. Ferrini, J. Furlani, V. Arangio-Ruiz (eds.), *Fontes iuris Romani antejustiniani. In usum scholarum*² (3 vols.) (Florence, 1940–3; repr. Florence, 1968–72)
Fontes	K. G. Bruns, Th. Mommsen, O. Gradenwitz (eds.), *Fontes iuris romani antiqui*⁷ (2 vols.) (Tübingen, 1909; repr. Aalen, 1958 and 1969)
ILCV	E. Diehl ed., *Inscriptiones Latinae Christianae veteres* (Berlin, 1925–1931)
ILS	H. Dessau, *Inscriptiones Latinae selectae* (5 vols.) (Berlin, 1954)
Ius Graecoromanum	C. R. Zacharia, A. Lingenthal (eds.), *Ius Graecoromanum. Vol. 1. Novellae et aureae bullae imperatorum post Justinianum* (Athens, 1931; repr. Aalen, 1962)
Jones, *LRE*	A. H. M. Jones, *The Later Roman Empire* AD *284–640: A Social, Economic, and Administrative Survey* (Norman, Okla., 1964)
MGH AA	*Monumenta Germaniae historica, Auctores antiquissimi*
MGH Epist.	*Monumenta Germaniae historica, Epistulae*
MGH Leg.	*Monumenta Germaniae historica, Leges*
MGH Poet.	*Monumenta Germaniae historica, Poetae Latini*
MGH SRM	*Monumenta Germaniae historica, Scriptores rerum Merovingicarum*
MGH SS	*Monumenta Germaniae historica, Scriptores*

Nov. Anth.	*Novellae Anthemii*
Nov. Just.	*Novellae Justiniani*: C. E. Zacharia, A. Lingenthal, *Imp. Iustiniani PP. A. Novellae quae vocantur sive constitutiones quae extra codicum supersunt* (Leipzig, 1881); R. Schoell, W. Kroll (eds.), *Corpus iuris civilis. Volumen tertium. Novellae* (Berlin, 1895)
Nov. Maj.	*Novellae Maioriani*
Nov. Marc.	*Novellae Marciani*
Nov. Sev.	*Novella Severi*
Nov. Theo.	*Novellae Theodosii*
Nov. Val.	*Novellae Valentiniani*
PG	J.-P. Migne (ed.), *Patrologia Graeca*
PL	J.-P. Migne (ed.), *Patrologia Latina*
PLRE I	A. H. M. Jones, J. R. Martindale, J. Morris (eds.), *The Prosopography of the Later Roman Empire. Volume I. AD 260–395* (Cambridge, 1971)
PLRE II	J. R. Martindale (ed.), *The Prosopography of the Later Roman Empire. Volume II. AD 395–527* (Cambridge, 1980)
PLRE III	J. R. Martindale (ed.), *The Prosopography of the Later Roman Empire. Volume III. AD 527–640* (Cambridge, 1993)
PLS	*Patrologia Latina, supplementum*
RE	Paully-Wissowa-Kroll, *Real-Encyclopädie der klassischen Altertumswissenschaft*
RHD	*Revue historique de droit*
RHDFE	*Revue historique de droit français et étranger*
RIDA	*Revue internationale de droits de l'antiquité*

SC	*Sources chrétiennes*
ZSS GA	*Zeitschrift der Savigny-Stiftung für Rechtsgeschichte. Germanistische Abteilung*
ZSS KA	*Zeitschrift der Savigny-Stiftung für Rechtsgeschichte. Kanonistische Abteilung*
ZSS RA	*Zeitschrift der Savigny-Stiftung für Rechtsgeschichte. Romanistische Abteilung*

For other journal abbreviations, see the list in *L'année philologique*; for additional full source citations, see the Selected Bibliography below.

Introduction

Ralph W. Mathisen

In his study of the role of imperial Quaestors in the making of late Roman law, as first among a number of 'large issues' Tony Honoré asks, 'In what way did law shape the later empire?'[1] This is a very good question, and can lead to an even broader question, 'In what way did law shape—not just the Roman Empire—but Late Antiquity as a whole?' For Late Antiquity (*c*.260–640)[2] was a crucial transitional period. It saw the gradual replacement of Mediterranean classical society, government, and religion by a strictly western European, Christian society that eventually would culminate in the modern-day western European states. It also marked a crossroads where the post-Roman eastern Byzantine world diverged from the post-Roman western medieval world and the post-Roman eastern Islamic world.[3]

The evolution of the law was a most significant manifestation of these developments, for the law was an institution that had the potential to impact virtually every aspect of public and private life. Yet, given the mass and depth of past scholarship on late Roman law, it is remarkable that—with the exception of the significance of the law for the Christian church—there has been so little specific investigation of the interrelationship between law and society.[4] This is not to

[1] T. Honoré, *Law in the Crisis of Empire 379–455* AD*: The Theodosian Dynasty and its Quaestors* (Oxford, 1998), p. vii.

[2] The chronological time span represented by the three volumes of the *Prosopography of the Later Roman Empire* (Cambridge, 1971–93).

[3] See R. W. Mathisen, H. Sivan (eds.), *Shifting Frontiers in Late Antiquity* (Aldershot, 1996), 1.

[4] See e.g. W. Boyd, 'The Ecclesiastical Edicts of the Theodosian Code', *Columbia Studies in History, Economics and Public Law*, 24 (1905), 1–125; L. de Giovanni, *Chiesa e stato nel Codice Teodosiano: Saggio sul libro XVI* (Naples, 1980); F. de Marini,

say, of course, that legal sources have not been utilized. Any investigation of the history and society of Late Antiquity must perforce make use of the legal documents, which have been regularly excavated for nuggets relating to this or that area of inquiry. But studies looking at the specific interaction between law and society—that is, at how social changes effected the creation of new law, and at how the issuance and application of legislation had a direct impact on society—are few.[5]

During Late Antiquity, the law was a dynamically developing, multi-faceted institution. A lot was happening. Earlier Roman law was catalogued in the Hermogenian and Gregorian Codes (293 and 295), the Theodosian Code (438), and the Code of Justinian (534).[6] Innovations in provincial,

'Codice Teodosiano e Concilio di Efeso', *Atti dell'Accademia Romanistica Constantiniana*, 5 (1983), 105–22; A. di Mauro Todini, *Aspetti della legislazione religiosa del IV secolo* (1990); J. Gaudemet, *La Formation du droit séculier et du droit de l'église aux IVe et Ve siècles* (Paris, 1979); E. J. Jonkers, 'Application of Roman Law by Councils in the Sixth Century,' *RHD*, 20 (1952), 340–3; and W. Ullmann, *The Church and the Law in the Earlier Middle Ages: Selected Essays* (London, 1975).

[5] For aspects of the relationship between law and society, see e.g. A. Arjava, *Women and Law in Late Antiquity* (Oxford, 1996); C. A. Bourdara, 'Le Dossier byzantin de sainte Euphèmie: quelques aspects juridiques', *RHDFE* 66 (1988), 383–9; W. Davies, P. Fouracre (eds.), *The Settlement of Disputes in Early Medieval Europe* (Cambridge, 1986); J. Gaudemet, 'Les Abus des potentes du Bas-Empire', *Irish Jurist*, 1 (1966), 128–35; S. Giglio, *Il tardo impero d'Occidente e il suo senato: privilegi fiscali, patrocinio, giurisdizione penale* (Naples, 1990); J. Evans Grubbs, *Law and Family in Late Antiquity: The Emperor Constantine's Marriage Legislation* (Oxford, 1995); P. D. King, *Law and Society in the Visigothic Kingdom* (Cambridge, 1972); F. S. Lear, 'The Public Law of the Visigothic Code', *Speculum*, 26 (1951), 1–23; A. C. Murray, *Germanic Kinship Structure: Studies in Law and Society in Antiquity and the Early Middle Ages* (Toronto, 1983); W. Ullmann, 'Public Welfare and Social Legislation in the Early Medieval Councils', in G. J. Cuming, D. Baker (eds.), *Councils and Assemblies* (Cambridge, 1971), 1–35; and A. Wacke, 'The Potentiores: Some Relations between Power and Law in the Roman Administration of Justice', *Irish Jurist*, 13 (1978), 372–89.

[6] For the development of Roman imperial law, see e.g. S. J. J. Corcoran, *The Empire of the Tetrarchs: Imperial Pronouncements and Government* AD *284–324* (Oxford, 1996); M. Fortina, *La legislazione dell'imperatore Costante* (Novara, 1955); J. Harries, 'The Roman Imperial Quaestor from Constantine to Theodosius II', *JRS* 78 (1988), 148–72; J. D. Harries, I. Wood (eds.), *The Theodosian Code* (Ithaca, NY, 1993); T. Honoré, *Emperors and Lawyers* (London, 1981); G. B. Ladner, 'Justinian's Theory of Law and the Renewal Ideology of the "Leges barbarorum"', *Proceedings of the American Philosophical Society*, 119 (1975), 191–200; S. I. Oost, 'Galla Placidia and the Law', *CP* 63 (1968), 114–21; and W. E. Voss, *Recht und Rhetorik in den Kaisergesetzen der Spätantike: Eine Untersuchung zum nachklassischen Kauf- und Übereignungsrecht* (Frankfurt-am-Main, 1982).

local, and 'vulgar' law incorporated elements of indigenous custom and the enactments of local officials.[7] The barbarian rulers of the western European successor states issued laws that sometimes utilized previous Roman legislation and sometimes were created *de novo*, but which always were suited to their own particular needs.[8] And an entirely new branch of law appeared, ecclesiastical canon law, which in some ways co-operated but in others competed with secular law.[9] Nor did these developments occur independently of each other, rather there was a complex interaction among them, with each having effects upon the other. The end result was a synthesis that set medieval law markedly apart from, yet still not separate from, its classical forebears.

These legal developments were intimately connected to, and driven by, the societies in which they arose, for, in a kind of symbiosis, changes in the law were tied to social evolution. Law and society interacted in a complex dance of

[7] See e.g. T. Honoré, 'Ausonius and Vulgar Law', *Iura*, 35 (1984), 79–82; E. Levy, 'Vulgarization of Roman Law in the Early Middle Ages', *Mediaevalia et Humanistica*, 1 (1943), 14–40; idem, *West Roman Vulgar Law: The Law of Property* (Philadelphia, 1951); L. Mitteis, *Reichsrecht und Volksrecht in den ostlichen Provinzen des römischen Kaiserreich* (Leipzig, 1891); and A. J. B. Sirks, 'Shifting Frontiers in the Law: Romans, Provincials, and Barbarians', in Mathisen and Sivan (eds.), *Shifting Frontiers*, 146–57.

[8] e.g. G. Astuti, 'Note critiche sul sistema delle fonti giuridiche nei regni romano-barbarici dell'Occidente', *Atti della Accademia Nazionale dei Lincei. Rendiconti: Classe di scienze sociale*, 25 (1970), 319–48; K. F. Drew, 'The Barbarian Kings as Lawgivers and Judges', in R. S. Hoyt (ed.), *Life and Thought in the Early Middle Ages* (Minneapolis, 1967); eadem, 'The Germanic Family of the Lex Burgundionum', *Mediaevalia et Humanistica*, 15 (1963), 5–14; F. Franz, 'Das legislative Werk Chilperics I', *ZSS GA* 78 (1961), 1–38; L. A. Garcia Moreno, 'Legitimate and Illegitimate Violence in Visigothic Law', in G. Halsall (ed.), *Violence and Society in the Early Medieval West* (Rochester, NY, 1998); and H. Nehlsen, 'Alarich II als Gesetzgeber. Zur Geschichte der "Lex romana visigothorum"', *Studien zu den germanischen Volksrechten für Wilhelm Ebel* (Frankfurt, 1982), 143–203.

[9] See e.g. J. Gaudemet, *Les Sources du droit de l'église en occident du IIe au VIe siècle* (Paris, 1985); F. Maasen, *Geschichte der Quellen und der Literatur des canonischen Rechts in Abendlande*, i (Graz, 1870); G. le Bras, 'Un moment décisif dans l'histoire de l'église et du droit canon: la renaissance gélasienne', *RHDFE* 9 (1930), 506–24; H. Mordek, *Kirchenrecht und Reform im Frankenreich. Die* collectio vetus gallica, *die älteste systematische Kanonessammlung des fränkischen Gallien* (Berlin, 1975); E. Schwartz, 'Die Kanonessammlungen der alter Reichskirche', *ZSS KA* 25 (1936), 61 ff.; A. M. Stickler, *Historia iuris canonici latina* (Rome, 1974); A. Strewe, *Die Canonessammlung des Dionysius Exiguus in der ersten Redaktion* (Berlin, 1931); and H. Wurm, *Studien und Texte zur Dekretalensammlung des Dionysius Exiguus* (Amsterdam, 1964).

interdependence in which changes in society resulted in the creation of new kinds of authority, which in turn triggered the creation of new kinds of law. As Jill Harries notes in her study below:

> The content of living law was not produced by jurists in their studies but by wider social and cultural changes, which could feed into the written law through the courts, representations from officials, or the decisions of emperors, who were themselves products of the contemporary social and cultural environment.

Social developments such as the barbarian settlement and the rise of the Christian church both inside and outside the imperial frontiers resulted in the development of new sources of legal authority. Competing legal systems, such as the canon law of the church on the one hand, and barbarian legislation on the other, either complemented or challenged established Roman practices. But—with a single exception—there never was any question of Roman law being totally, or even largely, superseded. Both barbarian and canon law continued to recognize the authority of many elements of Roman law. Some barbarian law codes, the Visigothic *Breviarium Alaricianum* ('Breviary of Alaric') and the Burgundian *Lex Romana Burgundionum* ('Roman Law of the Burgundians'), subsumed large chunks of existing Roman law *in toto*. Others, such as the Code of Euric of the Visigoths, the Burgundian Code, and the Salic Law of the Franks, more subtly used Roman legal form and theory to provide a contextual format whereby barbarian rulers could create their own law *de novo*.

At the same time that social evolution effected the creation of new kinds of law and authority, the evolution of the law affected society in a multi-dimensional manner. Applications of the law brought many kinds of intersections involving geography, social status, the economy, literary culture, ethnicity, gender, and religion. There were interactions, as well as a blurring of boundaries, between legal theory and practice, the Greek east and the Roman west, secular and ecclesiastical, Roman and barbarian, male and female, Christian and non-Christian (including pagans, Jews, and Zoroastrians). At the same time, one observes inconsistencies, and even conflicts, between *lex scripta*, or written law, and actual practice. As a consequence, *consuetudo*, local social custom, could sometimes influence the manner in which the law was implemented, as when arbitration was used in place of adjudication.

The following studies will investigate some of the linkages between law and society during Late Antiquity. In particular, they will consider, on the one hand, how the development of new kinds of authority was manifested in the law, and, on the other, what kinds of specific impacts legal innovations had on society. The topic of the creation of new kinds of law is addressed first. John Matthews discusses the role played by continuing traditions of Roman jurisprudence in the compilation of the 'Breviary of Alaric', published in 506 under the auspices of the Visigothic king Alaric II. It was wholly Roman in both content and format, and included commentary ('interpretations') written by Gallic jurisprudents, who, as Matthews writes, 'knew that they did not live under Roman authority any longer, and in some cases phrased their commentaries to accommodate the new political environment'. During the Middle Ages, the Breviary continued to exist alongside several barbarian law codes.

Antti Arjava then examines points of convergence and divergence, as seen for example in differing views on the status of women, between Roman and barbarian family law. Aspects of Roman family law—seen in continuity of language and subject matter—were incorporated into barbarian law codes at the same time that increasingly assertive elements of barbarian custom were merged as well. Subsequently, Michael Jones turns his attention to Britain, the exception to the 'rule of continuity', where native custom was the strongest and largely eclipsed Roman legal traditions. But even here, he concludes, elements of Roman law survived, after a hiatus in the fifth century, having been revived by ecclesiastics in order to meet their own particular local needs.

New legal authority also coalesced in the hands of the church. Jill Harries evaluates the ways in which bishops came to serve as the settlers of disputes, often as arbitrators, a form of negotiation that took place outside formal courtrooms, and from which there was no appeal. She discusses what law could and could not do, and what alternatives there were to the formal episcopal adjudicatory role, known as *episcopalis audientia* ('episcopal hearing') or *iudicium episcopale* ('episcopal judgment'), in which bishops served as judges at a hearing that was very much like that of a secular judge.

Noel Lenski and Leslie Dossey then expand on the issue of the significance of *episcopalis audientia* by looking at how bishops judged cases that involved not only ecclesiastical issues, but secular ones as well. In the latter case, there were ambiguous areas of overlap where it was unclear just which jurisdiction—secular or ecclesiastical—took precedence, and this could contribute to a sense of legal uncertainty. Turning to the east, Victoria Erhart then analyses the development of Christian canon law in the Sasanian Empire, using the evidence of church councils to show how the Syriac Christian church attempted to establish its authority, and Christian society attempted to function, in a potentially hostile environment. Not only did the 'Church of the East' successfully create legal institutions that fostered its longevity under the Sasanids, but in the seventh century, after the Muslim conquest, some of its practices were even adopted by the new regime.

The consideration of the impact of law and authority on society begins with two studies looking at intellectual issues. Gillian Clark examines examples of potential inconsistencies between Roman law and 'God's law', and studies the effect that legal training and ideas of Roman law had on that most fundamental of Christian institutions, Biblical exegesis. She demonstrates how legal arguments were used to justify the perpetuation and use of the pagan cultural heritage. Geoffrey Greatrex continues the theme of the intellectual impact of the law by scrutinizing the ways in which the growing importance of the law during Late Antiquity affected the professional and social status of lawyers, and caused them, rather then the educated senatorial elite as in the past, to become the primary writers of history, another means by which the Roman cultural heritage was preserved.

There then follow two studies that deal with the effects that legal enactments emanating from the imperial government had upon that most characteristic Roman social institution, the senatorial aristocracy. Dennis Trout looks at the interaction between emperors and senators as the latter attempted to negotiate the shoals of legal subleties in order to retain something of their pagan cultural heritage, only to be overwhelmed, ultimately, by the tidal wave of Christianization. And Ralph Mathisen assesses how emperors subtly used their position as the issuers of law to aggrandize their roles as the dispensers of rank and status by the use of honorifics in legal documents, a practice that not only indicated how the emperor perceived senatorial officials, but also would have influenced how senators perceived themselves.

In a study of the significance of ethnic designations and distinctions relating to legislation banning Roman–Jewish marriage, Hagith Sivan next shows how both Roman emperors and Jewish rabbinic authorities could use the law to define and maintain 'communities of faith'. She argues that the resultant policies depict a new intrusiveness of the law into social areas that previously had been off-limits.

The remaining four studies are presented in pairs, of which one contribution relates to late Roman and the other to the post-Roman barbarian world. The first two look at implications of changes in legal thought for gender roles, and, in particular, at growing attempts by the state to regulate the lives of women. Judith Evans Grubbs explores ways in which late Roman legislation attempted to impose increasing controls over less privileged women, and Catherine Peyroux turns to barbarian Europe in her analysis of the ways in which sixth-century Gallic bishops strove to impose their control over women religious. In both cases, however, there were occasional difficulties in the enforcement of such regulation.

Ultimately, the volume turns to economic issues. Boudewijn Sirks approaches the late Roman colonate from a new perspective, seeing in it a manifestation of an agricultural credit system, but denying that there was a direct link between it and medieval serfdom. And Kathy Pearson uses the Salic Law of the Franks to demonstrate the role that law played in the maintenance of the economic livelihood of early medieval France, and what it shows about the strategies for survival adopted not only by the newly arrived Franks but also by the Romans who remained after the barbarian occupation.

In general, these studies not only offer new insights into many discrete aspects of the evolution of the law during Late Antiquity, but also provide new ways in which 'the law', broadly writ, can be used as a source to provide new kinds of insights into the many tranformations that occurred during this portentous period. More specifically, the discussions of the interaction between law and society presented in this volume all present, either directly or indirectly, a picture of a far-reaching transformation in the manner in which political and religious authority was created and exercised through the medium of the law. New kinds of authority were manifested not only in the production of *lex scripta* but also in the application of *consuetudo*. Indeed, it is only by recognizing the manner in which and the extent to which new kinds of law represented new kinds of authority that one can truly comprehend the extent of the crucial role that law, in all its manifold forms, played in the changing society of Late Antiquity.

Finally, one special indicator of the effectiveness of the new kinds of authority is the manner in which they accommodated themselves to the old authority, in the same way that the new barbarian and canon law accommodated themselves to classical, Roman law. And in this regard, the transformation of the law can serve as a metaphor for the way that Late Antiquity itself accommodated itself to the culture and traditions of antiquity while at the same time transforming itself into something quite different.

PART I

Law and the Manifestations of New Authority

I

Interpreting the *Interpretationes* of the *Breviarium*

John F. Matthews

Mommsen's edition of the *Codex Theodosianus* (Theodosian Code), begun in 1898 and published in 1905 after the death of its initiator on 1 November 1903, is a truly amazing achievement.[1] It is not, however, a book for the faint-hearted or casual reader. The complex presentation, with its exhaustive documentation of manuscript readings and other sources, can give an impression of finality, when it is really intended to show the variety of alternative possibilities that have to be considered. Nor is it easy to track down, in the dense Latin print of his Prolegomena, Mommsen's justification for an important editorial policy in which he differed from the advice of his collaborator Paul Krüger. This was the decision not to include in the printed version of the incomplete early books of the Code texts recovered from the *Codex Justinianus* (Code of Justinian) of a century later; Krüger's partial edition of the Theodosian Code, published two decades after Mommsen's, is technically far less accomplished than its predecessor, but in its first five books includes from the *Codex Justinianus* more than two hundred and thirty texts not printed by Mommsen.[2]

The extent to which Mommsen's decision on this point has resulted in an under exploitation of the possibilities for the reconstruction of these early books is perhaps not widely realized by readers of the Theodosian Code—a lack

[1] T. Mommsen, P. M. Meyer (eds.), *Theodosiani libri XVI cum constitutionibus sirmondianis et leges novellae ad Theodosianum pertinentes*, with apparatus criticus by P. Krüger (3 vols.) (Berlin, 1905; repr. 1970–1).

[2] P. Krüger (ed.), *Codex Theodosianus, fasc. I, libri I–VI* (Berlin, 1923).

of awareness that is aggravated by the extreme rarity of Krüger's edition.[3] What will be said in this investigation, however, is based on a connection, not subject to dispute, between the Theodosian Code and the *Breviarium* of the Visigothic king Alaric II (484–507).

A puzzle for unwary readers of Mommsen's edition, as indeed of Hänel's edition of 1842 and Krüger's of 1923, is the appearance after many laws, especially in certain books, of the word 'INTERPRETATIO', followed by what appear to be more or less detailed ancient comments on the laws. The word does not appear to occur with any obvious pattern or regularity, and the comments are on baffling levels of inconsistency—sometimes difficult, sometimes simple, sometimes superfluous, and often in the strangely inconsequential form, 'This law needs no interpretation'. One law is even said to be 'so clear that it needs no interpretation'.[4]

Just what are these 'interpretations'? To many, they clearly remain a mystery. This is evident from a research seminar given at Oxford some years ago, in which an *interpretatio* was cited as if it were the Theodosian Code text, and appeared in the seminar handout without the original constitution to which it belonged. When the speaker was asked about this, he seemed not to understand the distinction between law and interpretation. One purpose of this paper, therefore, is to clarify the nature of the interpretations and to explain their function.[5]

In fact, the apparently random distribution of the *interpretationes* is an illusion. It arises from the nature of Mommsen's text, which is both an edition of the Theodosian Code as extant in the manuscripts, and a reconstruction of its early books, where the manuscripts are incomplete. It is to be explained in terms of the sources for these early books of the Code, of which the most important (leaving aside the *Codex Justinianus*) is the *Breviarium* of the Visigothic king

[3] For this and what follows as to the character of the Theodosian Code, see chapter 5 of J. F. Matthews, *Laying Down the Law: A Study of the Theodosian Code* (New Haven, 2000).

[4] 'Ista lex tam evidens est, ut expositione non indigeat' (*CTh* 9. 27. 1).

[5] The *interpretationes* have received surprisingly little scholarly attention. For an early discussion, see C. Lécrivain, 'Remarques sur l'*Interpretatio* de la "Lex Romana Visigothorum"', *Annales du Midi*, (1889), 145–82.

Alaric II, otherwise known as the *Lex Romana Visigothorum*.[6] The *Breviarium*, published in 506, is a compilation of selections from various legal texts of Roman origin, including: (1) the Theodosian Code, published in the eastern and western parts of the Roman Empire respectively in 437 and 438 and containing imperial constitutions from the period from Constantine I (306–37) until the time of publication; (2) the Gregorian and Hermogenian Codes, both published in the 290s and containing texts, mainly imperial rescripts, of the third century; (3) some *Novellae* ('new laws') of Theodosius II (402–50) and Valentinian III (425–55) from the period after the publication of the Theodosian Code; and (4) extracts from Roman jurists, namely Papinian, Paul's *Sentences*, and Gaius' *Institutes*. With the exception of Gaius, which was itself an elementary handbook and could be thought not to need them, all these texts were equipped with explanatory commentary in the form of an *interpretatio*.

The puzzle referred to above regarding the apparently irregular appearance of the interpretations thus arises from the role of the *Breviarium* as a main source for Books 1–5 of the Theodosian Code as Mommsen (and Hänel) presented it.[7] These are the books on the sources of law (Book 1); on private law, following the order of the Praetor's Edict (Books 2–4); and as expressed in the *ius civile*, essentially the substantive legislation of Roman emperors as transmitted by jurists (Book 5). Given the poor state of the manuscript evidence for these books, it is a happy circumstance that these topics were the main preoccupation of the compilers of the *Breviarium*. For large parts of Books 1–5 of the Theodosian Code in Mommsen's edition we are, essentially, reading the *Breviarium*, and this, paradoxically, is what makes the *interpretationes* seem to be part of the Theodosian Code. In

[6] For the *Breviarium* in general, see J. Gaudemet, *Le Bréviaire d'Alaric et les Epitome*, Ius Romanum Medii Aevi I.2b (Milan, 1965); C. de Wretschko, 'De usu Breviarii Alariciani forensi et scholastico per Hispaniam, Galliam, Italiam regionesque vicinas', in Mommsen, *Theodosiani*, 1. cccvii–cccxv; and R. Lambertini, *La codificazione di Alarico II* (Turin, 1990).

[7] See Matthews, *Laying Down the Law*, passim. For Books 6–16 of the Code, there is good support from manuscripts 'R' (Paris: Books 6–8) and 'V' (Vatican: Books 9–16), and for Book 16 from the expanded versions of the *Breviarium* mentioned below.

effect, Mommsen edited the Code and *Breviarium* simultaneously, and published them as a composite text. An edition of this part of the *Breviarium* could simply be extracted from Mommsen's edition of the Code, and if this were done the relationship of the *interpretationes* to the *Breviarium* would be instantly clear, for every text chosen for inclusion would have its respective interpretation. On the other hand, an edition of the Code by itself would need to delete the interpretations.

Accepting this connection between the Code and the *Breviarium*, we now can pose a more precise question. What is the nature of the connection and where do the *interpretationes* come from? There are essentially two alternative solutions, though as will be seen they are not exclusive. Either the interpretations are part of a broader tradition of juristic comment on the Theodosian Code in the period since its publication;[8] or they are to be connected with the *Breviarium* itself, being specifically written for it and published as part of it in 506.

Of these alternatives, the second is unquestionably correct, if for no other reason than that the fit with the *Breviarium* is so tight. As noted above, all *Breviarium* texts (except for Gaius' *Institutes*) are equipped with one, even in the negative form, 'This law needs no interpretation.' This was done for the sake of formal completeness; every text included in the *Breviarium* was to possess an *interpretatio*, even if there was nothing for it to say. On the other hand, no text in the Theodosian Code that was not selected for the *Breviarium* possesses one, except for a pair of manuscript pages, now in the Vatican Library, belonging to Book 4 of the Code.[9] But these fragments clearly were intended to supplement the *Breviarium* from the complete Theodosian Code, and have *interpretationes* in imitation of it.[10] Even if there were a

8 On which see Arjava in this volume.

9 *Codex Vaticanus reginensis* 520, fols. 94–5: see Mommsen, *Theodosiani*, I. lxxxvii–lxxxvii.

10 See Mommen, *Theodosiani*, I. lxxxvi–lxxxvii, 185, 189–90. The laws in question are, in Mommsen's edn., *CTh* 4. 8. 8; 4. 10. 2–3; 4. 11. 1–2; 4. 12. 1–3, 5–7. There is some doubt as to their exact location, and indeed as to the order of titles, in this part of the *Theodosian vs Code x*. For interpolations in the *Breviarium*, see T. Mommsen, 'Interpolationen im Theodosischen Breviar', *Neues Archiv der Gesellschaft für ältere deutsche Geschichtskunde*, 25 (1900), 587–92.

continuing tradition of juristic comment on the Theodosian Code in the later fifth century, and there is no reason why there should not have been, the *interpretationes* are to be connected explicitly with the composition of the *Breviarium*.

This conclusion is supported by the *interpretatio* to *Breviarium* 1. 4. 1 (= *CTh* 1. 4. 3), the so-called 'Law of Citations', which was part of an imperial letter directed to the Roman senate on 7 November 426; other parts of the original letter, in Krüger if not in Mommsen, are recovered from the *Codex Justinianus*.[11] The *interpretatio* to this law commented on the jurists referred to in it (Papinian, Paul, Gaius, Ulpian, Modestinus, and others whom they cited), and added that 'Gregorianus and Hermogenianus'—who were referred to as if they were individual jurists rather than the compilers of Codes—were ratified in the Theodosian Code by an earlier law entitled 'De constitutionibus principum et edictis' ('On the constitutions of emperors and on edicts').

This reference is to *CTh* 1. 1. 5, of 429, which cites the Hermogenian and Gregorian Codes as precedents for the Theodosian Code itself.[12] The *interpretatio* is doubly perplexing. In the first place, a text of 426 could not have adduced a later law as validation. The law to which it refers, as represented by the *interpretatio*, was 'earlier' than *CTh* 1. 4. 3 not in time, but because it was located in a title of the published Theodosian Code that was earlier in sequence. Secondly, the law of 429 which was used to justify the inclusion in the *Breviarium* of extracts from the Gregorian and Hermogenian Codes was not even included in the *Breviarium* itself. Not that there was any reason to do so, for *CTh* 1. 1. 5 was concerned with the implementation of the Theodosian Code, which the *Breviarium* was to supersede. Yet, by citing it the *interpretatio* paradoxically implied that the full text of the Theodosian Code continued to remain in effect even after the publication of the *Breviarium*. The compilers of the *Breviarium* clearly wanted to ensure that all

[11] See T. Honoré, *Law in the Crisis of Empire 379–455* AD: *The Theodosian Dynasty and its Quaestors* (Oxford, 1998), 249–51. The 'Law of Citations' is a much misunderstood text, but this is not the place to argue it.

[12] *CTh* 1. 1. 5: 'Ad similitudinem Gregoriani atque Hermogeniani codicis, cunctas colligi constitutiones decernimus, quos Constantinus inclitus et post eum divi principes nosque tulimus edictorum viribus aut sacra generalitate subnixas,' etc.

the sources they excerpted possessed judicial authority derived from Roman sources, and thus authorization for citing the Gregorian and Hermogenian Codes, which were not covered by 'The Law of Citations', was drawn from *CTh* 1. 1. 5.

Having established the validity of the sources cited in the *Breviarium*, the *interpretatio* concluded by saying, 'We have chosen from these jurists, from Gregorianus, Hermogenianus,[13] Gaius, Papinian, and Paul, those things that seemed needful for cases of the present times' ('quae necessaria causis praesentium temporum videbantur'). It is to this phrase that we now might turn, on the understanding that the reference to the 'present times' is to the time of publication of the *Breviarium*.

As with other late Roman acts of legal codification, notably the Theodosian Code and the *Digest* of Justinian, the circumstances of the publication of the *Breviarium* of Alaric are well documented. They are set out in a *Commonitorium* ('memorandum') addressed by the king to the *comes* Timotheus, the senior civil official in his domain (we should see him as a successor to the late Roman praetorian prefect).[14] The *Commonitorium* gave royal authority to the *Breviarium* as a digest of 'leges Romanae' and 'antiquum ius'—that is to say, acts of primary legislation and juristic opinion, a distinction between complementary sources of law well understood in Roman jurisprudence. It also noted that the project had been approved by an assembly, or council, of bishops and nobles, that is to say the Roman leaders in the Visigothic kingdom, and that it had been carried out by 'prudentes', or Roman jurists in the kingdom. Then, the laws had been selected and explained: 'excerpta vel [= et] clariori *interpretatione* conposita'. Like the Theodosian Code in its day, the book was to be definitive for the future, and the manufacture of copies was to be the responsibility of the *vir spectabilis* Anianus; he is the counterpart of the Roman *constitutionarii* who had been given responsibility for the preparation of

[13] That is, their Codes, as explained above.

[14] See Mommsen, *Theodosiani*, 1. xxxii–xxxvii, for the texts referred to here. For Timotheus, Anianus, and Goiaricus, see *PLRE II*, 1121 (Timotheus 4), 90 (Anianus 1), 517 (Goiaricus).

texts of the Theodosian Code.[15] Lastly, the *Breviarium* was intended for use in the 'forum', or court, of Timotheus, and no other law or legal definition was to be cited there. In this provision, as in the responsibility of Anianus for the integrity of the text of the *Breviarium*, the precedent of the Theodosian Code is again obvious.

We also possess enabling legislation, including a 'subscriptio' of Anianus which was written 'Aduris', that is, at Adoure-sur-Aire near Toulouse, the capital of the Visigothic kingdom; and a 'praescriptio', issued over the name of the *vir inlustris*, count Goiaricus (Goar), in which, echoing Alaric's *Commonitorium*, the laws were described as 'selected and clarified, according to instructions': 'electae vel, sicut praeceptum est, explanatae'.[16]

The evidence leaves little room for doubt on two important points: the laws were intended for use, and the *interpretationes* were an integral part of the project. Now, of course, what legal minds ('prudentes') may intend for 'use' may reflect wishful thinking and an optimistic view of their own importance, together with a respect for irrelevancies from the past. It is unlikely that the early sixth century really needed such an explanation of Roman citizenship and Latin rights as was given in the *interpretatio* to *Breviarium* (= *CTh*) 2. 22. 1.[17] On the other hand, the *interpretatio* to 3. 17. 3 speaks of the guardianship of minors as a present concern; 'quotiens de pupillorum tutela tractatur, debet . . .' ('however often there are dealings regarding the guardianship of minors, it is fitting . . .'). If there were Roman courts in early sixth-century Gaul, and the *interpretationes* are evidence that there were, this was just the sort of issue that one would expect to arise. It reflects the emphasis given by the editors of the *Breviarium* to questions of Roman private law, and especially to the law of property, gift, and succession.

[15] See the 'Gesta Senatus de Theodosiano publicando', §§1, 7, etc. and the law of 443 addressed to them (Mommsen, *Theodosiani*, 1. 1–4); note also *PLRE II*, 81–2 (Anastasius 14), and 731 (Martinus 5).

[16] Mommsen, *Theodosiani*, 1. xxxii. *Explanatae* is Mommsen's necessary correction of the MSS *exemplatae* or *explanari*.

[17] Under the title 'De hereditatis petitione'. For convenience, all references to the *interpretationes* are to Mommsen's edition of the *CTh* text included in the *Breviarium*, and not to the *Breviarium* itself.

The editors of the *Breviarium*, and the writers of its *interpretationes*, were working in early sixth-century Gaul under a barbarian king on the Roman law of an earlier period. The situation is one with real historical possibilities. If the writers show that Roman law continued to be relevant for their own time, then they also might show, both in their selection of laws and in their interpretations of them, an awareness of what made their own time different from what preceded—the time in which the original texts had been created. They might reveal gaps in perceptions between the fourth and early fifth and the early sixth centuries, over which their selections and their interpretations should provide a bridge.

If we are right to think that the same people were responsible for both selecting and commenting on the laws, some general questions might be quickly addressed by looking at their selection of texts. To put the converse of this question, what sorts of things did they omit? We can begin with the later books of the Theodosian Code, those least well represented in the *Breviarium*. (The question is distorted by the fact that the *Breviarium* is itself our main source for Books 1–5 of the Theodosian Code. Nevertheless, the balance of the content of the *Breviarium* in favour of the early books of the Code is perfectly clear.)

From Book 7 of the Theodosian Code, which contains twenty four titles and 175 individual laws, the *Breviarium* has chosen just one text, the very first in the book. A law of Constantine of 323, it concerned the facilitation by Romans of barbarian 'depredation'. Perhaps with an eye to his Visigothic master, the author of this law's *interpretatio* has replaced the term 'barbarians' by 'any enemies at all', and makes no use of the phrase 'wicked faction' ('scelerata factio') that is present in the original. No other law was selected from this entire book, which concerned late Roman military administration, and was clearly a matter of no interest in early sixth-century Gaul.

From Book 14 of the Theodosian Code, which contains twenty seven titles and ninety nine individual laws, again a single text was chosen (*CTh* 14. 7. 1). It covered two aspects of the situation of 'collegiati', or guild members. It recalled them, together with their property, to their municipalities, in order to ensure the performance of their obligations to their place of origin; and it dealt with the children of 'collegiati' by women of free or unfree status. The *interpretatio* was concerned more with the second aspect than the first. It neglected the important connection between property and origin,[18] but commented more explicitly than the original text on marriages between partners of unequal or equal status; the abstract juridical expressions 'non aequale' and 'iustum coniugium' were explained in practical terms, as exemplified by relationships of 'collegiati' with 'colonae' or 'ancillae' (neither is in the original text), and with women of free status ('ingenuae'), respectively.[19]

Book 6 of the Theodosian Code consists of thirty eight titles and 209 laws on 'dignities'—public offices, their duties and functions, and the grades of precedence attaching to them—affecting minor offices as well as the most important in the late Roman administration. From the entire book, the *Breviarium* selected the two laws from the fifth title, 'Ut dignitatum ordo servetur' ('That the order of ranks might be preserved'), which dealt with the principle of maintaining the correct grades of distinction attaching to public office. Consciously or not, the *interpretationes* provided a change of emphasis. Where the Theodosian Code seems to have been concerned with the defence of grades of precedence against improper claims of seniority, the *interpretationes* read as if the issue was the presumption of office by men who had not received it at all.

From the example of these three books, from which only a very few laws were chosen for inclusion in the *Breviarium*, we can at once see the chasm that has opened up between the late Roman Empire and the Visigothic period. The *Breviarium* dropped all reference to the Roman army, its

[18] Whereas the *Theodosian vs Code* text regards *civitates* and the 'places' of origin as different ways of saying the same thing, the *interpretatio* seems to distinguish them: 'ad civitatis suae officia cum rebus suis vel ad loca, unde discesserunt, revocentur' (the *CTh* phrase 'loco originario' has a different, more tendentious connotation).

[19] The *interpretatio* to *CTh* 9. 29. 2 (on harbouring 'latrones') similarly gives a more explicit description of differences of social rank; the phrase 'pro qualitate personae' is glossed as 'si ingenua et vilior persona est, si vero melior,' etc., 'where 'ingenua et vilior' means 'free but of lower social rank'.

recruitment, organization, and supply; and to the organization of social life at Rome, Constantinople, Carthage, and Alexandria; which respectively formed the main topics of Book 7 and 14 of the Theodosian Code. It ignored the detailed rules of precedence and conduct which formed the essence of the late Roman administration, that were found in Book 6, retaining only the general principle of respect for legitimately acquired dignities and their author the 'princeps', with punishment for those who 'presumed' to usurp them without authority. This was a matter of interest to any ruler, whether Roman emperor or barbarian king.

A similar result obtains with Book 13, which consists of eleven titles on Roman taxation, and 127 laws in all. The *Breviarium* includes only three of these laws, concerning (1) people who sold things that they produced themselves but did not buy and sell for a living (*CTh* 13. 1. 13); (2) the improper transfer of tax burdens from the powerful to men of inferior status (*CTh* 13. 10. 1); and (3) the respective time limits for appeals against tax assessments of men who were present in their communities and those who were absent on public service (*CTh* 13. 10. 5). Practically the whole panoply of Roman tax law and its administration, including such topics as immunity for professors and physicians, the position of artists and manual workers, and the estates and duties of shipowners, was omitted. As to the four laws chosen for inclusion from Book 15 (fifteen titles, 116 laws), in every case the *interpretatio* changes the emphasis, and even the meaning, of the original text. For *CTh* 15. 1. 32, on the restoration of defences and the heating of baths, the *interpretatio* ignored the heating of baths (reasonably enough; who had Roman baths in the early sixth century?), and converted the burden imposed on public estates to the direct responsibility of the fisc (i.e. the imperial exchequer). For *CTh* 15. 1. 9, a law of Julian addressed from Antioch to the prefect of Egypt, a reference to the building of private accommmodation above public workhouses ('ergasteria') was broadened to include houses built in any public space.

It is surprising to find in the *Breviarium*, with the comment that it 'needs no interpretation', a law addressed to the *comes Orientis* ('Count of the East') on established water rights and the irrigation of fields and pleasure gardens (*CTh* 15. 2. 7). Water rights hardly present the same issues in the Middle East as in south–western Gaul, but the general principles were evidently thought worth maintaining. The fourth and last of the laws included in the *Breviarium* from Book 15 of the Theodosian Code (15. 14. 14) referred to the circumstances of the recent barbarian invasions, where, as in the case referred to above (*CTh* 7. 1. 1), 'barbarian' was changed to 'enemy' depredation. The editors of the *Breviarium* perhaps did not realize that the barbarian invasions referred to (it is a law of 416) were precisely those of Alaric and Athaulf, the ancestors of the present Gothic regime of southern Gaul. Apart from these few examples, the whole domain of Roman public works and entertainments was omitted; nothing here on aqueducts, road repair, imperial portraits, men and women of the stage, pimps and procurers, or wild beast shows and gladiators. Whether for better or for worse, it represents a considerable narrowing of social experience.

From Book 12, a book of nineteen titles and 273 laws, were chosen eleven examples for inclusion in the *Breviarium*, but nine of these were from the 192 laws of the first title, producing together a rudimentary set of rules for membership of curial orders. The other two texts involve the appointment of *exactores* and *susceptores*, local officials responsible for the collection of taxes in municipalities (*CTh* 12. 6. 20, 22). The effect is a radical narrowing of the range of reference of the original book of the Theodosian Code to those elements that might be relevant to Roman communities in the Visigothic kingdom. A particularly important omission is the title on civic embassies and the decrees that authorized them (*CTh* 12. 12). At one stroke this eliminated the most commonly used means of communication between the cities of the Roman Empire and their emperor. For *CTh* 12. 1. 19, on the age at which curial obligations could be imposed upon individuals, the *interpretatio* ignores the complaint in the Theodosian Code that youngsters of seven or eight years of age were being nominated, stating only the general principle that these obligations were acquired at the age of eighteen. In this as in other texts, the term 'munus' for a civic obligation is replaced by 'servitium'. The latter word evokes not so much slavery as the idea of a legal service of any kind that one person may owe to another, or the 'servitude' or obligation to others that may attach to a piece of property. On any reading it is an abandonment of the notion, which although declining still meant something in the fourth century, of a 'munus' as a contribution made by an individual to his community through a sense of civic duty rather than by coercion.[20]

Perhaps the most interesting of these examples of omission is Book 16, eleven titles containing 201 laws on religion in its various aspects. Again, eleven texts are selected, six of them from the forty seven laws of the second title 'De episcopis, ecclesiis, et clericis' ('On bishops, churches, and the clergy'). Several of them concern the discipline of the clergy and their immunity from taxation; and two limit episcopal jurisdiction to church matters, civil cases and criminal jurisdiction being reserved for the regular courts. It also is noteworthy that neither of the two extant laws from Book 1 of the Theodosian Code, 'On the jurisdiction of bishops', was included in the *Breviarium*.[21] It would not be surprising if the Roman institution of episcopal jurisdiction over secular litigation, which might well have worked against its interests, was discouraged by the Visigothic regime.

This leaves five texts chosen from other titles of Book 16. One sets limits on episcopal jurisdiction (*CTh* 16. 11. 1), and the remaining four concern relations between Christians and Jews, in the shape of conversions from Christianity to Judaism, and the treatment of slaves by Jewish owners.[22] The concentration on these topics is all the more striking when we consider what has been omitted. There is nothing on the Catholic faith and heresy (a point worthy of note, the Visigoths being Arians); and nothing on monasticism, baptism,

[20] Cf. *CTh* 12. 1. 55, 170; 10. 3. 2, etc.; and esp. 16. 2. 2; 'ab omni munere, id est ad omni officio omnique servitio.'

[21] *CTh* 1. 27, two laws; not in the MSS of the Code or *Breviarium* but restored from other sources. A third text should be added from the *Codex Justinianus* (1. 4. 7). For episcopal jurisdiction, see also Dossey and Lenski in this volume.

[22] *CTh* 16. 8. 5, 7; 9. 1; 7. 3. Of these, *CTh* 16. 8. 5 and 16. 9. 1 were edited in the Theodosian Code from the same original text. Of the four texts, only *CTh* 16. 9. 1 carries an *interpretatio*; the others 'do not need it'. For Jewish–Christian relations, see also Sivan in this volume.

apostasy, or paganism. The only glancing reference to these latter subjects is found in *CTh* 16. 7. 3, drawn from the title 'De apostatis'. But even here, all that was retained was an extract relating to Jews, and the rest of the law, which involved Manichees, was omitted in the *Breviarium*.[23] Given this dearth of opportunities for the clergy represented in the *Breviarium*, it is not surprising that several of its manuscripts have versions of Book 16 supplemented from the full text of the Theodosian Code.[24]

As already noted above, the vast majority of laws selected for inclusion in the *Breviarium* were chosen from the first half of Book 1, on the sources and authority of the law; from Books 2–5 on private law; and from Books 8–11 on property and inheritance, the criminal law, the interests of the fiscus, and appeal procedures. Omitted, as has been seen, were almost all references to Roman offices and institutions, the army, taxation, public works and services, civic life, and the organization of the great cities, entertainments and games, and religion. In all of this, we see how the process of selection and omission expressed a sense of 'what is needful for cases of the present times'. Put the other way round, by its silence on certain matters, the *Breviarium* offered a statement of what is 'no longer needful', that is, of the extent to which the later Roman Empire and its institutions no longer had any practical applications in the first years of the sixth century.

Apart from what has been omitted, the commentaries on the texts included in the *Breviarium* may reflect a more positive awareness of the differences between the fourth and early fifth centuries and their authors' own time. What follows is by way of example only; the material invites a careful and comprehensive study.

[23] This law presents a complex situation, as can be seen from Mommsen's apparatus to the text (*Theodosiani*, i. 884–5). Most mss. of the *Breviarium* omit the part about the Manichees, with a reference to the *Novellae* and the comment that the rest (an extract on the Jews) did not need interpretation. One MS ('E') includes the full text from the Theodosian Code. A reference to 'arae et templa' is passed over rapidly in the first sentence of the law.

[24] As can be seen from the apparatus of Mommsen's edition, see *Theodosiani*, 1. lxv–lxviii, lxxxii–xcii, and the table at xc–xci. The main examples are the MSS known as 'EYDO' (respectively at Ivrea, Berlin + the Vatican, Paris, and Oxford).

The shortest form of *interpretatio*, as mentioned, is the commonly found expression, 'haec lex interpretatione non eget' ('This law does not need interpretation'). Sometimes, especially on some more complex problems of private law, the writers refer to longer discussions in other *interpretationes*, as on the *Novellae* of Theodosius II and Valentinian III (see below). On other occasions, as in the case of the law on sacrilege (*CTh* 6. 5. 2), they may say that a legal problem needs elucidation from 'ius', that is, from juristic writing. This is not a sign of incompleteness or haste, as Mommsen argued, but a recognition that the 'leges' that comprised the *Breviarium* sometimes had to be considered in the context of juristic opinion, for which a different sort of commentary was required.[25] Other interpretations resemble little essays, which sometimes are longer than the text commented on, and which can accumulate within a title into quite a substantial discussion. An example of this is title 8. 18 just mentioned, where three *interpretationes*, taken together, give an extensive account of questions relating to maternal property. Here, three texts, *CTh* 8. 18. 1, 2, 9, refer to Theodosius II's *Novella* 14, while the *interpretatio* on the latter refers back to the title in the Theodosian Code.

The manner of expression of the *interpretationes* varies, partly, no doubt, because of the different personal conventions of individual commentators, and partly because commentators, like all of us, desired to express themselves differently from time to time. There seems to be little reason to suppose that the different modes of expression reflect different traditions of juristic comment or different types of source.[26] At times, we read, 'this law says that'; or 'the emperor here wishes that'; or, still in the imperial first person plural, 'these are our instructions'; and so on.

But the compilers knew that they did not live under Roman authority any longer, and in some cases phrased their

[25] *Theodosiani*, I.xxxv. For other examples, see *CTh* 2. 4. 1, 6; 8. 13. 2; 9. 39. 3 (on calumniators). *CTh* 3. 13. 2 refers (hesitantly) to Paul, as (with more confidence) does 3. 16. 2.

[26] See F. Wieacker, 'Lateinische Kommentare im Codex Theodosianus,' *Symbolae Freiburgenses* (Leipzig, 1933), 259 ff.; and W. E. Voss, *Recht und Rhetorik in den Kaisergesetzen der Spätantike: Eine Untersuchung zum nachklassischen Kauf- und Übereignungsrecht* (Frankfurt-am-Main, 1982), 43–50.

commentaries to accommodate the new political environment. As the source of the laws, the emperor (normally a collegiate plurality) was sometimes referred to as 'princeps', but when he entered more actively into its procedures he could become 'the master(s) of things' ('domini rerum'), a phrase presumably designed to encompass a barbarian king (*CTh* 9. 41. 1; 11. 16. 11). The imperial *comitatus*, or court, was transformed into 'the place where the masters of things are to be found' (*CTh* 12. 1. 20). And in the *interpretatio* for *CTh* 1. 16. 7, appeals to praetorian prefects and their deputies for reference to the emperor were directed to 'our masters' ears' ('dominicis auribus').

The *interpretationes* sometimes begin with a brief general statement of principle or legal definition. For example, the *interpretatio* on *CTh* 1. 2. 5 distinguishes between two sorts of *praescriptio*, 'moratoria', which offered a delay, and 'peremptoria', which ordered a resolution, observing that the first kind can be given by rescript, the second not; none of this general definition was in the original text. The *interpretatio* on *CTh* 4. 1. 1, under the title 'De cretione vel bonorum possessione' ('On Claiming and Entering Possession of an Inheritance'), referred to the 'antiquum ius' as it once had been administered by the urban praetors in Rome, with the comment that this issue now was covered by 'leges'—that is, imperial legislation—so that explanation was not necessary ('quod explanari opus non est, quia legibus utrumque sublatum est'). The *interpretatio* on *CTh* 2. 15. 1 begins with a formal definition of 'dolus malus ('wicked trickery'),' while those on *CTh* 10. 10. 2 and 9. 39. 3 define 'delatores' ('informers') and 'calumniatores' ('false accusers') respectively, and that on *CTh* 4. 13. 1 explains 'vectigalia' as indirect taxes levied on transported goods. And the long *interpretatio* of *CTh* 8. 12. 1 begins by describing the various possible forms of 'donatio' (deeds of gift). In these and other cases, the *interpretatio* provides a comment on the name of the Theodosian Code title before moving on to individual texts within it.[27]

[27] In similar fashion, the *interpretatio* to *CTh* 3. 2. 1 defines 'commissoriae cautiones.'

The writers of the *interpretationes* also defined terms that may no longer have been familiar, or offered a paraphrase; and they sometimes omitted or added details for clarity and relevance to their own day. On *CTh* 9. 15. 1, setting out the famous penalty for parricide (included, no doubt, for legal–historical reasons rather than for its contemporary relevance), the commentator explained the meaning of 'culleus', the sack into which the parricide was sewn with serpents, before being drowned in the sea or a river and left without burial. A similarly antiquarian comment comes at *CTh* 9. 16. 4, where the writer explained forgotten terms from the old pagan religion; added to those who summon up demons and deities for foretelling the future were the 'divini' called 'harioli,' while a 'haruspex' was 'one who collects auguries'. Neither is a very precise or correct definition. In another context (*CTh* 9. 19. 1) a 'tabellio', or 'secretary', is 'now called an *admanuensis*'. The *interpretatio* to *CTh* 8. 2. 5 (cf. 13. 10. 1) explains 'tabularii' as 'those who handle public accounts', while *CTh* 10. 1. 2 glosses 'rationales' and 'magistri rei privatae' as 'administrators of our masters' households' ('ordinatores domorum dominicarum').

A law about imperial coinage (*CTh* 9. 22. 1) forbade the clipping of *solidi* and observed that it made no difference to the value of a coin whether the imperial portrait shown on it was large or small, provided that its weight was correct; the *interpretatio* commented on the first of these issues and paid no attention to the second, which was indeed a feature rather specific to late Roman and Byzantine coinage.[28] In another case, *CTh* 1. 34. 3 required that governors did not take personal staff members to provinces with them as *domestici* and *cancellarii* but must only use personnel chosen 'on the record' ('sub fide gestorum'), who would remain in the province for three years after the governor's departure in case there was legal action against him; the *interpretatio* emphasized that any such adviser must not come from the governor's own province or from any other region unless he was 'publicly assigned by the choice of the citizens' ('publice

[28] As in the distinction between the so-called 'divided' and 'undivided' legends. The former allowed room for a larger imperial portrait, the latter limited the space for it.

civium electione deputatus'). Whatever the precise nature of the respective procedures, that envisaged in the *interpretatio* is rather different from that in the original legislation.[29]

Not surprisingly, the *interpretationes* commit misunderstandings and make mistakes, as in the case of *CTh* 4. 4. 4, where a law issued at Constantinople and addressed to the prefect of the city is taken to relate to Rome. The *interpretatio* on *CTh* 2. 1. 12 neglects the point that the court of five nobles known as the 'iudicium quinquevirale' was specifically intended to apply only to Roman senators.[30] Interpretations also can apply laws out of their proper context, as in the case of the law mentioned above on private building on public property originally addressed to the prefect of Egypt, or that on water rights, addressed to the *comes Orientis* (*CTh* 15. 1. 9; 2. 7). They may offer a single explanation to cover the contents of an entire title, as when they remark, in language derived from the Theodosian Code title as well as from the specific text in question, that occasions for public rejoicing are not a cause for enforced exactions in the name of a thanksgiving (*CTh* 8. 11. 5), or explicate Easter amnesties by commenting on a single representative law in the title (*CTh* 9. 38. 8). The *interpretatio* on *CTh* 9. 34. 1, under the title 'De famosis libellis' ('On defamatory documents'), goes beyond the law under discussion by giving a general description of how such *libelli* may be posted up or left on the ground for people to find them—adding the penalty of beating with a cudgel, which is not specified in the original text.

There are also all sorts of minor variations and points of difference. The naming of a fine of 50 lb of silver mentioned in the *interpretatio* to *CTh* 11. 36. 20 comes not from that law but from two predecessors in the same title which were not included in the *Breviarium* (*CTh* 11. 36. 15–16). One law glosses 'centesima', an interest rate of 1 per cent, as

[29] The *Codex Justinianus* version of *CTh* 1. 34. 3 (*CJ* 1. 51. 8) adds the phrase 'ex eodem officio' after 'sub fide gestorum.' There is a difference between this and the 'choice of the citizens'.

[30] The court was established in 376, in reaction to the trials of senators conducted under Valentinian; *CTh* 9. 1. 3, and see J. F. Matthews, *Western Aristocracies and Imperial Court,* AD *364–425* (Oxford, 1975, repr. 1998), 66.

'tres siliquae in anno per solidum' ('three siliquas yearly per solidus') (*CTh* 2. 33. 2); and another explains a point of law through an imagined intervention in direct speech: 'si forte dicat aliquis' ('If, perhaps, someone says') (*CTh* 4. 4. 5). In addition, a law on 'milites' or 'privati' behaving like robbers and bandits (*CTh* 9. 14. 2) becomes a general reference to 'anyone' who behaves in that fashion.

All of this means that the *interpretationes* do everything that commentators are expected to do; they expound, summarize, give the meaning of terms, abbreviate or expand as seems appropriate. In some cases they also 'update' in a more fully circumstantial manner, and this paper will conclude with a few examples of this practice:

(1) Constantine's law of 315 against kidnappers (*CTh* 9. 18. 1) had laid down the penalties of condemnation to gladiatorial combat with the certainty of death or, in the case of slaves, of exposure at the first opportunity to wild beasts. The law was included in the *Breviarium* with a brief *interpretatio* naming the penalty of death without specifying the means of execution, and with no distinction between slave and free. In early sixth-century Gaul there no longer were gladiatorial shows or 'venationes' involving victims, even had the penalties laid down in the Roman law still been thought appropriate. The essential rule of law was retained in a form adapted for the later period. In a similar way, a law advising provincial governors how they should conduct themselves in office (*CTh* 1. 16. 9) received an *interpretatio* that simply omitted as irrelevant the part of the law insisting they should not be distracted from serious business by attending shows and games.

(2) Another law of Constantine, on deeds of gift (*CTh* 8. 12. 1), required that written documentation of the gift be provided, either by the donor himself, 'or by him, whom opportunity has provided'. The long *interpretatio*, which begins with an explanation of the different types of gift (see above), expanded this general remark into a reference to the literacy or illiteracy of the intending donor; the 'man whom opportunity has provided' was a man who could read and write in cases where the donor could not, and where written authentication of the gift was required. This may also have

been the situation envisaged by Constantine, but the *interpretatio* went beyond the original law to make explicit the application of the rule that was most obviously relevant in the writer's day.

(3) A law on prison custody (*CTh* 9. 3. 7) ordered that every Sunday prisoners were to be brought out from their cells, given food, taken to the baths 'under trusty escort', and questioned about their treatment, adding at the end of the text that a Christian priest would be present to ensure observance of the law. The *interpretatio* threw the emphasis onto 'Christiani vel sacerdotes' (presumably meaning simply Christian priests)[31] and gave to them the duty of providing food. This was a change from the situation set out in the original text; the clergy now themselves performed the specified services rather than ensuring by their admonition that the governor did so.

(4) Constantine's law on magic arts (*CTh* 9. 16. 3) is most justly famous for the exception that it provides for harmless 'white magic' used as a remedy for illness or to secure the prosperity of crops in country districts. The *interpretatio* ignored the exception, which was actually the main point of law at issue in the original text, referring only to 'malefici vel incantatores vel inmissores tempestatum ('necromancers or enchanters or the summoners of tempests')'. The last of these categories was not in Constantine's law at all—except by contrary implication, in the exemption of those who averted such storms from the threat of criminal prosecution. It is also noteworthy that this, and two other *interpretationes* from the same title, speak of the 'invocation of demons'—a phrase used nowhere in the original title of the Theodosian Code and reflecting a distinctly more doctrinaire level of Christianization than that pervasive in the fourth century.

(5) A particularly interesting case is *CTh* 2. 8. 19, issued at Rome by Theodosius I in 389, a substantial law defining legal holidays. All days are defined as 'iuridici' except for the following: two months allowed for the mitigation of the summer heat and the harvest; the Kalends of January; the

[31] C. Pharr, *The Theodosian Code and Novels and the Sirmondian Constitutions* (Princeton, NJ, 1952: repr. New York, 1969), 230, translates, 'Christians, that is, by the priests'.

birthdays of Rome and Constantinople, 'because it was in these places that the laws ('iura') were born'; Easter Day and the seven days preceding and following; Sunday ('dies solis'); and the emperors' birthdays and the beginnings of their imperium ('diebus, qui vel lucis auspicia vel ortus imperii protulerunt').

The *interpretatio* to this law offered variations relating to both the time and place of these legal holidays, which presumably were a matter of personal interest to its author, one of the 'prudentes' or legal experts, whose role in preparing the *Breviarium* was mentioned earlier. It begins with a misunderstanding of the first point, where it claimed that the law allowed four months for gathering harvests. On a plain reading, the law did not say this: the two months allowed for summer heat and for harvesting were the same and not separate periods. According to the *interpretatio*, the actual time allowed for legal holidays was to be based upon the 'character of provinces' and the 'presence of landowners' ('pro provinciarum qualitate et pro praesentia dominorum'). Two periods were set out, from 24 June to 1 August for the harvest and from 23 August to 15 October for the vintage. The days between 1 and 23 August were allowed for the conduct of legal business. This was a situation much more suited for the conditions of southern Gaul than for those of the city of Rome, and the general rule was, as the *interpretatio* said, to suit province and personal circumstance.

As for the other holidays mentioned, the Kalends of January and the birthdays of Rome and Constantinople were ignored—the former was viewed as a pagan holiday now superseded, and neither Rome nor Constantinople was of much interest in early sixth-century Gaul. Sunday was allowed as a holiday, but had evolved from 'dies Solis' ('day of the sun') into 'dies dominicarum ('day of the Lord')', and came earlier in the sequence:[32] the two weeks' Easter holiday likewise was maintained, and Christmas Day and Epiphany were added to the existing schedule of holidays, their regular observance having developed in the period since the

[32] The version of the law in the *Codex Justinianus* (3. 12. 6) glosses the phrase 'dies solis' with the words 'quos dominicos rite dixere maiores,' as does *CTh* 8. 8. 3, of 386, together with its *interpretatio* (*Brev.* 8. 3. 1).

original law. Finally, the birthday and the beginning of the emperor's reign were retained as holidays, although the emperor was transformed into a 'princeps' ('dominus noster' here having become a designation for Christ) and his 'imperium' into a 'regnum'. Like other changes mentioned above, this would allow the application of the rule to a Gothic king.

(6) It already has been seen that in *CTh* 7. 1. 1 the Roman compilers showed their understanding of Visigothic sensitivities by altering 'barbarian' to 'enemy' depredation. The same delicacy of touch is found at *CTh* 15. 14. 15, where the 'disaster of barbarian devastation' ('clade barbaricae depopulationis') of the original text is expressed in the *interpretatio* as 'fear of the enemy' ('hostium terrore'). On the other hand, Valentinian I's law against intermarriage between Romans and barbarians (*CTh* 3. 14. 1) is retained in the *Breviarium* and even strengthened, with the expansion of the reference to cover barbarians 'of any nation whatsoever' ('cuiuslibet gentis').[33] The comment would suggest that there was little intermarriage between the Gothic and Roman populations under the Visigothic regime, a separation that might help to explain Alaric II's endorsement of a code of Roman law for the use of the Romans in his kingdom.

There are many such examples in the *interpretationes*, of words, formulas and comments that present significant differences from the original texts in question. Many of them reflect the change in various dimensions—regional, political, social, and cultural—that had occurred between the conditions of the late fourth and those of the early sixth centuries. Others resulted from developments within the law itself and within enduring Roman institutions like the church. Some expressed the antiquarian interests of jurists, and others, no doubt, their wishful thinking, not to mention errors and misunderstandings. Still others were merely haphazard and

[33] For detailed discussion of this law, see H. S. Sivan, 'Why not Marry a Barbarian? Marital Frontiers in Late Antiquity (The example of *CTh* 3. 14. 1)', in R. W. Mathisen, H. S. Sivan (eds.), *Shifting Frontiers in Late Antiquity* (Aldershot, 1996), 136–45, where it is argued that Valentinian's law concerned the events in North Africa narrated by Ammianus Marcellinus. Whether or not this is so, it is certain that the author of the *interpretatio* knew nothing of it.

of no great significance. But it seems clear that a consideration of the two issues discussed above—the selections and omissions made by the editors of the *Breviarium*, and the character of the *interpretationes* that they wrote—can yield valuable historical insights into the 'shifting frontier' between Roman and barbarian in the domain of Roman law.

In general, the *interpretationes* fully bear out the alternative and perhaps more descriptive appellation for the *Breviarium* as the *Lex Romana Visigothorum*. By the early sixth century the Roman Empire had largely disappeared, but, however selective and simplified, this was still a handbook of Roman law. With the exception of intermarriage (which was prohibited) and the one or two other examples mentioned, where the editors seem to have evinced a certain tact in referring to barbarians, nothing within the texts gives any indication that there were Goths living anywhere around. It clearly was envisaged by both the editors and by Alaric II, as well as by the nobles and bishops who endorsed the *Breviarium*, that Roman law would continue to define relations among the Romans living in the Visigothic kingdom. There is nothing to be found, as there is in the earlier 'Code of Euric', on relations between Romans and Goths, or between the Roman and any other system of law and courts, but that, and the relationship between the 'Code of Euric' and the *Breviarium*, is another story.

2

The Survival of Roman Family Law after the Barbarian Settlements

Antti Arjava

One of the most intriguing unsolved questions of early medieval history concerns the nature of the endurance of Roman social practices during the sixth and seventh centuries. The sources are not particularly rich on this issue in any of the new Germanic kingdoms,[1] and legal texts are the kind of evidence that pays more than casual attention to the secular life of the Roman population.[2] Consequently, legislation provides a context in which the interaction of Roman and barbarian culture can be investigated. The purpose of this study is to examine the vicissitudes of Roman family law after the late fifth century, when the promulgation of new imperial constitutions ceased in the west.

The paucity of texts is only one of the obstacles to a comparison between Roman and Germanic law in the early Middle Ages. It also can be difficult to distinguish one from the other. Many customs relating to marriage and the family have been found not just in the Classical World, but in different cultures all over the Eurasian continent: only the details and terminology varied.[3] Thus, a practice appearing in a

[1] See e.g. R. Collins, *Early Medieval Spain: Unity in Diversity, 400–1000*, 2nd edn. (London, 1995); P. J. Geary, *Before France and Germany: The Creation and Transformation of the Merovingian World* (New York, 1988); C. Wickham, *Early Medieval Italy: Central Power and Local Society 400–1000* (London, 1981); and I. Wood, *The Merovingian Kingdoms 450–751* (London, 1994).

[2] Hagiographical sources and the works of Gregory of Tours do provide some casual and passing glimpses, but they do not really answer the questions posed below.

[3] See especially J. Goody, *The Oriental, the Ancient, and the Primitive: Systems of Marriage and the Family in the Pre-Industrial Societies of Eurasia* (Cambridge,

Germanic law code and containing elements with similarities in Roman law, or vice versa, is not necessarily a result of simple borrowing. It can equally well attest a parallel development in the two cultures, which then of course may have made their subsequent fusion easier. For this reason particular attention might be devoted to those aspects of family law that were the most peculiar to the Romans: the paternal power (*patria potestas*) and the strong position of women. If traces of them are found in early medieval sources a good case could be made for a Roman survival. But before doing so one must look at the legal situation in the successor kingdoms more generally.

The Germanic rulers did not assume legislative authority over the Romans. Both populations continued to follow their own legal traditions. In the turbulent decades of the late fifth and early sixth centuries, Roman jurisprudents commented on and rewrote earlier juridic texts to make them simpler and more accessible to their countrymen. The *Lex Romana Visigothorum* ('Roman Law of the Visigoths'), now generally known as the *Breviarium Alaricianum* ('Breviary of Alaric'), issued in the year 506 by the Visigothic king Alaric II (484–507), was by far the largest of these new compendia and also was the most faithful to Roman law as its compilers did not tamper with the texts of the constitutions that they included in the collection. The résumés (*interpretationes*), which had been added to the original laws in several stages before they were included in the *Lex Romana Visigothorum*, display an equal reluctance to innovate.[4] They sometimes updated the laws they explained by taking account of later constitutions, but did not produce new legal principles themselves.[5]

1990); in a similar vein, from the viewpoint of legal history, see E. Levy, *West Roman Vulgar Law: The Law of Property* (Philadelphia, 1951); and idem, *Gesammelte Schriften* (Cologne, 1963).

[4] It would seem that the *interpretationes* were written at several stages, and were appended to the entire *CTh* and not just to the *Breviarium*, for there are *interpretationes* extant even for laws (e.g. *CTh* 4. 12) that were not included in the *Breviarium*. For discussion of the addition of the *interpretationes*, and a rather different view, see Matthews in this volume.

[5] On the *Breviarium* in general, see J. Gaudemet, *Le Bréviaire d'Alaric et les Epitome*, Ius Romanum Medii Aevi I.2b (Milan, 1965) = idem, *La Formation du droit canonique médiéval* (London, 1980); and note also Matthews in this volume.

Two shorter codes that appeared in the late fifth or early sixth century, the *Edictum Theoderici* (*ET*) ('Edict of Theoderic') in Ostrogothic Italy and the *Lex Romana Burgundionum* (*LRB*) ('Roman Law of the Burgundians') in the Burgundian kingdom, also preserved the essence of post-classical Roman law, even if they usually paraphrased it rather freely.[6] For example, the rules concerning divorce, the remarriage of widows, sale of children into slavery, betrothal, the abduction of women, and the guardianship over children, were more or less in line with the constitutions to be found in the *Codex Theodosianus* (*CTh*) ('Theodosian Code'), issued in the Roman Empire in 438.[7] The *Lex Romana Burgundionum* had several chapters on inheritance as well, clearly aiming to reproduce the system of Roman succession in a fairly comprehensive way (*LRB* 10, 28, 45). The *Edictum Theoderici*, on the other hand, passed over inheritance with a few very general clauses (*ET* 23–4, 28–33): it was not intended to be an exclusive source of law, but had to be supplemented from other collections, such as *Codex Theodosianus*. This may be because, unlike the *Breviarium* and *Lex Romana Burgundionum*, it was intended for both Romans and barbarians and therefore omitted areas in which the traditions were different. In any case, all these collections were compiled by Roman jurists from Roman law for a primarily Roman population. Although they do have some barbarous elements it is not quite correct to term them 'barbarian codes', as is often done in the Anglo-Saxon scholarship.[8]

When the Germanic peoples settled on Roman territory, they had no experience with written law. The Visigoths lived for decades in southern Gaul at a time when imperial administration still survived in western Europe. It therefore is no wonder that they were the first to create a written code for

[6] See *FIRA*, 683–710 (*ET*), and 713–59 (*LRB*).

[7] On divorce, see *LRB* 21; *ET* 54; *CTh* 3. 16; on remarriage, *LRB* 16; *ET* 37; *CTh* 3. 8; on betrothal, *LRB* 27; *CTh* 3. 2, 3. 5; *CJ* 5. 3; on abduction, *LRB* 9; *ET* 17–20; *CTh* 9. 24; on the sale of children, *ET* 94–5; *Sententiae Pauli* 5. 1. 1; on guardianship, *LRB* 36; e.g. *CTh* 3. 17. 4; *Nov. Theod.* 11.

[8] See G. Clark, *Women in Late Antiquity: Pagan and Christian Lifestyles* (Oxford, 1993), p. xii.

themselves, the *Codex Euricianus* ('Code of Euric') in the 470s.[9] Although it is preserved only in a few palimpsest fragments and as a substratum in later Germanic codes, it is easy to see how much it owed to Roman models. The diction reprises imperial legal language, and sometimes either the technical subject matter or close verbal affinities demonstrate the Roman derivation of individual statutes. It has been suggested on this basis that *Codex Euricianus* applied to both Goths and Romans (that is, it was a territorial law), but it seems rather that it was intended only for cases where at least one party was a Goth.[10] This seems natural, given that a ban on intermarriage between Goths and Romans persisted long into the sixth century.[11] In any case, some parts of Visigothic family law directly reflected Roman law as it was applied in the west in the late fifth century. Such borrowings appear, for example, in the rules that covered the remarriage of widows and widowers, the sexual relationships between free women and slaves, and the succession of spouses and of grandchildren on intestacy.[12] Additional similarities certainly would appear if the earlier stratum of Visigothic law were better known. In the course of time new legislation accumulated and partly replaced the Roman elements. Thus, the first fully extant Visigothic code, the *Lex Visigothorum* (*LV*) ('Law of the Visigoths') from the mid seventh century, was not more Roman even though it was expressly intended for

[9] See *MGH Leg.* 1. 1. 1–32; and H. Nehlsen, *Lex Visigothorum, Handwörterbuch zur deutschen Rechtsgeschichte*, ii (Berlin, 1978), 1966–79; also K. Zeumer, 'Geschichte der westgotischen Gesetzgebung I–IV', *Neues Archiv der Gesellschaft für ältere deutsche Geschichtskunde*, 23 (1898), 419–516; 24 (1899), 39–122, 571–630; 26 (1901), 91–149.

[10] For the territorial hypothesis, see Collins, *Spain*, 25–30; but for contra, see P. D. King, 'King Chindasvind and the First Territorial Law-Code of the Visigothic Kingdom', in E. James (ed.), *Visigothic Spain: New Approaches* (Oxford, 1980), 131–57.

[11] See *CTh* 3. 14. 1, preserved in the *Breviarium*; and *Lex Vis.* 3. 1. 1.

[12] On remarriage, see *Cod. Eur.* 321, 322; *Lex Vis.* 3. 2. 1; *CTh* 3. 8. 1–3, 8. 18. 3; *CJ* 6. 56. 4; *Nov. Sev.* 1 (463); *LRB* 16; *ET* 37; on women and their own slaves, *Lex Vis.* 3. 2. 2; *CTh* 9. 9. 1; *Nov. Anth.* 1 (468); on women and alien slaves, *Lex Vis.* 3. 2. 4; *CTh* 4. 12; on the succession of spouses, *Cod. Eur.* 334 = *Lex Vis.* 4. 2. 11; *CTh* 5. 1. 9; on that of daughters' children, *Cod. Eur.* 327; *CTh* 5. 1. 4 + *int.*; *LRB* 10. 2; A. Arjava, *Women and Law in Late Antiquity* (Oxford, 1996), 95–7, 101–3, 125, 168, 172–6, 225–7.

both Goths and Romans.[13] After its issuance, Roman law could no longer be applied in Spanish courts (*LV* 2. 1. 10).

No other Germanic people showed as much willingness to absorb Roman law as the Visigoths. The Burgundians, for example, made use of only the Latin legal vocabulary in the *Lex Burgundionum* (*LB*) ('Law of the Burgundians'), published *c*.500. Although they also commissioned the *Lex Romana Burgundionum* for their Roman subjects just a little later and although the latter derived its structure and titles from the former, a comparison between the two works reveals few similarities in subject matter.[14] Only in exceptional cases did the Burgundians adopt material from the *Codex Theodosianus* and its *interpretationes* for themselves.[15] It is as if they had consciously avoided an assimilation into the society of the conquered.

The Frankish codes, such as the early sixth-century *Pactus legis Salicae* ('Rule of Salic Law'), show no traces of Roman family law.[16] Although it is far from clear how much influence the *Pactus* had on subsequent Frankish legal practice,[17] it indicates that in the Merovingian kingdom Franks and Romans each retained their own legal systems. Romans continued to use the *Breviarium* and the *Codex Theodosianus* even after the Visigoths had been driven out of most of southern Gaul in 507 and thereafter. Roman legal autonomy was even reconfirmed by the king *c*.600.[18] Nevertheless, the dividing line may not have been clear. For example, in 633/4 an

13 *MGH Leg*. 1. 1. 33–456.

14 See e.g. *LB* 12, 14, 29, 39; with *LRB* 9, 10, 18, 19.

15 On the remarriage of widows, see *LB* 24 with *CTh* 3. 8. 2–3; on divorce, *LB* 34. 3–4 with *CTh* 3. 16. 1; on marriage without parental consent, *LB* 12. 5 with *LRB* 9. 2; *CTh* 9. 24. 1; but this may equally well have been influenced by Visigothic law (to which the *Burgundian Code* is indebted for many rules), *Lex Vis*. 3. 4. 7.

16 For the *Lex salica*, see also Pearson in this volume.

17 For this question, see A. C. Murray, *Germanic Kinship Structure: Studies in Law and Society in Antiquity and the Early Middle Ages* (Toronto, 1983), 128–33; and C. Schott, 'Der Stand der Leges-Forschung', *Frühmittelalterliche Studien*, 13 (1979), 29–55 at 48–9.

18 *Praeceptum Chlotharii* 4: *MGH Capitularia regum Francorum* 1. 19; note also Greg. Tur. *Hist*. 4. 46; *Vita Desiderii* 1: *MGH SRM* 4. 564; *Vita Boniti* 2: *MGH SRM* 6. 120; and see also I. Wood, 'The Code in Merovingian Gaul', in J. Harries, I. Wood (eds.), *The Theodosian Code: Studies in the Imperial Law of Late Antiquity* (Ithaca, 1993), 161–77.

heiress of a noble Frankish family mentioned in her last will the 'Theodosian law'.[19]

How quickly intermarriage blurred the concept of ethnicity is unclear. In eighth-century Italy it was still mandated that a Lombard woman who married a Roman thenceforth lived under Roman law, as did their children.[20] In Gaul, one Frankish capitulary in 768 authorized 'Romans' and 'Salians' to use their own law but in the same clause also confusingly referred to people who lived according to the law of their *provincia* or *patria*.[21] And another of 864 presented *lex Romana* as being applied in particular regions.[22]

Anyone wishing to consult Roman law in early medieval Gaul would not have been thwarted by any lack of source material. Copies of the *Breviarium* and the *Codex Theodosianus* seem to have been readily available in the Merovingian kingdom, and more manuscripts survive from the ninth century than from any other period.[23] But the extent to which these venerable statutes were put into practice or even correctly understood is difficult to assess. Authentic charters are very rare before the eighth century, and the gap is only partially filled by the collections of *formulae*. Many individual items in the formularies undoubtedly date to the sixth century and several may go back to Latin documentary practice in the western Empire. Some, like the eighth-century *Formulae Marculfi* ('Formulae of Marculf'), are predominantly Germanic in vocabulary and substance, whereas others, like the rather earlier *Formulae Andecavenses* ('Formulae of Angers'), preserve more Roman elements. What all of them suggest is a sort of mixed legal culture. The eighth-century *Formulae Turonenses* ('Formulae of Tours') in particular cites phrases from old imperial ordinances, but they do not

[19] J. M. Pardessus, *Diplomata, chartae, epistolae, leges aliaque instrumenta ad res Gallo-Francicas spectantia* (2 vols.; Paris, 1843–9), no. 257; see also J. Guerout, 'Le Testament de sainte Fare: matériaux pour l'étude et l'édition critique de ce document', RHE 60 (1965), 761–821.

[20] *Leges Liutprandi* 127, cf. 91; see also *LB* 100, discussed below.

[21] *Pippini capitulare Aquitanicum* 10: *MGH Capitularia regum Francorum* 1. 43.

[22] *Edictum Pistense* 13: *MGH Cap. Reg. Fr.* 2. 315.

[23] See e.g. J. Gaudemet, 'Survivances romaines dans le droit de la monarchie franque du Ve au Xe siècle', *Tijdschrift voor Rechtsgeschiedenis*, 23 (1955), 149–206, at 174–7.

always have much to do with the legal problem in question.[24] One wonders if there still existed a living tradition of Roman law.

Even if a wholesale confusion between the Roman and barbarian legal traditions appeared during later Merovingian and Carolingian times, this was not typical of the period immediately after the barbarian settlements. At that stage, the most common error was a misunderstanding of technical juridic concepts that one rarely encountered in everyday life. One such was the *ius liberorum* ('rights based on children'), originally an instrument of imperial population policy: a certain number of children ensured privileges for the parents, notably in the law of inheritance. Even after many of them had been abolished by Constantine (*CTh* 8. 16. 1), the *ius liberorum* was still required if a mother was to inherit something from her child, or if a married couple wanted to bequeath their property to each other. This was paradoxical because in practice such a mutual will was likely to be drawn up precisely in cases where the couple did not have surviving descendants. In such cases, one needed to acquire the *ius liberorum* as an imperial favour. And dispensations were indeed granted so lavishly that by the end of the fourth century the initial logic of the system had vanished (*CTh* 8. 17; *Nov. Val.* 21. 1).

As a result, in the *Breviarium* the chapter *De iure liberorum* (*CTh* 8. 17) was excluded as superfluous, although the term still appeared in the chapter *De legitimis hereditatibus* ('On legal inheritances') (*CTh* 5. 1). Moreover, whereas the *interpretatio* to *CTh* 5. 1 explained the phrase quite correctly, that to *Nov. Val.* 21. 1 obviously misunderstood it and in any case presented it so misleadingly that it could only create more confusion. Elsewhere, in the *Lex Romana Burgundionum* the *ius liberorum* was suppressed altogether (*LRB* 10. 5). By the end of the sixth century, understanding of the proper sense of the *ius liberorum* had been lost, and in the

[24] Cf. e.g. on abduction marriage, *Form. Turon.* 16 with *Sent. Paul.* 2. 19. 2 *interpretatio* (see Arjava, *Women*, 37–41); on divorce, *Form. Turon.* 19 with *CTh* 3. 16. 1. *interpretatio*; on wards, *Form. Turon.* 24 with *CTh* 3. 18. 1. *interpretatio*. See also Gaudemet, *Survivances*, 149–206 = idem, *La formation du droit canonique médiéval* (London, 1980), 178–82.

Merovingian and Visigothic *formulae* it was thought to mean simply the mutual will of a married couple without children, an idea shared also by Isidore of Seville, writing in Visigothic Spain in the early seventh century.[25]

Another word that underwent a semantic change was *dos*, the dowry. In imperial Roman law it always denoted the assets that the bride brought with herself into the marriage.[26] In the fourth century it received a counterpart, *donatio nuptialis* (bride-gift), which was the groom's contribution. Through a process that is far from clear the bride-gift gradually overshadowed and finally replaced the dowry in western Europe.[27] Thus, from the sixth century onward the word *dos* was used to refer not to the dowry but to the bride-gift. The traditional meaning survived in the letters of Sidonius (*Epist.* 1. 11. 5, 7. 2. 7–8), in the *Edictum Theoderici* (*ET* 54), and in the *Breviarium*, although an *interpretatio* to the *Sentences of Paul* (2. 21B. 1) indicates that the term now needed explaining to avoid confusion. On the other hand, the new practice prevailed in the *Lex Romana Burgundionum*, in the Germanic laws, in the *formulae*, and in many sixth-century literary sources.[28] Here, Germanic habits may have speeded up a development that had begun much earlier within the Empire.

The two cultures also converged in the punishment for adultery. Since the beginning of the Principate, Roman husbands had not been legally permitted to kill adulterous wives who were caught *in flagrante delicto* (although in some cases they had the right to kill the man). Homicides of honour undoubtedly remained a real possibility, but such private self-help did not suit the ideology of the developed Roman state, which had imperial courts to handle criminal charges.[29] By the early sixth century, however, even tradition-bound Roman jurists could not imagine that such high standards could be

[25] *Form. Andecav.* 41; *Form. Vis.* 24; and Isid. *Orig.* 5. 24; see Arjava, *Women*, 77–80, 125–6.

[26] For the impact of law on marriage, see also Erhart and Sivan in this volume.

[27] Arjava, *Women*, 52–62.

[28] See e.g. *LRB* 21; *LB* 62. 2; *LV* 3. 1. 5–6; *Form. Andecav.* 34; *Form. Turon.* 14; *Form. Vis.* 14–20; Greg. Tur. *HF.* 1. 47, 9. 20; Caes. Arel. *Serm.* 87. 3; Leander, *Regula* praef.; Arjava, *Women*, 52–62.

[29] See Arjava, *Women*, 193–202.

maintained. The *Breviarium* and the *Lex Romana Burgundionum* did not even mention a statutory penalty for adulterers who were convicted in court. Rather, they permitted the husband to murder an adulterous couple on the spot.[30]

This also was the viewpoint of most Germanic laws, and Gregory of Tours vividly depicts the application of private violence in such cases.[31] It would be tempting to explain this apparent change in Roman law either as an influence from Germanic custom or at least as a consequence of the disappearence of imperial authority. The *Lex Romana Burgundionum* (*LRB* 25), however, referred to a constitution of the emperor Majorian (457–61) that had made private retribution legal. If this citation is correct (as is quite possible, even though most scholars have rejected it as an error because the cited law is not extant) it would suggest that here, too, the provincial compilations remained true to an imperial model.

The cornerstone of Roman family law, and an essential element of the law of property and inheritance, was the concept of *patria potestas* ('paternal power').[32] In theory, a father exercised almost absolute authority over his descendants until his own death. Children who were *in potestate* had no independent ownership rights; everything they acquired belonged to their *paterfamilias* just as if they had been his slaves. A father could support his descendants by allowances or he could allow them to control property independently (*peculium*), although he could reclaim it if he wished. *Patria potestas* was an ingenious way to manage inheritance and family property in a society where earned income was rare and most offspring were dependant on a father's estate for their survival. It also was a system of control that gave the older generation of males unusual power over their descendants.

[30] *LRB* 25; for Italy, see Cass. *Var.* 1. 37. In the *Breviarium*, the new idea appeared in the *Sentences of Paul* in an exceptional case of textual alteration, which permitted a husband to kill his wife; see *LRV, Paul. Sent.* 2. 27. 1, with *Collatio Romanarum et Mosaicarum legum* 4. 12. 6: *FIRA* 2. 543–89 = *Sent. Paul.* 2. 26. 7: the restyling of this passage may have been almost unconscious, as phonological changes had made the two versions nearly identical; see Arjava, *Women*, 198–200.

[31] *LB* 68; *LV* 3. 4. 4–6; *Edictum Rothari* 211–13; Greg. Tur. *Hist.* 5. 32, 6. 36, 8. 19.

[32] See e.g. A. Arjava, 'Paternal Power in Late Antiquity', *JRS* 88 (1998), 147–65.

After the universal grant of Roman citizenship in 212, *patria potestas* became a legal fact to be reckoned with in all provinces. One can only guess at the problems that many ordinary inhabitants of the Empire must have encountered when faced with this strange new concept of family authority (Gaius, *Inst.* 1. 55). It is quite possible that many of them did not perfectly understand the legal definition of *potestas*: they may have regarded it as a kind of guardianship rather than an absolute domination.[33] Nevertheless, the fundamental principles of paternal power figured prominently in the rescripts of Diocletian issued in the 280s and early 290s and preserved in the *Codex Justinianus*. Its continued existence is reflected in the efforts made in the fourth and fifth centuries to ensure that fathers did not deprive their children of their maternal inheritance.[34] In addition, the concept of *patria potestas* permeated the *Corpus juris civilis* of Justinian (527–65), and it is impossible to believe that this recurrent topic was wholly fictional.[35]

On the other hand, as a matter of practice people increasingly connected *patria potestas* with minor children. Apart from the fact that in pre-modern demographic conditions a great number of fathers were already dead before the adulthood of their children, many children were artificially released from paternal power. This procedure, called emancipation, seems to have been an exceptional measure in the early Empire, being used for special political or family reasons. Beginning in the early fourth century, several sources suggest that a father was likely to consider the possibility of emancipating his children when they married or reached adulthood. It depended, however, entirely on his own decision.[36] According to Augustine, in contemporary Roman North Africa it was 'sometimes' expedient for children to be emancipated and receive property from their parents: a son's

[33] For the evidence of the papyri, see Arjava, 'Paternal Power', 155–9.

[34] See Arjava, *Women*, 98–105.

[35] See *Inst.* 1. 9 and 1. 12. The laws sometimes reveal that people felt the impact of *potestas* on their everyday life, see e.g. *Nov. Just.* 74. praef. 2.

[36] *CTh* 8. 18. 2: 319; *Conc. Hipp.* 1: 393 (*CCL* 149. 20); *CTh* 8. 13. 6 + 8. 18. 9 + 8. 19. 1: 426; *Nov. Val.* 35. 10: 452 + *interpretatio* (not mentioning emancipation but probably meaning it); note also *LRB* 26; and *Cod. Eur.* 321.

marriage or office-holding might be such a moment. Yet, many fathers refused to do so because they did not want to lose the authority deriving from their control over family property.[37]

Patria potestas certainly was known to Roman jurisprudents working north of the Alps in the late fifth and early sixth centuries. It appears in the *Breviarium*, not only in numerous titles but also in the *interpretationes*, seemingly without any need for further explanation. The *Lex Romana Burgundionum*, on the other hand, discussed it only indirectly; it does not mention *emancipatio*, although *filiusfamilias* appears three times.[38] These few citations provided a very inadequate description of the old *patria potestas* and would have rendered it difficult to understand without prior knowledge of Roman law. Nevertheless, they give the impression that the paternal power had not been forgotten.

Little is known about relations between parents and children among the Germanic peoples. Only the Burgundian and Visigothic codes discussed them to any extent. With regard to the *patria potestas*, the Visigoths, as usual, were more ready to utilize Roman models than other barbarian peoples. For example, they copied the paternal usufruct of the maternal inheritance directly from contemporary imperial law: Gothic children received two-thirds of their maternal estate when they married, or one half when they reached the age of twenty, very much like children living under Roman law who were emancipated.[39] What the children received from external sources, such as the king, they could keep as their own. Late Roman law already had come very near this with the institution of a separate account, the *peculium castrense*, for soldiers and civil servants.[40] Although *patria potestas* has left only such isolated traces in the seventh-century versions of the *Lex Visigothorum*, it is possible that in their earliest law the Goths had been prepared to embrace it to a somewhat wider extent. But this cannot be demonstrated, because

[37] Aug. *Serm.* 45. 2: *CCL* 41. 517.

[38] *LRB* 9. 4, 14. 4–5, 22. 1–2, 26. 1, 38. 1; note also *ET* 93, 95, 128.

[39] *Cod. Eur.* 321 = *LV* 4. 2. 13; cf. *CTh* 8. 18. 1–2; *Nov. Val.* 35. 10: 452 + *interpretatio*; *LRB* 26.

[40] *Cod. Eur.* 305; *LV* 4. 5. 5, 5. 2. 2. For the *peculium castrense* in Roman law, see Arjava, 'Paternal Power', 148–52.

the *Codex Euricianus* is so poorly preserved. In other Germanic societies the idea of a lifelong paternal authority seems to have been foreign. For example, in the *Lex Burgundionum* nothing resembling *patria potestas* can be found.[41]

The fate of the *patria potestas* among the former Roman provincials is equally difficult to trace. In the early seventh century, in his *Etymologiae* ('Etymologies'), Isidore of Seville explained the word *peculium* in terms that implied that adult people were no longer *in potestate* (Isid., *Orig.* 5. 25. 5). Yet, on the other hand, a Visigothic *Cartula mancipationis* ('Formula of Emancipation') reads:

> Ancient custom and the rulings of law have laid down that fathers having children under their authority should understand that, at the time when they see that [the children] have reached their majority, when freedom has been requested from the fathers, the fathers, moreover, should grant it, if they wish[42]

This text indicates that it had become customary to emancipate children after they had come of age, even if doing so was still, at least in theory, regarded as optional. In the seventh century the formula was certainly used by people who wished to continue Roman traditions. But whether it reflected Gothic custom as well cannot be known.

Elsewhere, in Gaul, no similar *formulae* have been preserved. There, paternal power has left virtually no trace.[43] Nor is it mentioned by Gregory of Tours. But there is some evidence from another region, the Rhaetian Alps, where Roman law appears not only in charters of the eighth and ninth centuries but also in a contemporary adaptation of the *Breviarium*, the so-called *Lex Romana Curiensis* ('Roman Law of Chur'), complied at or near Chur in *c.*800. This work preserved, in principle, the concepts of *patria potestas* and *emancipatio*. However, it glossed them in a way that shows that children now were released from paternal power rather automatically

[41] See *LB* 1, 24. 5, 51. 1–2, 75, 78.

[42] '[pri]sca consuetudo et legum decreta sanxerunt ut patres filios in potestate habentes tempore, qui perfectos in eos esse praespexerint annos, postula<ta> a patribus absolutione percipiant, quod tamen patres ipsi si voluerint concedant': *Formula Visigothorum* 34: I. Gil (ed.), *Miscellanea Wisigothica* (Seville, 1972), 103.

[43] For a possible exception, see *Form. Turon.* 23, probably modelled after Gaius, *Epit.* 1. 5. 1.

at their marriage.[44] It is tempting to assume that, in a similar manner, *patria potestas* gradually fell into desuetude in all corners of the former Empire.

Women's succession rights were another important area where Roman and Germanic law diverged. On intestacy, Roman daughters and sisters inherited precisely the same share as sons and brothers. Of course, Romans often left wills in which females may have received somewhat less than their intestate portion. But even if there was considerable individual and perhaps social variation, there is no reason to suspect that daughters in the Late Roman Empire were greatly discriminated against. For example, in 536 Justinian addressed a law to the governor of Armenia Prima demanding that only Roman law should thenceforth be observed in that newly organized region.[45] It stressed that the Armenians were to repudiate their barbarous custom of excluding women from inheritances, because such an injustice separated them from all the other peoples of the realm. Even allowing that the situation may have been somewhat over-simplified, the law implies that inheritance practices were expected to be relatively uniform throughout the Empire. In the west, all the western sources of Roman law likewise confirmed that daughters and sons were equal heirs to their parents in the immediate post-settlement period.[46]

Most Germanic codes, on the other hand, gave preference to sons in the inheritance, at least, of ancestral land.[47] One can only speculate regarding the origins of such a male-dominated inheritance system. The Germans may have imported it from their ancestral abodes (where it is questionable how far they recognized private land-ownership at all), or they could have adopted it during their travels, or they may have developed it only after they found permanent homes

[44] E. Meyer-Marthaler, *Römisches Recht in Rätien im frühen und hohen Mittelalter* (Zurich, 1968), esp. 131–8.

[45] *Nov. Just.* 21; see further Arjava, *Women*, 62–71.

[46] *LRB* 10, 45. 4; Gaius, *Epit.* 2. 8; and the *Breviarium*, passim.

[47] *LB* 14. 1, 51; *Pact. leg. Sal.* 59; *Lex Rib.* 57; *Edict. Chilp.* 3: *MGH Cap. reg. Franc.*1. 8; *Edict. Roth.* 158–60, 181, 199; K. Kroeschell, 'Söhne und Töchter im germanischen Erbrecht,' in G. Landwehr (ed.), *Studien zu den germanischen Volksrechten, Gedächtnisschrift für W. Ebel* (Frankfurt, 1982), 87–107; Murray, *Kinship*, 177–212.

within the Empire. It also may be that the diverging devolution of property, where daughters could expect to inherit a fair portion of their parents' estate, was a phenomenon of relatively stable and peaceful societies, such as Graeco-Roman Egypt, and the Roman Empire in general. These conditions were not found among the intrusive Germans. Still, the Visigoths once again adhered to the Roman custom, at least in part already incorporated into the *Codex Euricianus*.[48]

In the Merovingian kingdom, too, many Franks appear willing to have forsaken their customary inheritance pattern. This is attested in several testamentary *formulae* of Germanic origin. One reads as follows:

> An ancient but impious custom prevails among us that sisters do not have a share of the paternal land along with their brothers. But I have pondered this impiety (and decided that), as God has given you to be equally my children, in the same manner I have to love you equally, and after my death you shall equally enjoy my property[49]

Although the genesis of these *formulae* cannot be dated and it is not possible to estimate how often Franks used them in practice, it nevertheless is clear from many sources that women in early medieval Europe could own considerable landed estates, which they had inherited from their parents.[50] It is difficult to say if this was due to cultural reasons (the adoption of Roman customs by the Germanic minority) or if it had a more material basis (that is, some change in the roles of gender and property in Frankish society). Nor can we assess the role played here by the Roman nobility, which had gradually merged with the new rulers.

Thus, in the late Roman and sub-Roman cultural environment women were important owners of property, but could

[48] *CE* 320, 327; *LV* 4. 2. 1/5/9/10; see F. de Arvizu, 'La Femme dans Le Code d'Euric', *RHDFE*, 62 (1984), 391–405. The reading and interpretation of the fragments of the *CE* is still disputed.

[49] 'Diuturna sed impia inter nos consuetudo tenetur, ut de terra paterna sorores cum fratribus porcionem non habeant; sed ego perpendens hanc impietate, sicut mihi a Deo aequales donati estis filii, ita a me estis aequaliter diligendi et de res meas post meum discessum aequaliter gratuletis' (*Form. Marc.* 2. 12: *MGH Form.* 78; see also *Cartae Senonicae* 45: *MGH Form.* 205).

[50] See Arjava, *Women*, 72 n. 138.

they use it independently? The guardianship of women had long been rather nominal in Roman society, and as of the fifth century it no longer appeared in legal codes. It also was an established principle of Roman law that the husband could not interfere in his wife's economic affairs without her authorization.[51] Laws to this effect were included in the *Breviarium* and discussed in the so-called *Consultatio veteris cuiusdam iurisconsulti* ('The Consultation of a Certain Ancient Jurisconsult'), a short juridic treatise that is generally dated to the late fifth century.[52] Therefore, at least in theory, the strong position of women continued to be perceived as a characteristic of Roman legal culture. The Germanic codes, on the other hand, by no means presented a uniform approach. The Visigothic pattern did not differ radically from the Roman one: women had no guardians, nor did the husband have unlimited powers over his wife's goods, albeit he certainly was the leading figure in the family.[53] The Frankish codes did not discuss women's legal capacity at all.

The *Lex Burgundionum* was explicitly male oriented: 'We prescribe that if a Burgundian or Roman woman of her own free will joins a husband he will have power not only over the wife herself but in a like manner over all her property, too'.[54]

This did not of course apply to marriages between two Romans, but only to marriages of Burgundian men; the compilers evidently understood that there was a difference between the customs of the two ethnic groups. In Italy, finally, the chasm between Romans and Lombards was even greater. The latter placed women perpetually under male power (*mundium*), of either the husband or a blood relative or the king.[55]

[51] For these practices see Arjava, *Women*, 133–46.

[52] *CTh* 2. 12. 4 + *interpretatio*; 3. 1. 3 + *interpretatio*; *Epit. Cod. Greg. Vis.* 3. 6. 5: *FIRA* 2. 655–65; *Consultatio veteris cuiusdam iurisconsulti* 1, 2. 1–5, 8. 1–3: FIRA 2. 593–613; see also Cass. *Var.* 4. 10. 2.

[53] *LV* 2. 3. 6, 3. 1. 4, 4. 2. 15 (= *CE* 323), 4. 2. 16, 4. 2. 20, 5. 2. 3, 5. 2. 7.

[54] 'Quaecumque mulier Burgundia vel Romana voluntate sua ad maritum ambulaverit, iubemus, ut maritus ipse facultatem ipsius mulieris, sicut in ea habet potestatem, ita et de omnes res suas habeat' (*LB* 100).

[55] *Edict. Roth.* 186, 195–7, 204; *Leg. Liut.* 22.

From all this it would appear that it made a tremendous difference whether a woman was born under Roman or Germanic law. But in actual practice, the distinction may not have been as great as it seemed. Roman general opinion had always recommended that a wife should have her estate administered by her husband,[56] and the jurists agreed: it was only in cases of conflict that they stressed female autonomy. In spite of their theoretical independence, most women in practice shared the management of their households with their spouses. As almost no Latin private documents have survived before the late fifth century, it is impossible to verify how the western notarial practice took account of married women's property rights. But beginning in the sixth century evidence from all over the former Empire—Greek papyri from Byzantine Egypt, Latin papyri from Gothic and Byzantine Italy, wooden tablets from Vandal Africa, and *formulae*, along with charters from Frankish Gaul—concur in suggesting a reality very different from that found in imperial law. Only widows (or women whom we must assume to be widows) disposed independently of their assets. Married women either acted together with a husband or recorded his authorization.[57] It is striking that deeds involving married couples usually did not even specify the ownership of the property in question: it might have belonged to the husband or the wife, but obviously such information was not important for the validity of the transaction.[58]

What, if any, legal theory lay behind these practices is not clear. Because widows were permitted to act independently,

[56] See Arjava, *Women*, 127–33, 139–46.

[57] See the *Tablettes Albertini*, passim, in *Actes privés de l'époque vandale* (Paris, 1952); Ravenna papyri: *Pap. Tjäder* 12–15, 17, 20, 23, 25, 28, 30, 35. 25, 37, 43–4, 46, 49, in J.-O. Tjäder, *Die nichtliterarischen Papyri Italiens aus der Zeit 475–700* (2 vols.; Stockholm, 1982); *Form. Andecav.* 25, 27, 37, 46, 59; *Form. Marc.* 2. 3–5, 2. 32, 2. 39; Pardessus, *Dipl.* 140, 196, 256, 364, 384, etc.; see further Arjava, *Women*, 143–54. On Greek papyri, note J. Beaucamp, *Le Statut de la femme à Byzance (4e–7e siècle), ii: Les Pratiques sociales* (Paris, 1992), 212–47; eadem, 'L'Égypte byzantine: biens des parents, bien du couple?', in D. Simon (ed.), *Eherecht und Familiengut in Antike und Mittelalter* (Munich, 1992), 61–76.

[58] *Pap. Tjäder* 12, 14–15, 23, 25, 43–4; see also I. Heidrich, 'Besitz und Besitzverfügung verheirateter und verwitweter freier Frauen im merowingischen Frankenreich', in H.-W. Goetz (ed.), *Weibliche Lebensgestaltung im frühen Mittelalter* (Cologne, 1991), 119–38 at 128–9.

'female frailty' does not seem to have been a primary motivating element. There seems rather to have been an idea of a joint family enterprise, a concept that had been totally alien to classical Roman law. Yet, the phenomenon emerges so universally it is hard to believe it had not existed prior to the barbarian settlement. Two Gallic *formulae*, one from the sixth century (*Form. Andecav.* 1b), and the other from the eighth (*Form. Turon.* 20), may preserve traces of the development. Both are mandates by a wife who granted an unlimited authorization for her husband to take care of her legal and financial affairs. The latter even cited an *interpretatio* from the *Breviarium* (*CTh* 2. 12. 4), which, however, is not quite accurate, given that this constitution pointed out that the husband could only represent his wife in a particular matter specifically defined by the mandate. In any event, like fathers who emancipated their children, these individuals did not wish simply to disregard Roman law but to use its methods to achieve results that ran counter to its original principles.

In conclusion, it appears that in the period following the collapse of the imperial goverment in the west, from the mid fifth century through the early sixth century, Roman family law survived fairly well the transformation of the political and ethnic landscape. The *interpretationes*, the *Breviarium*, and the *Lex Romana Burgundionum* display an interest in, an ability to understand, and a desire to preserve the legal framework of the Roman family. These works exhibit few traces of conscious innovation, and mistakes were rare, in part, perhaps, because most concepts of family law were inherently easy to understand and did not pose problems for anyone who had at least elementary legal training. Paternal power, the general system of succession, rules over remarriage, and many other aspects of family law were transmitted, perhaps somewhat simplified (which was not necessarily a very bad thing), but still in easily recognizably Roman form. On the other hand, some technical concepts of imperial jurisprudence, such as the *ius liberorum*, were evidently passing into oblivion, and the diminishing importance of the old dowry can be seen in the change of vocabulary.

Some might suggest that this conservatism was the result of a lack of understanding and self-confidence, so that the compilers of the *Breviarium* refrained from changing the texts of the *Codex Theodosianus* merely because they did not know how to do it properly. However, the *Lex Romana Burgundionum* and the *Edictum Theoderici* were very free renderings of Roman law, and in the 470s Roman advisers had provided an innovative mixture of Roman and Gothic norms for Euric. So it is difficult to see why the jurists of Alaric II could not have found a way to introduce changes into the existing legal order if they had thought it desirable. The law remained the same because that was exactly how the compilers wanted it to be.

How far the immigrants themselves were willing to assimilate the legal achievements of their subjects is another problem. Visigothic legal history is obscured by difficulties of the textual tradition: it is often difficult to determine whether a given Roman trait was already in the *Codex Euricianus* or was only added later, that is, whether Visigothic law became Romanized or Germanized as time went on. However, it is sufficiently clear that from the early years of their settlement the Goths were more open to Roman influence than other barbarian peoples. Whether this means that social conditions among them had already come closer to those among the Romans, or only that being the first Germans to legislate they were more dependent on Roman models, might be difficult to prove, given our very meagre evidence. But as the Goths retained most of their adopted principles in their successive codes, we may suspect a combination of the two causes.

The developments after the early sixth century are inevitably shrouded in mystery. The habits of different ethnic groups were certainly combined, although there is no evidence on how this came about. This is a conclusion that must sound both very unsatisfactory and not at all novel. If any progress in the future is possible beyond that, it may come from a more careful study of the formularies and charters, which suggest that well into the early medieval period at least some people tried to preserve formalities that had their origins in a distant past and a bygone culture.

Finally, this survey also may have implications for another debated issue: the extent of legal integration during the Roman Empire itself. The fact that such large collections of imperial law were considered worth the trouble to compile and recopy even after the fall of the western empire suggests that they had great practical value for a large number of former Roman citizens. And if people in remote Alpine valleys preserved Roman elements in their customary law right through the early Middle Ages it is difficult to believe that they had neglected Roman legislation while the Empire still survived. It should not, of course, be presumed that imperial constitutions or juristic commentaries *per se* had a wide currency. Even today most people learn the individual legal rules in force in their society only when they get personally involved in a dispute. In this sense laws are probably never 'embraced' by the populace at large. But it seems reasonable to conclude that on the eve of the barbarian settlement the Empire's inhabitants were more or less familiar with the general tenor of their family law, as far as any population can be said to be aware of its own legal system. And as a result they made concerted efforts to preserve the laws that regulated their family lives even after the regulating authority disappeared.

3
The Legacy of Roman Law in Post-Roman Britain

Michael E. Jones

A logical approach to a study of the transmission and influence of Roman law in post-Roman Britain would be to look both at late Roman legislation associated with Britain and at legal systems operating within the former Roman diocese during the early Middle Ages, and then to try to squeeze these two endpoints together to meet in the historical context of Late Antiquity. Unfortunately, this method would fail at both ends. The Romano-British imprint on late Roman law codes is astonishingly slight, and provides no safe basis for anything beyond speculation. The legal systems of early medieval Britain, and in particular the Welsh and Anglo-Saxon laws, show no evidence of significant, direct influence of Roman law traceable to the Roman governance of Britain. The exceptional lack of impact of Roman law on Roman and post-Roman Britian surely deserves discussion and explanation.

With regard to Roman law, of the more than 3,500 entries in the Theodosian Code of 438 CE, only a single enactment was certainly directed to Britain: *CTh* 11. 7. 2, a rescript from the emperor Constantine (306–37) of 20 November 319, was addressed to Pacatianus, vicar of Britain. The short text stated that decurions were liable for taxes owed on their property together with the liability of their *coloni* and *tributarii* (taxable dependants). They were not liable, however, for property and *coloni* of other decurions.[1] The law therefore

[1] 'unusquisque decurio pro ea portione conveniatur, in qua vel ipse vel colonus vel tributarius eius convenitur et colligit; neque omnino pro alio decurione vel territorio conveniatur. id enim prohibitum esse manifestum est et observandum

documents the existence of the colonate in Britain and also associates decurions with the problem of tax collection and liability, one of the most serious and intractable problems to beset the empire.

In similar fashion, the *Digest* of Justinian (527–65) also preserves only one piece of legislation addressed to governors of Britain. A rescript of Septimius Severus (193–211) and his son Caracalla dealing with an inheritance problem was directed to Virius Lupus, 'governor of Britain'.[2] The *Digest* also includes one other possibility, a citation from a letter of Hadrian to Pomponius Falco. No details of Falco's office are preserved, but a Pompeius Falco served as governor of Britain under Hadrian (117–38) before retiring to private life. The legal issue dealt with the validity of the will of a legionary who had committed suicide, perhaps while campaigning against northern British peoples (*Digest* 28. 3. 6. 7).

The *Digest* also cites two other cases concerning Britain. The jurist Javolenus Priscus, who served in Britain as *legatus iuridicus* ('Judicial Legate') *c.*84–6, discussed a principle of inheritance linked to a dispute about the will of the chief pilot of the Roman fleet in Britain (*Digest* 36. 1. 48). Another entry concerns the status of a woman condemned to hard labour in the saltworks for an unspecified crime. While serving this sentence she was abducted by brigands from across the frontier and sold. A centurion named Cocceius Firmus redeemed her. He was evidently her original owner, and won a judgment that the government was liable for her abduction from

deinceps, quo iuxta hanc nostram provisionem nullus pro alio patiatur iniuriam' (*CTh* 11. 7. 1). C. E. Stevens, 'A Possible Conflict of Laws in Roman Britain', *JRS* 37 (1947), 132–4, speculates that the law dealt with obligations of landholders to take over waste or abandoned land and that it may reflect a clash between native British custom and Roman law. But given that the same principle also was expressed in later legislation referring to Africa and Italy (*CTh* 11. 1. 31; 8. 8. 10), it would not seem to be directly connected to British native landholding customs. It may be that the principle espoused in *CTh* 11. 7. 12, 'decurions shall demand payment of decurions', is a more likely source of the problem in Britain and elsewhere.

[2] 'quae sententia rescripto imperatoris nostri ad Virium Lupum Brittanniae praesidem comprobata est . . .' (*Digest* 28. 6. 2. 4). In addition, the *Codex Justinianus* also preserves a number of rescripts issued while emperors were campaigning in Britain, but their content does not seem to be directly relevant to British conditions: note *CJ* 3. 32. 1 and other edicts of Severus and Caracalla issued from York in 210 (*CJ* 3. 1. 2, 6. 4. 1, 8. 37. 2, 8. 44. 3, 8. 53. 1).

the saltworks. The imperial treasury had to refund to him her purchase price.[3]

These citations, few as they are, document Britain's participation in the legal life of the Roman world. The paucity of references to Britain in the codes, however, is curious and striking. After all, approximately a tenth of the entire Roman army was garrisoned there for three centuries. The later British diocese eventually included five provinces and a population estimated at between three and six million inhabitants. A number of factors may have resulted in the scarcity of British material in the law codes. The means by which the codes were assembled may provide a partial explanation, for by the late 420s British archives, even if they survived, no longer would have been accessible, given that British ties with the empire had been severed from *c*.410. The stormy political history of the British diocese also might have resulted in a disinclination to include British documents preserved in the imperial archives of Rome, Ravenna, and Constantinople, not to mention the consideration that no British legislation could even have existed for the period 410–37.[4] Moreover, during the years 383–88 and 407–10, Britain was controlled by usurpers whose legislation, even where it survives, was not included in the lawcodes; and for the period 383–410, Britain was ruled by emperors who also controlled Italy for only eight years.[5] In addition, legislation relating to Britain might have been excluded based on the compilers' occasional policy of excluding laws that no longer had any basis, which could have minimized references to Britain.

Moreover, the lack of legislation dealing with Britain also may reflect the failure of Romano-Britons to manipulate the imperial system effectively.[6] For in many ways the rulings

[3] *Digest* 49. 15. 6. For the British origin of this case, see E. Birley, *Roman Britain and the Roman Army* (Kendal, 1976), 51–2, 87–103.

[4] Regarding the provision of source material for the Theodosian Code, J. F. Matthews, 'The Making of the Text', in J. Harries and I. Wood (eds.), *The Theodosian Code: Studies in the Imperial Law of Late Antiquity* (Ithaca NY, 1993), 19–44, stresses the importance of provincial archives, while B. Sirks, 'Sources of the Code', ibid. 45–67, focuses on the role of the central archives.

[5] N. Higham, *Rome, Britain, and the Anglo-Saxons* (London, 1992), 69.

[6] J. Harries, 'The Background to the Code', in Harries and Wood (eds.), *Theodosian Code*, 9–15.

preserved in the law codes represent the successful use of influence. Legal cases that reached the emperor often had to survive a series of appeals through the imperial hierarchy, including provincial governor, vicar, praetorian prefect, and consistory. Successful requests, reports, and proposals that led to legislation also had to filter successfully through the bureaucratic hierarchy. To sidestep the hierarchy and reach the emperor's ear more directly required even greater leverage and patronage. Those most able to do so belonged to the senatorial aristocracy, that is, they were *clarissimi* as opposed to *curiales*, who had much less stature. Significantly, however, there is no substantial evidence for the existence of senatorial families either resident in Britain or of British origin.[7]

Finally, yet another possible explanation for the thinness of British legislation in the law codes concerns the relationship of native and Roman law. The extent to which the Roman administration tolerated the persistence of local, non-Roman law among peoples of the provinces who were not Roman citizens is a vexed question.[8] In theory, if both parties in a case were non-citizens and willing to be judged locally, their dispute could be resolved according to native law. Provided such cases were not referred upward to a Roman magistrate, there would be no Roman record for potential inclusion in the law codes.[9] Thus, an inverse relationship might exist between the continued practice of native law in a given region and that region's representation in the law codes.

These possibilities for the lack of reference to Britain in the law codes all result from a lack of evidence that promotes speculation even as it inhibits analysis. The handful of legal vignettes provide tantalizing glimpses into the operation of

[7] King Cogidubnus, or perhaps his son, provide one possible example of a British senator from the first century: see A. Birley, *The Fasti of Roman Britain* (Oxford, 1981), 209. Otherwise, inscriptions suggest that Britons sought senatorial patronage from outside the province, perhaps to compensate for the lack of British *clarissimi*: two such were M. Vettius Valens (second century) and Julius Asper (third century) (Birley, *Fasti*).

[8] For local law in the east, where the evidence is much more extensive, see L. Mitteis, *Reichsrecht und Volksrecht in den ostlichen Provinzen des römischen Kaiserreich* (Leipzig, 1891).

[9] A. Lintott, *Imperium Romanum* (London, 1993), 159.

Roman law in Britain, but cannot provide a reliable basis for answers to essential questions. What was the relation between native and Roman law in Britain, particularly after Caracalla's *Constitutio Antoniniana* of 212, which granted citizenship to all of the *gentes* within the empire?[10] And what was the legacy of Roman law in the immediate post-Roman era in Britain? Some insight into these issues might be sought in the Welsh and Anglo-Saxon laws that formed the early medieval legal systems operating within the former diocese of Britannia.

It has been said that 'Welsh law was not quite what one might expect.'[11] This is particularly the case when looking for Roman influences. Wales, of course, was long part of the Roman empire. Although Irish settlement affected the western areas of Wales in the late Roman and immediate post-Roman period, and population from the Romano-British lowlands may have moved into Wales in response to the Anglo-Saxon invasions, much of the population was essentially indigenous throughout the Roman and early Medieval eras. Theoretically, this should offer good potential for the uninterrupted transmission of Roman legal custom and practice into the early Medieval period. In fact, however, the degree of Romanization of different parts of Wales varied greatly. On the one hand, south-eastern Wales formed the Romanized *civitas* of the Silures within the Roman province of Britannia Prima. On the other hand, the mountainous areas of Wales were long under military government and it seems were never incorporated into a *civitas* structure. In addition, in the latter regions there is little evidence for a developed Roman material culture or for the spread of Roman institutions. In this sense Roman Wales may be considered to have been a cultural frontier area.[12]

The medieval Welsh laws survive in some forty manuscripts, which represent three redactions perhaps dating to the twelfth and early thirteenth centuries. Six are written in Latin; it is unclear whether the Welsh or Latin texts are older.

[10] For the edict, see Plutarch, *Mor.* 814F; Dio Cassius 77 (78). 9. 5; Justinian, *Digest* 1. 5. 17; and *Pap.Giessen* no. 40. col. 1.

[11] T. M. Charles-Edwards, *The Welsh Laws* (Cardiff, 1989), 2.

[12] See W. Davies, *Wales in the Early Middle Ages* (Leicester, 1982), 85–7.

The laws do exhibit some regional aspects, but otherwise are essentially homogeneous. Unsupported tradition associates them with King Hywel Dda (904–50). The entire Welsh legal tradition is often called simply the 'Law of Hywel' (*lex Hoeli; Cyfraith Hywel*). The laws contain a mixture of archaic and more recent material. Indeed, elements of the substance and language of the laws certainly predate the rule of Hywel. It is, however, often difficult to distinguish between early and later material and a central problem of analysis is recognition and separation of different chronological strata.[13]

The laws are organized topically into what are called 'tractates', for example, 'Law of Women', 'Corn Damage', and 'Laws of the [Royal] Court'. The result is something between a textbook and a legal commonplace book. There seems to be no close parallel elsewhere.[14] There are very few records of actual court proceedings, and although the lawbooks sometimes can be supplemented with material from literature, inscriptions, charters, and narrative historical sources, the law is presented in principle rather than in action.[15] These principles define a traditional native and tribal law centered on the kindred, oath-taking, and compensation.[16] Interestingly, unlike Roman law and Germanic barbarian law, the authority of Welsh law derived from ancient custom as a law of a people rather than legislation associated with royal or imperial power of a monarch.[17]

Native Welsh law included an awareness of its distinctiveness from other laws, particularly the canon law of the Church and English law. This sense of distinction was no doubt nourished by frontier conflict with the Anglo-Saxons,

[13] See D. Jenkins, trans., ed., *The Law of Hywel Dda* (Llandysul, 1986), pp. xi–xxxvi; Davies, *Wales*, 203–5; and Charles-Edwards, *Welsh Laws*.

[14] Jenkins, *Law of Hywel*, p. xxvi. Ireland provides some similarities, but these are probably better explained as outgrowths of a common Celtic social pattern rather than as direct influence or borrowing: see Jenkins, *Law of Hywel*, p. xxxiv; and Charles-Edwards, *Welsh Laws*, 23.

[15] The lawbooks have a strongly didactic quality and may well have been produced for lawyers, judges, or men ambitious for judicial office.

[16] Charles-Edwards, *Welsh Laws*, 9. Key concepts include *braint* (status, right); *sarhaed* (insult and also compensation for insult); *cenedl* (kin, kindred), and *galanas* (enmity, homicide, feud and compensation for homicide). See the glossary in Jenkins, *Law of Hywel*, 309–94.

[17] See Jenkins, *Law of Hywel*, pp. xxxiv–v.

Anglo-Normans, and later English kings. Rival law was not only alien, it was also often hostile and aggressive. For medieval Wales legal unity in the sense of shared law evidently predated political unity.[18]

Evidence of direct Roman influence on Welsh law is difficult to find, either in the form of explicit reference within the lawbooks and maxims, or in the legal process of which the written law was a component. A complicating element, moreover, is that Welsh legal developments were part of the great twelfth-century European revival of Roman law. This means that any Roman elements in the Welsh lawbooks could have resulted from the medieval revival rather than being a direct inheritance from the Roman occupation of Britain. For example, the form of proof in Welsh called *arddelw*, which evidently derived directly from the Roman *exceptio*, can be shown to have been an assimilation of new practice from the high Middle Ages in which a concern for argument displaced the earlier Welsh native practice of a conflict between sets of witnesses.[19] Another factor that confuses the issue even more is the possibility of independently evolved equivalents. The Welsh *sarhaed* (insult) in its legal sense closely resembles the *iniuria* of Roman law, and the Latin term is used as a translation of the Welsh in the lawbooks. There is no indication of a direct relation, however, and the concept is common to a number of different and seemingly unrelated legal systems.[20]

There is one significant set of legal texts whose underlying tradition can be traced back to the later Roman empire. These are records of land transactions (charters) purportedly carried out in southern Wales from the sixth through the eleventh centuries, and which exhibit peculiarities in structure, phraseology, and delivery that are geographically

[18] See Charles-Edwards, *Welsh Laws*, 11.

[19] See Charles-Edwards, *Welsh Laws*, 38, 63–6, 87. An *exceptio* was a reply made by a defendant that allowed the truth of the plaintiff's assertion but claimed an additional consideration that nullified the effect. In English law the *exceptio* appeared in *Glanville* and flourished in 'Bracton', about 1230: see F. Pollock, F. W. Maitland, *History of English Law*^{2} (Cambridge, 1968), 2. 611–20.

[20] See Jenkins, *Law of Hywel*, 379; also B. Nicholas, *Introduction to Roman Law* (Oxford, 1962), 215–16.

limited to the 'Celtic' west.[21] They are not contemporary records, but narrative descriptions in retrospective form, and are preserved in early medieval texts such as the *Life of St. Cadog* (late seventh, or eighth century), the *Lichfield Gospels* (eighth or ninth century), and the *Book of Llandaf* (twelfth century). Although the medieval process of copying and editing has corrupted the texts, close study of the witness lists and diplomatic formulae confirms that a number of the charters derive from genuine earlier manuscripts.[22] The earliest example potentially free of dubious elements is a grant 'from Peibio to Dubricius' probably made in the second quarter of the sixth century.[23] If this charter is genuine, it predates the earliest recorded Anglo-Saxon charters by a century and represents an independent practice.[24]

These early charters describe transactions between Welsh rulers and the churches of southern Wales. The granting of land seems to have taken place in a hybrid context. On the one hand, on the ecclesiastical side, forms and formulae, including the written charter, witnesses, and the alienation of property in perpetuity, derived ultimately from the late Roman private deed.[25] Comparison of early medieval forms of donation in Wales and on the continent reveal some significant similarities.[26] On the other hand, from the standpoint of the donors, tribal custom rather than Roman practice seems to have been at work. Even kings evidently were unable to alienate land without the consent of family members.

[21] See W. Davies, 'The Latin Charter-Tradition in Western Britain, Brittany and Ireland in the Early Mediaeval Period', in D. Whitelock, R. McKitterick, D. Dumville (eds.), *Ireland in Early Mediaeval Europe* (Cambridge, 1982), 258–80; and F. Seebohm, *Tribal System in Wales* (London, 1895), 201.

[22] See Charles-Edwards, *Welsh Laws*, 74.

[23] *Liber Landavensis* 72a: see Davies, 'Liber Llandavensis: Its Construction and Credibility', English Historical Review, 88 (1973) 351.

[24] See W. Davies, *An Early Welsh Microcosm* (London, 1978); and eadem, 'Liber Landavensis', 335–51. But for a rejection of these charters as evidence for pre-ninth-century Welsh history, see K. R. Dark, *Civitas to Kingdom* (Leicester, 1994), 140–8.

[25] Davies, 'Charter-Tradition', 274–6, compares formulae from the charters with the language of imperial rescripts, and the use of witnesses with Constantinian legislation on property transfer; see also E. Levy, *West Roman Vulgar Law: The Law of Property* (Philadelphia, 1951), 1–148; and Seebohm, *Tribal System*, 227–8.

[26] See Seebohm, *Tribal System*, 192–7, 210–26, a comparison to Alamannic and Bavarian laws; and Davies, 'Charter-Tradition', 262.

Rents and payments, moreover, correspond to traditional food rents mentioned in the Welsh law codes.[27]

How did late Roman form of legal documents, specifically the Latin charter tradition, reach western Britain in the immediate post-Roman era? Paucity of records permits no secure answer, but the geographical and chronological distribution of the charters is suggestive. They are confined to western Britain, and are first found in the sixth century. This presents a gap between the periods and areas of Roman occupation, and indicates that the charters were a post-Roman import into Celtic areas rather than the product of a practice that survived continuously from the Roman period. The clear ecclesiastical context of the charters suggests that this importation was tied to the spread of monasticism in western Britain beginning in the later fifth century.[28] Newly established monasteries required land for subsistence, and the donation of land required grants, something for which pre-Christian Celtic customary law had no procedure. The early charters may therefore be a Welsh solution to the novel problem of alienating land from the kindred in order to donate it in perpetuity to the church. The charters, familiar to churchmen with continental experience, solved the problem.[29]

It is tempting to link the charter evidence with the corpus of Christian inscribed stones from western Britain dating from the late fifth to the eleventh centuries.[30] Several of these monuments use formulae found in the charters.[31] Nor does the British sequence of inscribed stones show any real continuity with Roman Britain. The fashion and idea for such

[27] On alienation, see Davies, *Microcosm*, 162; for Welsh custom, see Seebohm, *Tribal System*, 198, 231–3.

[28] See Seebohm, *Tribal System*, 193–8, 204–5; and Davies, 'Charter-Tradition', 279–80, who dates the origin of the charters to the first half of the fifth century. For monasticism, see C. Thomas, *Celtic Britain* (London, 1986), 123, 135.

[29] Seebohm, *Tribal System*, 197–8; and Thomas, *Celtic Britain*, 132.

[30] See V. E. Nash-Williams, *The Early Christian Monuments of Wales* (Cardiff, 1950), nos. 240, 255; and C. Thomas, *And Shall these Mute Stones Speak? Post-Roman Inscriptions in Western Britain* (Cardiff, 1994).

[31] See Nash-Williams, *Early Christian Monuments*, nos. 240, 255; and see J. Higgit, 'The Stone-Cutter and the Scriptorium: Early Medieval Inscription, in Britain and Ireland', *Epigraphik*, (1988), 149–62.

inscriptions may well have come from outside Britain, perhaps through limited contact with Christian Gaul.[32]

The evidence for the nature and practice of Welsh law, drawn from the lawbooks, literature, inscriptions, charters, and other written texts suggests a lack of direct transmission of the Roman legal system into post-Roman, western Britain.[33] Nor does one find evidence for such a connection by looking for conformity of Welsh law with Roman law in a more general sense.[34] It does not seem possible to trace 'a pattern of gradual devolution from late Roman society'.[35] There are no obvious stepping-stones that connect the British and Celtic roots of the Welsh legal tradition with the end of the Roman governance of Britain.[36] Therefore, instead of a devolutionary relationship between Roman law and native British legal traditions one perhaps should consider the possibility of revolution and discontinuity.

The history of law during the Roman era in Britain doubtless reflects the dual trends of Romanization and the survival of native tradition.[37] But more so than in other provincial areas, conditions in Roman Britain seem to have favoured the survival of native legal custom. Because Britain was never completely conquered by Rome, a zone of independent British kingdoms survived between the Pictish territories of the far north and the frontier of the Roman diocese. Within this zone native British Celtic law persisted. The Roman diocese of Britain was itself subdivided into zones of military and civil governance, partially reflecting the highland and lowland division of Britain's geography. Within the area under military government, the habits and practice of Roman civil law may never have become strongly rooted. During the fluid but

[32] See Nash-Williams, *Early Christian Monuments*, 1; followed by Thomas, *Celtic Britain*, 139–40. For possible non-Gallic or Spanish contacts, see Davies, 'Liber Landavensis', 351; and Thomas, *Celtic Britain*, 135, 145.

[33] See Jenkins, *Law of Hywel*, p. xxxiv.

[34] See Lintott, *Imperium Romanum*, 160, who suggests that conformity with Roman law is an obvious yardstick of the degree of political and social coherence in the Roman empire.

[35] For contra, see Davies, *Early Welsh Microcosm*, 160.

[36] For contra, see Charles-Edwards, *Welsh Laws*, 75.

[37] See J. Hines, 'Britain after Rome: Between Multiculturalism and Monoculturalism', in P. Graves-Brown, S. Jones, C. Gamble (eds.), *Cultural Identity and Archaeology* (London, 1996), 257–9.

obscure conditions of the fourth century and after, areas of the military zone including the Pennines, mid-Wales, and the south-western peninsula may even have passed from effective Roman government into the hands of native dynasties.[38] If so, these areas may also have returned to the practice of native law and custom—if, indeed, they ever really left it. Ultimately, the periodic rebellions in Britain over the one hundred and fifty year period ending in 410 seem to have created intervals of de facto self-government in Britain. The revolt of Magnus Maximus, for example, severed Britain from the central empire in 383. Although he was killed in 388, restoration of Roman control in Britain was delayed until 395. Such intervals of self-government may have permitted or even encouraged the practice of native British legal traditions.[39]

Even if Celtic customs may have been maintained in the 'wilder west' of Britain, it does appear that Roman law superseded native law in the lowland and civilian zone of Roman Britain.[40] By the end of the Roman era in Britain, that is, the close of the fourth century and the first half of the fifth century, writings by Britons suggest the existence in the island of rhetorical schools preparing students for careers in Roman administration. Such training necessarily would have included exposure to the language and procedures of the Roman law courts.[41] The famous British heresiarch Pelagius, if his enemies may be believed, left Britain *c.*380 and travelled to Rome, perhaps, to study law.[42]

[38] See D. Dumville, 'The Idea of Government in Sub-Roman Britain', in G. Ausenda (ed.), *After Empire: Towards an Ethnology of Europe's Barbarians* (Woodbridge, 1995), 178–80.

[39] See Dumville, 'Idea', 178.

[40] See Stevens, 'Possible Conflict', 133; and Dark, *Civitas*, 2, 29, 216, 223.

[41] See M. Lapidge, 'Gildas's Education and the Latin Culture of Sub-Roman Britain', in M. Lapidge, D. Dumville (eds.), *Gildas: New Approaches* (Woodbridge, 1984), 28–33.

[42] For possible motives for Pelagius' departure from Britain, see B. R. Rees, *Pelagius: A Reluctant Heretic* (Woodbridge, 1988), pp. xiii–xiv. See Lapidge, 'Gildas's Education', 31, for the suggestion that Pelagius had rhetorical training before leaving. If the monk described by Jerome, *Epist.* 50, is Pelagius—and if the description is accurate—then Pelagius was a 'home grown dialectician' ignorant of Aristotle and Cicero who composed illogical syllogisms in uneducated circles, one who 'has reached perfection without a teacher, so as to be a vehicle of the spirit and a self-taught genius' (trans. W. H. Fremantle, *The Principal Works of St. Jerome* (Grand Rapids, 1979), 80–1). This does not sound like the product of an established rhetorical school, even in Britain.

If Roman law was in fact predominant in lowland Britain during the later Roman period, then any explanation for the transmission or non-transmission of the Roman legal tradition in Britain must be embedded in the historical context of the fifth and sixth centuries, the most probable period of transition between late Roman law on the one hand and Anglo-Saxon law along with the re-emergence of Celtic law on the other. The most crucial source for this transitional period is Gildas's *De excidio britanniae* ('On the Ruin of Britain'). Composed sometime between *c.*485 and 540, *De excidio* is a jeremiad warning the Britons of God's impending wrath and denouncing the contemporary secular and ecclesiastical rulers for their corruption, oppression, and moral failings.[43]

Without doubt, Gildas had a keen interest in justice, or more precisely, in the abuse of justice. His writings have been cited as evidence both for the survival of Roman law and for the displacement of Roman law by Celtic custom.[44] The scholarly disagreement stems in part from the thinness and ambiguity of the evidence, and in part from Gildas's style and purpose. In the final analysis, Gildas was not interested in the existence or lack of existence of a clash between native and Roman legal tradition and practice but in the biblical struggle between God's law and human sin. In short, Gildas was not a lawyer but a preacher.

Arguments for the survival of legal practice based on Roman law in Gildas's world can be based on Gildas's vocabulary, on his ideas of political legitimacy, and on the rhetorical structure of the *De excidio*. Regarding the first of these, Gildas mentioned 'regula recti indicii' ('the rule of correct judgment'), which has been seen as a reference to Roman law.[45] This is possible, although Welsh law too, at some point, also became written law, so Gildas's statement just as easily could have been an early reference to Celtic law.[46]

[43] For text and translation see M. Winterbottom (trans.), *Gildas, The Ruin of Britain and Other Works* (Chichester, 1978). For a discussion of the range of dates with references see M. E. Jones, *The End of Roman Britain* (Ithaca, NY, 1996), 42–6.

[44] See P. Schaffner, 'Britain's *Iudices*', in Lapidge and Dumville (eds.), *Gildas*, 151.

[45] See J. Morris, *The Age of Arthur* (London, 1973), 134.

[46] See T. P. Ellis, *Welsh Tribal Law and Custom in the Middle Ages* (2 vols.; Oxford, 1926), 2. 196.

Gildas also used words such as *iudices* ('judges': *De excidio* 27), *testes* ('witnesses': 37. 4), and *respondeo* ('answer to': 37. 3) that bore technical meanings in the vocabulary of Roman law.[47] The use of these words could have reflected a familiarity with the language and procedures of Roman law courts and hence the possible survival of those courts. On the other hand, however, in late Roman parlance such words also had a wide range of meaning. *Iudex* could refer to a judge at law, but also to a provincial governor, a barbarian king, or an official of unspecified rank.[48] Such imprecision broadens the possibilities of Gildas's intended meaning and weakens any certainty of an association between his vocabulary and continued Roman legal practice. Indeed, even if one arbitrarily limits his use of *iudex* to mean a judge at law, the actions performed by *iudices* in the *De excidio* still can be paralleled with examples drawn from the later Welsh lawbooks. This is also the case with the royal judicial authority and powers of police of the kings that appear in Gildas's account.[49] Ultimately the context of the linguistic terms for judges, witnesses, and testimony in the *De excidio* is too thin in detail and too ambiguous to serve as a certain indicator of either Roman or Celtic law. In fact, the closest parallels to Gildas's language and thought are probably to be found in the Old Latin and Vulgate bibles. The Old Testament and the laws of the prophets probably best explain Gildas's points of reference and intended meaning when he deliberately interweaves contemporary criticism with biblical texts.[50]

Much the same thing may be said of arguments for the continuity of Roman style government and law that are based on Gildas' ideas of political legitimacy. He employed

[47] 'Respondeo', for example, referred to evidence provided by jurisconsults. See Morris, *Age of Arthur*, 134; Lapidge, 'Gildas's Education', 46–7; and Dark, *Civitas*, 2, 216.

[48] See Schaffner, 'Britain's *Iudices*', 153.

[49] See Dumville, 'Idea', 188–9; and B. Bachrach, 'Gildas, Vortigern and Constitutionality in Sub-Roman Britain', *Nottingham Medieval Studies*, 32 (1988), 129. For the Welsh parallels, see D. A. Binchy, *Celtic and Anglo-Saxon Kingship* (2 vols.; Oxford, 1970), 2–22.

[50] See Schaffner, 'Britain's *Iudices*', 154. For Gildas's use of scripture in his portrayal of British *judices*, *reges*, and justice, compare *De excidio* 63 with Sap. 6. 2. 11, *De excidio* 43 with Isaiah 1: 23–4, *De excidio* 50.6 with Jerome 22. 3–5, and *De excidio* 51 with Habakkuk 2: 12–13, 1: 2–4.

a variety of terms for rulers in Britain including *reges* (kings), *duces* (generals), *rectores* (governors), *iudices* (judges) and, most significantly, *tyranni* (tyrants). Some have seen in Gildas's use of this Roman political vocabulary and his condemnation of illegitimate tyrants evidence for the survival or restoration of Roman-style government and law. Close examination of *De excidio*, however, reveals no precise and consistent parallels with Roman constitutional practice.[51] In Gildas's eyes contemporary rulers were legitimate or illegitimate not because of Roman constitutional theory but because of their private and public morality, a morality based primarily on the Old Testament.[52]

The few explicit statements concerning Roman law in Gildas's synopsis of the Roman past may well provide a more reliable guide to the probable fate of Roman law in Gildas's own day than the necessarily indirect evidence of vocabulary and rhetorical structure. Gildas is usually considered to have been a Romanophile who looked back with approval on Britain's Roman past. It is surprising and significant, therefore, that his characterization of Roman law was ambiguous and even hostile. Although the 'stiff-necked, haughty, and ever rebelling' Britons were in need of the corrective of law (*De excidio* 4. 1), and the Romans brought 'the laws of obedience' (*De excidio* 5. 2) to the island, the Roman law was very harsh and the Roman governors who administered the law were brutal (7, 14). The only Roman laws specifically mentioned by Gildas were the 'wicked edicts' of the Roman persecution of Christianity (12), along with a reference to the great variety of death penalties of this period (8, 9. 2).

Gildas never seems to have accepted the Roman law as his own. He strongly saw himself as a Briton rather than a Roman, and his fellow citizens (*cives*) as Britons rather than Romans. Gildas' *patria* (homeland) was Britain rather than

[51] For continuity or restoration of Roman-style government, see Higham, *Rome*, 84–116; Morris, *Age of Arthur*, 132–3; and Bachrach, 'Gildas', 135. Dumville, 'Idea', 177–91, however, argues that Britain had been ruled by kings (tyrants) for three generations before Gildas.

[52] See Dumville, 'Idea', 190, for Gildas as 'a mediator of biblical (that is, Old Testament) ideas of kingship into the Insular Celtic World'.

Rome. In Roman imperial eyes, such separatist sentiment and British identification may even have been deemed treasonable under late Roman law. These attitudes tell strongly against the transmission of Roman law into Gildas's Britain.[53] Gildas suggests that Roman law and custom had ended in Britain long before he wrote the *De excidio*. They were part of Britain's historical past but not part of Gildas's own present. Indeed, perhaps the single most important clue to the fate of Roman law in sixth-century Britain comes when Gildas said regarding the usurper Magnus Maximus (383–8), 'At length the tyrant thickets increased and were all but bursting into a savage forest. The island was still Roman in name, but not by law or custom[54] ('nomen Romanum nec tamen morem legemque tenens'). Gildas believed that Roman rule in Britain ended with Magnus Maximus and the tyrants (*De excidio* 13) and that Roman law ended along with it.

This surprising statement finds confirmation in an unlikely quarter. Writing sometime after 498, the pagan Greek historian Zosimus described how a tyrant from Britain, Constantine III (407–11), stripped Britain of troops to campaign in Gaul, where he met catastrophic defeat. At the same time—about 410—the barbarians attacked a weakened Britain. In Zosimus's words, Constantine 'was not able to oppose them . . . which allowed the barbarians over the Rhine to make unrestricted incursions. They reduced the inhabitants of Britain and some of the Gallic peoples to such straits that they revolted from the Roman empire, [they] no longer submitted to Roman law and reverted to their native customs.'[55] Now, Zosimus is not the most reliable historian of Late Antiquity, and his statement that Roman law was abolished in Britain has been viewed with deep scepticism.[56] Nevertheless, when a similar story is retailed by a sixth-

[53] See E. A. Thompson, 'Gildas and the History of Britain', *Britannia*, 10 (1979), 303–18; and Dumville, 'Idea'. For a recent full discussion of Gildas's attitude toward the empire and the Roman past see Jones, *End of Roman Britain*, 123–30.

[54] *De excido* 13. 1 (trans. Winterbottom).

[55] Zosimus 6. 5: R. T. Ridley (trans.), *Zosimus: New History* (Canberra, 1982), 128–9.

[56] See Jones, *LRE*, 191; and E. Stein, *Histoire du bas-empire*, J.-R. Palanque (trans.) (Paris, 1949), vol. i, 252.

century odd couple such as Gildas and Zosimus, it may well have had some basis in fact.

An abrupt and revolutionary end to Roman law in Britain just such as this would explain an otherwise perplexing coincidence—the disappearance of the Roman legal tradition from post-Roman Britain and the emergence in early medieval Britain of vernacular, customary, and non-Roman law among the successor states of both the Britons and Anglo-Saxons. Indeed, if Roman law did disappear so quickly with scarcely a trace, one might wish to reconsider just how 'Romanized' Britain ever was in the first place.

4
Resolving Disputes: The Frontiers of Law in Late Antiquity[1]

Jill D. Harries

Frontiers, whether physical or in the mind, are crucibles of change. In law, and especially in the laws governing the handling and settlement of disputes, one such frontier is the boundary between written law and the 'law' that operates beyond it, by means of custom and local usage. Much of what might be defined as legal activity in the area of dispute settlement is in fact not catered for by what is written, and still less by what is codified, but is defined by traditional forms of behaviour and strategies rooted in contemporary social practice. During Late Antiquity, getting a dispute resolved in one's favour—or indeed at all—entailed the exploitation of forms of power that fell outside the remit of lawyers to discuss or even acknowledge. Yet these alternative kinds of power also impacted on the operation of law itself, both because custom can change law, and because the written law may be used as merely one of many options to achieve a desired result.[2]

To take one example, in the year 481 a deacon of the Christian church at Lycopolis in Egypt, one Theophilus, found himself embroiled in two disputes with clerical superiors.[3] His bishop, Cyrus, owed him money, and two priests, who happened to be brothers, had illegally taken possession of

[1] This paper was written while I was a Visiting Fellow at All Souls College, Oxford, in 1996–7. I am grateful to the College for its generosity and to Stephen Cretney and David Parkin for bibliographic suggestions on legal anthropology.

[2] For an accessible discussion of the theory of dispute settlement, see S. Roberts, *Order and Dispute: An Introduction to Legal Anthropology* (London, 1979).

[3] For text, translation, and commentary, see H. B. Dewing, 'A Dialysis of the Fifth Century in the Princeton Collection of Papyri', *TAPA* 53 (1922), 113–27.

his wardrobe and various items of linen and bedding, which, as it later transpired, they had passed on to a third party. Relying, perhaps, on their superior social status, neither priests nor bishop would take any notice of the deacon's ever more obstreperous complaints—until he threatened to take all three to court. The two priests were to be brought before the head of the tax-collectors in the Thebaid, a man called Makarios, whereas the bishop was threatened with arrest and prosecution before a judge. At this point, the priests gave way and agreed to go before Makarios, but as an arbiter. There they would be expected to set out their arguments within a specified time, or pay a penalty (*poena*) for not fulfilling the terms of the initial agreement. In the meantime, the bishop still held out, despite receiving 'sharp reminders' from his deacon, until, abandoned by his confederates, he 'humbled himself' to accept the judgment of intermediaries (*mesoi*), who would consist of Makarios and one other.

Three points emerge from the story thus far. One is that socially inferior people were not necessarily weak, or unable to impose their will on those more powerful than themselves. Theophilus' strategy was to use the threat of legal proceedings to force his opponents to submit to some form of adjudication by third parties. It succeeded, we may suspect, not for financial reasons—bishops were surely better placed to sustain the costs of litigation—but because the social opprobrium of being dragged into court by his own deacon was too much for the bishop to contemplate. Secondly, the parties resorted to the same man, Makarios, first as judge, then as intermediary, but they nevertheless perceived a clear difference between adjudication by an arbiter and by a judge in a formal court, and preferred the former. Arbiters were more flexible in that they were not explicitly bound by Roman (or any other) law and their decision, being final, prevented expenses being incurred by further litigation, although it should be noted that, in practice, decisions tended to conform to the spirit, if not the letter, of established law. And thirdly, while it was obviously out of the question for the bishop to act as judge in his own case, there also seems to have been no thought of referring the dispute to judgment by other bishops.

Having heard the statements of all the parties, the adjudicators gave judgment in favour of Theophilus on all counts. Cyrus was to pay sixteen gold pieces and was then freed from further liability, although he also of his own free will (we are told) agreed to compensate the third parties who had received Theophilus' wardrobe. The two priests were to hand over the goods listed in the document of agreement to Theophilus; these included various fashion items, such as a Damascene shirt and other garments of non-local provenance, as well as blankets, pillows, and a lady's facecloth. On fulfilment of these conditions, all disagreement between the parties would be ended. To formalize the settlement, a document, known as a *dialysis*, or arbitration agreement, was drawn up, in which were set out the course of the dispute, the agreement reached, the assent of the parties to the agreement, a penalty clause, stipulating a sum of money considerably in excess of what was in dispute, and the signatures of the four participants and four witnesses. Theophilus' assent was written by one Claudius Heracleides in Theophilus' presence and at his dictation, as he could not write his name.

The Lycopolis *dialysis* is a rarity because it survives in a more or less complete state and tells the story of a dispute from start to finish. Apart from the victory of the David-figure, Theophilus, over the Goliaths, his superiors in the local church establishment, it reveals that the law, in this case the law on arbitration, had only limited relevance to the handling of many disputes. Although the Lycopolis *dialysis* is a legal document, it is the end product of a struggle in which manipulation of social pressures, in particular the threat of shaming superior clergy by involving them in formal legal proceedings, and the canvassing of various options for resolving the dispute led to the informal, but nonetheless binding, hearing before the two arbiters.

This does not indicate a failing in the law, but an important limitation on its operation: the law was very little concerned with the comprehensive circumstances of disputants, only the matter immediately at issue. But the document also reveals a variant on what was, according to Justinian's *Digest*, standard arbitration practice. Once arbitration has been agreed on, the disputants at Lycopolis opted, not for the usual one, but for two consecutive binding agreements, the first stipulating a penalty for failing to turn up and speak, which was equivalent to the *compromissum*, or agreement to the conditions of arbitration discussed by the classical jurists (*Digest* 4. 8. 11), the second enforcing the final settlement. The creation of the *dialysis* was doubtless regarded as a useful safeguard, and was typical of the late Roman fondness for putting things in writing, a habit of mind not confined to the imperial bureaucracy.

Local procedures, such as that used at Lycopolis, coexisted with Roman law, being based partly on custom and partly on innovations, like the double agreement, which seemed useful at the time. Lawyers of the Roman Empire accepted the importance of custom, *consuetudo*, as standing in place of law. In the eighty-fourth book of his ninety-book *Digest*, the great Hadrianic jurist Salvius Julianus, codifier of the Praetorian Edict, set out what became, through the medium of Justinian's *Digest*, the definitive statement on custom and law:

In situations where we do not use written law, what is sanctioned by custom and habit should be upheld . . . Ancient law is upheld in place of law not without reason and it too is law, which is held to be founded on habit.[4]

Julianus then affirmed that the will of the sovereign People was the basis of all law. His 'populus' was no longer the 'populus' of the Roman Republic, expressing its will through the constitutional procedures of the popular assemblies, but the 'People' or society at large, whose opinions became known—and therefore binding—by its actions. Thus 'laws' that were followed by common consent, whether written or not, were valid, while laws that were not followed but fell into desuetude by common consent were effectively abrogated, even though nothing had been formally done:

For seeing that the statutes themselves have authority over us for no reason other than that they were passed by the verdict of the

[4] 'De quibus causis scriptis legibus non utimur, id custodiri oportet, quod moribus et consuetudine inductum est . . . inveterata consuetudo pro lege non immerito custoditur, et hoc est ius . . .' (*Digest* 1. 3. 32).

People, it is right that those laws too which the People have endorsed in unwritten form will have universal authority. For what difference does it make whether the People declares its will by vote or by the things it does and the facts? Therefore it is very right and proper that it should follow that laws may be abrogated not only by the decision of the legislator but also through desuetude, by the tacit consent of all.[5]

Julianus' analysis of *consuetudo* in some respects runs counter to modern perceptions that Roman law was made by the elite for the elite, as shown in the greater leniency of the penalties to which the upper classes were subject. Certainly, as a system of control and as an intellectual construct, Roman law was the property of the elite. But Julianus' statement reflects a profounder awareness of how law is created than can be gained merely by constructing a prosopography of the rich and noble authors of the texts. The content of living law was not produced by jurists in their studies but by wider social and cultural changes which could feed through into the written law through the courts, representations from officials, or the decisions of emperors, who were themselves products of the contemporary social and cultural environment.

Julianus' emphasis on the 'populus' thus also creates a new perspective on the ideology of legislation by 'universal consent', which was a feature of the terminology used by emperors and others to legitimize their actions. While acclamation, the best-known form of expression of the popular will, was occasionally exploited to validate laws, as seen in the grant of privileges to his veterans by Constantine I (306–37) (*CTh* 7. 20. 2: 326), or the senatorial acclamations accorded to the *Theodosian Code* and recorded in the *Gesta Senatus* for 25 December 438, the emperor's usual method of ensuring 'universal consent' was consultation. Moreover, emperors also continued to make frequent references to practices as being endorsed (or not) 'by both law and custom', or 'law and reason', referring both to custom as followed in legal

[5] 'nam cum ipsae leges nulla alia ex causa nos teneant, quam quod iudicio populi receptae sunt, tenebunt omnes: nam quid interest suffragio populus voluntatem suam declaret an rebus ipsis et factis? quare rectissimi etiam illud receptum est, ut leges non solum suffratio legis latoris, sed etiam tacito consensu omnium per desuetudinem abrogentur' (ibid.).

matters and to commonly held standards of equity (*aequitas*) or fairness, by which legal outcomes could also be judged.

Given the acknowledged importance of *consuetudo*, and the probability that it would sometimes operate in ways not catered for by Roman law or legal philosophy, more sensitivity might have been expected from Constantine and his successors in handling the state's dealings with that most custom-based of Christian institutions, the episcopal 'hearing' (*definitio* or *audientia*).[6] The right of a bishop to adjudicate disputes among his flock had grown up as part of the operation of Christian communities, which regulated themselves independently of the formal procedures of Roman, or any other kind of, formal law.

When the third-century author of the *Didascalia apostolorum* turned to the handling of disputes by bishops, the language used was that of mediation and negotiation. The bishop was the physician of his flock and, when a dispute arose, his duty was first to seek to reconcile the conflicting parties and only as a last resort to convene a formal hearing, attended by priests and deacons, who acted as an equivalent of the *consilium* of the judge. Even then, the hearing was to be conducted on a Monday, to allow time for reconciliation of the parties by the following Sunday.[7] When serious misconduct was involved, which damaged the Christian community as a whole, the sanctions were penance or, at worst, expulsion from the community. The effectiveness of expulsion, or excommunication, should not be underrated. Believers debarred from the Church could expect not only retribution hereafter, but also social isolation from their former 'brothers and sisters'.

Although the bishop acted as an adjudicator once the hearing was convened, the ideology of mediation or negotiation, as set out in the *Didascalia*, is in many ways fundamentally at odds with that of 'adjudication', which comprises both formal processes before a judge, and all types of arbitration. The legal anthropologist Philip Gulliver has argued that dispute settlement can be analysed in terms of two main

[6] For *episcopalis audientia*, see also Lenski and Dossey in this volume.

[7] *Didascalia Apostolorum* 2. 47: for an edition and translation of the Syriac text, see A. Vööbus (ed), *CSCO* 175 (Louvain, 1979).

models, adjudication (judicial decisions, arbitration) and mediation/negotiation, and that the distinction is based on the locus of the decision-making.[8] Adjudication, he argues, 'is essentially characterised by the fact that decision-making and the outcome of the issues in dispute are controlled by a third party exercising some degree of accepted authority' and the disputants therefore address themselves to him. 'In negotiation, by contrast, the disputants are interdependent in the absence of authority', they interact with each other and reach a joint decision, which both are morally obliged to accept. Likewise mediation leaves the final decision with the disputing parties; the mediator is 'a facilitator but not an adjudicator'. But the difference is not expressed only in terms of who decides. In Gulliver's view, the cultures of the two forms of settlement diverge widely. Adjudication is likely to be based on 'concern for values and a definition of disputes in terms of values', norms would be applied with attention also given to decisions one way or the other, acts, rather than actors and past behaviour, but excluding the wider context.

The negotiatory model allows for 'a definition of disputes in terms of interests . . . and a concern for the personal qualities and dispositions of the disputants, for the future of their and others' rights or relationships . . .'. In other words, the negotiator or mediator would take account of the wider social context and be allowed some flexibility, while the adjudicator would be expected to apply the rules. All this does not preclude the use of both methods in dispute settlement, a process that, as we have seen, could be conducted in ingenious ways. Of relevance to the role of the bishop also is Gulliver's concession that in practice the distinction between arbiter and mediator could break down: 'occasionally mediators virtually take control and make effective decisions'.[9]

Although Gulliver's analysis may be challenged on some counts, for example that by combining judge and arbiter he risks underestimating the extent of flexibility available to

[8] P. H. Gulliver, *Disputes and Negotiations: A Cross-Cultural Perspective* (New York, 1979), 20.

[9] Gulliver, Ibid., 209.

the arbiter in taking factors other than rules into account, it nevertheless highlights the fundamental problem of assimilating episcopal hearings into the existing framework of Roman law, which was geared entirely to the regulation of adjudicatory procedures. Constantine's legislation allowing the cases of lay people who were not members of Christian congregations to be referred to the 'episcopale judicium' skirted the problem by simply treating the bishop's 'judicium' as another kind of court, and allowing it the special privilege of inappellable decisions.[10] Had bishops chosen to insist on their rights, haul pagans into their courts on a large scale, and operate, arbitrarily, on the basis of the so-called *lex Christiana*, the long-term consequences for the Roman legal system could have been catastrophic.

Constantine's legislation, however, had very little immediate effect and, after its repeal by Julian (361–3),[11] may have been quietly allowed to lapse, thus resulting in its exclusion from the *Codex Justinianus*, which, unlike its Theodosian predecessor, was strict in excluding defunct laws. The reason for its ineffectiveness was its irrelevance. Where bishops were required to adjudicate between Christians and possible non-Christians, both could accept his decision, provided both were willing, under the existing rules and conventions governing arbitration. Thus, a hearing of the 330s, recorded on a papyrus from Hermopolis,[12] was conducted by the bishop, Plusianon, in the outer court of his local church. The disputants were a nun, who would have been under the bishop's jurisdiction anyway, and some people of doubtful standing and unknown religious persuasion, called the 'tenants of Besarion'. The dispute was labelled a 'diaite' (spelled phonetically in the papyrus as 'diete'), or 'arbitration', and the award made by the bishop was called a 'dietikon', or arbitration award. The informal *consilium* consisted of a deacon and a lay local councillor, Dioscorides. There clearly was a Christian context for these proceedings—the nun, the bishop as adjudicator, and the place of the hearing—but even

[10] *Sirm.* 1: 33; for discussion, see J. D. Harries, *Law and Empire in Late Antiquity* (Cambridge, 1998), 196–7. For the 'episcopale iudicium', see Lenski in this volume.

[11] Julian, *Epist.* 435D–438C.

[12] *FIRA*^{2} 3. 574–6.

without Constantine's legislation, the bishop was in many communities a prominent figure to whom local people would have resorted informally for the resolution of their disputes with their neighbours.

Lawyers seeking to impose Roman legal classifications on episcopal hearings turned naturally to the theory of arbitration procedure. The section on arbitration in Justinian's *Digest* emphasized the limited role of the 'praetor', who represented the state as enforcer of law. He was involved because he might have to deal with the legal consequences of the parties failing to honour their agreement. The point about arbitration was that it was a voluntary arrangement, and the parties therefore were obliged both morally and legally to accept the outcome as final. But it was also 'like' a formal judicial hearing; both the arbiter and the *judex* were, in Gulliver's terms, adjudicators—as was also the bishop, when presiding at his own hearings. Like episcopal verdicts, from which no appeal was allowed, the award of the arbiter was final; it 'finished' the case (*Digest* 4. 8. 1: Paulus).

In order to ensure either that an outcome was reached, or that it was clear whose fault it was if negotiations broke down at any point, a formal agreement to go to arbitration, known as a *compromissum*, was a prerequisite (*Digest* 4. 8. 11. 1). The classical jurists also spent much energy discussing the conditions under which the arbiter or the disputants could be released from the obligations outlined in the *compromissum*. Its contents, on which much could depend, would have included the name(s) of the arbiter(s), the stipulation of the *poena* ('penalty'), the forfeit for non-compliance, the time limit for reaching a decision, the subject matter of the dispute, whether the cases were multiple or single, the mention or non-mention of heirs (which affected what happened if one or both parties died), and protection against fraud or malice. Composition of this document allowed formal arbitration to proceed to a conclusion, but, in informal cases, where the agreement of the parties was deemed sufficient, it would have been dispensed with and the law rendered irrelevant.

Given that resort to the bishop was supposedly on the basis of consent (*pace* Constantine), that the formality of the *compromissum* only became relevant in the event of non-compliance, and that the bishop's judgment was final, the Egyptian assimilation of the bishop, Plusianon, to the arbiter was a natural interpretation of his social role. It might not even have been clear to the people involved at the time that he was conducting an 'episcopal hearing' at all, although he himself may have differentiated between his routine judgments of his flock and the resort to his arbitration by outsiders. What mattered was that the close relationship in the secular world between the *judex* and the arbiter, as expressed in Paulus' comment that arbitration was 'like' a court, was one that allowed the bishop, as adjudicator, to fudge the exact legal technicalities of his role and act as he saw fit.

By the late fourth century, renewed interest was taken in episcopal courts by lawyers. Various factors had become more clear. One was that ecclesiastical should be taken as separate from secular jurisdiction; bishops, wrote Theodosius I (379–95), had their own courts and 'nothing in common with the laws of the state' (*Sirm.* 3: 384). Secondly, the uncertainty over whether a bishop was a *judex* in the full sense or an arbiter persisted in the language of the legislation, even in that of the relatively sophisticated quaestor of Arcadius in 398, who re-emphasized the importance of the consent of litigants choosing to go before a bishop in civil cases, allowing them, if they consented, to receive the *judicium* ('judgment') of the bishop 'arbitri more residentis' ('in the manner of an arbiter hearing a case') (*CJ* 1. 4. 7: 27 July 398). So strong was the conviction at the court of Valentinian III (425–55) that episcopal hearings were a form of arbitration that the quaestor of 452 drafted a regulation that when disputes among clerics were brought before the bishop, he had *licentia judicandi* ('the right of passing judgment'), but only after a binding *compromissum* had been agreed, and the same was to apply to the laity, provided they agreed (*Nov.Val.* 35 praef.: 15 April 452).

This flexible use of terminology reflects a peculiarity of late Roman jurisdiction in civil cases, that the differences in practice between the role of the *arbiter* and that of the *judex* were sometimes not great. It may be recalled, for example, that in the Lycopolis dispute the arbiter was the same person who initially had been asked to act as *judex* and that both sides were expected to present their cases before the arbiter, just as they would have done in a formal court. From the point of view of the bishop, Cyrus, whose main idea was to stay out of court, the advantage of the arbitration procedure was that it was less confrontational and allowed him to avoid the ignominy of facing a formal charge brought by his aggrieved deacon.

On the other hand, a *judex* often would have had to behave like an arbiter. One of the jobs of the arbiter was to establish facts before proceeding to make his award and, as the parties were expected to agree, some negotiation might also have been in order. The same scrupulous care was required by Constantine of his *judices*, whom he ordered to conduct full enquiries, be patient, listen to the litigants, and ask questions repeatedly to ensure that everything relevant to the case had been revealed; this would allow the case to be concluded, not by the judge's unilateral decision but by the agreement to it of the litigants themselves (*CTh* 1. 18. 1).

A further variant on the judge's role as investigator was the procedure when one party to a case obtained an imperial rescript on a point of law. Again, the judge's main concern was with the facts; he was to find out what they were and, if they were in accordance with the assumptions behind the rescript (which must often have reflected the representations of the petitioner), then judgment would be given in accordance with the ruling of the rescript. In many respects, therefore, *judex* and arbiter acted as adjudicators in similar ways. Even the notion that the arbiter, unlike the *judex*, could make a ruling on whatever basis he liked and did not have to conform to strict law[13] is unlikely to have mattered much in practice. An arbiter who disregarded existing law and custom in favour of some whimsical system of his own was unlikely to improve his standing with the conflicting parties (or be asked to serve again).

When, therefore, the bishop took on the job of adjudicator in his court, the definition of his role as *judex* or as arbiter

[13] As endorsed by Seneca, *De Beneficiis* 3. 7. 5, who argued that a formal trial was better than arbitration if one had a good case, because judgment by a *judex* was in accordance with *lex* and *iustitia* and not unpredictable things like *humanitas* and *misericordia*.

was of little practical significance, except to lawyers, who, as we have seen, attempted from afar to impose Roman legal constraints on an originally non-Roman private system of dispute settlement. In purely theoretical terms, their attempt was a reasonable one. Whereas the decisions of provincial *judices* could be appealed to the praetorian prefects' courts or even to the emperor, episcopal decisions were not subject to the right of appeal, and this required some justification (*CTh* 1. 27. 2). Moreover, the state was committed to enforcing episcopal decisions, if required, and therefore felt itself entitled to a say in how they were reached. But where the law ceased to be operable was in the ramifications of episcopal powers as settlers of disputes beyond the confines of their courts. As adjudicators of disputes among Christians, bishops inherited from their pre-Constantinian predecessors an ideology of conciliation. This meant that, outside the formal hearing, bishops might lay aside their powers as adjudicators in order to act in traditional Christian fashion as negotiators or mediators, thus, in Gulliver's terms, shifting the locus of decision-making to the disputants and away from the adjudicator.

The bishop as mediator takes us into modern theories and practice of Alternative Dispute Resolution ('ADR'), in which the mediator acts as a facilitator to bring together disputants willing to employ their services.[14] However, while mediators have to try to appear neutral, it can also be argued that, by their very presence, they 'become a party in the negotiations' and 'therefore . . . cannot be neutral or merely a catalyst'.[15] Nor are mediators devoid of self-interest or, necessarily, impartial; Gregory of Nazianzus, for example, was employed by his local governor to mediate in a dispute between a father and daughter, in the justified expectation that, given his views on Christian marriage, he would take the daughter's side.[16] Mediators could be linked to one party in the dispute, although acting for both, or might hope, by offering their assistance, to gain 'credit, prestige, and leader-

[14] For an accessible guide to ADR, see A. F. Acland, *Resolving Disputes without Going to Court: A Consumer Guide to Alternative Dispute Resolution* (London, 1995).

[15] Gulliver, *Disputes*, 214.

[16] Gregory of Nazianzus, *Epist.* 144–5.

ship' among the parties, sometimes at the expense of competitors for leadership among the group.[17] Moreover, the role of mediator covers a spectrum of meaning, from the virtually passive observer, whose presence nonetheless affects the behaviour of disputants, through convener, enunciator of values and norms, prompter, and leader, to virtual arbitrator.[18] This range of meanings allowed the bishop considerable scope for initiative, but it also enabled the exercise of episcopal power. Although acting as a conciliator, the bishop was also, inevitably, exerting and displaying his *auctoritas*, and was motivated by concern for his own position as well as the interests of his clients.

In no bishop is this mixture of roles and motives more clearly seen than in Ambrose of Milan, whose famous arbitration in the late fourth century of the quarrel among the bishop Marcellus; his brother, the *vir clarissimus* Laetus; and their sister, allowed him to utilize the full gamut of episcopal techniques for dispute resolution. The altercation concerned an estate owned by Marcellus, who wished to donate it to the sister for her support during her lifetime, and to the church thereafter. Laetus challenged his right to do this and took the case through secular procedures, until it began to run out of time at the court of the Praetorian Prefect.[19] At this point the advocates on both sides advised resorting to an outsider and Ambrose was chosen—'so great was their eagerness as Christian men that a prefect should not judge in the case of a bishop'.[20] Ambrose accepted the commission, although not as *judex* but as arbiter. While the implied contrast between his roles as *judex* amd arbiter may have carried with it a reference to his formal *audientia*, it is more likely that Ambrose used the comparison to stress the consensual nature of his role; as arbiter, with the consent of the parties, he would seek to persuade them to agree, acting as arbiter-cum-mediator, rather than enforce a judgment, which could cause offence. Ambrose did see his role in quasi-legal guise—and referred at the end, metaphorically, to the arbitral *poena*,

[17] Gulliver, *Disputes*, 215–17. [18] Gulliver, Ibid., 220.

[19] For time limitations, see *CTh* 2. 4. 1: 318, 4: 385; and chapters 2. 6–7 (passim).

[20] Ambrose, *Epist.* 82. 2.

but in fact his arbitration was conducted on informal lines without benefit of formal *compromissum* or *poena*.

To resolve the dispute, Ambrose moved into mediation mode. Going between the parties, he ascertained the positions of the two sides. Marcellus made the first offer, to cede the estate to Laetus, provided the sister had the use of it in her lifetime. Laetus welcomed the offer but observed that women were incapable of running estates properly and he was afraid it would deteriorate. All the men were impressed by this. Ambrose now pronounced his arbitral *sententia*, that Laetus would receive the estate and pay a stipulated amount of the produce to the sister. Although acting as adjudicator, Ambrose also expatiated on the benefits of his verdict to all, and in particular argued that Marcellus had shared responsibility for the decision; there were two bishops acting as arbitrators (he said), not one. The manner in which the whole episode was represented in Ambrose's letter on the subject reveals two aims; on the one hand, to play down his own role in reaching the final decision, and, on the other, to advertise his effectiveness as a resolver, by 'universal consent', of a difficult and long-running dispute. He also showed that, by the use of a little ingenuity, it was possible to merge the mediatory and the adjudicatory modes of dispute resolution into a single operation.

The handling and settlement of disputes is an area of activity profoundly relevant to the operation of law. Much of law is devoted to the regulation of property—its ownership, possession, and transmission—and most disputes were about property in some shape, whether they came before the *judex* or the formal or informal arbiter, or were resolved by mediation or negotiation between the parties. But Roman law was not invoked in all such cases. Where formal arbitration was used, the Roman state took an interest only because the *poena* might require enforcement. Many disputes would have been solved by informal arbitration, where the *compromissum* was dispensed with and the authority of the adjudicator, be he a bishop or some other local big man, the desires of the parties, and the conventions and pressures prevalent in small face-to-face communities were sufficient to ensure compliance. The continuing acknowledgement of the importance of custom, *consuetudo*, in late Roman law is an expression of a fact known to many a provincial *judex*: that the locals had their own ways of doing things, which were legitimate, provided they did not clash overtly with the *lex scripta*.

Custom and tradition also explain both the effectiveness of bishops' methods of conflict resolution among their flocks and the inability of Roman lawyers to explain *episcopalis audientia* in their own legal terms. The adjudication of bishops was rooted in pre-Constantinian Christian community values, of which Roman law had taken no cognizance. These were gradually adapted, as bishops' powers—and their clientele—expanded with the Christianization of the Roman Empire. The flexibility and freedom of action allowed to the early Christian bishops, who had operated outside the law (but not illegally) remained. Thus, while legally sanctioned *episcopalis audientia* was acknowledged—and puzzled over—by lawyers, a large area of episcopal activity lay outside its scope, as did many forms of dispute resolution engaged in by the versatile denizens of the later Roman Empire.

When, therefore, we try to understand the law of Late Antiquity, we must appreciate the cultural ambience of the text, and, in particular, what it does not say. Roman *lex scripta* expressed rules on a limited number of topics, which reflected the values and perspectives of the elite. It acknowledged, but did not elaborate on, the importance of custom and equity. What it did not do was reveal the real dynamics of how law worked, was enforced, exploited, or circumvented in communities in which written law was only one of several influences on social behaviour and coexisted with other forms of power, some of which, like the exploitation of shame by the deacon Theophilus, were available even to the ostensibly weak. To understand written law, we must understand that not all law is written. There is much more to the law of Late Antiquity than the *Theodosian Code* or the *Corpus iuris civilis*.

5
Evidence for the *Audientia episcopalis* in the New Letters of Augustine

Noel E. Lenski

Much ink has been spilled over the *audientia episcopalis*, that is, the legal authority granted to bishops to act as *iudices* ('judges') in civil cases.[1] Nevertheless, many questions remain unanswered. The new letters of Augustine, published in 1981, provide a remarkable resource for shedding light on some of them,[2] and can help to flesh out our picture of the ecclesiastical courts in practice.[3] Although individual letters have been examined for information on episcopal jurisdiction, no synthetic treatment of legal issues utilizing the letters as

[1] For bibliography, see M. Rosa Cimma, *L'episcopalis audientia nelle costituzioni imperiali da Costantino a Giustiniano* (Turin, 1989); note also V. Busek, 'Episcopalis audientia, eine Friedens- und Schiedsgerichtsbarkeit', *ZSS KA* 28 (1939), 453–92; J. G. Keenan, 'A Christian Letter from the Michigan Collection', *ZPE* 75 (1988), 267–71; J. C. Lamoreaux, 'Episcopal Courts in Late Antiquity', *JECS* 3 (1995), 143–67; F. Martroye, 'Saint Augustin et le compétence de la juridiction ecclésiastique au Ve siècle', *MSAF* 10 (1911), 1–78; K. L. Noethlichs, 'Materialen zum Bischofsbild aus den spätantiken Rechtsquellen', *JAC* 16 (1973), 28–59 at 41–5; W. Selb, 'Episcopalis audientia von der Zeit Konstantins bis zur Nov. XXXV Valentinians III', *ZSS RA* 84 (1967), 162–217; A. Steinwenter, 'Zur Lehre von der episcopalis audientia', *BZ* 30 (1929), 660–8; and G. Vismara, *Episcopalis audientia* (Milan, 1937). See also Harries and Dossey in this volume.

[2] J. Divjak (ed.), *CSEL* 88 (Vienna, 1981); for discussion see H. Chadwick, 'New Letters of St. Augustine', *JThS* 34 (1983), 425–52; and C. Lepelley, 'La Crise de l'Afrique romaine au début du Ve siècle, d'après les lettres nouvellement découvertes de Saint Augustin', *CRAI* (1982), 445–63.

[3] For material related to the *audientia episcopalis* in the remaining corpus of Augustine, see C. Lepelley, *Les Cités de l'Afrique romaine au bas-empire*, i. *La Permanence d'une civilisation municipale* (Paris, 1979), 389–402; and Martroye, 'Compétence'.

a group has been attempted.[4] The following study will consider four questions. What can the new letters tell us about who used episcopal courts? What can they reveal about how well a bishop understood the law? How do they illuminate the enforcement of episcopal decisions? And what do they tell us about how a bishop conceived of his legal role?

The question of who used episcopal courts can be further parsed: were the courts open to all or only to ecclesiastics, and over what kinds of cases did bishops have authority, religious or civil? The letters suggest a fairly clear answer to the first of these. Of the seven that explicitly discuss legal issues, six involve clerics or ecclesiastical matters: *Epist.* 7* describes a bank deposit owed to the church of Hippo; *Epist.* 8* a property suit against a bishop;[5] *Epist.* 9* the scourging of a priest; *Epist.* 10* slave raids that had affected Augustine's clergy; *Epist.* 15* the rape of a nun; and *Epist.* 20* the crimes and misdemeanours of a suffragan bishop. All of these cases impinged in some way on the church or its clergy. Only *Epist.* 24*, a series of legal questions on the *locatio* ('hiring') of child labour, has no relevance to the church. The corpus thus conforms to and supplements what we learn from the law codes: while a bishop could have authority over any civil suit, he had exclusive jurisdiction over cases involving clerics. Moreover, at least in the new letters, Augustine seems to have preferred to confine his legal activity to clerical cases, although occasionally, as in *Epist.* 24*, he did take on others.[6]

The second part of this question, regarding the kinds of cases over which bishops had authority, is in part subsumed under the first. Contemporary legal sources indicate that episcopal courts could consider all civil disputes provided that both parties agreed to the venue.[7] Furthermore, the

[4] *Les lettres de saint Augustin découvertes. Communications présentées au colloque des 20 et 21 Septembre 1982* (Paris, 1983), particularly P.-A. Février, 'Discours d'église et réalité historique dans les nouvelles Lettres d'Augustin', 101–15, which offers a synthesis of some legal issues.

[5] J. Rougé, 'Escroquerie et brigandage en Afrique romaine au temps de Saint Augustin (*Epist.* 8* et 10*)', in *Les lettres*, 177–88 at 177–8, is decisive on Victor's identity as a bishop.

[6] Ambrose held to the same principle, *De officiis* 2. 125.

[7] *CJ* 1. 4. 7 (398); *CTh* 1. 27. 2 (408); cf. *Nov. Val.* 35 (452); on which see Cimma, *Audientia*, 84–92, 111–19. *Sirm.* 1 (333) actually had permited unilateral appeal but

late Roman law codes indicate that all cases against clerics, whether criminal or civil, had to be referred to episcopal courts, that is, all bishops enjoyed a *privilegium fori* over their own clergy.[8] An excellent example of the effects of the latter requirement is found in *Epist.* 8*, where the Jew Licinius hoped to recover some land from which he had been ejected by a bishop Victor. Licinius originally had purchased the land from his own mother, but she subsequently sold the same property to Victor as part of a larger estate. Although Victor's legal claim to the property was entirely unfounded, he had denied Licinius' initial suit in his own court. This forced the Jew to bring the case not to the public authorities but to Augustine. In sum, the case involved an *emptio* or *venditio* ('sale') in which the seller did not have title. It would have been perfectly suitable for public courts were it not that a bishop was involved.[9]

Other letters also attest to the sorts of cases over which a bishop presided. In *Epist.* 9*, Augustine sought help from his friend and fellow bishop Alypius in a case where a priest, found guilty of raping a nun, had protested at the beating he received at the hands of the clergy on the the grounds that he was immune from such treatment because of his curial descent. Augustine hoped that Alypius, then resident in Italy, would offer support against the priest, who had taken his appeal to pope Celestine (422–32).[10] In this instance, Augustine was not acting as a judge but as a legal adviser, and not in a civil but in a criminal case involving *stuprum* and the illegal whipping of a curial. Criminal sexual charges recur in *Epist.* 15*, where Cresconius, an estate manager had raped a nun. Particularly instructive is *Epist.* 20*, which reveals that

was superseded by these laws: see Cimma, *Audientia*, 36–55, 62–9. Christians had long been expected to have legal quarrels adjudicated by a bishop: *Didascalia apostolorum* 2. 45–53.

[8] *CTh* 16. 2. 12: 355; *Sirm.* 3: 384, 15: 412, 6: 425. This right wavered over time: Cimma, *Audientia*, 97–132. In North Africa it was reinforced by canon law: clerics were forbidden by the ninth canon of the Council of Carthage of 397 (*CCL* 149. 36) to turn to secular courts.

[9] See Rougé, 'Escroquerie', 177–83.

[10] Such an appeal would have been directly contrary to one of the canons of the Council of Carthage 424, 'that no one dare to appeal to the church of Rome' ('Ut nullus ad Romanam ecclesiam appellare audeat') (*CCL* 149. 266).

Augustine's court cleared a suffragan bishop, Antoninus, of four capital sex charges, the details of which are not revealed.[11] Antoninus had been appointed by Augustine to preside over the see of Fussala, 60 km south of Hippo. Once consecrated, he wrought havoc in his diocese through peculation, depredation, and intimidation. He let out a piece of church property and used the rent to buy a villa, after forcing its sale at a ridiculously low price (*laesio enormis*). He then began to embellish the villa with property seized from other people (*rapina*); he occupied people's land and stole their crops (*furtum*); he bought a second property in a partnership (*societas*) and then refused to divide the proceeds with his partner; he also compelled the brother of the partner to sell his share in the property and then refused to pay the price (*metus* and *dolus*).[12] Eventually, Augustine required Antoninus to answer all these charges as delictal, or civil, actions. Interestingly, many of Antoninus' offences also could have resulted in criminal charges. Augustine's legal authority thus extended to criminal cases in the instance of clerics. Although he was willing to take on such charges where necessary, as in the rape cases, he preferred to avoid them where actions could be limited to delict, as with Antoninus.

Another interesting case arises in *Epist.* 7*, where a tribune named Bassus had been given a mandate by his commander to deposit a large sum of the latter's money with two bankers. The commander then ordered Bassus to retrieve the sum and pay it to the church of Hippo. Unfortunately, Bassus died in the middle of the transaction, as did one of the bankers. When Bassus' widow refused to carry through the mandate and sought an injunction from another tribune, Augustine asked his friend, the bishop of Sitifis (where the widow resided) to

[11] On *Epist.* 15* see M.-F. Berrouard, 'Un tournant dans la vie de l'Église d'Afrique: les deux missions d'Alypius en Italie à la lumière des Lettres 10*, 15*, 16*, 22* et 23*A de Saint Augustin', *REA* 31 (1985), 46–70. On *Epist.* 20* see S. Lancel, 'L'Affaire d'Antoninus de Fussala: pays, choses et gens de la Numidie d'Hippone saisis dans la durée d'une procédure d'enquète épiscopale (*Epist.* 20*)', in *Les lettres*, 267–85.

[12] On legal issues, see W. W. Buckland, *A Text-Book of Roman Law from Augustus to Justinian* (Cambridge, 1963), 576–85 (*furtum, rapina*), 593–5 (*metus, dolus*); A. J. B. Sirks, 'La laesio enormis en droit romain et byzantin', *Tijdschrift voor Rechtsgeschiedenis*, 53 (1989), 296–8 (*laesio enormis*); and Justinian, *Digest* 17. 2. 45 on actions against a partner who stole from a *societas*.

investigate further and to appeal to the Count of Africa for redress.[13] Here, as in *Epist.* 9*, Augustine acted again only as a legal adviser. Indeed, he seems to have hoped that this case, which involved church property but not a cleric, would be settled by the public authorities. One senses here, as will be confirmed below, that Augustine preferred to avoid entanglement in secular disputes wherever possible.

In addition, *Epist.* 10* was directed to Alypius, again in Italy, for assistance in a number of cases involving the forced enslavement and sale of locals, including some of his own clergy, at the hands of long-distance slave traders. Augustine appears to have had authority to bring criminal charges against the traders, but he used his legal authority to free their victims.[14] Finally, *Epist.* 24* shows Augustine preparing himself for a case wherein an estate manager had leased out the labour of his children to the owner of an estate, but after the father's death, the owner argued that the children were his slaves. Augustine, who was soon to hear the case, sought counsel from Eustochius, an otherwise unattested legal adviser.[15]

The new letters thus indicate that a bishop could handle a wide array of civil cases. Though most of his attention was devoted to issues involving clerics, he did not shy from civil suits even where the church was not involved. A bishop also could have criminal jurisdiction, though here his authority seems to have been limited to cases that somehow involved clerics.

The second question posed above asks how much law a bishop knew.[16] Of course, the answer depends entirely on the bishop. Some recent research has played down the legal

[13] On *Epist.* 7* see J. Andreau, 'La Lettre 7* document sur les métiers bancaires', in *Les lettres*, 165–76.

[14] On *Epist.* 10* see J. Szidat, 'Zum Sklavenhandel in der Spätantike (Aug. epist. 10*)', *Historia*, 34 (1985), 560–71; M. Humbert, 'Enfants à louer ou à vendre: Augustin et l'autorité parentale (*Epist.* 10* et 24*),' in *Les lettres*, 189–204; and Rougé, 'Escroquerie', 183–7.

[15] See C. Lepelley, 'Liberté, colonat et esclavage d'après la Lettre 24*: la juridiction épiscopale *de liberali causa*', in *Les lettres*, 329–42; and Humbert, 'Enfants'.

[16] The new letters (with the exception of *Epist.* 20*) have little to say regarding judicial procedure in episcopal courts. On this issue, see Steinwenter, 'Lehre'; and Keenan, 'Letter'.

learning of the average bishop,[17] but the new letters indicate that Augustine, at least, knew a good deal. Although it has been suggested that Augustine seems to have had little formal legal training, his familiarity with the law is attested well by his use of legal vocabulary and metaphors.[18] An additional example of this could be added from *Epist.* 3*, where Augustine responded to a woman who had vowed her daughter's virginity while the girl was ill but later hoped to substitute a vow of her own widowhood so that the daughter could marry. Using legal terminology, Augustine refused the proposition: he claimed that the woman's widowhood was in her *potestas* ('legal power'), but that the vow regarding her daughter was unchangeable because it pertained to *aliena* ('the property of someone else').[19] Although Augustine understood well the concept of *potestas*[20] and would have known it did not apply in this instance, he used the authority of legal language to strengthen his argument about an entirely religious matter.

Of course, Augustine's knowledge of the law stretched beyond the lexical. He even collected imperial constitutions. Twice in the new letters he mentions laws that he had in his possession. In *Epist.* 10* he cited a *lex* of Honorius (395–423) addressed to the prefect Hadrian on transporting slaves, and in *Epist.* 24* he mentioned a number of *constitutiones* ('laws') relevant to the *locatio operarum* ('hire of services') of children.[21] In both instances Augustine included copies of the laws in his correspondence.[22] In *Epist.* 10*, he even appealed

[17] See R. S. Bagnall, *Egypt in Late Antiquity* (Princeton, 1994), 223–5; Lamoreaux, 'Episcopal Courts', 159.

[18] See J. Gaudemet, *Le Droit romain dans la littérature chrétienne occidentale du IIIe au Ve siècle* (Varese, 1978), 127–66; and A. Nonnoi, 'San Agostino e il diritto romano', *RISG* 9 (1934), 531–45. Augustine himself (*Conf.* 3. 3 [6]) claimed that his studies were aimed at training him for the 'fora litigiosa'.

[19] *Epist.* 3*. 2. 5–3. 2; cf. 3. 8; 4. 3. Interestingly, Augustine's own mother had made a similar unfulfilled vow for his safety as a child: *Conf.* 1. 11 (17).

[20] e.g. *Epist.* 24* 1. 4; see Gaudemet, *Droit romain,* 137–8.

[21] None of these laws survives; Humbert, 'Enfants', 193–8, collects the extant laws on the hire and sale of children.

[22] *Epist.* 10*. 3. 5–4. 3; *Epist.* 24*. 2. 4–5. In *Epist.* 113–5 (*CSEL* 34. 660–2), Augustine claims to have sent copies of another law, still extant (*CTh* 9. 2. 6: 409), to two imperial officials; *Cont. epist. Parm.* 1. 12. 19 (*CSEL* 51. 41–2) shows familiarity with a series of laws; and *Epist.* 91. 8 (*CSEL* 34. 432) indicates that the bishop of Calama also kept imperial laws. Augustine even knew the *Codex Gregorianus*:

to Alypius to lobby officials in Ravenna for a law that could more effectively hamper the sale of kidnapped *ingenui* ('freeborn citizens'). Two years earlier, he had made similar demands for the issuance of constitutions on matters unrelated to civil law.[23] Augustine, therefore, did not simply accumulate copies of laws, he also solicited new laws.

In addition, Augustine sought legal advice in *Epist.* 24* from a jurisconsult, and from Alypius in *Epist.* 9*. Indeed, Augustine's frequent reliance on Alypius for help with legal matters makes good sense, for the latter had been trained as a lawyer.[24] Although some have seen Augustine's requests for advice as a sign of his ignorance of the law, his questions actually demonstrate remarkable learning. The queries advanced in *Epist.* 24*, for example, are precisely those that dog modern scholars attempting to pinpoint the minutiae of child indenture.[25] Similarly, it would seem that Augustine merely feigned ignorance of the proper punishments for decurions in *Epist.* 9* as a pretence intended to cover the transgressions of those he was defending. A later section of this same letter even demonstrates Augustine's legal astuteness with his countercharge against the priest with whom he was haggling based on the latter's suppression of evidence, a violation of imperial law.[26] But perhaps the best evidence for Augustine's legal knowledge comes from *Epist.* 8*. 1. 3, where he demonstrates his understanding of contract law in contradistinction to what he calls the 'ignorantia iuris' ('ignorance of the law') of his correspondent. Augustine, therefore, certainly knew his law.

At *De adulterinis coniugiis* 8 [7] (*CSEL* 41. 389–90) he cites a passage 'apud Gregorianum' which is preserved as *Digest* 48. 5. 14. 5. I owe this reference to Judith Evans Grubbs.

[23] *Epist.* 22*. 1. 2, 2. 3; 23A*. 1. 2. On the success of the last request see Berrouard, 'Deux Missions', 53–6. Ambrose also had a number of laws at his disposal, on which see M. Sargenti, R. B. Bruno Siola, *Normativa imperiale e diritto romani negli scritti di S. Ambroggio* (Milan, 1991).

[24] Aug. *Conf.* 6. 8 (13), 9 (14), 10 (16); 8. 6 (13). At *Conf.* 6. 9 (15) Augustine refers to Alypius as a future 'multarum in ecclesia tua causarum examinator' ('examiner of many arbitrations in your church').

[25] Humbert, 'Enfants', 191–3, 198–201; see also Lepelley, 'Liberté', 332–5.

[26] *CTh* 1. 2. 6 = *CJ* 1. 22. 4, which forbids appeals based on false evidence. Augustine cites the same principle at *Tract. in Iohannis Evan.* 7. 11 (*CCL* 36. 73).

Epist. 20* indicates that another bishop did too. Many of the schemes concocted by the renegade bishop Antoninus seem to have been based on legal dodges. For one thing, Antoninus knew enough to dispose quickly of anything he had stolen, thereby frustrating actions *in rem* ('assertions of ownership of a thing') against him.[27] Other ploys, aimed at beautifying the villa he was constructing outside Fussala, indicate that Antoninus (or at least the *defensor ecclesiae* with whom he was colluding) had an elaborate legal imagination. The roof of the villa was built from tiles illegally removed from a property Antoninus held in partnership. Other bits of it were erected from another man's house which he had torn down after acquiring it in exchange for a house he had illegally obtained.[28] In fact, to hear Augustine tell it, 'some would claim there is practically nothing in the construction of that house which does not appear to have been taken from someone else's house'.[29] Now, any first-year Roman law student knew that anything Antoninus built into the house on his estate could not be reclaimed as long as the house stood.[30] Antoninus thus may have been using the house to provide a legal loophole allowing him to acquire long-term possession of his loot. It was perhaps for this reason that Antoninus struggled so hard to retain his position in Fussala and maintained to the end his demand, 'Give me back the house I built in your village!'[31] Nor did Antoninus' legal legerdemain stop with this elaborate haven for his ill-gotten gains. Many of his rackets were conducted under the umbrella of his episcopal legal authority, and, had he won back his see after his expulsion, he apparently planned to continue with further suits.[32] Antoninus, therefore, seems to have been well versed not only in the theory but also in the practice of certain points of law.

The third question raised above asks what the new letters can tell us about the enforcement of episcopal decisions. A bishop's most obvious means of coercion, and one limited to

[27] *Epist.* 20*. 29. 2; 31. 1.

[28] *Epist.* 20*. 30. 1–2; 31. 1; cf. 6. 3–4.

[29] *Epist.* 20*. 31. 4.

[30] Gaius 2. 73; Justinian, *Inst.* 2. 1. 29–30: see Buckland, *Text-Book*, 212–3.

[31] Aug. *Epist.* 30. 31. 3; cf. 17. 3; 24. 2–3; 25. 1.

[32] *Epist.* 20*. 10. 1; cf. *Epist.* 209. 9 (*CSEL* 57. 351–2).

episcopal courts, was excommunication. After convicting the estate manager Cresconius of rape, Augustine excommunicated him even before pushing for further penalties.[33] In his decision against Antoninus, Augustine ordered him to return any stolen property and attempted to enforce his decision with excommunication; Antoninus himself had done this as a means of coercion.[34] In the case of the presbyter who had raped the nun, excommunication was mooted but not eventually used. Here, Augustine argued, it would have been totally ineffective against a man who cared nothing for spiritual penalties. For this reason he preferred the punishment that the priest actually received, whipping.[35]

Even though this particular instance was illegal because the priest was a decurion, this incident demonstrates that bishops could use corporal punishment as an alternative to the more spiritual castigations customarily associated with ecclesiastical courts. Indeed, elsewhere Augustine distinguished between torture and mere 'virgarum verbera' ('blows from switches') (*Epist.* 133. 2: *CSEL* 44. 82) which, he claimed, were often used in episcopal courts. Augustine's monks had certainly beaten a *notarius* who had consorted with nuns before fleeing to join Antoninus' coterie, and Augustine himself recommended that the bishop Victor administer a whipping to the Jew Licinius should Licinius be shown to have committed *iniuria* ('gross insult') against his mother.[36] *Epist.* 10*. 4. 1–4 even implies that Augustine could have chosen to enforce the law of Honorius demanding that illegal slave traders be beaten with lead-tipped whips, a punishment tantamount to a death sentence because of the gravity of the wounds inflicted.

Given this broad authority for enforcing their judgments, one might ask what personnel and apparatus a bishop had at his disposal to impose such penalties. A law of Constantine from 333 commanded the Praetorian Prefect to enforce episcopal judgments.[37] Nowhere in the new letters, however,

[33] *Epist.* 15*. 4–5.
[34] *Epist.* 20*. 20. 2.
[35] *Epist.* 9*. 2. 1–6; cf. ibid. 1. 3, 3. 2, 4. 1.
[36] *Epist.* 20*. 5. 1; *Epist.* 8*. 2. 2.
[37] *Sirm.* 1: 333; cf. *CTh* 1. 27. 2: 408. *CTh* 16. 2. 31: 409 offered military assistance to African clerics.

is this collusion between civil and ecclesiastical authorities attested. On the contrary, in *Epist.* 9*. 2. 1, Augustine laments that only the church, not public authorities, enforced the law on rape. So, too, *Epist.* 10*. 5. 1 indicates that imperial authorities were largely absent from the local scene when it came to enforcing laws on illegal slave trading, leaving the responsibility entirely to Augustine himself. Indeed, in *Epist.* 22*, Augustine sought advice on how to elect a *defensor civitatis* (a local legal official under the authority of the Praetorian Prefect) to help champion the interests of his community against *improbi* ('wicked people'), among whom he ranked regional imperial officials.[38] Even so, the same letter reveals a profound lack of knowledge about the procedure for selecting such a *defensor civitatis*, and has been taken as supporting evidence for the widely held assumption that such officers were a rarity in North Africa early in the fifth century. The state, therefore, was hardly a real presence for the enforcement of justice at the community level.

In the state's absence, the church filled the void. Beginning in the early fifth century one begins to hear of a parallel local official in North Africa termed the *defensor ecclesiae*. In 407 the Council of Carthage called for and obtained imperial sanction for such officers, apparently to help with the enforcement of the laws against the Donatists.[39] That the *defensor ecclesiae* also played a larger role as a law enforcement factotum is confirmed, moreover, by *Epist.* 20*: in Fussala, Antoninus used his *defensor ecclesiae*, along with town *vigiles* ('watchmen'), locally garrisoned soldiers, and even members of the clergy, to enforce his decisions.[40] Even though Augustine indicates that Antoninus overstepped his authority by threatening his congregation with 'court cases, public officials, and military attacks',[41] the issue here was more the

[38] *Epist.* 22*. 2. 1–4; with F. Jacques, 'Le Défenseur de cité d'aprés la Lettre 22* de Saint Augustin', *REA* 32 (1986), 56–73. *Reg. Eccl. Carthag. Exc.* 75 = *CCL* 149. 202 already had requested the appointment of *defensores* 'adversus potentias divitum' ('against the powers of the rich') in 410. See also *Epist.* 23*. 1 and *Epist.* 115 (*CSEL* 34. 662) for the influence of the wealthy and powerful.

[39] *Reg. eccl. Carthag. exc.* 97 (*CCL* 149. 215); with *CTh* 16. 2. 38: 407, *CJ* 1. 55. 8: 409; and Possidius, *Vita Augustini* 12: *PL* 32. 43; note also B. Fischer, 'Defensor ecclesiae,' *Reallexikon für Antike und Christentum*, iii (Stuttgart, 1957), 656–8.

[40] *Epist.* 20*. 6. 1; cf. 29. 4.

[41] *Epist.* 209. 9 (*CSEL* 57. 351–2).

treacherous ends to which Antoninus put his henchmen than the fact that he employed them as enforcers.[42] When he was charged with ordering his *defensor ecclesiae* to arrest and detain a man as part of a plot to deprive him of his property, Antoninus defended his action by claiming that the man had been arrested not for this, but on a separate, valid charge. He apparently had the authority to order the *defensor* to arrest people, and did so in this case to try to deflect charges against this false arrest by arguing that it was based on just cause.[43] Bishops thus had considerable latitude in the types of punishment they could mete out and in the means they could use for enforcing their decisions.

The final question posed above asks how bishops perceived their legal role. Twice in the new letters Augustine complained of the burdens of worldly jurisdiction.[44] This sentiment recurs throughout his corpus, most famously in a passage from the *De opere monachorum* ('On the Work of Monks') where he praised the simplicity of monastic life over his pressing need 'to endure the highly tumultuous perplexities of other people's legal cases about worldly business'.[45] Indeed, Augustine was said regularly to have spent mornings and sometimes all day hearing cases.[46] Augustine thus regarded his legal duties as burdensome, even annoying. Nevertheless, in this same passage, he went on to say that legal jurisdiction was a pastoral demand incumbent on all bishops because of St Paul's injunction that worldly disputes between Christians be brought to 'the holy'.[47]

[42] This legal authority is to be distinguished from the vigilante enforcers often used by bishops of the period, on which see P. Brown, *Power and Persuasion in Late Antiquity* (Madison, 1992), 146–52.

[43] *Epist.* 20*. 29. 3–4; cf. 6. 4. Optatus of Timgad also used soldiers to enforce corrupt decisions: see Aug. *Cont. lit. Petil.* 2. 23 (53) (*CSEL* 52. 51–2). And Basil of Caesarea (*Epist.* 268) had ecclesiastical officials at his disposal who could arrest law breakers.

[44] *Epist.* 9*. 2. 1; 24*. 1. 2.

[45] *De opere monachorum* 28 [37] (*CSEL* 41. 586–8); cf. *Epist.* 33. 5; 48. 1 (*CSEL* 34. 22, 137); *Ennarat. in Psalm.* 25. 2. 13; 118. 24. 3 (*CCL* 38. 150; 40. 1745).

[46] Possidius, *Vita Augustini* 19 (*PL* 32. 50). Elsewhere, Epiphanius of Salamis also set aside mornings for legal decisions (*Vita Epiphanii* 55: *PG* 41. 93); and Augustine suggested that Ambrose of Milan too spent much of his day with 'catervae negotiosorum hominum' ('crowds of men of business') (*Conf.* 6. 3 [3]).

[47] 1 Cor. 6: 1–6. Augustine also cited Paul as the basis for his legal inquiries at *Epist.* 24*. 1. 2; cf. *Ennarat. in Psalm.* 80. 21; 118. 24. 3 (*CCL* 39. 1133; 40. 1745); Possidius, *Vita Augustini* 19 (*PL* 32. 50).

In keeping with this command, Augustine was concerned that Christians should be adjudicated only before bishops, and was worried that church members should not wrangle in court unless absolutely necessary. In *Epist.* 20* he lamented that the church would become a spectacle for Jews, pagans, and heretics because of the legal disputes surrounding Antoninus. The same sentiment recurs in *Epist.* 8*, where bishop Victor was pushing his unfair claim against the Jew Licinius.[48] To avoid embarrasssment, Augustine discouraged Victor from forcing his case to court. This pressure to avoid legal action, which surely occurred on other occasions, helps to explain the paucity of examples in which disputes settled by bishops proceeded to the stage of adjudication.[49]

Augustine's conviction that his legal activities fulfilled a pastoral responsibility also affected the tenor of his approach to cases at law. The new letters reveal what one might call a soft touch in legal dealings. For example, Augustine was ready to forgo his church's strong claim to the money withheld by Bassus' widow in *Epist.* 7*. Instead, he preferred to let civil authorities handle the case so he would not be seen squabbling with the widow.[50] Moreover, in a famous case of 425 Augustine gave up a legacy offered to the church of Hippo by a monk in order to avoid disputing a *querela* from the monk's children.[51] More dramatically, when he enforced the law against renegade slave traders in *Epist.* 10*, Augustine only pushed his authority far enough to free the captives, not to torture their captors.[52] And in the case of Cresconius, who had committed rape, Augustine insisted that the presiding bishop promise not to inflict a harsh sentence before allowing him to learn the details of the case.[53]

[48] *Epist.* 20*. 26. 2; 8*. 1. 8, referring to 1 Cor. 10: 32.

[49] For the settlement of disputes without formal adjudication, see Harries in this volume.

[50] *Epist.* 7*. 2. 1–3. On the strength of Augustine's legal claim see Fevrier, 'Discours', 166–7; 171–2.

[51] *Sermo* 355. 3–4; 356. 2, 11 (*PL* 39. 1570–72; 1575; 1579); see also Possidius, *Vita Augustini* 24 (*PL* 32. 53); and F. van der Meer, *Augustine the Bishop*, (trans.) B. Battershaw, G. R. Lamb (London, 1961), 600–6.

[52] *Epist.* 10*. 3–4; 7–8. For Augustine's opposition to torture see *De civitate dei* 19. 6 (*CCL* 48. 670); *Epist.* 14*. 2. 1–2 (*CSEL* 88. 83); *Epist.* 104. 2, 17 (*CSEL* 34. 582, 594); *Epist.* 133. 2; 134. 2 (*CSEL* 44. 82, 85).

[53] *Epist.* 15*. 3. 3–4. 6.

At times, this forbearance was carried so far that it backfired. When Augustine punished Antoninus by mere excommunication, he opened the way to further disputes that nearly forced his own resignation.[54] Though expulsion was a possible, indeed the logical punishment, the lighter penalty offered Antoninus the grounds he needed to build an appeal to Rome.[55] Augustine thus interpreted his legal authority as an aspect of his pastoral duties, and he exercised it in a corresponding spirit of charity that at times could lead him to excessive leniency.

Finally, to expand upon the answer to the question of how bishops understood their legal role, it must be said that the boundaries of their activity were not neatly defined. For one thing, there was no single word used to describe an episcopal court. The preferred modern term 'audientia episcopalis' certainly is cited in the legal sources, but these same sources prefer 'episcopale iudicium' and also mention several other terms.[56] In the new letters, Augustine, too, favours 'episcopale iudicium' though he generally shortens this to 'iudicium'.[57] There thus was slippage in the terminology, and the most popular designation, *iudicium*, was shared with the term used of public courts. Given this overlap, we can imagine that the boundary between episcopal and public jurisdiction was often blurred; in the real world this could not be helped.

Cases like that found in *Epist.* 7*, involving church property but not ecclesiastics, had the potential to create problems of jurisdiction. Although the widow sought redress from a civil official and Augustine himself hoped for the

[54] *Epist.* 20*. 8. 1–2. Augustine felt tremendous guilt over his poor choice in Antoninus, especially because it had violated several North African canons (Council of Carthage [390] can. 12; *Brev. Hippon.* 1, 2, 20: *CCL* 149. 18, 33, 39). A number of decisions from the Council of Hippo of 427 seem to have been aimed at preventing the kinds of mistakes Augustine had made (*Conc. Hippon.* can. 1–3, 5: *CCL* 149. 250–1).

[55] *Epist.* 209. 7–8 (*CSEL* 57. 350–1). On the procedures for expulsion see Noethlichs, 'Materialen', 49–51. On Antoninus' appeal see C. Munier, 'La Question des appels à Rome d'après la Lettre 20* d'Augustin', in *Les lettres*, 287–99.

[56] *Audientia episcopalis*: *CTh* 16. 2. 12; *Sirm.* 6; *CJ* 1. 3. 25. *Episcopale iudicium*: *CTh* 1. 27. 1, 2; 11. 36. 20; 16. 2. 12, 23; *Sirm.* 1, 2, 9; *Nov. Val.* 35; *Nov. Maj.* 11. *Episcopalis definitio*: *CTh* 1. 27. *Causa ecclesiastica*: *CTh* 11. 36. 20; *Sirm.* 3. Note here that individual constitutions sometimes use different terms.

[57] *Episcopale / ecclesiasticum iudicium*: 8*. 1. 8; 9*. 4. 3; 20*. 6. 4, 7. 3. *Iudicium*: 9*. 1. 2, 3. 3, 4. 2; 20*. 12. 4, 15. 2, 30. 1–2, 31. 1. *Causa*: 9. 1. 1–2, 3. 1.

same, he wrote to a bishop to request that he investigate the matter, hoping that the bishop's report would have an effect on the public official's decision. Similarly, in *Epist.* 20* one of the plaintiffs brought his case against Antoninus' *defensor ecclesiae* before the imperial courts. In this instance, jurisdiction was ambiguous because the *defensor* had been acting as the agent of a cleric. Moreover, although the suit originated in the public court, the case was eventually settled by the intervention of Augustine.[58] And in *Epist.* 209. 5, related to the same affair, Augustine indicated that at one point even Antoninus faced possible actions in public court before the Proconsul of Africa. It seems, therefore, that even though there were *de iure* lines between episcopal and public jurisdictions, as Augustine knew well,[59] the sticky reality of daily life prevented bishops and public officials from maintaining well-defined boundaries.[60]

Ultimately the blurred frontier between secular and ecclesiastical jurisdiction could lead to serious injustices. Fortunately for Hippo, Augustine worked hard not to abuse his episcopal powers. Thus, in the case of the monk's legacy, from which his own church stood to benefit and which presented a serious conflict of interest, he refused to take advantage of his authority and deprive the monk's children of their inheritance. But on the other hand, the new letters also show that not all bishops were as even-handed in the exercise of the spiritual, judicial, and executive authority concentrated in their hands. Bishop Victor of *Epist.* 8* was investigating a charge of *iniuria* against Licinius at the very time that he was engaged in a property suit with this same man. Although Victor was certain to lose his property case, if he found grounds for the *iniuria* charge he could have enjoyed the satisfaction of having his victorious legal opponent whipped. And in *Epist.* 20*, Antoninus hid behind legality in his committing of crimes and delicts. By the time he was removed, his parishioners were so intimidated by the legal system that

[58] *Epist.* 20*. 29. 4. [59] *Epist.* 9*. 4. 3.

[60] Ambrose *Epist.* 24 (*CSEL* 82. 170–5) settled a case involving a bishop that already had gone before the Praetorian Prefect; and Augustine himself regularly intervened in secular criminal trials (*Epist.* 90, 113–16, 133–4, 151–3, 15*–16*, 23*A).

they refused to give their names in testimony before the episcopal Primate of Numidia.[61]

When a bishop wished, he could enthusiastically abuse his legal powers. And even if he did not, as in Augustine's case, the failure to distinguish between ecclesiastical–pastoral and secular–legal responsibilities could still compromise justice. When Augustine's *iudicium* acquitted Antoninus on charges of *stuprum*, Augustine reported that the decision was greeted by his clergy with 'fraternal joy'.[62] Given the sentiment in favour of this fellow cleric, one can imagine that Augustine was inclined to show leniency toward Antoninus in this capital case. Even when Antoninus' offences became too egregious for Augustine to excuse, his refusal to depose the scoundrel led to a continuation of the crisis. Whether for good or ill, then, a bishop's authority at the local level was virtually beyond question.

[61] *Epist.* 20*. 21. 2. 3.

[62] *Epist.* 20*. 8. 4; cf. *Epist.* 209. 4 (*CSEL* 57. 349).

6

Judicial Violence and the Ecclesiastical Courts in Late Antique North Africa

Leslie Dossey

Late Roman clerics were occasionally accused of flogging, imprisoning, or otherwise coercing fellow clerics and laypersons. This phenomenon is potentially important for understanding the judicial role of the Christian church, for an essential part of Roman dispute settlement was the ability to coerce people to court and oversee the interrogation and corporal punishment that attended even civil suits.[1] This study will focus on the use and significance of judicial violence in ecclesiastical contexts in North Africa during the fourth and fifth centuries.

It should be emphasized at the outset that the coercive power of the western church was fundamentally a popular movement, occasionally recognized by emperors at certain bishops' request, but more often suppressed. Emperors jealously reserved the use of force to secular (preferably imperial) officials. When they gave bishops the authority to judge, they did not include the power to coerce: a ruling of Constantine I (306–37) specified that secular officials were to enforce bishops' judgments: 'whether judgment should have been made by bishops about minor or great matters, we wish their execution to pertain to you, who hold highest office among judges, and to all other judges.'[2] Constantine's successors

[1] For this practice, see Sirks in this volume; for bishops' judicial roles, see also Harries and Lenski in this volume.

[2] *Sirm.* 1: 'Siue itaque inter minores siue inter maiores ab episcopis fuerit iudicatum, apud uos, qui iudiciorum summam tenetis, et apud ceteros omnes iudices ad exsecutionem uolumus pertinere.'

tried to prevent bishops from even judging the criminal and civil suits that were likely to involve corporal punishment. Gratian denied that the church had any jurisdiction in criminal matters, even when clerics were involved (the African church, however, did not agree).[3] In 399, Honorius assured the proconsul of Africa that bishops were to judge only matters of religion; other litigation went to the civil judges.[4] In 408, a western edict affirmed that bishops could only judge civil suits when both parties agreed (as with ordinary arbitration).[5] Imperial officials were to execute their decisions.[6] Even in religious matters, such as the conversion of schismatics, the secular powers were to perform any necessary coercion.[7]

The question remains, however, of whether the late Roman clerics accepted these imperial restrictions on their ability to arrest, interrogate, and punish miscreants. Mindful of Christ's rebuke when a disciple cut off a royal slave's ear (Matt. 26: 51–2), few clerics could justify shedding blood with a sword.[8] Their reasons, however, sometimes were the result more of sacral concerns than opposition to violence per se; as an anonymous North African treatise on clerical celibacy explained, 'Clerics do not shed blood nor bear iron because of the dignity of the holy priesthood', and compared it to avoiding women.[9] Nor did most clerics advocate the use of force against heretics and schismatics, at least when writing for an imperial audience.

[3] *CTh* 16. 2. 23: 376. The African church claimed criminal jurisdiction over clerics: *Breviarium Hipponense* 9 (*CCL* 149. 36), from the Council of Carthage of 397.

[4] *CTh* 16. 11. 1: 399, Honorius to Apollodorus, Proconsul of Africa; cf. *CJ* 1. 4. 7: 398 for the east. For the efforts of Honorius and Arcadius to restrict the civil jurisdiction of bishops to arbitration, see M. R. Cimma, *L'Episcopalis audientia nelle costituzioni imperiali da Costantino a Giustiniano* (Turin, 1989), 81–96, and C. Lepelley, *Les Cités de l'Afrique Romaine au bas-empire*, i (Paris, 1979), 389–95.

[5] For episcopal arbitration, see Harries in this volume.

[6] *CTh* 1. 27. 2: 408; *CTh* 1. 27. 3: 408: 'Per publicum quoque officium ne sit cassa cognitio, definitioni exsecutio tribuatur'.

[7] Marcellinus, the imperial tribune who enforced the decrees of the Council of Carthage of 411, ordered decurions, landlords, and village leaders to close Donatist churches and transfer their property to the Catholics: *Edictum cognitoris*, S. Lancel (ed.), *Actes de la conférence de Carthage en 411* 2. 73 (*SC* 224. 974–6); see also *CTh* 16. 5. 52: 412, which orders landlords to flog Donatist *coloni*, and magistrates to collect fines.

[8] Petilianus cited this verse against Augustine: *Cont. Petil.* 2. 88. 194.

[9] Ps.-Cyprian, *De singularitate clericorum* 33: *CSEL* 3. 209.

Augustine of Hippo, when criticizing Donatists, certainly trod the official line. In his treatise against the Donatist bishop Petilianus of Cirta, he argued that clerics should not use 'clubs and carnage' to defend their churches, but rather ought to avail themselves of the legitimate secular powers.[10] At the Council of Carthage of 403, the bishops echoed his words when complaining to the proconsul of Africa about Donatist violence. They also asked for the assistance of secular magistrates to force their Donatist rivals to meet with them.[11] After the Council of Carthage of 411, the Catholic bishops relied on imperial *executores* and landlords to force the Donatists back into their congregations.[12]

The corporal discipline of one's own clerics or parishioners also seems to have been contrary to canon law, at least by the sixth century. When discussing the punishment of misbehaving clerics or laymen, the early church councils focused on the non-corporal kind, such as excommunication, public penance, or loss of ecclesiastical office, although they did not explicitly prohibit beating.[13] The Apostolic Canons —apocryphal decrees from a 'Council of the Apostles' at Jerusalem—forbade corporal punishment entirely, decreeing regarding a bishop, priest, or deacon who 'strikes believers for sinning or unbelievers for wrong-doing, and wants to be feared on account of this, we command that he be deposed'.[14] This canon, which actually dates to late fourth-century Syria, became part of eastern canon law, although it was little known in the west until the sixth century and not in North Africa

[10] Aug. *Cont. Petil.* 2. 19. 43.

[11] Letter of Council of Carthage to proconsul Septiminus (*c.*403) (*SC* 224. 1120): 'Aut si putant se habere aliquid veritatis, non eam furiosis circumcellionum violentiis contra publicam quietem sed tranquilla rationis redditione defendant.'

[12] See P. Brown, 'Religious Coercion in the Later Roman Empire: The Case of North Africa', *Historia*, 47 (1963), 283–305 = Idem, *Religion and Society in the Age of Saint Augustine* (New York, 1972), 301–31, esp. 322, 327–9. The key reference to *executores* in the councils is *Reg. eccl. Carthag. excerpta* 123: *CCL* 149. 226.

[13] For these decrees, see J. Gaudemet, *L'Église dans l'empire romain* (Paris, 1958), 70–7, 182–3.

[14] *Apostolic Canons* 27: M. Metzer (ed.), *Les Constitutions apostoliques, SC* 320 (Paris, 1985), 280–2. The Apostolic Canons were originally an appendix to a longer work, the Apostolic Constitutions, although they had a separate transmission.

until the seventh.[15] In the early sixth century, an apocryphal collection from Rome, the *Constitutum Silvestri*, added its own injunction against bishops, priests, or deacons punishing their clerics by beating them.[16] By the late sixth century, the church of Rome, at least, recognized that corporal punishment violated the canons. Gregory the Great criticized the patriarch of Constantinople for flogging a priest for heresy: 'What the canons say about bishops who want to be feared for their blows, you well know. For indeed we have been made pastors, not persecutors.'[17] As we shall see, however, Gregory did not always follow his own advice.

Only in the early medieval period do western church councils begin to allow that corporal punishment might sometimes be warranted; the Council of Braga (675), for example, urged clerics to refrain from beating laymen 'except for the more serious and mortal sins'.[18] But the Byzantine church, more closely controlled by the emperor, never made even this concession. The First–Second Synod of Constantinople (861) ridiculed the notion that a cleric who was forbidden from striking someone with his own hand could

[15] For the provenance of the Apostolic Constitutions in the region of Antioch *c.*380, see Metzer, *Constitutions*, 55–62. They were regarded as authentic in sixth-century Constantinople and at the Byzantine Trullan council (691): J. Gaudemet, *Les Sources du droit de l'Église en Occident* du IIe au VIe siècle (Paris, 1985), 25 n. 55. Can. 27 first appears in western collections of canons in the early sixth century, when it was incorporated into Dionysius Exiguus' Latin collection of eastern canons: A. Strewe (ed.), *Die Canonessammlung des Dionysius Exiguus in der ersten Redaktion* (Berlin, 1931), 7. By this time, however, there were western doubts about their authenticity as expressed in the Pseudo-Gelasian *De libris recipiendis et non recipiendis*: *PL* 59. 163, itself dated to the early sixth century. Can. 27 appears in North African collections for the first time in the seventh century: Cresconius, *Breviarium Canonicum* 29: *PL* 88. 852.

[16] *Constitutum Silvestri*, can. 17: *PL* 8. 839: 'Nemo enim quemquam peccantem clericum caede attingat, non presbyter, non diaconus, non episcopus supra clericum uel seruitorem ecclesiae ad caedem perducat.' This document pretends to be the decrees from a council under Pope Silvester (*c.*324), but was probably composed at Rome at the beginning of the sixth century: Gaudemet, *Sources*, 139–40.

[17] Greg. Mag. *Regest*. 3. 52: 'Quid autem de episcopis qui uerberibus timeri uolunt, canones dicant, bene fraternitas uestra nouit. pastores etenim facti sumus, non persecutores.'

[18] 'Et ideo qui gradus iam ecclesiasticos meruerunt, id est presbyteri, abbates sive leuitae, excepto grauioribus et mortalibus culpis nullis debent uerberibus subiacere', Council of Braga (675), can. 6: J. Vives, (ed.), *Concilios visigóticos e hispano-romanos* (Barcelona, 1963), 377.

order a beating. If the canonical punishments did not work, the clerics should call in the secular magistrates.[19] On balance, the late antique bishop had little legal justification for using physical coercion against anyone.

On the basis of imperial law and conciliar decrees, scholars generally agree that the late Roman church did not adopt the judicial violence used by the the secular courts, and legal historians, whatever their debates over the precise nature of *audientia episcopalis*, concede that non-spiritual enforcement belonged to imperial or municipal officials.[20] Even in matters where bishops had uncontested jurisdiction, such as the correction of clerics for minor infractions, they are presumed to have applied only canonical punishments—excommunication, penance, or deposition from clerical office.[21]

Yet, when we turn from normative law to practice it becomes clear that clerics throughout the late Roman empire were more involved in beating people than the law allowed. Even in the Greek east, where injunctions against corporal punishment appear earlier,[22] clerics did not refrain from beating miscreants. A fifth-century Syriac rule for clerics enjoined in splendid ambiguity, 'Do not scourge anyone, but if there is a reason because of which you are compelled to scourge, either scourge to frighten or send the guilty ones to

[19] *First–Second Synod* 9: P.-P. Joannou, (ed.), *Discipline générale antique* (Grottaferrata, 1962), 463. Cf. the influential ninth-century rule of the Stoudios monastery in Constantinople: 'Discipline with the whip, although suitable for those in the world, was properly judged unacceptable by our fathers' (*Hypotyposis of Stoudios* 25: *PG* 99. 1713).

[20] See Cimma, *Episcopalis audientia*, 76; F. J. Cuena Boy, *La 'episcopalis audientia'* (Valladolid, 1985), 52–3; Gaudemet, *L'Église*, 247–9; and C. Gebbia, 'Sant'Agostino e l'episcopalis audientia', *L'Africa romana: Atti del VI convegno di studio, Sassari, 16–18 dicembre 1988* (Sassari, 1989), 683–95, esp. 691, 694.

[21] See M. F. Martroye, 'Saint Augustin et la compétence de la juridiction ecclésiastique au Ve siècle', *Mémoires de la Société Nationale des Antiquaires de France* 7th ser., 10 (1911), 1–78; Gaudemet, *L'Église*, 182–3; Gebbia, 'Sant'Agostino', 692–4; and P. Saint-Roch, *La Pénitence dans les conciles et les lettres des papes des origines à la mort de Grégoire le Grand* (Rome, 1991), who notes (100–1) that imprisonment in monasteries was used by the sixth century.

[22] In addition to Apostolic Canon 27, the *Didascalia apostolorum* told bishops not to use force or violence when correcting laity: *Didascalia* 7: R. H. Connolly (trans.), *Didascalia apostolorum: The Syriac Version* (Oxford, 1929), 64. The *Didascalia* was a book of instructions for bishops, originally composed in Greek in the third century, probably in the region of Antioch, but only surviving in Syriac, Latin, and other translations.

the judges of the world'.[23] The Egyptian desert fathers had even less compunction about corporally disciplining monks or troublesome laity. According to the monastic rule of Pachomius, a monk who stole secretly was to be beaten thirty-nine times and then kept outside the gates until he had performed suitable penance.[24] Palladius described three date palms at a church on Mt. Nitria where miscreant monks or robbers were bound and whipped.[25] The Coptic-speaking archimandrite Shenoute, perhaps best known for punching the bishop Nestorius at the Council of Ephesus in 431, admitted to striking 'with canes and our own hands when incited with rage against someone whose mind is inflated with pride'.[26] Shenoute provided copious scriptural justification for his violence, focusing on injunctions that fathers discipline their sons.[27] He extended his sphere of influence to the laity, becoming particularly renowned for castigating the rich for oppressing the poor.[28] Part of the reason holy men like Shenoute managed to exercise as much coercion as they did was their location on the fringes of the empire, in the villages and deserts where imperial and municipal authority was weak. Bishops and abbots close to Constantinople had to tread more warily. The issue, in short, was not whether clerics could morally justify using force, but whether the secular powers would allow them to get away with it.

In the western empire, bishops and abbots could corporally punish their own clerics and monks without much secular opposition. An example of North African discipline

[23] 'Rules of Rabbula for the clergy' 35: A. Vööbus (trans.), *Syriac and Arabic Documents regarding Legislation relative to Syrian Asceticism* (Stockholm, 1960), 45.

[24] *Regula Pachomii* 120: P. B. Albers, (ed.), *S. Pachomii abbatis Tabennensis regulae monasticae, Florilegium patristicum* 16 (Bonn, 1923), 55. The same penalty was applied to fugitives and, in *Regula* 84, to those who engage in the 'pessimam consuetudinem', perhaps meaning homosexual sex.

[25] Palladius, *Hist. Laus.* 7. 15–19: J. A. Robinson, (ed.), *The Lausaic History of Palladius* (Cambridge, 1898), 25.

[26] Shenoute, 'De iis, qui e monasterio discesserunt', in H. Wiesmann (trans.), *Sinuthii archimandritae vita et opera omnia*, iii, *CSCO. Scriptores coptici*, ser. 2, vol. 4 (1906), 86.

[27] Shenoute, 'De confessione peccatorum': Wiesmann, *Sinuthii*, 102, alluding to Prov. 3: 11 and Hebr. 12: 6 ('Whom the Lord loves He disciplines; He whips every son He receives').

[28] Besa, *The Life of Shenoute* 81: D. Bell (trans.) (Kalamazoo, 1983), 65.

is found in an early fourth-century letter from a bishop Purpurius to the neighbouring Bishop Silvanus of Cirta about Silvanus' deacon Nundinarius: 'He gave to me with his own hand the pamphlet of court proceedings on account of which he was to have been stoned at your order. It is not true that a father castigates a son against the truth, and I know that those things recorded in the pamphlet are true.'[29] Purpurius questioned the justness of Silvanus' judgment, not his right to stone his 'son'. Most bishops, however, contented themselves with merely beating their clerics. Augustine allowed members of his episcopal monastery to be beaten for conversing with nuns (Aug. *Epist.* 20*. 5. 1). Over a century later, the bishop of a small North African town corporally disciplined his clerics with such vigour that they appealed to Gregory the Great (after getting no sympathy from the North African ecclesiastical authorities).[30] Gregory disapproved of this bishop's excessive cruelty, yet on another occasion he insisted that the bishop of Naples publicly flog his subdeacon and expel him from the city for falsely accusing one of his fellow clerics.[31]

In the west, early monastic rules advocated flogging miscreant monks as a matter of course. Some, like the Rule of Benedict, suggested doing so with paternal affection,[32] but others were more vengeful: the Rule of the Master bade abbots to 'smite' impenitent monks 'to the point of death' before expelling them.[33] In Cassian's *Institutes*, monks were to be 'corrected with blows' for such things as eating secretly, conversing with women, keeping private possessions, and swearing.[34] In early medieval Gaul and Spain, bishops specified the precise number of lashes. Aurelianus, the bishop of Arles in the mid sixth century, limited it, as in the Rule of Pachomius, to thirty-nine lashes,[35] and the seventh-century bishop Fructuosus of Braga ordered that monks caught talking with nuns receive a hundred lashes in public,

[29] Optatus, App.1, *Gesta apud Zenophilum*: *CSEL* 26. 189.

[30] Greg. Mag. *Regest.* 12. 8–9.

[31] Greg. Mag. *Regest.* 11. 53.

[32] Bened. *Regula* 2. 28: *CSEL* 75. 24.

[33] *Regula mag.* 13. 69: A. de Vogüé, (ed.), *SC* 105. 46.

[34] Cassian, *Institutiones* 4. 16. 3: J.-C. Guy, (ed.), *SC* 109. 142.

[35] Aurelianus, *Regula ad monachos* 41: *PL* 68. 392.

even if penitent.[36] The rules justified such punishments with the familiar theme of paternal discipline.[37] Western bishops and abbots, therefore, did not recoil from the use of corporal punishment in individual cases when the culprits were in their power.

But could the church use physical coercion against lay men and women without suffering legal retribution? In matters of religion, bishops appear sometimes to have done so, especially if acting against only a few dissidents rather than an entire congregation. In the probably hagiographical *Altercatio Heracliani* from late fourth-century Illyricum, an Arian bishop Germinius of Sirmium beat laymen accused of heretical preaching. Procedurally, the *Altercatio* resembles a municipal inquest, with a bishop taking the place of a magistrate: 'They led Heraclianus and Firmianus and Aurelianus from the prison . . . the bishop presiding in his cathedra, with the whole clergy, in the presence of all the people.'[38] The bishop interrogated Heraclianus (whom he had baptized) about preaching heresy. In the course of this apparently religious trial, the bishop's deacon and lector beat Heraclianus to make him confess (*Alt.* 346). Eventually, the Arian priests and deacons urged the bishop to send the accused on to the governor 'so that they may be killed, because they have made sedition' (*Alt.* 350). The bishop refused, choosing instead to expel Heraclianus from the community. The reader is left to decide whether the bishop was merely publicly excommunicating a wayward member of his flock, or interrogating—and releasing—a citizen accused of the secular crime of sedition. Whatever the nature of the accusation, the bishop is portrayed as using the procedures proper to municipal courts, including judicial torture and imprisonment.

The *Altercatio* may, of course, be a malicious fabrication by the Catholics against the Arians. Yet we know that Catholic bishops also on occasion applied flogging, imprisonment, or worse against religious dissidents. When he learned that a bishop in Sardinia had idol worshipers in his diocese,

[36] Fructuosus, *Regula communis* 15: *PL* 87. 1123. The number is probably derived from Pachomius.

[37] Aurelianus, *Regula* 42; Benedict, *Regula* 2. 29 (citing Prov. 23. 14).

[38] *Altercatio Heracliani laici cum Germinio episcopo Sirmiensi*: *PLS* 1. 345.

Gregory the Great ordered him to castigate 'uerberibus cruciatibusque' ('with blows and tortures') those of servile birth (under which category he seems to have included *coloni*), and to imprison those of free birth, 'so that the agony of the body might be able to bring them to the desired health of mind'.[39] In 411, the Catholic bishop of the small town of Abora in Africa Proconsularis informed the imperial representative Marcellinus and the entire Council of Carthage that, in his community, 'If the name of Donatists should be heard, he is stoned.'[40] Perhaps in this case he was correct, but it is at least as likely that the bishop of this predominately Catholic community would have arrested, tried, and expelled a Donatist in a quasi-judicial ceremony, much like the bishop of Sirmium in the *Altercatio Heracliani*.[41]

These examples of physical coercion of laity have so far involved religious disputes, where the church had, after all, the authority to judge, if not to enforce. Clerics had to be more careful when they involved themselves in civil or criminal cases. The laity whom they would have been most likely to punish corporally for secular misdeeds were *coloni* and paupers, whom Romans had always deemed most in need of beating. In the emperor Leo's edict on asylum of 466, slaves or *coloni* who had stolen their master's property and fled to the church were to be returned by the *defensor civitatis* ('Defender of the City') to their masters 'after punishment has been meted out in accord with ecclesiastical discipline and the nature of the offense', or their master had sworn to

[39] Greg. Mag. *Regest.* 9. 205. 35: 'Ferventi comprehendere zelo te uolumus et, siquidem serui sunt, uerberibus cruciatibusque, quibus ad emendationem peruenire ualeant, castigare. si uero sunt liberi, inclausione digni districtaque sunt in paenitentia dirigendi, ut, qui salubra et a mortis periculo reuocantia audire uerba contemnunt, cruciatus saltem eos corporis ad desideratam mentis ualeat reducere sanitatem.'

[40] *Actes de la conférence de Carthage en 411* 1. 133: *SC* 195. 750, 'Trifolius episcopus plebis Aborensis, coram viro clarissimo tribuno et notario Marcellino suprascripta mandavi et subscripsi Carthagini. quo recitato, idem dixit: nomen si illic auditum fuerit donatistarum, lapidatur.' For Brown, 'Coercion', 307, this is an example of a bishop acting as the local 'leader of public opinion', creating an atmosphere of religious discrimination which could lead to a popular riot against minorities.

[41] Stoning, rather than execution, was probably a means of expulsion here; both Donatist and Catholic bishops expelled laity of the other sect: see *Actes de la conférence de Carthage en 411* 1. 133 (*SC* 195. 758–60) and 1. 198 (*SC* 195. 852).

pardon them (*CJ* 1. 12. 6. 9). The malefactors doubtless found ecclesiastical discipline gentler than the private vengeance of their masters. Nevertheless, the ecclesiastical punishment for theft also was likely to have been corporal. A letter attributed by Bede to Gregory the Great shows little compunction about flogging thieves: when Augustine, bishop of the English, asked him what to do about men stealing from the church, Gregory advised corporal punishment, for, he explained, even fathers beat their well-beloved heirs.[42]

Paupers fed by the church were even more in their bishop's power. In the 590s, the bishop of Tarentino 'castigated with rods' a female resident of the episcopal poor house. The woman subsequently died, although probably not from the beating. Gregory (who was already annoyed with the bishop for having a concubine) considered the beating sufficiently 'contrary to the office of the priesthood' to suspend him for two months.[43] The problem seems to have been that the bishop flogged the woman excessively and perhaps with his own hands: when Gregory ordered the bishop of Naples to flog his subdeacon, he also bid him to name a 'vicedominus' and 'maior domus' to oversee guesthouses or internal disputes (*causae*).[44]

Augustine's new letters suggest that, in addition to the poor, bishops also disciplined local smallholders.[45] Bishop

[42] Greg. Mag. *Regest.* 11. 56: *MGH Epist.* 2. 334. The authenticity of this 'Libellus responsionum' is debated. Norberg omits it from his 1982 edition of Gregory's letters (*CCL* 140–141A), while Minard includes it in his 1991 edition, considering it 'très probablement authentique' (*SC* 370. 59, 371. 490–521).

[43] Greg. Mag. *Regest.* 3. 44–45.

[44] Greg. Mag. *Regest.* 11. 53. For an opinion that bishops were expected to appoint lesser clerics or laymen to govern their episcopal guesthouses and poorhouses, see *Statuta ecclesiae antiqua* (*c.*475) 17, 'Ut episcopus gubernationem uiduarum et pupillorum aut peregrinorum non per se ipsum, sed per archipresbyterum uel archidiaconum agat' (*CCL* 149. 345).

[45] They also show Augustine himself using corporal punishment in suits judged by the church: see Aug. *Epist.* 8* (the Jew Licinius), *Epist.* 9* (man of the curia who raped *sanctimonialis)*, *Epist.* 20*. 5 (notary in episcopal monastery), and *Epist.* 133. 2 (to Marcellinus): 'qui modus cohercitionis et a magistri artium liberalium et ab ipsis parentibus et saepe etiam in iudiciis solet ab episcopis haberi', on which, see J. Lamoreaux, 'Episcopal Courts in Late Antiquity', *Journal of Early Christian Studies*, 3 (1995), 143–67, 163–4. For Augustine's use of coercion based upon his unusual degree of influence, see W. Eck, 'Der Episcopat im spätantiken Afrika: organisatorische Entwicklung, soziale Herkunft und öffentliche Funktionen', *Historische Zeitschrift*, 236 (1983), 266–95. See also Lenski in this volume.

Antoninus of the village of Fussala imprisoned the owner of a nearby farm for an unspecified fault (Aug. *Epist.* 20*. 29. 4).[46] Another case shows that offenders did not have to be Christians. When the mother of the Jewish smallholder Licinius was injured by her son's wife, she sold her son's fields to the local bishop (or possibly priest) Victor. Augustine, hearing about this transaction, charitably suggested that Victor had purchased the fields as a way to punish Licinius for harming his mother. Augustine advised Victor to give back the land and formally judge the dispute. If Victor judged Licinius and his family guilty, he should publically flog Licinius and have Licinius flog his wife and slave-girl (thus recognizing Licinius' power as *paterfamilias*).[47] As long as bishops did not profit from their authority, they could get away with punishing the petty violence and thefts of the humbler members of their communities.

In some cases, the church applied corporal punishment to save an accused from harsher treatment in the secular courts. When the nephew of the bishop of Sipontum committed fornication (*stuprum*) with the unmarried daughter of a deacon, Gregory the Great ordered him to be castigated corporally and then imprisoned in a monastery. This was not a case of the church reserving the right to judge its own clerics, because the nephew did not hold any clerical office. As Gregory explained to the bishop of Sipontum (who no doubt resented Gregory's interference), he was exercising moderation, in consideration of the heavy punishment proscribed by secular law.[48] In such cases, corporal punishment, if not excessive, could even be portrayed as an act of mercy.

As long as the church contented itself with punishing those who were poor, dependent, or eager to avoid the secular courts, it seems to have met with little governmental opposition. But when a cleric raised his hand to punish someone of superior dignity he committed a grievous crime.[49] Immunity from such punishment was one of the most valued privileges of Roman decurions and senators. It was

[46] For these cases, see also Lenski in this volume.
[47] Aug. *Epist.* 8*. For the *paterfamilias*, see Arjava in this volume.
[48] Greg. Mag. *Regest.* 3. 40, 3. 42.
[49] See Lamoreaux, 'Episcopal Courts', 164, regarding Aug. *Epist.* 9*.

confirmed by the emperor Constantine and respected by the governors of fourth-century North Africa.[50] With the imperial courts reluctant to torture or flog members of the elite, bishops (much less priests or deacons) did so at their peril. The image of a person of lesser status beating his superior was profoundly disturbing. A rule of the jurist Gaius that made its way into the early medieval law-codes was that 'an injury is a grave one which is inflicted in public or in the forum by a *humilior* on an *honestior*'.[51] Many North African communities in the fourth century had priests and bishops of humble social origins promoted to a position of power over landlords of curial or senatorial birth. This could lead to a crisis of authority, if clerics tried to discipline men of high status in the same way as they did petty thieves.[52]

Until the publication of Augustine's new letters, the Donatist circumcellions were the main religious group in North Africa to be accused of using physical coercion against men of high birth. According to the Catholic bishop Optatus of Milevis, *c.*340 two Donatists calling themselves 'generals of the saints' (*duces sanctorum*) took over the market village Octava. Against their bishops' wishes, they issued documents to prevent creditors from collecting their debts, and 'if anyone delayed in obeying their commands, an insane mob would suddenly fly up'.[53] The two also reversed the role of masters and slaves in a very physical way: 'masters, struck down from their vehicles, ran along like slaves, in front of their own slaves who were sitting in the place of the masters.'[54] When the Donatist bishops proved unable to correct these 'generals', a real general was called in and killed them on the spot.

[50] The proconsul Aelianus did not torture a lying decurion because of the latter's curial status, see the authentic *Acta purgationis Felicis episcopi Autumnitani* 10: J.-L. Maier, (ed.), *Le dossier du Donatisme*, i (Berlin, 1987), 49–56. Constantine referred to this case in a letter to Probianus (apud Aug. *Epist.* 88. 4); for discussion, see Lepelley, *Cités*, 1. 214, 323.

[51] *Leges Burgundionum. Lex romana* 5. 1: *MGH Leges* 3. 599, derived from Gaius 3. 225, F. de Zulueta, (ed.), *The Institutes of Gaius*, i (Oxford, 1946), 228.

[52] A point made at the Council of Braga (675), can. 6: Vives, *Concilios*, 376–7, 'Nouimus quosdam ex fratribus tantis caedibus in honoratos subditos efervescere quantas poterant latrocinantium promereri personae.'

[53] Optat. 3. 4: *CSEL* 26. 82. [54] Ibid.

In 417 Augustine described similar Donatist attacks on local notables. In order to prove the need to continue the repression of the Donatists, he wrote to the imperial tribune Boniface:

Demented flocks of wicked men disrupted the quiet of the innocent in various suits . . . Through fear of their clubs and fires and immediate death the ownership deeds of the worst slaves were broken, so that they departed free men . . . Whoever ignored their hard words were forced to do what they had ordered by means of harder rods . . . Some heads of households, born to a honest position and nobly educated, were removed scarcely living after their blows (Aug. *Epist.* 185. 15: *CSEL* 57. 14).

As in Optatus, Donatists were freeing slaves, preventing the collection of debts, and inflicting humiliating corporal punishments on well-born Romans. And like Optatus, Augustine expected the imperial officials to be eager to stop such things from ever happening again.

The scholarly tendency has been to view the 'generals of the saints' and other circumcellions as extremists acting outside the Donatist church altogether.[55] Yet in Augustine's letters, their leaders, when named at all, were Donatist priests, deacons, subdeacons, and other clerics.[56] In addition, Augustine's new letters show Catholics using coercion in much the same way. In the early 420s, the clerics of Hippo descended upon a slave ship about to embark and impounded 120 slaves against the will of their owners. They took them to Hippo and Augustine manumitted them one by one, after determining that each had been illegally

[55] For the circumcellions as terrorists disconnected from the Donatist episcopal leadership, see R. A. Markus, 'Christianity and Dissent in Roman North Africa: Changing Perspectives in Recent Work', in D. Baker, (ed.), *Schism, Heresy and Religious Protest* (Cambridge, 1972), 21–36. For them engaging in economically motivated banditry, see Z. Rubin, 'Mass Movement in Late Antiquity: Appearances and Realities', in I. Malkin, Z. W. Rubinsohn (eds.), *Leaders and Masses in the Roman World: Studies in Honor of Zvi Yavetz* (Leyden, 1995), 156–68. For them as Berber revolutionaries, see W. H. C. Frend, 'Town and Countryside in Early Christianity', in D. Baker (ed.), *The Church in Town and Countryside* (Oxford, 1979), 25–42. See also B. Kriegbaum, *Kirche der Traditoren oder Kirche der Martyrer?* (Innsbruck, 1986), 16–43, for bibliography.

[56] Aug. *Epist.* 35. 105. Based on Augustine's evidence for circumcellion leadership, it has been suggested that Axido and Fasir had clerical positions, but Optatus is not explicit: see O. Seeck, *Geschichte des Untergangs der antiken Welt*, iii (Berlin, 1921), 338.

enslaved.[57] Although bishops had the authority to free slaves in church, this sort of rescue went beyond the law, and, indeed, Augustine faced a lawsuit from the slave merchants (Aug. *Epist.* 10*. 8). One wonders how such heavy-handed tactics would have been portrayed by an unsympathetic Donatist writer.

Another letter reports that clerics apprehended a man, among those who 'held honour in the curia or forum', in the act of raping a nun in the church, where she had presumably fled for sanctuary (Aug. *Epist.* 9*. 2. 44). The clerics flogged him, a type of punishment from which someone of his status was immune in the secular courts, and precisely the sort of thing the Catholics had been criticizing the Donatists of doing. The rapist appealed to Celestine, the bishop of Rome, who ordered the African church to prosecute the clerics for *iniuria*. Augustine, outraged by the pope's decision, complained to his friend and primate Alypius:

> For you know how much this sort of complaint is accustomed to wear us down, and how these evils would be left unpunished except for the government of the church and how they ought to be vindicated by the church, when they are not able to be through public laws. What therefore ought a bishop or his clerics do, not about the various sins of this sort, but about the crimes of men? (*Epist.* 9*. 2. 43).

Augustine went on to defend using 'the discipline of flogging' on those who cared nothing for excommunication and whom the secular courts would not touch because of their influence.

Neither the circumcellions nor the clerics of Hippo encountered official opposition for using physical coercion *per se*, but for employing it against the wrong people. There were potent restraints against anything that smacked of overturning the established social order. Augustine explained that

[57] He questioned the captives, and then held them until their relatives came to claim them with letters from their local bishops attesting their free status: Aug. *Epist.* 10*. 8. 168–9. For *Epist.* 10* and 24* showing that bishops had a jurisdiction over the manumission of slaves that went beyond arbitration, see G. Vismara, 'Le *causae liberales* nel tribunale di Agostino vescovo di Ippona', *Studia et documenta historiae et iuris*, 61 (1995), 365–72, and C. Lepelley, 'Liberté, colonat et esclavage d'après la lettre 24*: la juridiction épiscopale *de liberali causa*', in *Les Lettres de saint Augustin* (Paris, 1983), 329–42. Neither discusses the use of coercion.

whenever clerics tried to defend anyone against the powerful, they were accused before the authorities of 'impeding the public necessities' (*Epist.* 22*. 3. 2), a euphemism for taxes. The Catholics of Hippo were facing the same sort of rhetoric as their Donatist rivals.

In the later fifth century, when North Africa was under Vandal rule, we find some hints that the increasingly high birth of Christian clerics brought their attitudes toward corporal punishment more in line with secular tradition. The primary Catholic sources (Victor of Vita, and Ferrandus, a deacon of Carthage) overflow with sympathy for the 'delicate' noble men and women forced by the Vandals to suffer judicial torture.[58] One of the high-points of Ferrandus' biography of Fulgentius of Ruspe is his portrayal of an encounter between a Vandal priest and Fulgentius while the latter was still a monk. Fulgentius had been preaching in the countryside near Sicca Veneria. The Arian priest of a nearby estate, hearing of this, sent his guards to arrest Fulgentius and his companion.[59] The priest accused them of public sedition: 'Why have you come secretly from your regions to overthrow the Christian kings?' He ordered his officials to flog Fulgentius until he confessed his crime. Fulgentius' companion begged the priest to flog him instead, because Fulgentius would perish under torture on account of his noble delicacy (*Vita Fulgentii* 10. 18–19). Reporting how the priest, undeterred, tortured them both, Ferrandus sympathetically described Fulgentius as 'a man of so delicate a body, as one born from an *illustris* family, scarcely tolerating the violent blows of rods' (ibid. 11. 20). The Arian bishop of Sicca also was disturbed that someone of Fulgentius' status was tortured: hearing of Fulgentius' ordeal, he offered to prosecute his own priest (ibid. 11. 22). Such elitist attitudes are a far cry from the hagiographical literature of fourth-century North Africa, in which decurions prayed to be tortured in the company of their low-born companions.[60]

[58] For Vandals torturing nobles, see Vict.Vit. *Hist. persec.* 3. 21–7. Huneric's own edict ordered corporal punishment only for public officials: ibid. 3. 9–10.

[59] Ferrandus, *Vita Fulgentii* 9. 17–18: *PL* 65. 125.

[60] *Vitae Saturnini et Dativi* 8: Maier, *Dossier* 1. 70; *Vitae Mariani et Iacobi* 8: H. Musurillo (ed.), *The Acts of the Christian Martyrs* (Oxford, 1972), 204.

The age was passing when holy men like Shenoute or the 'generals of the saints' tried to bring God's justice to the present world. The leaders of the Catholic church of Africa had become more protective of elite immunity than their Vandal rulers, and after the Byzantine reconquest in 533, these bishops came back into power. Sixth-century bishops concentrated on the power of the word rather than the rod, at least when opposing the powerful. When bishop Verecundus of Junca defended his city from an invading army in 548, he did not, in the grammarian Corippus' words, use fortifications, but rather 'tamed the tribes with the strength of the word'.[61] Even when speaking to his own congregation, Verecundus eschewed physical punishment: 'I do not permit [the enemies of God] to be punished, even though they do things worthy of punishment'.[62] Whether Verecundus would have withheld his paternal discipline from the poor of his diocese is not so clear.

The history of clerical coercion is full of contradictions. As the church came to mimic the procedure of the secular courts, by necessity it adopted some of the methods of Roman interrogation and punishment (flogging in particular) and found the scriptures to justify doing so. At the same time, clerics' ability to coerce was limited both by imperial law and by church canons. In practice, there appears to have been a tacit acceptance that the church could punish corporally those in its own power (clerics and monks) or those whose low social status made beating inconsequential. But when clerics tried to coerce the wealthy and influential, they found themselves labelled social revolutionaries, but so would have most municipal magistrates.

What does this use of corporal punishment mean for our broader understanding of authority of the Christian church? Were Christian clerics just one more group ready to undermine the authority of the late Roman state and oppress the poor, or do they represent the emergence of a new type of communal government? In their own eyes, at least, they

[61] Corippus, *Iohannes* 7. 484. Although Corippus did not name the *sacerdos* of Junca, the identification with Verecundus of Junca, who died four years later, is likely.

[62] Verecundus, *In cant. 28*: *CCL* 93. 48.

were rulers of congregations, exercising their authority in the only way a late Roman could comprehend—through discipline. As a sermon attributed to Augustine explained, when discussing the need to correct sinners:

All discipline is exerted for this purpose, just as is fitting and suitable for anyone who rules, not only a bishop ruling his congregation, but also a pauper ruling his household, a husband ruling his wife, a father ruling his offspring, a judge ruling his province, a king ruling his people.[63]

The author placed bishops alongside the other recognized powers—the *paterfamilias*, *iudex*, and *rex*, all of whom had the authority to employ corporal punishment, and all of whom exercised this authority.

[63] Ps.-Aug., *De generalitate eleemosinarum*: *PL* 40. 1229, 'Huic officio omnis inuigilat disciplina, sicut cuique regenti apta et accomodata est, non solum episcopo regenti plebem suam, sed etiam pauperi regenti domum suam, diuiti regenti familiam suam, marito regenti coniugem suam, patri regenti prolem suam, iudici regenti prouinciam suam, regi regenti gentem suam.' For a reattribution to Augustine; see C. Lambot, 'Sermon sur l'aumône à restituer à saint Augustin', *RB* 66 (1956), 149–58.

7
The Development of Syriac Christian Canon Law in the Sasanian Empire

Victoria Erhart

Canon law in the 'Church of the East', that is, the Christian church located within the Sasanian (or 'Persian') Empire, developed in an atmosphere influenced by customs and ecclesiastical practices in the Byzantine Empire as well as by laws and customs in force in the Zoroastrian society of the Sasanian Empire. By far, the most important primary source is the *Synodicon Orientale*, a collection of canons of the synods of the Church of the East for the period 410–775.[1] Without it, we would know virtually nothing about the religious and social life of the eastern Christians at this time. The *Synodicon* was compiled in the early ninth century under the direction of Catholicos Timothy I (780–823). It exhibits signs of some limited editorial revision, most of which concerns the anachronistic use of ecclesiastical titles and does not detract from the collection's historical value.[2] In the following discussion, the legislation of the Church of the East, and in particular that concerning celibacy and marriage, will be examined, as will be its tendency to expand into areas not usually considered matters of religious concern, specifically property and inheritance laws.

[1] J. B. Chabot (ed.), *Synodicon Orientale* (Paris, 1902).

[2] See S. Gero, 'The See of Peter in Babylon: Western Influences on the Ecclesiology of Early Persian Christianity', in N. Garsoïan, T. Mathews, R. Thomson (eds.), *East of Byzantium: Syria and Armenia in the Formative Period* (Washington, DC, 1982), 45–51.

Christianity may have been present in Persia from early in the second century.[3] Until the beginning of the fifth century, the church in the Sasanian Empire functioned autonomously without regard to the decisions of the Byzantine church. All this changed at the Synod of 410,[4] when the Church of the East agreed to standardize its liturgical practices, ecclesiastical administration, and doctrinal statements based upon those of the Byzantine church. This decision occurred through the efforts of bishop Maruta of Maipherqat, a Byzantine ambassador to the shah's court.[5]

Henceforth, the Church of the East agreed to abide by the decisions of the Byzantine church councils of Ancyra (314), Neocaesarea (314/19), Antioch (324), Gangra (*c*.340), and Laodicea (347/95),[6] and to accept the Creed as it had been articulated at the Council of Nicaea in 325.[7] It also agreed to observe Christian holy days on the same day as in the Byzantine Empire,[8] and to rearrange its ecclesiastical administration along the lines followed by the church in the Byzantine Empire.

The twenty-one canons of the Synod of 410 mainly concern the election of bishops, priests, and deacons; their qualifications, duties, and ranks within the hierarchy; and the ranking of episcopal sees. Assigned first place, naturally, was the administrative capital of the Sasanian Empire, Seleucia-Ctesiphon. Its bishop therefore ranked as the 'Catholicos', or head bishop, of the church in Sasanian territory. Other bishops were ranked according to the status of their city in the Sasanian provincial administration, thus following the

[3] For early Syriac-speaking Christianity in Persia and northern Mesopotamia, see R. Murray, *Symbols of Church and Kingdom* (Cambridge, 1975).

[4] Chabot, *Synodicon*, 253–75: Synod of 410.

[5] For Maruta, see A. Vööbus, *The Canons Ascribed to Maruta of Maipherkat and Related Sources*, *CSCO* vols. 439–40, *Scriptores Syri*, vols. 191–2 (Louvain, 1982).

[6] For these councils, see H. R. Percival (ed.), *The Seven Ecumenical Councils of the Undivided Church*, in *Nicene and Post-Nicene Fathers* 14 (repr. Grand Rapids, 1977), 57–160.

[7] For Nicaea, see W. H. C. Frend, *The Rise of Christianity* (Philadelphia, 1984), 492–517. For the creed used in the Church of the East prior to Nicaea, see Murray, *Symbols*.

[8] Chabot, *Synodicon*, 266–7: Synod of 410, canon 13. The Church of the East also agreed to standardize the observance of Epiphany, Christ's Nativity, the Paschal feast and Lent.

Byzantine practice whereby the secular position of a city generally determined its ecclesiastical status. Liturgical celebrations, including the Eucharist, were to be conducted according to 'the western ministry that the bishops Isaac and Maruta have shown us'.[9] This insistence on uniformity in church affairs and liturgical celebrations brought the Church in the Sasanian Empire, at least initially, a measure of stability.

The canons of Ancyra, Neocaesarea, Gangra, Antioch, and Laodicea again were recognized at the Synod of 420.[10] This synod, however, insisted that all the signatories were to be given a copy of the canons, apparently because there was widespread disagreement over just what they were. The canons of these councils had been accepted, moreover, not as much for their ability to address problems pertinent to the local situation as because of the esteem in which most Syriac church leaders held the western church and its representative, Maruta.

On the other hand, however, there were those for whom imitation of the Byzantine church proved problematic. They argued at the Synod of 424[11] that the Church of the East was sufficient unto itself, saying that 'those things that had been defined by the earlier fathers of the Church of the East would be confirmed by the authority of the word of God',[12] and suggesting that there be no further appeals to Byzantine church leaders regarding matters of church doctrine or discipline. In particular, they believed that no questions concerning the head of the Church of the East should be referred to Byzantine ecclesiastics.[13]

From the Synod of 424 onward, a gradual process of separation between the Church of the East and its Byzantine counterpart began, a process that was greatly influenced by political as well as theological events. There were episodes of military hostilities between the Sasanian and Byzantine Empires that drove a wedge between further attempts at ecclesiastical communication (Socrates, *HE* 7. 18). The period

[9] Chabot, *Synodicon*, 266: Synod of 410, canon 13.

[10] Chabot, *Synodicon*, 276–84: Synod of 420.

[11] Chabot, *Synodicon*, 285–98: Synod of 424.

[12] Chabot, *Synodicon*, 292.

[13] Chabot, *Synodicon*, 295–6.

424–86 also was one of repeated outbreaks of persecution of Christians within the Sasanian Empire. Shahs Yazdigird I (399–420) and his son Bahram V (421–39) instituted repressive measures against Christians in an attempt to inhibit the growth of Christianity in largely Zoroastrian areas. They also punished the entire Christian community when some Christians refused to repair Zoroastrian fire temples that Christians had damaged (Theoderet, *HE* 5. 39). Yazdigird II (439–57) was accused of ordering the massacre of 153,000 Christians, and Peroz (459–84) imprisoned many Christian leaders who were released only when he negotiated a treaty with the Byzantine emperor Zeno (474–91) in 464.[14] It probably is a result of these difficulties not only that the *Synodicon* records no synods for the period 424–86, but also that the Church of the East knew virtually nothing of ecclesiastical developments in the Byzantine Empire, such as the Councils of Ephesus of 431 and 449 and the Council of Chalcedon of 451, during this period.

Even during the time that it was bringing its administrative and liturgical practices in line with those of the Byzantine church, the Church of the East also attempted to accommodate itself to local social and cultural norms, for Sasanian society was officially Zoroastrian and at times even openly hostile to Christianity. The church could not function entirely removed from the much larger non-Christian society in which it existed. Over the years, it promulgated a number of canons that sought to render Christian practices more acceptable to the Zoroastrian majority.

Two areas of accommodation concerned celibacy and marriage. Syriac Christianity had a long tradition of strict asceticism. In its earliest period, full membership in the church was reserved only for those who were permanently celibate.[15] But celibacy was offensive to Zoroastrian sensibilities. It was seen as a rejection of the principle of creativity and fruitfulness, and therefore was thought to have more in common with the other principle in Persian dualism:

[14] A. Scher (ed.), *Chronique de Séert* (Histoire Nestorienne), *Patrologia Orientalis*, 7 (1910), 112–13.

[15] A. Vööbus, *Celibacy, A Requirement for Admission to Baptism in the Early Syrian Church* (Stockholm, 1951).

darkness and evil. In other ways, too, Christian behaviour was perceived as being offensive to Zoroastrians. Church discipline was a concern. Under Catholicos Babowai (457–84), it was said, 'The faithful were in charge of the affairs of the church, offered the eucharist in their homes and confirmed baptism outside the church. The bishops allowed women to enter the baptistry in order to see the baptism; shameful acts were practiced; adultery was frequent; monks and priests were illegitimately married.'[16] All of these activities implied liturgical irregularity and impropriety.

Concerns such as these were addressed at the Synod of 486, which, among other things, attempted to address issues of behaviour that offended Zoroastrian religious sensibilities. For example, the Church of the East adopted a liberal view toward the marriage of clergy. The synod's third canon was the first step in a long process of establishing a legally married clergy. There would be no more 'spiritual marriages' in which husband and wife lived together as brother and sister. Clergy of the rank of deacon, priest, or bishop had two choices. They could be fully celibate and live as members of a monastic community or they could enter a legally recognized marriage. Only married men were allowed to enter the diaconate, and bishops could not forbid a priest to marry or, in the case of widowers, remarry.[17]

The church also mitigated its tradition of strict asceticism, particularly for members of the clergy who were more likely to be located in urban locations and had a higher degree of contact with Zoroastrians. Those who practised asceticism were kept out of sight: the second canon of the Synod of 486 stated that ascetics, however well intentioned, were to remain outside of towns or put themselves under the authority of a monastery.[18] This was done, in large measure, because wandering ascetics were promoting doctrines and practices at odds with the Christian community's accepted teachings. Occasionally, this internal dissension spilled over into the church's relations with the Zoroastrian population and the Magian clergy, and the bishops wanted to keep any confrontations from occurring.

16 Scher, *Chronique de Séert*, 99.
17 Chabot, *Synodicon*, 303–5.
18 Chabot, *Synodicon*, 302–3.

Subsequently, the Synod of 497 extended the earlier position on clerical marriage: any Christian cleric, from the Catholicos down, could contract a marriage.[19] In the ensuing years, Sasanian society was convulsed by the Mazdakite movement, which advocated that all property as well as all women should be held in common.[20] The movement flourished under the shah Kavad I (488–531), who was deposed at one point in his reign by members of the Sasanian nobility who saw in his support for the movement an attempt to shatter the relations among the higher ranking Sasanian aristocratic families and thus weaken the overall power of the nobility *vis-à-vis* the shah. One chronicle reported:

Kavad supported the doctrine of Zoroaster, who recognized two great and eternal principles[21] and the common holding of women, to the extent that no man was united to one woman to the exclusion of another. He even constructed throughout the entire empire temples and houses in order to bring together the most voluptuous men and women, devoting themselves to immorality. He caused much pain to the Magians because of their wives and their children . . . The Magians asked him to anull the laws in which he prohibited the practice of the Zoroastrian religion. He refused, saying to them: 'Magianism [Mazdakism] commands a woman should not at all be prevented from uniting secretly to another husband as his own; and, if she wants to have a child by another husband as his own, she may do so'. They used schemes to kill him but were unable to do so. Then, at the end of ten years of reign, they were able to depose him.[22]

The Christian community was influenced not only by aspects of the Mazdakism, but also by the societal and fiscal reforms of Kavad's successor, Khusrau I (531–79).[23] One result was stricter regulations on Christian marriage issued by the Synod of 544. The Catholicos at this time, Mar Aba the Great (540–52), wrote a letter to all the bishops and clergy outlining a Christian theology of marriage. According to him,

[19] Chabot, *Synodicon*, 312.

[20] For the Mazdakite movement, see P. Crone, 'Kavad's Heresy and Mazdak's Revolt', *Iran*, 29 (1991), 21–42.

[21] That is, of good and evil.

[22] Scher, *Chronique de Séert*, 125.

[23] See Z. Rubin, 'The Reforms of Khusro Anushirwan', in A. Cameron (ed.), *The Byzantine and Early Islamic Near East, iii.: States, Resources and Armies* (Princeton, 1995), 227–97.

God established marriage for the purpose of perpetuating the human race through legitimate union. In the same way that Adam had only one wife, so must Christians have only one spouse. Mar Aba then listed thirty-four forbidden degrees of relationship for marriage. Nor were Christians to marry pagans or Jews.[24] Canon 5 applied the terminology of marriage and remarriage to the relationship between a bishop and his see, which resembled a proper marriage. Should a bishop want to leave the see to which he was wedded for another one, he was guilty of adultery. He was to be deprived of his rank in the church and denied any further participation in ecclesiastical matters until he performed appropriate penance.[25]

Canon 10 further circumscribed marriage. Priests, deacons, and clerks (which may refer to Christians holding positions in the Sasanian civil service) were not to marry non-Christian, that is, Zoroastrian, women because there was a great concern about apostasy by the children of mixed marriages, and apostasy by children of Christian clergy or officials brought particular dishonour on the Christian community. Clergymen who ignored this canon were stripped of their right to exercise the priesthood.[26]

This attempt to maintain a distance between Christian clergy and officials and Zoroastrians also was an attempt to forestall persecution of the entire Christian community. For if a Christian priest married a Zoroastrian woman who then converted to Christianity, both she and the priest were liable to severe punishments. Conversion from Zoroastrianism to Christianity was a capital crime for all parties involved. Excessive evangelical activity by Christians among Zoroastrians could result in widespread persecution of the church throughout Sasanian territory. Bishops were concerned that the entire church not be put at risk as a result of Zoroastrian apostasies. Thus, they attempted repeatedly to forestall this danger by legislating against intermarriage and by discouraging conversions, at least from the Zoroastrian community.[27]

[24] Chabot, *Synodicon*, 335–6. [25] Chabot, *Synodicon*, 357–8.
[26] Chabot, *Synodicon*, 359–60.
[27] For intermarriage, see also Sivan in this volume.

In 562, a fifty years' truce was arranged ending the conflict between the Byzantine emperor Justinian (527–65) and the Sasanian shah Khusrau I (531–79). Christians in Sasanian territory were guaranteed freedom to build churches, to assemble for worship, and to bury their dead in graves in the ground, a practice that was particularly abhorrent to Zoroastrians. On the other hand, the Christians agreed not to try to convert Zoroastrians.[28] These terms show the Byzantine government taking a continuing interest in the welfare of the Christians resident in the Persian Empire.

A Synod held in 576 attempted, among other things, to deal with a revival of Messalianism, an ascetic movement that did not recognize marriage as either an admirable or a legal state and encouraged husbands and wives to separate. As before, the Zoroastrians found this scandalous.[29] The seventh canon decreed that marriage was a state that had been ordained by God and that anyone who regarded it as illegitimate was in violation of the canons of the Fathers.[30]

But the problem with Messalianism continued. The Synod of 585 promulgated several canons that were devoted to marriage and were explicitly anti-Messalian. Canon 13 reissued Mar Aba's work on Christian marriage of thirty years earlier. The synod argued that in a legitimate marriage love for God was reflected in the love of the two principals for each other. The canon ended with a version of Mar Aba's list of forbidden relationships.[31]

This synod also legislated against the apparently Messalian practice of males and females living in the same monastery, decreeing that those who had adopted monastic garb must live in a same-sex monastery lest they cause scandal.[32] It also issued a canon further specifying what constituted a legitimate Christian marriage. Dyophysite Christians were to marry only Christians holding the same Christological belief in order to ensure that they would persevere in their own

[28] Menander Protector, fr. 6. 1: see R. C. Blockley (trans.), *The History of Menander the Guardsman* (Liverpool, 1985), 74–7.

[29] Chabot, *Synodicon*, 375. See also A. Vööbus, 'Les Messalliens et les réformes de Barçauma de Nisibe dans l'église perse', *Contributions of Baltic University*, 34 (1947), 1–27.

[30] See also canon 1: Chabot, *Synodicon*, 377–8.

[31] Chabot, *Synodicon*, 409–11.

[32] Chabot, *Synodicon*, 406–7.

faith. They also were not to allow their children to marry heterodox Christians, apparently Syriac-speaking henophysite Christians who later formed the Jacobite church, lest the resulting quarrel cast Christianity as a whole into disrepute.[33] This ruling provides a rare insight into interactions among the different segments of the Christian community. For when two Christians holding different Christological positions married, it was presumed that one would have to give up his or her Christology in order to maintain domestic harmony. The canon also demonstrates, once again, the need felt by the Christian minority to cause as little disruption as possible in Sasanian society. And, taken together, such canons illustrate the development of increasing restrictions upon what constituted a Christian marriage until ultimately they dictated the manner in which one type of Christian could marry another.

In general, the five fifth-century synods dealt primarily with ecclesiastical matters; no surprise, perhaps, given that the church was just beginning to emerge as a permanent presence in Sasanian society.[34] But by the sixth century, the Syriac Christian community had established itself as a legitimate and permanent entity. Numerous Christians achieved high rank and influence in Sasanian society as doctors, court advisers, and civil servants. Bishops functioned as ambassadors in the complex diplomatic relations between the Byzantine and Sasanian empires.[35] Professing Christianity was not necessarily a deterrent to advancement in Sasanian society as long as one was born into it and was not a convert.

The growing wealth and stature of the Christian church seems to have led to an increasing desire by church leaders to issue legislation dealing with areas of civil jurisdiction, most

[33] Chabot, *Synodicon*, 418. Here, Dyophysite Christians (once referred to as 'Nestorians') accepted a two-nature Christology, but not that promulgated at Chalcedon in 451, which is never cited in the *Synodicon*.

[34] A few isolated canons from this period concerned issues such as concubinage and the use of amulets or incantations (Chabot, *Synodicon*, 264: Synod of 410, canons 3–5).

[35] See R. C. Blockley, 'Doctors as Diplomats in the Sixth Century A.D.', *Florilegium*, 2 (1980), 89–100; and note also N. Garsoïan, 'Le Rôle de l'hiérarchie chrétienne dans les rapports diplomatiques entre Byzance et les Sassanides', *Revue des Études armeniennes*, 10 (1973), 119–38.

particularly property and inheritance. Bishops and monastic leaders began to function as religious judges in addition to their sacerdotal duties. This new policy is illustrated by the first synod in the sixth century, held under Mar Aba in 544. In addition to the marriage legislation discussed above, the synod also issued a canon detailing how gifts or bequests to the church were to be handled.[36] Donations were to be given into the custody of the archdeacon (a typically western practice which had been promulgated earlier in canon 15 of the Synod of 410) and used by the faithful for the benefit of the church. The increasing wealth of the Church of the East here resulted in the reinstatement of the traditional policy for managing donations.

The next synod, held in 554, introduced legislation regarding the management of property acquired by churches and monasteries. It did not belong to the bishop or abbot, but was the property of the group to whom it had been given. Now, this injunction is no more than standard Christian practice, so its issuance seems to imply that bishops and abbots had in fact been acting contrary to it. And this suggestion would seem to draw confirmation from the consideration that the canon was promulgated under a Catholicos, Joseph, who was subsequently deposed from office for, among other things, the alienation of church property.[37]

Subsequent synods were faced with dealing with the ramifications of a number of troublesome issues that arose in the Sasanian world. The Sasanian and Byzantine Empires again were engaged in military hostilities, including a Byzantine siege of the fortress city of Nisibis, after the Byzantine emperor Justin II (565–78) broke the truce of 562. The plague had broken out, and would continue to wreak havoc for another decade. Dissident Christians continued to leave the Church of the East in favour of a community centred on the henophysite Christology articulated by Jacob Baradaeus. And the Church of the East was still dealing with disaffection caused by the autocratic behaviour of the previous shah, who had been driven from office. As a result, the church was forced to expend much energy maintaining and

[36] Chabot, *Synodicon*, 560: canon 35.

[37] Scher, *Chronique de Séert*, 176–88.

reasserting its traditional social and economic prerogatives, including even the control of its own finances.

The Synod of 576 introduced legislation regarding bequests made to churches, which, according to Sasanian law, had been legal at least since the 540s. Canon 11 stated that heirs who did not comply with the terms of wills that granted money, property, or slaves to a church, monastic foundation, or charitable institution under the auspices of the church were anathematized until such time as the terms of the bequest were honoured. This canon seems primarily intended to cover cases where some part of the Christian community was the beneficiary, although in some instances non-Christians also may have benefited, as in a provision pertaining to the manumission of slaves on their owners' death which did not stipulate that the slave had to be a Christian.[38] If the Christian owner had promised the slave manumission upon the owner's death, the Christian heirs were obliged to fulfil the pledge.

The same synod also returned to the issue of church property, and to problems relating to how to control gifts of merchandise or money to churches, monasteries, and hospices, for there seems to have been a continuing problem with people trying to use church property for private advantage.[39] It proclaimed that gifts conveyed to the church belonged entirely and completely to the church. The need to promulgate such an obvious regulation once again leads one to wonder how successfully the church was able to enjoy its perquisites.[40] Canon 26 decreed that accurate records of donations were to be kept in institutional archives. And in canon 20, the synod addressed the complex issue of how to separate church property from a bishop's private property after the bishop's death.[41] A bishop was permitted to leave private property to whomever he wished but neither the proceeds from property conveyed to the church nor the property itself could be claimed by the bishop's family. It had to be used

[38] Chabot, *Synodicon*, 378–9. [39] Chabot, *Synodicon*, 384.

[40] Catholicoi Joseph (552–66) and Ezekiel (569–81) were rather despotic. Both were accused of alienating church property, a crime for which Joseph was deposed by the shah.

[41] Chabot, *Synodicon*, 384–5.

to support clergy, pilgrims, or those in need.[42] Regulations such as this could suggest that there was a recurrent problem with bishops and their heirs appropriating church property.

Legislation issued by the Synod of 585 also dealt with church property. Canon 6 confronted the issue of clergy and lay people who put church property in their own name, whether by using church money or by any other means.[43] Such persons were considered guilty of theft and were placed in the same category as those who, in Rom. 2:22, saw the world God had created yet continued to worship the creations rather than the Creator. In other words, they did not respect the holy altars and were therefore guilty of idolatry. Canon 7 revisited the problem of misappropriation of church property by heirs who refused to abide by the terms of a will.[44] Nor were Christians to be extravagant with religious bequests. It seems that a few prime bishoprics and monasteries were amassing great wealth and consequent prestige while other less desirable but no less deserving institutions were suffering financially.[45] For example, canon 10 noted that a number of churches and monasteries were in ruins or disrepair; perhaps warfare or a population decline caused by the plague resulted in the abandonment of small shrines and monasteries. Canon 11 decreed that new monasteries were not to be built, or even old ones rebuilt, unless there was a guarantee of sufficient revenue to support them. And canon 12 attempted to distribute wealth more equitably among major urban churches and monasteries and smaller rural ones: the churches at important cities like Seleucia-Ctesiphon and Nisibis were becoming large and ornate, and attracting an inordinate amount of donations from persons whom the bishops felt were doing so for reasons of ostentation.

The synod also attacked usury, claiming that some clergy and lay people, having become quite wealthy, were making loans at interest to both Christians and non-Christians. This practice already had been forbidden to clergy by the Synod of 410;[46] it now was prohibited to all Christians. The synod declared that 'even 1 per cent is too much', suggesting that

[42] Ibid., 385. [43] Ibid., 404–5.
[44] Ibid., 405–6. [45] Ibid., 408–9.
[46] Canon 4, citing canon 17 of the Council of Nicaea (Chabot, *Synodicon*, 264).

some persons were charging even greater interest rates. The bishops argued that usury was similar to gangrene, which if present in just one spot eventually could kill the entire body.[47]

The issues considered in 585 expanded into even wider areas. Canon 22 stated that bishops must either be guardians or appoint guardians for the property and interests of orphans, indicating that they had a legal obligation to do so. It is not clear that these orphans had to be professing Christians in order for the bishop or his representative to act as guardian. Paradoxically, however, the very next canon stated that bishops were not to involve themselves in legal matters, and one wonders how this apparent inconsistency was resolved.[48] Furthermore, canon 24 declared that upon the death of her husband, a wife had the right to receive back her dowry even if this was not stipulated in the will. Nor could heirs or creditors make any claims against the dowry. In addition, a woman also could qualify to participate in the inheritance from her husband's estate.[49]

In this case, it seems that canonical legislation, even when it did not strictly pertain to ecclesiastical matters, was perceived as being as equally valid as Sasanian civil law, about which, however, we are woefully ill informed.[50] Even if the dowry was not mentioned in the will, it had a protected status that the church insisted upon regardless of Sasanian civil law. And at the same time that canon law was beginning to acquire, in the Christian community, equal status with civil law, clergymen were acquiring some of the functions of a civil judge.[51] For a document appended to canon 14 of the Synod of 585 described how property should be divided up upon a man's death, and priests had the power to annul wills that did not adhere to the approved plan of division.[52] It has been suggested that this formula may have provided a

[47] Chabot, *Synodicon*, 412–13: Synod of 585, canons 15–16.

[48] Chabot, *Synodicon*, 415–6. [49] Ibid., 417.

[50] For a brief discussion, see A. Christensen, *L'Iran sous les Sassanides* (Copenhagen, 1944).

[51] For this phenomenon, see also Lenski and Dossey in this volume.

[52] Chabot, *Synodicon*, 440–1.

precedent for similar forms of distribution of inheritances in early Islamic law codes.[53]

The Syriac Christian community was able to expand its jurisdiction into areas having more to do with civil than church matters because of a very fortunate set of circumstances. Shah Hormizd IV (579–90), and even more so Khusrau II (590–628), were very tolerant of, if not outright favourable to, Christianity. Khusrau II had a Christian wife, Shirin, who supported the Christian community whose Christological views were different from those of the Church of the East. Khusrau II was so grateful for the assistance he received from the Byzantine emperor Maurice (582–602) that he dedicated a large gold cross to St Sergius and had it sent to the saint's shrine at Sergiopolis/Rusafa. He made additional dedications to Sergius after his wife bore a son.[54] It is intriguing to speculate about what might have happened had the Sasanian Empire become at least nominally Christian. Effective Sasanian rule, however, came to an end shortly after the end of Khusrau II's reign in 628, a year that marked the beginning of the Muslim conquest of Sasanian territory.

Thereafter, a wide range of matters came under the jurisdiction of the first Catholicos of the Islamic period, Henanisho I (686–699/700), including a number that were entirely civil, such as inheritances, civil contracts, marriage rights, and, significantly, punishments for a variety of civil crimes.[55] By the late seventh century, all cases involving Christians had to be presided over by either priests or bishops no matter what the topic.[56] Christians in previously Sasanian territory now had a complete and autonomous judicial system that was acknowledged by Muslim governments. One of the reasons that such a highly developed legal system for the Syriac Christian community appeared so soon after the Islamic conquest was that much of the groundwork already had been

[53] See A. Vööbus, 'A Calculation of Inheritances', and 'The Computation of the Inheritance of the Arabs', in *The Synodicon in the West Syrian Tradition*, ii (Louvain, 1976), 68–87, 95–7.

[54] For Khusrau's opinion and the dedications, see Theophylact Simocatta, *HE* 5. 13. 1–14; and Evagrius Scholasticus, *HE* 6. 21.

[55] See E. Sachau (ed.), *Syrische Rechtsbücher*, ii (Berlin, 1908), 2–51.

[56] Chabot, *Synodicon*, 484–5: Synod of 676, canon 6.

done during the later Sasanian period. Like so many of the fiscal and administrative systems that the Muslims appropriated from those whose territories they conquered,[57] they also inherited the tradition of autonomous legal systems for officially recognized religious minorities in the conquered territories. For example, it seems that the *millet* or *dhimmi* system for minority peoples during the medieval Islamic period had at least some of its antecedents in the Syriac Christian canonical legislation of the Sasanian period, which shows just how persistent the legislation of the Church of the East during Late Antiquity had been.[58]

[57] See M. Morony, 'Continuity and Change in the Administrative Geography of Late Sasanian and Early Islamic al-Iraq', *Iran*, 20 (1982), 1–49.
[58] See Vööbus, 'Calculation' and 'Computation'.

PART II

The Impact of Law on Society

8

'Spoiling the Egyptians': Roman Law and Christian Exegesis in Late Antiquity

Gillian Clark

The case of the unrighteous patriarch troubled the Christian writers of Late Antiquity.[1] The problem, briefly stated, was that the leaders appointed by God for Israel were, on the evidence of Scripture, themselves guilty of acts that, by late Roman standards, were illegal or immoral. Moses, the lawgiver of Israel, was a particularly striking example. His laws (though partially superseded by the New Testament) stood comparison with those of Rome; he was presented by Jews and Christians not only as a rival to the wisdom of the Greeks but as its unacknowledged source, superior to Homer and plagiarised by Plato.[2] But 'Moses committed murder, he despoiled Egypt, he waged wars, he both commanded and carried out many cruelties, he himself was not satisfied with one marriage-partner.'[3] That, according to Augustine, was the climax of an argument by Faustus the Manichean denouncing the Old Testament account of the patriarchs. A man who had shown himself to lack self-control in relation to anger, sex, and riches could not be either an exemplar of

[1] Many thanks especially to Jill Harries and Alan Watson; I am of course responsible for legal, and other, errors that remain.

[2] On the fourth-century *Mosaicarum et Romanarum legum collatio*, see the references in J. Evans Grubbs, *Law and Family in Late Antiquity* (Oxford, 1995), 100 n. 201. For Jewish legends of Moses, including the claim that he devised the alphabet, see E. Schürer, *The History of the Jewish People in the age of Jesus Christ* (rev. ed., Edinburgh, 1979), 2. 350; for Christian claims, note M. Frede, 'Celsus' attack on the Christians', in J. Barnes, M. Griffin (eds.), *Philosophia Togata II: Plato and Aristotle at Rome* (Oxford, 1997), 234–5.

[3] Augustine, *Contra Faustum* 22. 5: *CSEL* 25. 1. 595.

wisdom or a leader worthy to hold power. And any attempt to displace the responsibility to God, who had commanded or at least permitted the behaviour of Moses, made the problem more complicated.

Christians were taught not to offend against Roman law: they might disobey (and take the consequences) only if human law required something that God's law did not permit, most obviously idolatry.[4] They also were taught to live by the higher standards of divine law, refusing to take advantage of the human law's concessions to human weakness. For instance, Roman law did not forbid men to have extra-marital relationships with women who were not themselves married or marriageable, but God's law did.[5] How, then, could the patriarchs be defended? Had divine law changed between the Old and the New Testaments? Had God commanded actions that violated God's own law? Or did Christians have to concede that the patriarchs were not so righteous, and the Old Testament not so authoritative, after all? The answers to these questions exercised minds trained in the techniques of forensic debate. They illustrate the importance of law and legal argument in shaping the thought of educated men; at the same time, they illustrate the dangers of using theological writing to supplement extant Roman law.

The spoiling of the Egyptians was, at first sight, a good example of the unrighteous patriarch at work. In the third chapter of Exodus, when the people of Israel are still enslaved in Egypt, Moses flees to the desert because he has killed an Egyptian who hit an Israelite. God speaks to him from the burning bush, telling him that Israel will escape to a land of milk and honey. Moses is to ask permission for a three days' journey into the wilderness to sacrifice to Yahweh; God will force the Pharaoh to consent; and the Israelites will not go empty-handed, for every woman is to ask her neighbour and her guest for silver and gold vessels and clothes: 'You shall put the clothes on your own sons and daughters, and you shall despoil the Egyptians' (Exod. 3. 22). Everything happens as God said: 'The Lord gave the people favour in the eyes

[4] H. A. Deane, *The Political and Social Ideas of St. Augustine* (Columbia, 1963), 90–1, 146–50.

[5] Evans Grubbs, *Law and Family*, 203–25.

of the Egyptians, so that they gave them what they asked; and they despoiled the Egyptians.'[6]

This is a very satisfying story. The Egyptians themselves urge the Israelites to leave and enrich them with gold and silver and clothing, and the Israelites never engage to return this portable capital. But for those not in sympathy with the Old Testament, the mass departure of slaves with large amounts of their owners' property looked like deceit and theft. It could not be denied that the Israelites had in fact taken the gold and silver, and that the Egyptians had expected them to be returned, so an advocate would have to argue that what appeared to be a case of theft was something different. As Augustine remarked in his *De doctrina christiana* ('Christian Teaching'), people can learn to use arguments without a rhetorical education;[7] but most Christian exegetes did have that training, and Cicero's useful handbook *De inventione* ('Finding Arguments') shows what tactics they had learned to use when it could not be claimed that the act committed was right. The act could be compared with the purpose for which it was done (*comparatio*); the charge could be turned back against the plaintiff with a claim that he had provoked retaliation (*relatio criminis*), or displaced to someone else who was held responsible for an admittedly wrong act (*remotio criminis*).[8] All these were possible in the Egyptian case.

Philo, in his *Life of Moses* (1. 25. 41), briefly used the most obvious countercharge, suggesting that the Israelite acquisition of property was not greed or covetousness, but compensation for years of unpaid labour and retaliation for the injustice done to them: they took less than they were owed. Irenaeus, meeting a Valentinian Gnostic challenge to the Old Testament, used and added to this counter-charge: the Egyptians owed their own lives to the benevolence of the Israelite Joseph in time of famine.[9] But Irenaeus' main purpose was to turn the charge of theft back against his

[6] Exod. 12. 35–6; 'favour' translates the Hebrew that the Vulgate translated *gratia*.

[7] *De doctrina Christiana* 2. 132–5 (logic), 4. 6–13 (rhetoric): *CSEL* 80. 71–2, 119–21.

[8] Cic. *Invent.* 2. 72, 78, 83; discussion in R. D. Sider, *Ancient Rhetoric and the Art of Tertullian* (Oxford, 1971), 19, 74–5.

[9] *Adversus haereses* 4. 30: *SC* 100. 771.

Gnostic opponents. He argued that they had undermined their only Scriptural defence for retaining the goods they had acquired from pagan society. Why, he asked, had God let the Israelites take the gold and silver? He claimed authority for his answer by ascribing it to a presbyter who had it from people who had heard the apostles (or had himself heard them).[10] This answer was that those who denounced the Israelites for theft did not understand God's management. The exodus is a type (that is, a prefiguring) of the Christian exodus from paganism. If God had not permitted the Israelites to take Egyptian gold and silver and clothing, Christians would now be guilty of theft, for all Christians carry with them the possessions they acquired in their former life. Moreover, Christians have not themselves laboured to make the treasures they have taken from the Romans, and the Romans owe them nothing; but the Egyptians reduced the Israelites to slavery and forced them to work without reward. If a free man, abducted and enslaved, gradually acquired some property that was useful to him, he might be thought to have some of his master's belongings, but in fact he would have only a small return for what his labour had achieved. Anyone who accused him of not acting rightly would himself be seen as an unjust judge of the man who had been forcibly enslaved.

This claim would certainly have been disputed in court. Roman law did not consider the case of a captive population, but at least some jurists argued that when a free man was enslaved in good faith, what he acquired by his own work or by use of his owner's property belonged not to him but to the owner.[11] But Irenaeus argued not as a jurist, but as an advocate concerned with defeating his opponent. He was prepared to concede that the Israelite action was morally dubious if he could thereby defend Christian conduct that also was questionable. He concluded that, just as the Israelites used their Egyptian treasure to make God's tabernacle, so Christians must use their possessions in charity, to build God's tabernacle in themselves.[12]

[10] *Adv. haer.* 4. 27. 1, 30. 1: *SC* 100. 729, 771.

[11] *Digest* 41. 1. 19; see A. Watson, *Roman Slave Law* (Baltimore, 1987), 113.

[12] *Adv. haer.* 4. 30. 1–4: *SC* 100. 771–87.

Tertullian, also countering attempts to expurgate the Old Testament, returned to the legal defence of the Israelites. Typology appeared only in his opening remarks: cuttlefish are excluded from permitted foods because they are a type of those who, finding themselves observed, react like his Marcionite opponents and emit a cloud of obfuscation.[13] It cannot be shown that Tertullian was a practising advocate or jurist, but his liking for legal terminology is as evident in *Against Marcion* as elsewhere in his work, and God as just judge is one of its main themes.[14] When he reached the spoiling of the Egyptians, Tertullian imagined a lawsuit. The charge is 'fraus et rapina' ('deceit and theft'), and it is also brought against God, who told the Israelites to do it to the Egyptians.

Tertullian required the Marcionite heretic not only to act as *iudex* but also to arbitrate the rival claims.[15] The Egyptians claim back their gold and silver vessels; the Israelites, relying on the same documentation (namely the scriptures), present a counter-claim that they are owed wages for their labour. The case is already decided in that both sides agree that in the Old Testament, the Egyptians rightly renounced their claim to the vessels. But now the Israelites demand further compensation because the gold and silver was inadequate pay for their labour, and also because they could bring an action for injury in that they were free men enslaved, and could show the scars of floggings. Any judge, Tertullian claimed, would decide that the Israelites should be compensated not with a few gold and silver vessels, but with the entire property of the rich who owned such things and with contributions from the people as a whole. So the Israelites have a good case, and so does God, who gave them some comfort with a 'tacit compensation'; it was still too little, for the Egyptians should also have given the Israelites back their male children.[16]

Tertullian's assertions about what a judge would decide are no more reliable than those of Irenaeus. It is unlikely that a charge of *iniuria* would succeed unless a free man had

[13] *Adversus Marcionem* 2. 20. 1: *CCL* 1. 497–8.

[14] T. D. Barnes, *Tertullian: A Historical and Literary Study* (rev. edn., Oxford, 1985), 22–9, 325; Sider, *Rhetoric*, 78–83.

[15] See further Harries in this volume.

[16] *Adv. Marc.* 2. 20. 2–4: *CCL* 1. 498.

been knowingly and maliciously enslaved.[17] Moreover, any judge who was familiar with a decision of Marcus Aurelius would not have found in favour of the Israelites. This ruling, reported by the Severan jurist Callistratus and known to have been reaffirmed in 389 CE, classed as *rapina* not only violent crime, such as brigandage, but also seizure of property in general. Resort to force, rather than to due process of law, meant that even a good claim would fail: Marcus asked 'Do you think there is force only when people are hurt? It is force whenever someone reclaims, not through a judge, what he thinks is owed to him.'[18]

The Israelites, then, were not legally in the clear, and though the allegorical defence used by Irenaeus transferred the responsibility to God's long-term purposes for Christians, it also reflected anxiety about Christian relationships with non-Christian society. Egypt became an image for the *saeculum*, the realm of worldly and sensual concerns to which Christians are enslaved, and from which they may be liberated by God's grace: what then might they take with them on their spiritual exodus from their former life?[19] Irenaeus was concerned about Christian use of material possessions, but Origen interpreted the spoils of Egypt as, so to speak, cultural baggage. He argued that his student Gregory, trained both in Roman law and in Greek philosophy, could use that all-round education in the service of Christianity just as pagans used theirs in the service of philosophy, and he compared this to the Israelite re-use of the spoils of Egypt to build the tabernacle of the true God. The Egyptians were making bad use of their treasures, and it was bad for the Israelites to be enslaved in Egypt, but the Israelites were liberated and put the treasure to proper use.[20]

[17] I owe this point to Alan Watson. *Digest* 47. 10 deals with *iniuria*; the *Lex Iulia de vi* (*Digest* 48. 6) and the *Lex Fabia* on kidnapping (*Digest* 48. 15. 1) might also apply; Augustine, *Epist.* 10*: *CSEL* 88: 46–51, shows some of the problems, on which letter see also Lenski in this volume.

[18] 'Tu vim putas esse solum si homines vulnerentur? vis est et tunc, quotiens quis id, quod deberi sibi putat, non per iudicem reposcit' (*Digest* 4. 2. 13 = 48. 7. 7; reaffirmation, *CJ* 8. 4. 7); see O. F. Robinson, *The Criminal Law of Ancient Rome* (London, 1995), 30.

[19] A. di Berardino, 'Aegyptus', in C. Mayer *et al.* (eds.), *Augustinus-Lexikon* I (Basle 1986–94), 137–9.

[20] *Epist. ad Gregorium* 2ab: *PG* 11. 87–9; for Gregory's student experience see R. Lane Fox, *Pagans and Christians* (London, 1986), 516–28.

Origen's allegory does not suggest that he himself felt unease, but he was attacked by Christians and non-Christians for his appropriation of pagan learning. The starting-points were different, but the attacks coincided. The philosopher Porphyry complained of theft, arguing that Origen had illegitimately used the techniques of philosophical exegesis on a Scriptural narrative that was straightforward but morally suspect. Christian opponents complained that Origen's exegesis of Scripture was too much influenced by pagan philosophy: it was overly speculative and negated the plain sense of the text.[21]

When Augustine began to think about the spoils of Egypt, in the last years of the fourth century, it was the Christian complaint that had to be negotiated. The emperor Julian, while Augustine was still a schoolboy, had taken (so to speak) the Pharaoh's side, arguing that Christians had no right to cultural treasures that belonged to the worshippers of other gods. He failed to exclude Christians from teaching the classics, but Christians remained uneasy about the possessions they carried on what was, in many cases, a hardly detectable exodus from paganism. Pagans might charge Christians with theft; some Christians saw pagan culture as excess baggage, and found greater spiritual authority in the uneducated ascetics who had reclaimed the land of Egypt for God.[22]

Jerome, who claimed both cultural and ascetic credentials, addressed his famous account of a dream in his Syrian hermitage to Eustochium, an educated young woman from a distinguished Roman family who had committed herself to the ascetic life, and who had taken him as her spiritual adviser. His evocation of a lawcourt, and of the formal exchanges of martyr-acts, expressed his sense of being doubly on trial as a Christian: that is, both because he was one and because he was not. In the dream, dragged before the judge, he is asked the question, 'What is your status?', which decided how the

[21] Porphyry, cited by Eusebius, *Hist. eccl.* 6. 19; see further P. Sellew, 'Achilles or Christ? Porphyry and Didymus in Debate over Allegorical Interpretation', *HThR* 82 (1979), 79–100; and E. A. Clark, *The Origenist Controversy* (Princeton, 1992).

[22] See P. Athanassiadi, *Julian: An Intellectual Biography* (rev. edn. London, 1992), 123–4; and A. Cameron, *Christianity and the Roman Empire* (Berkeley, 1991), 29–46.

interrogation would proceed. In the tradition of the martyrs who would not identify themselves by Roman social rank, he replies only, 'I am a Christian', but the judge directly challenges his claim: 'You lie, you are a Ciceronian, not a Christian', and he is flogged until those present plea for mercy on the grounds of his youth.[23]

Augustine was faced with a complex of problems. He knew himself to be the product of an education that was designed to maintain a particular cultural and legal system, and his techniques of argument and exegesis derived from his experience of that education, both as student and as teacher. He had trained advocates; his closest friend Alypius had worked as a legal assessor; his episcopal duties included arbitration and adjudication.[24] In using the techniques of forensic rhetoric to defend the patriarchs and the God of the Old Testament against Manichean charges of injustice, he had to consider how any cultural and legal system, whether that of the Old Testament or that of Rome, stood in relation to divine law.[25] So his analysis of his own formation, in the *Confessions*, connects both with the anti-Manichean argument of the *Contra Faustum* ('Against Faustus') and with his exploration of exegesis and education in the *De doctrina christiana*; moreover, the Egyptian problem is one of the 'diverse questions' to which he responded during this period, and one of his sermons on the Psalms summarises his reflections on it.[26]

These works have different purposes and use different kinds of argument. Book 2 of the *De doctrina christiana* deals with the exegesis of unfamiliar signs (*signa ignota*) and with the subjects Christians need or need not study to understand

[23] Jerome, *Epist.* 22. 30: *CSEL* 54: 189–91; see further F. J. LeMoine, 'Jerome's Gift to Women Readers', in R. W. Mathisen, H. Sivan (eds.), *Shifting Frontiers in Late Antiquity* (Aldershot, 1996), 230–41; and P. Cox Miller, *Dreams in Late Antiquity* (Princeton, 1994), 210–14.

[24] See Lenski in this volume; for bishops as adjudicators and arbitrators, see also Harries and Dossey.

[25] Education and culture: P. Brown, *Power and Persuasion in Late Antiquity* (Madison, Wis. 1992). Human and divine law: R. Markus, *Saeculum: History and Society in the Theology of St. Augustine* (rev. edn. Cambridge 1988), esp. 87–104.

[26] *De diversis quaestionibus* 53: *CCL* 44A. 85–93; *Enarrationes in psalmos* 104. 28: *CCL* 40. 1547.

obscure passages of Scripture.[27] Augustine did not assume that education was intrinsically pagan, so Christians must choose between appropriating it and avoiding it. He distinguished study of what has already happened, or what God has made, from study of human conventions that may be useful or may be merely superstitious. Thus, for example, magic and astrology are human constructs, often involving pacts with demons (*De doct. chr.* 2. 74–91), whereas logic is not a human invention (ibid. 2. 117–31).

Augustine's interpretation of spoiling the Egyptians formed the conclusion of Book 2, recapitulating and justifying the advice he had given. As Egypt had 'idols and heavy burdens', so pagan learning has 'superstitious inventions and heavy loads of unnecessary effort' that are to be avoided. But Egypt also had authentic treasures, 'dug from the mines of providence', which could be put to good use. These include the liberal arts, some sound moral teaching, and some philosophic truths about the worship of the One God. The clothes taken by the Israelites represent human social institutions, which are necessary for this life and which can be used for good. Augustine affirmed a long Christian tradition of such despoiling. Cyprian, Lactantius, Victorinus, Optatus, Hilary of Poitiers, not to mention those still alive (probably Ambrose) and many Greeks, took treasures from Egypt in this sense; Moses himself was trained in all the wisdom of the Egyptians (Acts 7: 22). Pagan society would never have given these people treasures if it had realised that they would be used to eliminate idolatry. So 'what was done in the Exodus was without doubt figured so as to signify this.' Augustine added that this was without prejudice to any other equal or greater interpretation: when he referred back to this passage in the *Contra Faustum* he offered an alternative, that the gold and silver are the precious Gentile souls that came out of this world, the *saeculum*, as if out of Egypt, to join God's people, and the clothes are their bodily covering.[28]

[27] See B. Stock, *Augustine the Reader: Meditation, Self-knowledge and the Ethics of Interpretation* (Harvard, 1996), 201–4.

[28] *De doctrina christiana* 2. 144–7: *CSEL* 80: 75–6; on the dating of Books 1–3. 78 see R. P. H. Green, *Augustine: De Doctrina Christiana* (Oxford, 1995), pp. xi–xii; *Contra Faustum* 22. 91: *CSEL* 25. 1. 697–8.

Augustine was not much concerned, in the *De doctrina christiana*, to defend the conduct of the Israelites. A brief parenthesis (2. 144) offered suggestions that he developed elsewhere: 'the people, leaving Egypt, surreptitiously claimed [this treasure] for themselves as for a better use, not on their own authority but by God's command, and the Egyptians themselves, without realising it, gave them those things that they had not used well.' In his longest anti-Manichean work, *Contra Faustum*, he did not want to license any implication that the Old Testament could be salvaged only by allegory, and there he provided a moral defence.

Faustus the Manichean is represented as arguing that Augustine cannot maintain both the authority of the Old Testament writers and the morality of the patriarchs and prophets; the Manichaeans would prefer to reject the more scandalous stories as false. There follows a brief survey of what they find objectionable, and Moses concludes the examples of bad conduct by the patriarchs.[29] Augustine's much longer case for the defence postponed detailed discussion of what was typified or foretold by the actions of the patriarchs, and instead focused attention on their motives. He argued that 'sin is something done or said or desired contrary to the eternal law; and the eternal law is the divine reason, or God's will, requiring the natural order to be preserved and forbidding it to be disturbed.'[30] The natural order entails the rule of reason over desire. So Augustine could argue, for example, that Abraham had a child by Hagar not out of sexual lust but because of a natural desire for offspring.[31]

When Augustine's defence reached Moses, he began by emphasising the status of Moses as the lawgiver of Israel who, as Christ himself attested, foretold Christ.[32] Such praise of the defendant was a standard tactic for suggesting that he had not done wrong (Cic. *Invent.* 2 35–7), but Augustine then offered a startling *praeteritio* of some promising lines of defence.

[29] *Cont. Faust.* 22. 1 and 5: *CSEL* 25. 1: 591, 595.

[30] *Cont. Faust.* 22. 27: *CSEL* 25. 1. 621; for the importance of this formulation, see Markus, *Saeculum*, 90–1.

[31] *Cont. Faust.* 22. 30–2: *CSEL* 25. 1. 624–6.

[32] *Cont. Faust.* 22. 69: *CSEL* 25. 1. 665–6, referring to John 5. 46.

Let me leave out for the present [the argument] that when he struck the Egyptian, though God had not commanded it, nevertheless it was divinely permitted to a prophetic figure in order to be a sign of something that would happen in the future, for I am not now working from this [starting-point], but discussing these actions as if they had not been a sign of anything; having consulted the eternal divine law, I find that a man ought not to have been killed by one who had no duly authorised power, even though the man was aggressive and wicked.[33]

Augustine argued elsewhere that God's eternal law forbids murder, but not all killing is murder: a judge or a military commander may justly cause a death provided that he has the duly authorised power, *ordinata potestas*, which protects human society against anarchy, and provided that his motive is not to hurt (even in retaliation), but to prevent injustice.[34] Moses was no doubt motivated by desire to avenge injustice, but God had not authorised the proper use of that desire either directly or by allowing Moses to hold *ordinata potestas*. The best Augustine could do for Moses was to argue that killing the Egyptian was the kind of fault that shows potential for a particular virtue, just as wild olives are evidence that, in the same soil, cultivated olives will bear fruit.

Moses sinned by killing the Egyptian, but he would have sinned by not despoiling the Egyptians, because he would have disobeyed God. Was God, then, at fault? Augustine's answer was again concerned with the use of desire. God knows not only *facta*, things done, but also the human heart, *cor*, and God ordains what should happen to each one and through whom. In *De diversis questionibus* ('On diverse questions'), Augustine developed the argument that individuals, and the human race as a whole, progress through stages of virtue. Commands appropriate to the early stages may look like sins in comparison with what is appropriate to the later stages. The low point is wanting to deceive everyone, the high point is not wanting to deceive anyone, and the Israelites were at an intermediate level where it was appropriate for them to deceive an enemy; but even the deception of an enemy may

[33] *Cont. Faust.* 22. 70: *CSEL* 25. 1. 666.
[34] Deane, *Ideas*, 142–7; and Markus, *Saeculum*, 96.

be unjust (for instance, when there is a truce), so God's authorization was important. God, who is truth, does not deceive, but uses an appropriate agent. Augustine made a comparison with a judge, 'who judges that to execute a condemned man is unworthy of his role and wicked, but on his orders it is done by the executioner, who in accordance with his desire is so appointed to his office, that he who could execute even an innocent man by his own cruelty, executes a man condemned by the rule of law.'[35]

In the *Contra Faustum*, such an argument about the early stages of virtue might have strengthened the Manichean case for discarding some of the Old Testament, and there Augustine said only that the Israelites still wanted earthly things and the Egyptians misused God's creation (gold and silver) in idolatry, so the Egyptians deserved their punishment and the Israelites were suitable recipients of God's instruction, or rather permission. Perhaps there were 'other most hidden reasons' for the divine instruction, but our job is to obey God's commands, not to resist them by debate (*disputando*, a favourite word for being clever in the wrong context, like the present-day pejorative use of 'academic discussion'). Any objection that the 'true and good God' would not give such an instruction is ignorant human sentimentality ('inperita et falsa bonitas cordis humani'): God does punish the wicked, and God also decides what is allowed to whom.

The Israelites were owed remuneration for their labours; the Egyptians had unjustly dominated free men, and the property they lost had been misused against their creator. But these now familiar arguments support the central argument of obedience to the will of God. Moses would have been wrong to give the order himself, the Israelites would have been wrong to take the gold of their own free will, and perhaps sinned anyway by having such desires (as Augustine said in a sermon, they took the gold 'not without a certain surge of the carnal spirit'). But Moses himself was not guilty either of desire or of disobedience to God's orders.[36]

[35] *De div. quaest.* 53. 2: *CCL* 44A. 88.

[36] *Cont. Faust.* 22. 71–2: *CSEL* 25. 1. 669–70; *Ennar. in psal.* 104. 28: *CCL* 40. 1547.

In Book 3 of the *Confessions*, Augustine reflected on the ignorance that had led him to accept Manichean arguments about the unrighteous patriarch. He did not know the 'inner righteousness, which judges not from habit but from the wholly righteous law of the omnipotent God, by which the customs of places and times are formed in accordance with the places and times, while it is itself always and everywhere, not different in different times and places.'[37] According to God's law, the patriarchs were righteous, but people judge as if their local customs were the standard for all, forgetting their own experience of actions that are permitted at one time but not another, or in one place but not another, or to one person but not another; or indeed of words that fit the metre in one place but not another. These examples, which appear to support cultural relativism, could be strengthened with arguments Augustine used elsewhere about adultery: that what makes adultery wrong is neither positive law nor the Golden Rule (which does not of itself exclude wife-swapping), but desire dominating right reason. So a polygamous patriarch, living when polygamy was customary and motivated by desire for children, was more virtuous than a Christian motivated by desire for his one wife.[38]

But Augustine's argument in the *Confessions* did not endorse cultural relativism: he went on to say that local custom is not always a reflection of divine law. It is always and everywhere righteous to love God and one's neighbour, so it is always wrong to sin against nature, which God made, no matter what human custom allows. Augustine's example was sodomy, which was regarded as acceptable by all the men of Sodom, but which would be unacceptable even if all men everywhere approved it. Offences against human custom (assuming that the custom is not against nature) should usually be avoided, because the civil contract, strengthened by law and tradition, is of such importance to society. But if God gives a command that is against the custom or contract of anyone whatsoever,

[37] *Conf.* 3. 7. 13: *CCL* 27. 33–4. See further J. M. Quinn, 'Anti-Manichean and other moral precisions in *Confessions* 3. 7. 12–9. 17', *Augustinian Studies*, 19 (1988), 165–94.

[38] *De libero arbitrio* 1. 14–20: *CSEL* 74: 7–8; *De bono coniugali* 25. 33: *CSEL* 41. 228.

we must follow it, as we would follow an unprecedented order from the king. The context makes it clear that Augustine had in mind a general instruction, 'to be restored if it had been neglected, and established if it had not been', rather than a specific command such as that to despoil the Egyptians.[39] In *De doctrina christiana*, discussing the common use of the distinction between genus and species, he remarked that 'even laymen understand what is specific and what is general in any imperial edict'; in *De civitate dei* ('City of God') he commented both that one must be very sure a specific command (for instance, to commit suicide) is from God, and that some of God's commands are not to be generalised (for instance, the command to sacrifice Isaac).[40]

The remaining discussion in *Confessions* does not explicitly refer to the Egyptian case, but fits it well. The desire to do harm, Augustine said, is always wicked; but there are 'sins of those making progress', which (as he argued in more detail in *De diversis questionibus*) are sins when judged by the standard of perfection, but show promise. He did not give examples, but Moses' killing of the Egyptian could be one. There are acts that look wrong but are not sins, because they do not offend God or society, and we do not know what motivates the agent: 'when things are collected for use in accordance with the time, and it is unclear whether this is in the desire to have, or when people are punished by duly authorised power in the zeal to reform, and it is unclear whether this is in the desire to hurt.' We also do not know the 'articulus occulti temporis', the context in God's 'sacred history' that gives the action another significance: again, there are no specific examples, but the figurative interpretation of spoiling the Egyptians could be one.[41] Augustine's final comment to God fits the Egyptian case exactly:

When you suddenly command something unusual and unexpected, even if you have sometimes forbidden it, although you conceal the reason for your order in accordance with the time, and although it

[39] *Conf.* 3. 8. 15: *CCL* 27: 35; see further Deane, *Ideas*, 85–92.

[40] *De doctrina christiana* 3. 107–8: *CSEL* 80. 109; *De civitate dei* 1. 26: *CCL* 47. 27.

[41] Sacred history: Markus, *Saeculum*, 14–17.

is against the contract of some human society, who could doubt that it is to be done, when a just human society is one that serves you? But happy are they who know that you gave the order; for everything is done by those who serve you either to show something that is needed at the time, or to foretell the future.[42]

Augustine had solved the case of the unrighteous patriarch without claiming either that the Israelites were entirely in the clear, or that justice is relative to human societies, or that the Old Testament is a morally and theologically primitive text. He did it by using the training in legal and philosophical argument which, like Origen's pupil Gregory, he had taken from the Egyptians. And his solution to the problem carried with it a wider understanding of how positive law and human society stand in relation to the judgment of God.

[42] *Conf.* 3. 9. 17: *CCL* 27. 36–7.

9
Lawyers and Historians in Late Antiquity

Geoffrey Greatrex

For a Roman historian an education in the *artes liberales* was essential; only thus would he gain not only the skill in rhetoric that the genre required, but also familiarity with earlier histories, both Greek and Roman.[1] In addition, in the late Republic and early Principate most historians had some passing knowledge of the law.[2] In Late Antiquity, on the other hand, a significant number of historians (and chroniclers) were not merely acquainted with the law, but also had received a formal legal training.[3] It is in this sense that the term 'lawyer' will usually be employed below; advocates who had only a passing knowledge of the law also will receive some consideration here, but experts in the *minutiae* of jurisprudence (for instance in the imperial *scrinia*, or bureaux) and academic lawyers, exemplified by Tribonian, will not.[4] The aim of this

[1] M. Grant, *Greek and Roman Historians* (London, 1995), 30–3; C. W. Fornara, *The Nature of History in Ancient Greece and Rome* (Berkeley, 1983), 135–6; see also T. P. Wiseman, 'Practice and Theory in Roman Historiography', *History*, 218 (1981), 375–90. I am most grateful to numerous participants at the conference for their comments.

[2] See Cicero, *De Oratore* 1. 40, on advocates largely ignorant of the law; with J. A. Crook, *Legal Advocacy in the Roman World* (London, 1995), 10, on the term 'advocate'.

[3] The *quaestor* Ausonius is an example from Late Antiquity, on whom see J. Harries, 'The Roman Imperial Quaestor from Constantine to Theodosius II', *JRS* 78 (1988), 158 ff. and T. Honoré, 'Ausonius and Vulgar Law', *Iura* 35 (1984), 79–82.

[4] Harries, 'Quaestor', 163; T. Honoré, 'The Making of the Theodosian Code', *ZSS RA* 103 (1986), 172–3, on the experts in the *scrinia* (esp. of the *magister memoriae*). Tribonian, it should be noted, was interested in history: T. Honoré, *Tribonian* (London, 1978), 39; M. Maas, 'Roman History and Christian Ideology in Justinianic Reform Legislation', *DOP* 40 (1986), 26–8.

study is not only to demonstrate that during the late Empire there was a connection between trained forensic lawyers and historians but also to show that this represents a change from the earlier Roman period. Some suggestions also will be offered as to how and why this development came about, and what impact it had.

Whereas some historians of Late Antiquity are easily identifiable as lawyers, others can be labelled as such only with varying degrees of likelihood. Among the straightforward cases are the sixth-century church historian Evagrius and his near contemporary Agathias, who specifically cites his activities in the law courts of Constantinople.[5] Agathias's continuator Menander studied law, but apparently never practised in court;[6] one of his sources, however, the long-serving *magister officiorum* ('Master of Offices') of Justinian (527–65), Peter the Patrician, probably did practise as a lawyer in the capital.[7] The last classicizing historian of Late Antiquity, Theophylact Simocatta, who was originally from Egypt and wrote in the seventh century, received legal training in Constantinople, and went on to become a successful lawyer.[8] In the fifth century, the church historians Sozomen and Socrates both were lawyers, as was their sixth-century continuator Zachariah of Mytilene.[9] Nor does the list end

[5] P. Allen, *Evagrius Scholasticus, the Church Historian* (Louvain, 1981), 2; A. Cameron, *Agathias* (Oxford, 1970), 140–1; and M. Whitby, 'Greek Historical Writing after Procopius: Variety and Vitality', in A. Cameron, L. Conrad (eds.), *The Byzantine and Early Islamic Near East*, i. *Problems in the Literary Source Material* (Princeton, 1992), 29. Evagrius's brother, the historian John of Epiphania, also was an advocate: *PLRE III*, s.n. Ioannes 162; and Whitby, 'Historical Writing', 38.

[6] Menander, fr. 1. 5–7: R. C. Blockley, *The Fragmentary Classicising Historians of the Later Roman Empire* (2 vols.; Liverpool, 1981–13), p. 111; see also B. Baldwin, 'Menander Protector', *DOP* 32 (1978), 101–2; and Whitby, 'Historical Writing', 39.

[7] On Peter, *PLRE III*, s.n. Petrus 6; with Joh. Lyd., *De mag.* 2. 26; Proc. *Wars* 5. 3. 30; and P. Antonopoulos, *Peter the Patrician* (Athens, 1990), 25, 41.

[8] M. Whitby, *The Emperor Maurice and his Historian* (Oxford, 1988), 28–33.

[9] Socrates and Sozomen: J. Harries, 'Sozomen and Eusebius: The Lawyer as Church Historian in the Fifth Century', in C. Holdman, T. P. Wiseman (eds.), *The Inheritance of Historiography 350–900* (Exeter, 1986), 45–7. The evidence that Socrates was a lawyer is less secure than that for Sozomen: G. C. Hansen, *Sokrates. Kirchengeschichte* (Berlin, 1995), p. lv; see also T. Urbainczyk, *Socrates of Constantinople* (Ann Arbor, 1997), 13–14. Zachariah: P. Collinet, *Histoire de l'école de droit de Beyrouth* (Paris, 1925), 47.

there. Other historians, although they do not explicitly describe themselves as lawyers, may plausibly be identified as such based on the testimony of other sources, as well as internal evidence from their own writings.

A good example is furnished by Procopius, now generally accepted to have been a lawyer.[10] Several passages in his works point to a knowledge of the law, such as his reference to the law allowing dispossessed landlords thirty years to recover property in Spain; and his complaints about the ignorance of the quaestor Junillus on legal matters.[11] External evidence confirms this impression: one of the fragments of Menander refers to Procopius as 'the historian and advocate', and his appointment to the post of *assessor* ('Counsellor') of the Master of Soldiers of the East Belisarius in 529 also strongly implies a legal training.[12] Once Procopius is accepted as a lawyer, it becomes possible to apply a similar methodology to other historians.

The most common designation of Procopius among later writers is that of rhetor: he is so described by Agathias, writing very soon afterwards, as too by Evagrius and the *Suda*.[13] If, on this basis, the designation 'rhetor' indicates legal training,[14] it then might reasonably be suggested that the fifth-century historian Priscus of Panium, who is also called a *rhetor*

[10] Despite the doubts of earlier scholars; for discussion see T. Honoré, *Tribonian* (London, 1978), 6 n. 42, 243; see also A. Cameron, *Procopius and the Sixth Century* (London, 1985), 6.

[11] H. F. Hitzig, *Die Assessoren der römischen Magistrate und Richter* (Munich, 1893), 169 n. 608, pointing to *Wars* 3. 3. 3; see also *Wars* 1. 19. 26 (Roman law forbids the export of iron), *Anecd.* 19. 17–25 (Justinian's interference with the law for the sake of gain in the case of an heiress of Ascalon); Junillus, ibid. 20. 17; with *PLRE III*, s.n. Iunillus. See also *Anecd.* 28, 29. 17–25; and Menander, fr. 14. 2, for his description (although *PLRE III*, s.n. Procopius 2, points out that the reference may have come from the excerptor rather than Menander himself).

[12] As the legal advisers of governors and other officials (including praetorian prefects), *assessores* were expected to have a good grasp of the law: Hitzig, *Assessoren*, 79–82; with G. Greatrex, '*Assessores* kaj Historiistoj en la malfrua romia imperio', *Jura Tribuno Internacia*, 2 (1998), 33–50, who notes a few exceptions.

[13] For the use of these terms for Procopius, cf. *PLRE III*, s.n. Procopius 2, where the references are collected, and it is suggested that he was an advocate.

[14] Procopius himself seems to use the term rhetor in this way, *Anecd.* 26. 2, 35, 30. 18. This meaning for the term 'rhetor' is not unusual: see the *Suda* P 153 (ed.) Adler, 4. 293, with A., A. Cameron, 'The Cycle of Agathias', *JHS* 86 (1966), 15–16; B. Baldwin, 'Priscus of Panium', *Byzantion*, 50 (1980), 21.

by Evagrius, was likewise a lawyer.[15] Priscus served under the general Maximinus, and could have accompanied him as an *assessor*; one of his surviving fragments, a well-known defence of Roman law made at the court of Attila, may also be borne in mind in this context.[16]

The case of Hesychius of Miletus is rather more clear-cut. According to Photius, he was the author of a survey of universal history that extended from the Assyrian king Belus to the death of Anastasius (491–518), and included accounts of the reigns of Justin I (518–27) and Justinian. The *Suda* informs us that his father was an advocate, and inscriptions discovered at Miletus show that his son also was a lawyer: he is described as being distinguished among the rhetors (that is, the advocates) of the praetorian prefect, as well as a friend of the emperor Anastasius.[17]

A legal training also may be suggested by a historian's career or the content of his work. The chronographer John Malalas also was a rhetor, and, it has been suggested, gathered much of the material for his chronicle from the records of the *comes Orientis* ('Count of the East') at Antioch, where he worked. He clearly had some knowledge of the law, and he may have served in a legal capacity, perhaps as an *advocatus fisci* ('Advocate for the Fisc').[18] Among fourth-century figures, it

[15] Evagrius, *HE* 5. 24. B. Croke, 'Malalas, the Man and His Work', in E. Jeffreys, B. Croke, R. Scott (eds.), *Studies in John Malalas* (Sydney, 1990), 5, argues that Evagrius, as a lawyer himself, would have used the term rhetor (for lawyer) advisedly. Evagrius (e.g. *HE* 2. 2) also refers to Zachariah as a rhetor.

[16] *PLRE II*, s.n. Priscus 1, suggests he was the *assessor* of Maximinus 11 between 449 and 453, and that he may have served the *magister officiorum* Euphemius in the same capacity in 456: see fr. 33. 2 and Blockley, *FCH* 2. 394 n.144, who argues (1. 48–9) that he was serving Maximinus in an unofficial capacity; Baldwin, 'Priscus', 25, also doubts whether he was Maximinus's *assessor* (but accepts that he may well have been a lawyer, ibid. 19–21). For references to Priscus as a rhetor, *PLRE II*, ibid. and e.g. fr. 28 (from Evagr. *HE* 2. 5). The *Suda* calls him a sophist (II 2301 (Adler (ed.), 4. 196)), and notes that he published declamations; Blockley, *FCH* 1. 55. The speech during his embassy to Attila: fr. 8. 2. 455–508.

[17] Photius, cod. 69; and *Suda* H 611 (Adler (ed.), 2. 594), on Hesychius; also *PLRE II*, s.n. Hesychius 14 (his father is Hesychius 13). But *PLRE* omits the epigraphical evidence, for which see A. von Gerkan, F. Krischen, *Thermen und Palaestren* (Berlin, 1928), 168–9, esp. no. 341 (for his friendship with Anastasius and his position as a rhetor); also ibid. 170–1 for the identification of the Hesychius of the inscriptions with the historian.

[18] See Jeffreys, Croke and Scott (eds.), *Malalas*, 3, 10–11, 202, on his role as *rhetor* and knowledge of the law.

is believed that the historians/epitomators Aurelius Victor, Eutropius, and perhaps also Festus, had been advocates; the former two display an interest in the law in their works, while Eutropius's duties as *magister memoriae* ('Master of Record-Keeping') under Valens will have required him to deal with judicial affairs.[19] Lastly, there is the case of Zosimus, who is referred to by Photius as 'comes et ex advocato fisci' ('Count and Ex-Advocate of the Fisc'), again implying a knowledge of the law.[20] Other late Roman historians may also have been lawyers, but too little is known of them to be sure.[21]

One now might ask whether the legal studies of these historians distinguish them from earlier Roman historians. There is no doubt, for instance, that Tacitus pleaded cases in Rome in collaboration with Pliny the Younger.[22] Nevertheless, there were differences. The first Roman historians, beginning with Fabius Pictor, were senators.[23] He was followed by such as Sallust, Asinius Pollio, and Tacitus. In their youth, senators or would-be senators studied elements of the law as a matter of course. But 'the law' was not a formal course of study, and knowledge of it was acquired on an *ad hoc* basis. Cicero, for example, knew the Twelve Tables by heart and frequented the audiences held by the renowned lawyers Q. Mucius Scaevola and L. Licinius Crassus.[24] But as Cicero made clear in the *Pro Murena*, a detailed knowledge of the law, such as that possessed by Servius Sulpicius Rufus, was

[19] On Aurelius Victor, see, Dufraigne (ed., trans.), *Livre des Césars* (Paris, 1975), p. x; and H. W. Bird, *Sextus Aurelius Victor: A Historiographical Study* (Liverpool, 1984), 6 (more hesitant). On Eutropius, idem, *The Breviarium of Eutropius* (Liverpool, 1993), pp. viii–ix. On Eutropius's duties as *magister memoriae*, idem, 'Eutropius: His Life and Career', *EMC/CV* 32 (1988), 52–3. On Festus, ibid. 57; *PLRE I*, s.n. Festus 3.

[20] *PLRE II*, s.n. Zosimus 6; Phot. *Bibl.* cod. 98. On *advocati fisci*, see Jones, *LRE*, 509–10; in earlier times (as Crook, *Advocacy*, 52–3, 190 n. 100, argues), rhetoric, rather than legal knowledge, played the more important role in the selection of *advocati fisci*.

[21] e.g. Malchus, on whom see B. Baldwin, 'Malchus of Philadelphia', *DOP* 31 (1977), 92.

[22] See R. Martin, *Tacitus* (London, 1981), 29–30.

[23] See R. Syme, *Ten Studies in Tacitus* (Oxford, 1970), 1, 11–13; Fornara, *Nature of History*, 54–5; Wiseman, 'Practice', 379. Livy is a conspicuous exception.

[24] See K. M. T. Atkinson, 'The Education of the Lawyer in Ancient Rome', *South Africa Law Journal*, 87 (1970), 37–40; and M. L. Clarke, *Higher Education in the Ancient World* (London, 1971), 114–15.

not necessarily an asset. Elsewhere he argued that eloquence was more important than legal expertise, a point amply demonstrated by the low fortunes of legal experts (*iuris consulti* or *iuris prudentes*) in the first century BCE.[25]

Little changed in the early imperial period. There was still no formal legal training, and hence only a handful of senators and *equites* had the opportunity of acquiring a thorough grounding in the law; those who wished to become juriconsults attended informal gatherings of experts, such as those of Cassius Longinus.[26] Although the scope for oratory may have been less than it once was under the Republic, it appears that many senators still preferred to concentrate on rhetorical techniques than to gain a sound grasp of the law.[27]

It should, in fact, occasion little surprise that few senators opted to become experts in the law. There was no shortage of other avenues to advancement open to a senator, and juriconsults were always available to give advice when necessary, as in the role of *consiliarius* or *assessor*. The fact that Cicero, Pliny, and Tacitus argued cases in court does not imply that they were lawyers in the same way as historians of the late Empire. But by the time Zachariah, Evagrius, and Menander were undertaking their legal studies, prospective lawyers were required to follow a regulated course for a fixed period, at the end of which students would be granted a type of diploma.[28]

This process, which may fairly be termed 'professionalization', rendered the subject more academic and widely

[25] *Pro Murena* 19–30, esp. 22, 28 (where Cicero clearly distances himself from the juriconsult Sulpicius Rufus); also *Orator* 141–4; and *De Oratore* 1. 17–18 (in favour of general knowledge), 1. 248–50, although note 1. 165–71 (Licinius Crassus). See B. W. Frier, *The Rise of the Roman Jurists* (Princeton, 1985), 252–4, 263; Crook, *Advocacy*, 40–1.

[26] See Atkinson, 'Education'.

[27] Or so Vipstanus Messalla complains in Tacitus' *Dialogus*, 31, on which see C. D. N. Costa, 'The "Dialogus"', in T. A. Dorey (ed.), *Tacitus* (London, 1969), 25–6; see also H. I. Marrou, *A History of Education in Antiquity* (London, 1981), 287–9. Messalla laments the lack of a well-rounded education generally, which includes a knowledge of the law among other subjects. Crook, *Advocacy*, 180–1, argues persuasively for the continuing importance of oratory under the principate.

[28] J. H. W. G. Liebeschuetz, 'Hochschule', *RAC* 15 (1991), 878, and see discussion below. On *assessores* in the Republican and Imperial periods, see O. Behrends, 'Der Assessor zur Zeit der klassischen Rechtswissenschaft', *ZSS RA* 86 (1969), 192–226.

available.[29] Its evolution was gradual and uneven. By the early third century a knowledge of the law was regarded by Gregory Thaumaturgus as the 'best equipment for life', whether or not one wanted to become an advocate.[30] Gregory gained a rudimentary knowledge of the law at Neocaesarea in the early third century and was persuaded to continue his studies at the recently founded school in Berytus (Beirut). Although he never reached the city on account of his meeting with Origen at Caesarea, he nonetheless was able to practise law in his home town upon his return.[31] Evidently in this period formal training in the law was an asset, but hardly a requirement, for an advocate.

Rhetorical skill, of course, never ceased to be of fundamental importance to the advocate, but ignorance of the law became increasingly less acceptable.[32] The letters and speeches of Libanius provide good evidence for the situation in the late fourth century. Although unhappy at the rising number of those forsaking Antioch for Berytus and Rome, he was prepared to write favourable references for some of his students departing to study law.[33] It emerges quite clearly from his works that students were eager to pass on to the study of the law, sometimes at the expense of (Greek) rhetoric; they were also keen to learn Latin, which led them to pay rather less attention to Greek than Libanius thought appropriate.[34]

Even during Libanius's lifetime the pace of change was accelerating. A contemporary of his, a certain Apringius, had practised as an advocate in Antioch for ten years

[29] See Frier, *Roman Jurists*, ch. 7, esp. 272–3; note also F. Millar, *The Emperor in the Roman World* (London, 1977), 94–7.

[30] Greg. Thaum. *Panegyr. ad Orig.* 5. 60 (Crouzel (ed.)); with F. Schulz, *History of Roman Legal Science* (Oxford, 1953), 268.

[31] Ibid.

[32] See e.g. Clarke, *Higher Education*, 116; J. H. W. G. Liebeschuetz, *Antioch* (Oxford, 1972), 50, 242–5; Schulz, *History*, 269; and T. Honoré, *Law in the Crisis of Empire, 379–455 AD: The Theodosian Code and its Quaestors* (Oxford, 1998), 10.

[33] See Zachariah, *Disputatio de mundi officio*: *PG* 85. 1017–19, and R. C. McCail, 'The Education Preliminary to Law', *Byzantion*, 47 (1977), 366–7, on the reasons offered by a student at Alexandria in the sixth century for taking up study of the law in Berytus.

[34] See e.g. Libanius, *Epist.* 1375 (Foerster (ed.), 11. 420–1); and note *PLRE I*, s.n. Gaianus 6, Olympius 8; P. Petit, *Libanius et la vie municipale à Antioche au IVe siècle après J.-C.* (Paris, 1955), 367.

without having received a legal training, just as Gregory had in Neocaesarea; but in 364 he thought it worth while to journey to Berytus in order to gain an education in the law.[35] Libanius himself states that eloquent advocates were being laughed out of court, and that trained lawyers dominated proceedings.[36] It was becoming ever more evident to ambitious *curiales* that a training in Latin, the language of administration, and the law was their passport to important posts in imperial service and relief from their civic duties.[37] According to Libanius, a certain Peregrinus saw in the law a means to gain wealth, office, and power;[38] whether he succeeded or not is unknown, but the career of the sophist Anatolius shows that his hopes were not ill founded. A native of Berytus, he undertook a legal training and excelled in his studies. He then proceeded to Rome, where his courtroom skills quickly brought him promotion, eventually to the post of praetorian prefect of Illyricum.[39]

The growth of the imperial bureaucracy over the fourth century, and the opportunities it presented, were critical in encouraging the study of the law and Latin. Knowledge of both Greek and Latin assisted the career of the praetorian prefect Strategius Musonianus and perhaps also that of Ammianus Marcellinus.[40] The profession of advocate became

[35] Libanius, *Epist.* 1203 (Foerster (ed.), 11. 286–7), which also notes that children, men, and old men were flocking to study law.

[36] *Orat.* 2. 44 (in J. Martin (ed., trans.), *Libanios. Discours.* ii (Paris, 1988)); see also *Orat.* 18. 288 (Foerster (ed.), 2. 363); and Schulz, *History*, 269. Note also Honoré, 'Making', 175; and the evidence assembled in A. J. Festugière, *Antioche païenne et chrétienne* (Paris, 1959), 411–12.

[37] On the attraction of imperial service, see Jones, *LRE*, 513–14; Marrou, *History of Education*, 257–8, 289–91; Petit, *Libanius*, 362; P. J. Heather, 'New Men for New Constantines', in P. Magdalino (ed.), *New Constantines* (Aldershot, 1994), 18–21.

[38] Libanius, *Epist.* 1539 (Foerster (ed.), 11. 558).

[39] *PLRE I*, s.n. Anatolius 3; with R. J. Penella, *Greek Philosophers and Sophists of the Fourth Century A.D.* (Liverpool, 1990), 130–1. Libanius laments how even the sons of decurions were taking up the study of the law, which had hitherto been the preserve of the lower orders: *Orat.* 62. 21 (Foerster (ed.), 4. 356–7) and 48. 22 (3. 438–9); with Liebeschuetz, *Antioch*, 249.

[40] Liebeschuetz, *Antioch*, 248, drawing attention to Strategius (Amm. 15. 13. 1–2; with *PLRE I*, s.n. Strategius Musonianus. On Ammianus (whose post of *protector domesticus* may imply an origin in the 'official classes' of Antioch), see J. F. Matthews, *The Roman Empire of Ammianus* (London, 1989), 79–80, 467–8; and idem, 'The Origin of Ammianus', *CQ* 44 (1994), 268.

highly coveted, to such an extent that restrictions were imposed to limit the number of advocates allowed to practise in the various courts (above all those of the praetorian and city prefects).[41] But it was not until the second half of the fifth century that measures were introduced by which those wishing to plead at the court of the praetorian prefect had to have the sworn testimony of their professors to prove their knowledge of the law; soon afterwards, rules concerning the content and length of courses in the law were tightened.[42]

In spite of the increasing importance of a formal legal training, the role of rhetoric—and hence that of an education in the *liberales artes*—never disappeared. Indeed, in the western Empire it seems to have long retained its ascendancy over a training in the law, to judge from several careers, such as those of Ambrose of Milan and Maximinus, the prefect of Gaul.[43] But at length legal knowledge came to be highly prized here too: the *consiliarius* of the Visigothic kings Euric (466–84) and Alaric II (484–507), Leo of Narbonne, was praised by Sidonius for both his eloquence and his expertise in the law, while Cassiodorus regarded both as vital qualities for any quaestor.[44]

The enduring importance attached to rhetoric and a classical education, taken together with the growing attraction of the law, provides the key to understanding the proliferation of lawyer-historians in Late Antiquity. Only a restricted elite had access to the traditional education, and not all of those who received it pursued careers as advocates. Some, like Libanius, used their education to teach; others went on to

[41] *CJ* 2. 7. 8: 440, 2. 7. 11: 460.

[42] See Schulz, *History*, 270, 275; with Liebeschuetz, 'Hochschule', 878; and Collinet, *Histoire*, 258–9.

[43] Crook, *Advocacy*, 189–90; and J. Harries, in Harries and Wood (eds.), *Theodosian Code*, 7–8; Honoré, *Law*, 19–20, 263. Amm. 28. 1. 6, with *PLRE I*, s.n. Maximinus 7; and Harries, 'Quaestor', 168. Paulinus, *Vita Ambrosii* 5. 1 (Bastiaensen (ed.)); with N. B. McLynn, *Ambrose of Milan* (Berkeley, 1994), 37–9. See Amm. 30. 4. 14–16 on the ignorance of certain advocates.

[44] Sid. Apoll. *Epist*. 4. 22. 3, see also *Carm*. 23. 446–49, and *PLRE II*, s.n. Leo 5. For Leo's legal knowledge, note J. D. Harries, *Sidonius Apollinaris and the Fall of Rome* (Oxford, 1994), 130–1; I. Wood, 'The Code in Merovingian Gaul', in Harries and Wood (eds.), *Theodosian Code*, 171, 176, sees Leo as 'having a hand in the creation of the *Codex Euricianus*'. The attributes of the quaestor: Cassiod. *Var*. 6. 5. 3.

study philosophy or medicine.[45] Such men also produced literary works and one, Eunapius, actually turned his hand to historiography.[46] For the most part, however, their output consisted of philosophical treatises and orations.[47]

Young men with ambition, especially those from the middle ranks of society, having studied the *liberales artes*, preferred to go on to law school because of the opportunity for social advancement offered by a legal education.[48] But once one had received legal training, qualified as an advocate, and then either practised at the bar or served a general or other official as an *assessor*, progress in the provinces, courts, or *scrinia* might prove slow. If an ambitious lawyer wanted to distinguish himself from his contemporaries, how was he to attract the attention of the emperor or other important officials at court?

One means of setting oneself apart was by utilizing one's earlier training in the *liberales artes* and engaging in literary composition. Panegyric was one option, as exemplified by Procopius's *De aedificiis* ('On Buildings') or Evagrius's panegyric to Maurice's young son Theodosius. But the opportunity to compose panegyrics was open to anyone with sufficient education; many were written by *grammatici*, in particular from the Gallic schools. They were not usually commissioned by the emperor, and carried no guarantee of recompense

[45] See Liebeschuetz, 'Hochschule', 865, 878–9 on alternatives to the law. And note Libanius's delight at Firminus's decision to renounce a military career to teach instead: *Epist.* 1048 (Foerster (ed.), 11. 271); with Petit, *Libanius*, 360. On the value placed on the classical education (and especially rhetoric) in Late Antiquity, see M. L. Clarke, *Rhetoric at Rome*, rev. edn. (London, 1996), 142–3; R. A. Kaster, *Guardians of Language* (Berkeley, 1988), 26–8; and, P. J. Heather, 'Literacy and Power in the Migration Period', in A. K. Bowman, G. Woolf (eds.), *Literacy and Power in the Ancient World* (Cambridge, 1994), 183–4; also *CTh* 14. 1. 1.

[46] See Blockley, *FCH* 1. 1–5.

[47] Note also the emperor Julian's literary output, which followed a philosophical training: see, P. Athanassiadi, *Julian: An Intellectual Biography*, rev. edn. (London, 1992) 27–42. A sixth-century example is Choricius, and the 'Gaza school' more generally, on which see G. Downey, 'The Christian Schools of Palestine: A Chapter in Literary History', *Harvard Library Bulletin*, 12 (1958), 297–319; Choricius and his colleagues were clearly familiar with the works of Thucydides in particular, but made no attempt to write history.

[48] See Jones, *LRE*, 511, 513; and Honoré, *Tribonian*, 38–9, 187–8; and note also Kaster, *Guardians*, 124; F. S. Pedersen, *Late Roman Public Professionalism* (Odense, 1976), 43–4; and Crook, *Advocacy*, 190–4.

or recognition.[49] A more attractive alternative might have existed in the writing of a larger-scale work, a history, which gave scope for praise of the emperor (and others) in the context of an account of the great deeds wrought during his reign. A writer even could have doubled as a panegyricist by reading excerpts to a select audience.[50] Imperial service, whether in the law courts of Constantinople or at the side of a governor or general in the provinces, would have provided not only potential proximity to the emperor but also the raw materials from which a history could be written. The post of *assessor*, for example, would have offered a would-be historian the opportunity not only to witness events at first hand but also to come into contact with the decision-makers themselves.[51]

Circumstances favoured these kinds of literary endeavours. Late Roman emperors, like their predecessors and successors, took a keen interest in literature, an attitude naturally praised by contemporary writers. John the Lydian went so far as to claim, regarding weaponry and literature, 'A man was not created emperor of Rome unless he happened to be someone outstanding for the instruction he had received in both fields.'[52] The emperor Anastasius 'showed due respect for literature', and until some point in the reign of Justinian

[49] C. E. V. Nixon, B. S. Rodgers, *In Praise of Later Roman Emperors* (Berkeley, 1994), 30–1; see also Kaster, *Guardians*, 123–4. Procopius (*Aedif*. 1. 1. 4–5) seems to express the hope for some sort of reward, as does Corippus, *Just*. praef. 41–8. Whether either received one is unknown. Evagrius was more successful: Allen, *Evagrius*, 2–3.

[50] Blockley, *FCH* 1. 55, suggests that Priscus may have incorporated declaimed speeches into his work; see below for a possible context. Matthews, *Ammianus*, 8–9, suggests that Ammianus may have read excerpts of his work to Theodosius I in 389/90.

[51] As in the case of Procopius: see Cameron, *Procopius*, 8. Evagrius and John of Epiphania also were *assessores*, as probably was Priscus as well (see above). And Sidonius Apollinaris (*Epist*. 4. 22. 3) notes how well suited Leo of Narbonne would have been to write history because of his close association with the Visigothic king Euric. See also Greatrex, '*Assessores*', on the links between *assessores* and historians generally.

[52] Joh. Lyd. *De mag*. 3. 33, T. F. Carney (trans.), *Bureaucracy in Traditional Society: Romano-Byzantine Bureaucracies Viewed from Within* (Lawrence, Kan., 1971). See M. Maas, *John Lydus and the Roman Past* (London, 1992), 29, for imperial interest in literature, aptly citing *CTh* 14. 1. 1; note also N. G. Wilson, *Scholars of Byzantium* (London, 1983), 2–4 (on later emperors); and Millar, *Emperor*, 88, 502–4.

there were literary competitions for retired advocates.[53] Actual instances of the commissioning of historical works are not difficult to find: Valens (364–78) asked first Eutropius, and then Festus, to compile their *Breviaria*, and Justinian commissioned John the Lydian to write an account of the Persian war at the opening of his reign.[54] The emperor Maurice (582–602), according to Menander, 'Loved the Muses, being especially solicitous for poetry and history', which encouraged the hitherto indolent historian to set about continuing Agathias's *Histories*.[55] Some of these writers were rewarded for their efforts. Eutropius, for example, was made proconsul of Asia following the publication of his *Breviarium*.[56] And Procopius may have received honorary illustrious rank for his literary efforts.[57]

The connection between law and historiography in Late Antiquity was very different from what it had been during the Republic and early Principate. Earlier Roman historians had picked up a smattering of law in the course of their traditional senatorial education; their late Roman successors were very often professional lawyers. As the law became more technical and its management more bureaucratized, its practice become more professionalized, and its practitioners came to be drawn increasingly from non-senatorial backgrounds, and in particular from provincial elites.[58] In a

[53] Anastasius: Joh. Lyd. *De mag*. 3. 47; Justinian: Procopius, *Anecd*. 26. 2.

[54] Kaster, *Guardians*, 228, takes Procopius to be referring to teachers and rejects his evidence; but the rhetors in question were advocates, as is clear from the context. See Bird, *Breviarium*, p. xxiv, on Valens' commissions. Justinian's request to John (*De mag*. 3. 26).

[55] Maurice: Menander, fr. 1. 18–28 (Blockley (trans.), quotations 19–20), and note Agathias's remarks (*praef*. 11–13) on how he was urged on by various people, especially Eutychianus (*PLRE III*, s.n. Eutychianus 1) to write history. Theodosius I, to whom the lost *annales* of Virius Nicomachus Flavianus were dedicated, is also said to have been much interested in history: *Epit. de Caes*. 48. 11; and Matthews, *Ammianus*, 10.

[56] See Bird, 'Eutropius', 56–71; note also B. Baldwin, *Studies in Lucian* (Toronto, 1973), 86, 94, on how in the second century sophistic performers advanced their careers in the same way.

[57] E. Stein, *Histoire du bas-empire*, trans. J.-R. Palanque (2 vols.; Paris, 1949), 2. 712; and Cameron, *Procopius*, 12 n. 456. Evagrius, *HE* 6. 24, reports that he received high honours from both Tiberius II and Maurice.

[58] See Crook, *Advocacy*, 39; and Schulz, *History*, 271–2. See also Harries, 'Quaestor', 169, on the increasing professionalization of the post of quaestor in the early fifth century.

similar fashion, the writing of history may also be viewed as having become professionalized. The senatorial historians of the late Republic and early Empire often took to their work late in their careers, to vindicate their actions or those of their faction; they may have wished to set the record straight or rebut the account of another historian, but they had little to gain personally from their work.[59] Dio Cassius, writing in the early third century, is perhaps the last of the senatorial historians: he had already entered the Senate when he began his literary compositions. But it was probably largely to these that he owed his subsequent advancement, first under Septimius Severus (193–211), and then under Severus Alexander (222–35).[60] Later Roman historians were even more 'professional' in their compositions: having risen from humbler, provincial, backgrounds by means of the law, they were writing not from a disinterested perspective, but in the hope that their literary efforts would bring them material remuneration, promotion in their careers, and social advancement.

One also might include a few words on the causes and impact of this transformation. The sweeping changes in the composition and provenance of the aristocracy in the fourth century meant that there was far less continuity in its membership, especially in the east.[61] A 'senatorial' historian therefore generally owed his rank as senator to an appointment in the imperial hierarchy, and so was in a quite different position from his predecessors. Few senators in Late Antiquity turned to historiography, and those who did preferred to deal with earlier periods: in the mid-sixth century, Peter the Patrician's history extended only to the reign of Constantius II (337–61),[62] while in the west in the early fifth

[59] Syme, *Studies*, 1–2, and see above. But this period also witnessed the emergence of 'professional literary men' composing histories: Wiseman, 'Practice', 380–1.

[60] See F. Millar, *A Study of Cassius Dio* (Oxford, 1964), 15–16: a work on portents presaging Severus's elevation to the throne no doubt helped to ingratiate him. Note that Dio, like Tacitus, fought court cases (ibid. 17–18). Note also the biographer Marius Maximus, also a senator under Severus: T. D. Barnes, *The Sources of the Historia Augusta* (Brussels, 1978), 101.

[61] See e.g. Jones, *LRE*, 526–9; and Heather, 'New Men', 12–14.

[62] Peter, it is true, also composed a work on his own embassy to the Persians: Menander (fr. 6. 2. 12–26) notes that Peter's account played up his own successes,

century, Nicomachus Flavianus edited the earliest books of Livy.[63] Writing about recent events could be dangerous, particularly for members of the aristocracy; as Ammianus and Procopius note, a historian had much to fear when dealing with current events and living emperors.[64]

As someone who had reached the pinnacle of the aristocracy,[65] a senator no longer had any need to write history—or at least 'classicizing history', dealing with recent events; he probably would only imperil himself by doing so. Late antique historians, while not usually members of the Senate, were members of the elite, who had risen through imperial service; but they were aiming for even further advancement. Thus, their more 'professional' histories, usually concerned with the recent past, tended to be positive in their assessments of the policies of the reigning emperor and his associates. On occasion, the desire to win favour could surpass reasonable bounds, as Lucian mockingly illustrates in his 'How to Write History.'[66] Yet, the emergence of the 'professional' lawyer-historians of Late Antiquity did not mark the end of critical historiography. They too were capable of offering criticism, even if (with one notable exception) their censures were reserved for previous emperors and disgraced officials.[67]

and this work thus resembles that of the earlier Roman historians, as it was a partisan account of the author's most important achievements, written not long before he died in 565, and aimed at posterity rather than contemporaries.

[63] J. F. Matthews, *Western Aristocracies and Imperial Court* (Oxford, 1975), 374 with idem., *Ammianus*, 10 and Harries, 'Quaestor', 158. Other senators, Ammianus complains, confined their literary interests to more low-brow material, 28. 4. 14.

[64] See Ammianus 28. 1 on the tribulations of the nobility at Rome under Valentinian, and 26. 1. 1 on the dangers of the recent past; with Matthews, *Ammianus*, 209–17, 204. Note also Procopius, *Anecd.* 1. 1–3; with A. Cameron, 'History as Text: Coping with Procopius,' in C. Holdsworth, T. P. Wiseman (eds.), *The Inheritance of Historiography* (Exeter, 1986), 68. The same problem had faced writers under the early principate: see Wiseman, 'Practice', 377.

[65] By the time of Peter the Patrician, the 'Senate' had become a much more restricted and selective body; see Jones, *LRE*, 529; and Mathisen in this volume.

[66] Lucian, *Quomodo historia conscribenda sit*, 8–9, 12–14.

[67] See Evagrius' criticisms of Justinian (*HE* 4. 30: Allen, *Evagrius*, 194–6). Procopius' *Anecdota* is the most notable example of criticism by such a historian (on which see G. Greatrex, 'Procopius the Outsider?', in D. Smythe (ed.), *Strangers to Themselves: The Byzantine Outsider*, (Aldershot, 2000). Lucian, *Quomodo historia conscribenda sit*, 8–9,12–14. The impact of a legal training on the method and style of historians in Late Antiquity must await treatment elsewhere.

10

Lex and *Iussio*: The *Feriale Campanum* and Christianity in the Theodosian Age

Dennis E. Trout

In the late summer or autumn of the year 384, the Urban Prefect Q. Aurelius Symmachus forwarded from Rome to Milan a *relatio* requesting the restoration of the Altar of Victory to the senate-house and the renewal of imperial subsidies for Rome's priestly colleges. Although the position of the emperor Valentinian II (375–92) was insecure—his elder brother, Gratian (367–83), had been killed at Lyon the year before and the usurper Magnus Maximus (383–8) now controlled Gaul and Spain—Milan's forceful bishop, Ambrose, persuaded Valentinian to deny the prefect's request.[1] Three years later, in the summer of 387, Maximus led his army from Gaul into northern Italy and Valentinian's court took refuge with the emperor Theodosius I (379–95) in the east. The following summer, Theodosius himself marched west, defeated Maximus, and reinstated Valentinian. Theodosius then stayed on in Italy for three years, not returning east until mid-391.[2] During that time he denied yet another senatorial petition for the restoration of support to Rome's traditional priesthoods—again following the intervention of Ambrose—

[1] Symm. *Rel.* 3; Amb. *Epist.* 17, 18, and 57: *PL* 16. See J. Matthews, *Western Aristocracies and Imperial Court, A.D. 364–425* (Oxford, 1975), 173–82, 203–11; N. McLynn, *Ambrose of Milan* (Berkeley, 1994), 166–8; D. Kienast, *Römische Kaisertabelle: Grundzüge einer römischen Kaiserchronologie* (Darmstadt, 1990), 328–30. I would like to thank Michele Salzman and Paul B. Harvey Jr. for comments upon an early draft and Heikki Solin and Peter Reid for responses to specific queries.

[2] Matthews, *Aristocracies*, 223–38; Kienast, *Kaisertabelle*, 330–7.

and appointed the pagan Symmachus to the consulship for 391.[3] Subsequently, in the months immediately before he returned east, Theodosius issued at Milan and Aquileia two laws that aggressively reiterated and further extended the earlier sanctions against traditional cults and temples.[4]

Midway through this course of events there occurred an incident that has received little notice in modern accounts of these religious and political confrontations. At Capua, on 22 November 387, a certain Felix published by order of the emperors a *feriale dominorum*, or 'calendar of the emperors'. The extant inscription, the so-called *Feriale Campanum*, is not a full annual calendar in the manner of the *fasti* of the Roman codex calendar of 354, nor does it even record imperial birthdays or anniversaries, as do both that calendar and the third-century *Feriale Duranum*.[5] Rather, the *Feriale Campanum* presented a select list of seven holidays (*feriae*) that were, with the exception of the *vota* of 3 January, primarily linked to the life and history of Capua and the surrounding *ager Campanus*. The implications of this text are significant not simply because it further documents the persistence of traditional ceremonies under Christian emperors, but especially because it credits those emperors with the validation of its holidays. Indeed, when the decidedly non-Christian and intensely local character of the calendar's *feriae* is viewed against the background of contemporary imperial legislation and the Altar of Victory affair, the imperial *iussio* that sanctioned it plausibly emerges as a concession granted in 387 by a beleaguered Milanese court to Italy's still

[3] Amb. *Epist.* 57. 4; R. Bagnall, A. Cameron, S. Schwartz, and K. Worp (eds.), *Consuls of the Later Roman Empire* (Atlanta, 1987), 316–17.

[4] *CTh* 16. 10. 10 and 11, of 24 February and 16 June 391. On Theodosius's movements see G. Rauschen, *Jahrbücher der Christlichen Kirche* (Freiburg, 1897), 333; T. Mommsen, P. M. Meyer, P. Krüger (eds.), *Theodosiani Libri XVI cum constitutionibus sirmondianis et leges novellae ad Theodosianum pertinentes* (Berlin, 1905; repr. 1970–1), pp. cclxix–xx. Note also P.-P. Joannou, *La Législation imperiale et la christianisation de l'empire Romain 311–476* (Rome, 1972), 87.

[5] Calendar of 354, at A. Degrassi (ed.), *Inscriptiones Italiae* 13. 2. 42 (hereafter Degrassi). On the calendar–*feriale* distinction see E. de Ruggiero, *Dizionario epigrafico*, s.v. 'feriale'; R. Fink, A. Hoey, F. Snyder, 'The *Feriale Duranum*', *Yale Classical Studies*, 7 (1940), 36–7; M. Salzman, *On Roman Time: The Codex-Calendar of 354 and the Rhythms of Urban Life in Late Antiquity* (Berkeley, 1990), 5–10; and J. Rüpke, *Kalender und Öffentlichkeit* (Berlin, 1995), 524–7.

influential pagan aristocracy. Although within only a few years imperial legislation quickly reaffirmed the direction established in the early 380s by the anti-pagan laws of Gratian and Theodosius, the imperial 'order' of 387 reveals the social and religious fault lines beneath those ostensibly confident legal proclamations.

The *Feriale Campanum*, discovered in 1829 in the amphitheatre at Capua, is inscribed on a piece of marble approximately three-quarters of a meter in height, slightly less in width, and a quarter of a meter in thickness.[6] Columns decorated with leaves and flowers flank the stone's central inscribed panel and the piece may have functioned as an altar at some point.[7] The first line of text, which records the supervision of the *sacerdos* Romanus, is squeezed into the upper margin as though added after the carving of the second line:

administrante Romano iun(iore) sacerdote
feriale dom(i)norum sic:
III nonas Ian. vota
III idus Febr. Genialia
kal. Mais lustratio ad [f]lumen Casilino
III idus Mai. Rosaria amp(h)i[t]eatri
VIII kal. Aug. lustratio ad flumen ad iter Dianae
VI kal. Aug. profectio ad iter Averni
idus Oct. vendemia Acerusae
Iussione dom(i)norum Felix votum
sollicite solvit X kal. Decembr.
Valentiniano III e[t] Eutropio <co(n)s(ulibus)>

With the priest Romanus Junior overseeing,
thus a 'calendar' of the emperors:

3 Jan	*vota*
11 Feb	the Genialia
1 May	a lustration at the river at Casilinum
13 May	the Rosaria of the amphitheater
25 Jul	a lustration at the river at/near the *iter Dianae*

[6] *CIL* 10. 3792; *ILS* 4918; and Degrassi, 13. 2. 46, with photograph and the text reproduced there.

[7] T. Mommsen, 'Epigraphische Analekten Nr. 8', *Berichte der sächischen Gesellschaft der Wissenschaften*, 2 (1850), 66 = idem, *Gesammelte Schriften*, 8 (Berlin, 1913), 17; Degrassi, 282.

27 Jul a procession at/near the *iter Averni*
15 Oct the Vendemia at Acerusa

By command of the emperors, Felix carefully fulfilled his vow 22 November during the consulship of Valentinian for the third time and Eutropius (387)

The inscription's Felix appears to be an agent of the imperial administration, sent from Milan or resident at Capua, the administrative centre of Campania.[8] His fulfilled vow is most likely represented in the publication of the text and the erection of the monument that bore it. The *sacerdos* Romanus, otherwise unattested,[9] may have been a provincial priest—an office known elsewhere in Italy but not documented in Campania[10]—or a Capuan *flamen*.[11] The choice between provincial and municipal affiliation hinges in part upon a debate over the scope of the *Feriale*.[12]

The text of the *Feriale Campanum* presents several lexical curiosities, and the stone itself shows signs of sloppy or incompetent carving. The use of the word *feriale* to denote an *index feriarum* is documented solely by this text, and *iussio* stands in here for the classical *iussus*.[13] Several egregious misspellings occur: TLUMEN for FLUMEN (1 May), AMPIIEATRI (13 May), and EE for ET in the final line, where the *lapidarius* ('stonecutter') also omitted the designation COSS ('consuls'). Moreover, the words *ad flumen* ('at the river') in the phrase *lustratio ad flumen* ('ceremony at the river') in line 7 may be a dittographic error generated by the words *lustratio ad flumen* two lines earlier.[14] Most surprising, perhaps, is the absence from the *Feriale* of the names of the *domini* ('emperors'), which raises issues about identity crucial to the text's interpretation, a point which will be discussed below.

[8] Mommsen, *Gesammelte Schriften*, 8. 17; Degrassi, 282. For the suggestion that Felix may have been the provincial governor, see G. Cecconi, *Governo imperiale e élites dirigenti nell'Italia tardoantica* (Como, 1994), 104–5, 216.

[9] G. D'Isanto, *Capua romana: Ricerche di prosopografia e storia sociale* (Rome, 1993), 291.

[10] Mommsen, *Gesammelte Schriften*, 8. 16–17; Degrassi, 282. See e.g. *ILS* 705: the Constantinian *sacerdos* of Tuscia-Umbria.

[11] Rüpke, *Kalender*, 530 n. 23.

[12] Cecconi, *Governo imperiale*, 103–5.

[13] *Thesaurus linguae latinae* (*TLL*), s.v. 'ferialis' and 'iussio'; Rüpke, *Kalender*, 525.

[14] A suggestion made by Paul B. Harvey Jr.

The *Feriale*'s provenance, the Capuan amphitheatre, was probably its place of original dedication.[15] Capua had been a leading city of Italy from the early Republican to the early Imperial period and had reasserted itself in the fourth century when it became the seat of the governor, usually a *consularis*, of Campania.[16] In the second century Florus recalled Capua as the *caput urbium*, once numbered among the world's three greatest cities; in the fourth century Ausonius ranked Capua eighth in his *Ordo urbium nobilium*, third in Italy behind Rome and Milan.[17] Moreover, the *Campani* themselves continued to be known in Late Antiquity for an addiction to gladiatorial games, as well as for the arrogance and love of luxury that had characterized them in the days of Cicero and Livy.[18]

Not surprisingly, then, three of the calendar's *feriae* apparently focus upon the Capuan amphitheatre. First, although the January *vota* pronounced *pro salute imperatoris* are widely attested throughout the imperial period,[19] the *fasti* of the codex calendar of 354 specifically assign *ludi* to the day, as do the mid-fifth-century *fasti* of Polemius Silvius.[20] Second, the *fasti* of 354 also record circus races at Rome for the Genialia of 11 February with games, the *ludi Genialici*, noted for the next day. The *fasti* of Polemius Silvius also record *circenses* and *ludi* for these days, although without specific reference to the Genialia.[21] Finally, as a spring floral holiday, the Rosaria also has rough parallels elsewhere. May floral festivals are known from other towns of the empire,

[15] Rüpke, *Kalendar*, 529. For fragments of an Augustan calendar found in the drains of the Capuan amphitheatre, though not necessarily published there, see G. D'Isanto, 'Iscrizioni latine inedite dell'antiquarium di S. Maria Capua Vetere', *Rendiconti dell'Accademia di archeologia lettre e belle arti di Napoli*, 59 (1988), 144–5; with Rüpke, *Kalender*, 106–8.

[16] M. W. Frederiksen, 'Republican Capua: A Social and Economic Study', *PBSR* 27 (1959) 80–130; idem, *Campania*, N. Purcell (ed.) (Oxford, 1984), 264–318; A. Chastagnol, 'L'Administration du diocèse Italien au bas-empire', *Historia*, 12 (1963), 362–6; and D'Isanto, *Capua romana*, 15–44.

[17] Florus 1. 11. 6; Aus. *Ordo* 46–63.

[18] Cic. *Att.* 7. 14; Livy 9. 40. 17; Ausonius, *Ordo* 58–60; *SHA Did. Jul.* 8. 3.

[19] e.g. Degrassi, 391.

[20] Degrassi, 13. 2. 42–43. On sacrifice as part of the early imperial ritual see e.g. *CIL* 6. 2041, *Acta* of the Arval Brothers. The *fasti* of Silvius (Degrassi, 13. 2. 43) further designate the day a *dies auspicalium*.

[21] Degrassi, 408; Salzman, *Roman Time*, 127.

and the *Feriale Duranum* records the decoration of military standards with roses on 11 and 23 May.[22] But a notation in the codex calendar of 354, where 'the market puts on roses' on 23 May,[23] permits us to envision the Capuan amphitheatre as a virtual 'rose bowl' on 13 May. In short, the Rosaria of 13 May is explicitly connected to the Capuan amphitheatre while two other festivals, the *vota* of 3 January and the Genialia of 11 February, can be so linked through comparison with Rome.

The calendar's remaining four festivals may have been celebrated with *ludi* in the amphitheatre as well, but they also clearly drew celebrants out of the city and into contact with both the countryside and the ancient religious history of Campania. The agrarian origins of October's vintage festival are obvious, while the *lustrationes* of 1 May and 25 July have been readily, and perhaps correctly, connected with the planting and harvesting of grain.[24] But explicit references in the *feriale*'s final three entries also evoke the legendary religious landscape of Campania. The *lustratio ad flumen ad iter Dianae* of 25 July alludes to the ancient temple of Diana Tifatina outside Capua, while the *iter Averni* and the *vendemia Acerusae* summon up the *lacus Avernus* and the *palus Acherusia* of the Phlegraean Fields near Cumae. Here of course Vergil's Aeneas met the Sibyl, priestess of Apollo and Diana,[25] to begin his underworld tour, but the religious and legendary associations of this volcanic area greatly predate the Augustan age.[26]

What religious implications lurk behind the words of the *Feriale*? Were *iter Dianae* and *iter Averni* simply topographical references, and did the term *lustratio* no longer bear troublesome associations with an ancient expiatory rite? Degrassi marvelled that Christian emperors sanctioned the

[22] See Fink *et al.*, '*Feriale Duranum*', 45, 115–20; J. Marquardt, *Römische Staatsverwaltung*[2] (Leipzig, 1885), 3. 311 ff.; K. Latte, *Römische Religionsgeschichte* (Munich, 1960), 73–4, 363.

[23] Degrassi, 247, 460–1: 'Macellus rosa(m) sumat'.

[24] Mommsen, *Gesammelte Schriften*, 8. 18–21; Degrassi, 283.

[25] Vergil, *Aen.* 6. 35: 'Phoebi Triviaeque sacerdos'. For Trivia as an epithet of Diana Tifatina see *CIL* 10. 3795.

[26] R. Peterson, *The Cults of Campania* (Rome, 1919), 45–79.

calendar's *ethnicae feriae*, but he accepted the explanation that Mommsen had offered a century earlier.[27] Mommsen mitigated his own discomfort by observing that the *Feriale* explicitly contradicted no earlier legislation: the calendar, for example, enjoined neither sacrifice nor temple attendance.[28] Furthermore, Mommsen portrayed the *Feriale*'s holidays as agrarian, civic, or political, but not 'religious', and therefore believed them capable of embracing Christian and pagan alike. The *sacerdos* Romanus, he noted with reference to a law of 386 restricting the office of 'chief civil priest' (*archierosyna*) to non-Christians, could have been construed by emperors as a civic official not a pagan priest.[29] Above all, Mommsen viewed the imperial *iussio* sanctioning the *Feriale* as a calculated effort by the emperors to find a neutral ground, outside the zone of personal religious affiliation, where the members of all cults could comfortably participate in official state festivals.[30] Now, the *Feriale* may indeed represent an attempt at consensus building, but the specific character of the text's holidays and its provocative language suggest that it is as much a document arising from concessions granted as from imperial initiatives freely undertaken.

In particular, the *Feriale Campanum* is provocatively non-Christian. Several of the calendar's *feriae*, as noted, pointedly refer to the pre-Christian religious traditions of Campania. The legendary associations of the Lacus Avernus and of Acheron-fed Acerusa, destination of July's *profectio* and site of October's *vendemia*, are self-evident to modern readers of Vergil, but some of the *Feriale*'s contemporaries could also have recalled that Hercules had preceded and Hannibal had followed Aeneas in sacrifing at this threshold to the underworld.[31]

Less obvious now, perhaps, are the implicit relationships among the calendar's *lustratio* at Casilinum, its *lustratio ad iter Dianae*, and the ancient cult celebrated on the Mons Tifata,

[27] Degrassi, 282. [28] *Gesammelte Schriften*, 8. 21–4.

[29] Mommsen, *Gesammelte Schriften*, 8. 22, citing *CTh* 12. 1. 112.

[30] *Gesammelte Schriften*, 23; followed by Peterson, *Cults*, 41–4; Cecconi, *Governo imperiale*, 106 n. 91; Rüpke, *Kalender*, 529 n. 22.

[31] Diod.Sic. 4. 22; Livy, 24. 12–13; Sil.Ital. *Punica* 12. 126–9; Sen. *Epist*. 55. 2–6.

some two miles west of Capua. As old as the city itself was the cult of Diana on the Mons Tifata, which was a rival in antiquity to the cults of Diana at Aricia and on the Aventine.[32] In the Republican and early Imperial era, the temple of Diana was a major site controlling significant property. During the late Republic, after Capua's loss of civic autotomy in 211 BCE, the temple apparently was managed by boards of *magistri*, who must have ceded their authority to the city's colonial administration after 58 BCE.[33] Already, however, the temple had attracted the attention of late Republican *duces*: an inscription documents a precinct wall built *de manubies* by Ser. Fulvius Flaccus, consul in 135 BCE;[34] and Velleius Paterculus (2. 25. 4), of Capuan background himself, knew the inscriptions recording land grants to the temple by Sulla. Moreover, a major renovation of the temple in 74 BCE may have been connected with the activities of Roman nobles,[35] whereas later boundary stones record that both Augustus and Vespasian recertified Sulla's donations.[36]

In addition, as the scene of frequent military action in the late Republic, the Mons Tifata likewise acquired a place in history.[37] And, as the repository of curiosities, the temple of Diana attracted antiquarian interest: Athenaeus knew that the temple housed a 'cup of Nestor' (466e, 489b), while earlier in the second century, Pausanias cited a skull that he had seen in the temple as evidence that elephant tusks are horns and not teeth (5. 12. 3). A fascinating but fragmentary verse inscription from the temple site attests to ritual continuity at least into the third century and probably into the

32 T. Mommsen, *CIL* 10 (Berlin, 1883), 366–8; J. Beloch, *Campanien*[2] (Breslau, 1890) 361–6; H. Nissen, *Italische Landeskunde* (Berlin, 1902), 2. 709–11; R. Peterson, *Cults*, 322–8; *RE* s.v. 'Tifata' and 'Tifitina'; and A. de Franciscis, 'Templum Dianae Tifatinae', *Archivo storico di terra di lavoro*, 1 (1956), 301–58.

33 On the *magistri*, see Frederikson, 'Republican Capua', 83–94; idem, *Campania*, 264–318. *CIL* 10. 3913 (*ILS* 5380) reveals a *duovir* paving the *via Dianae*, although *magistri* continued to be connected with the temple: see *CIL* 10. 3924 (*ILS* 6305), a five-year-old *magister fani Dianae* given the *equus publicus* in the second century CE.

34 *ILS* 22, with photograph at de Franciscis, *Templum*, Tav. 10.

35 *CIL* 10. 3935; de Franciscis, 'Templum', 316–22, 349; A. Degrassi (ed.), *Inscriptiones latinae liberae rei publicae*, 2 vols. (Rome, 1963), 721.

36 *CIL* 10. 3828 (*ILS* 251); *ILS* 3240.

37 e.g., Livy, 7. 29; 23. 36; 26. 5; Vell.Pat. 2. 25.

fourth.[38] It records the dedication to Diana Tifatina of certain 'wondrous objects' (*miracula*) by the poem's author, Laetus *signo* Delmatius. Laetus styles himself a 'silvarum cultor' ('devotee of the forests') and describes Diana as 'renowned among hunters'. His dedication appears to have been a hunting trophy, probably a deer's skull with antlers, a gift that recalls both Pausanias' tusked-elephant head and the silvan legends and iconography of Diana.[39]

Even though this temple is not specifically attested in later antiquity, there is no reason to suspect that the temple was not intact in 387. A tradition preserved in the *lectiones* of an 'ancient Capuan breviary' credits Capua's legendary first bishop and martyr, St Priscus, with subverting local enthusiasm for Diana, but any assault on the temple's cult may better be associated with the bishop of that same name martyred during the Vandalic sack of Capua in 456.[40] A church dedicated to Michael the Archangel may have been constructed on the site as early as the late sixth century, but the present Sant'Angelo in Formis, occupying the temple's podium and reusing its columns, arose in the tenth century.[41] Nevertheless, in 942 Pope Marino II could still reprimand Capua's bishop for allowing the people to dance and loiter at the site 'sicut quondam' ('just as in the past').[42]

This literary, epigraphical, and archaeological evidence provides a rich cultural and historical backdrop for the *Feriale*'s 'lustratio ad flumen Casilino' and 'lustratio ad flumen ad iter Dianae', but the exact location as well as the character of these

[38] *CIL* 10. 3796 = *ILS* 3261 = J. Buecheler (ed.), *Anthologia Latina*, 2. 1. 256 = E. Courtney (ed.), *Musa Lapidaria: A Selection of Latin Verse Inscriptions* (Atlanta, 1995), 139. The late date derives from the presence of the *signum*. See T. Mommsen, 'Sallustius=Salutius und das Signum', *Hermes*, 37 (1902), 443–55; I. Kajanto, *The Latin Cognomina* (Helsinki, 1965), 115; idem, *Supernomina: A Study in Latin Epigraphy* (Helsinki, 1966) 52–4; A. Cameron, 'Polyonomy in the Late Roman Aristocracy: The Case of Petronius Probus', *JRS* 75 (1985), 171–7.

[39] For similar dedications, see Courtney, *Musa Lapidaria*, 141–2. An unpublished text from Cosa was discussed by J. Bodel in a paper 'Diana Recepta' delivered at the 1998 meeting of the Americal Philological Asssociation and will be published in a forthcoming volume of the Cosa excavations.

[40] See de Franciscis, 'Templum', 350–1. For the 'Antiquo breviario Capuano' see *AASS*, Sept. I, 101.

[41] De Franciscis, 'Templum', 314–48; M. D'Onofrio and V. Pace, *Campanie Romane*, trans. D. Vaillant (La Pierre-qui-Vire, 1981), 169–78.

[42] *Regesto di S. Angelo in Formis* 5 (de Franciscis, 'Templum', 358).

rites is uncertain. The 'river' of May's *lustratio* must be the Volturnus, on whose banks Casilinum, the site of modern Capua, was located, just to the northeast of ancient Capua (now S. Maria Capua Vetere). The site of July's 'lustratio ad iter Dianae', however, is more difficult to determine. Mommsen suggested that it, too, was held at the Volturnus on a circuit that led eventually to the Temple of Diana Tifatina.[43] But if the 'ad flumen' of July's festival notation is, as suggested above, a dittographic error, then this *lustratio* may have been staged somewhere along the epigraphically attested *via Dianae* which left Capua through the *porta Volturni* and apparently proceeded rather more directly to the *vicus* of the temple on the Mons Tifata (*CIL* 10. 3913 = *ILS* 5380).

Regardless of exact venue, the appearance of *lustrationes* in an imperially sanctioned *feriale* of the year 387 is quite surprising, for by the later fourth century it seems that the term was either avoided or deployed primarily in anti-pagan invective. For centuries the word had signified a purification or expiatory ritual that concluded with sacrifice.[44] In the second century BCE, the Elder Cato had described the sacrificial *suovetaurilia* ('pig, sheep, and bull sacrifice') conducted for the lustration of the fields, while the Roman *vicennalia* ('twentieth anniversary') monument of Diocletian, as well as the arch of Constantine, redeploying a relief panel of Marcus Aurelius, still depicted the pre-sacrifice *pompa* ('ritual') of lustral animals.[45] Notably, neither the *fasti* of the Codex calendar of 354 nor the *fasti* of Polemius Silvius employed the term.[46] Moreover, as Mommsen argued, late-fourth-century bishops like Vigilius of Trent and Maximus of Turin railed against the persistence of lustral rites in the countryside, an indication that even if the Campanian *lustrationes* were connected with the agricultural cycle, that is no proof they were sufficiently sanitized for the needs of a

[43] Mommsen, *Gesammelte Schriften*, 8. 18–19.

[44] Marquardt, *Staatsverwaltung*, 3. 201–2; Latte, *Religionsgeschichte*, 41–2, 119; de Ruggiero, *Dizionario* s.v. 'lustratio'; *TLL* s.v. 'lustratio'.

[45] Cato, *De Agricultura* 141; I. S. Ryberg, *Rites of the State Religion in Roman Art* (Rome, 1955), 104–19; idem, *The Panel Reliefs of Marcus Aurelius* (New York, 1967), 37–43.

[46] Salzman, *Roman Time*, 118.

christianizing age.[47] Even at Cassiodorus's Vivarium in the early sixth century, *lustrationes* and *incantationes* still served to define the illicit magical rites of the *pagani atque Iudaei* ('pagans and Jews').[48] For several reasons, then, the parading of *lustrationes* by the *Feriale Campanum* was unusual, if not openly provocative.

The literary sources harbour one further piece of tantalizing evidence that may suggest another dimension of the *Feriale*'s riparian rites: the first-century *Punica* of Silius Italicus preserves a tale that mingles aspects of the cult of Diana Tifatina, the holidays of the *Feriale*, and the history of Capua. Writing his epic poem on the Hannibalic war at his Campanian villas in the Flavian age, Silius Italicus recalled how a tame white deer (*cerva*) sacred to Diana had lived at Capua for a thousand years until the Roman general Fulvius sacrificed it to the goddess. Until that time, the women of Capua had tended the animal by combing its hair and restoring its colour *umenti fluvio*, 'by bathing it in the river'.[49] Although Silius' poem may have been little read thereafter, the 'memory' of an ancient rite that brought Capua's people and Diana's cult 'ad flumen Volturnum' may still have had value for those interested in celebrating a 'lustratio ad flumen ad iter Dianae'.

In the end, the words of the calendar reveal little about either the ritual actions they cite or the religious self-understanding of those who gathered *ad flumen* or on the *iter Averni*. Yet, the evidence does project a thick context for the *Feriale Campanum* of 387 and suggests the predispositions of some of those who celebrated its festival cycle. However the *Feriale* fits into the context of religious conflict and political crisis at Rome and Milan in the mid to late 380s, the particu-

[47] Mommsen, *Gesammelte Schriften*, 8. 19. Vigilius, *Epist.* 2. 3: *PL* 13; Max.Taur. *Serm.* 106. 1: *CCL* 23. Note that although the 'harvest' *lustratio* of 25 July became a 'legal' holiday two years later when a law closed the courts, for agrarian purposes, during the mid-summer harvest and the vintage (*CTh* 2. 8. 19: 389), the 'sowing' *lustratio* of 1 May (see also the *Menologium Rusticum Colotianum* for May: Degrassi, 13. 2. 47) did not. Note also M. Salzman, 'The Christianization of Sacred Time and Sacred Space', in W. V. Harris (ed.), *The Transformations of Urbs Roma in Late Antiquity* (Portsmouth, 1999), 125–6.

[48] Cassiodorus, *Historia ecclesiastica tripartita* 6. 28. 4: *CSEL* 71. 344–5; with Sozomen, *HE* 5. 15. 5.

[49] Sil.Ital. *Punica* 13. 115–37; cf. Vergil, *Aen.* 7. 483–510.

larly concessionary qualities of the *iussio dominorum* that established it emerge more clearly.

The *Feriale Campanum*'s context was acutely political as well as religious, for at the moment of its dedication, November 387, Magnus Maximus, who had invaded Italy a few months earlier, occupied Milan. Thus, we might be tempted to identify the unnamed *domini*[50] responsible for the *iussio* that sanctioned the *feriale* as Maximus and his son Victor, who had joined his father as Augustus in 383 or 384.[51] Newly arrived in Italy, Maximus may have wished to reach out, but not too openly, to those members of the senatorial aristocracy who still maintained an allegiance to the kinds of pre-Christian traditions apparently glossed by the festivals of the *Feriale Campanum*. Indeed, in January of the next year, 388, Symmachus travelled to Milan to deliver a consular panegyric for Italy's 'new' emperor.[52] But Maximus, who recently had overseen the execution of the 'heretic' Priscillian and several of his followers at Trier, also was a strictly orthodox Christian emperor, one who earlier had hoped to win the support of the no less orthodox Theodosius.[53] Italy may have softened Maximus's stance, of course, but the evidence of the *Feriale* itself makes it more likely that the text's *domini* are

[50] The text's *domini*, who appear twice, must be emperors, not divinities or senators. By the later fourth century, this term had become standard imperial titulature: see T. Mommsen, *Römisches Staatsrecht*[2] (Leipzig, 1877), 2. 2. 739–40; and de Ruggiero, *Dizionario*, s.v. 'dominus VII'. It is attested for Magnus Maximus (*ILS* 788); and for Theodosius and Valentinian (*ILS* 781–5; 782 for *dominis* without *nostris*). Senators are never identified as such (see e.g. *ILS* 1243–84). And even though the expression 'iussione dominorum Felix votum solvit' is not unlike that used for dedications to divinities, such texts regularly identify the deity by name (see de Ruggiero, *Dizionario*, s.v. 'iussus I' and 'dominus VIII'). Moreover, this locution also was used for emperors, in exactly the way it was used in the *Feriale*; note, e.g. the *Corrector Italiae* who dedicated a temple 'iussu DD [dominorum] NN [nostrorum] Diocletiani et Maximiani Augg [Augustorum]': see de Ruggiero, *Dizionario*, s.v. 'iussus', who also notes actions taken 'iussu principis'; and G. Alföldy (ed.), *CIL* 6. 8B (1996), 4626, s.v. 'iussus'. In addition, a law of Constantine (*CJ* 3. 12. 3 [4]: 323) expressly forbade anyone other than an emperor to establish *imperiales feriae* (although it is not clear that this category was directly relevant in the case of the *Feriale*). For imperial and senatorial titulature, see also Mathisen in this volume.

[51] *PLRE I*, 962, s.v. Victor 14.

[52] Symm. *Epist.* 2. 30–31; with O. Seeck (ed.), *Q. Aurelii Symmachi quae supersunt* (Berlin, 1883), p. lvii.

[53] Sulp.Sev. *Chron.* 2. 50–2; Matthews, *Aristocracies*, 165–8.

Valentinian II, Theodosius, and technically, at least, Arcadius (383–408).

Several factors suggest that the *iussio* establishing the calendar originated at Valentinian's court, either after his flight east or, perhaps more likely, at Milan before he had evacuated the capital. Most tellingly, the *Feriale* was dedicated at Capua exactly on the anniversary of Valentinian's accession, which had taken place twelve years earlier, on 22 November 375, a coincidence that suggests that the *votum* of Felix was undertaken in anticipation of Valentinian's *dies imperii*.[54] Moreover, in 387 Valentinian was holding his third consulship, a fact duly recorded in the *Feriale*.[55] His consular colleague was Eutropius, author of the *Breviarium*, a primer of Roman history dedicated to Valens (364–78). Eutropius was a correspondent of Symmachus and apparently a man of pagan sympathies; by 387 he had served in the administrations of at least three emperors.[56] The implied association of the *Feriale* with Valentinian's imperial anniversary and the prominent notation of his consulship link the document to the courts of Valentinian and, indirectly, Theodosius. There are at least two possible explanations for the omission of the names and full titulature of the *domini*. It may simply have been because of lack of space on the crowded surface of a poorly inscribed stone. But perhaps a more likely explanation is to be sought in the aristocratic interplay that accompanied senatorial attempts to preserve their pagan heritage.

The *iussio dominorum* recorded by the *Feriale* may well indicate that what Valentinian and Theodosius were unwilling to do in 384 and 390, that is, to accept bids for the restoration of imperial support for Rome's traditional cults, they may have been willing to compromise upon in Campania in 387. Symmachus, who had been a member of the senatorial delegation sent in protest to Gratian in 382[57] and who had composed the official request of 384, was present in Milan in January of 387, when he attended the consular celebrations of Valentinian II and whence he wrote to Valentinian's

[54] Bagnall *et al.*, *Consuls*, 308–9; Kienast, *Römische Kaisertabelle*, 330.

[55] Bagnall *et al.*, *Consuls*, 308–9.

[56] *PLRE I*, 317, s.v. Eutropius 2; P. Schmidt, 'Eutrope', in R. Herzog (ed.), *Nouvelle histoire de la littérature latine* (Paris, 1993), 232–8; Symm. *Epist.* 3. 46–53.

[57] Symm. *Rel.* 3. 1; Amb. *Epist.* 17. 10.

consular colleague, Eutropius.[58] It would have been an apt moment to renew pressure for religious concessions. Moreover, any suspicions that Valentinian and Theodosius may have had about the loyalty of some Roman nobles subsequently would have been confirmed by Symmachus's own actions after Maximus took Italy, when, in January 388, he returned to Milan to deliver a panegyric in honour of Maximus.

Capua would have offered Valentinian's court a distinctly advantageous venue for the display of an imperial bid for the support of the non-Christian Roman nobility at a moment of uncertainty. Concessions made public here removed the matter from its overheated Roman context, yet offered compromise in a city rich in ancient traditions and in a region that was nearly the special reserve of Rome's noble families, Christian and pagan. Roman nobles frequently held the province's governorship. The *fasti* for the decade before the publication of the *Feriale* contain the names of two Anicii as well as the younger Nicomachus Flavianus, while two Avianii, both possibly related to Symmachus, held the post at some earlier time.[59] Moreover, Rome's aristocratic families continued to own extensive properties in Campania.[60] The eclectic pagan, Vettius Agorius Praetextatus, whiled away his leisure at Baiae;[61] while a disgruntled Ammianus Marcellinus complained that Rome's indolent senators considered a pleasure cruise from Lake Avernus to Puteoli an epic adventure, especially if attempted in the heat of summer.[62] Symmachus owned properties throughout the region: at Baiae, Naples, Puteoli, and Cumae; at Beneventum, where he admired the pagan sympathies of the populace; and, notably, at Capua, where he poured money into the upkeep of an old villa (*praetorium*).[63] From Capua he corresponded with Ausonius in

[58] *Epist.* 3. 52; with Seeck, *Symmachus*, p. cxxxiv.

[59] Fasti: Chastagnol, 'L'Administration', 363–5; *PLRE I*, 1093; Cecconi, *Governo imperiale*, 214–17. Avianius Vindicianus and Avianius Valentinus: *PLRE I*, 968, 936.

[60] On the background see J. D'Arms, *Romans on the Bay of Naples* (Cambridge, Mass., 1970).

[61] Symm. *Epist.* 1. 47, cf. 1. 48. [62] Amm. 28. 4. 18

[63] See *Epist.* 2. 4 (Cumae); 1. 3, 2. 26, 5. 93, 6. 9, 7. 25 (Baiae); 1. 8, 2. 26, 5. 93, 6. 66 (Puteoli); 2. 60 (Naples); 1. 3. 4 (Beneventum); 1. 10 (Capua). See D'Arms, *Romans*, 226–9; D. Vera, 'Simmaco e le sue proprietà: struttura e funzionamento di un patrimonio aristocratico del quarto secolo d.C', in F. Paschoud (ed.), *Symmaque* (Paris, 1986), 231–76, esp. n. 135.

379 or 380;[64] and it was probably in 385, two years prior to the *Feriale*'s dedication, that he informed Nicomachus Flavianus of his intention of spending the very month of November enjoying Capua and the locales of the *ager Campanus*.[65] Moreover, office holding, property ownership, and local influence were complementary. The pagan Nicomachi, for example, were *patroni originales* at Naples[66] and in 395 Symmachus successfully represented at the imperial court a group of Campanian *curiales* seeking tax concessions.[67]

This selective list is not meant to imply that the Christian elite had no interests in Campania. On the contrary, Constantine himself is said to have founded a basilica at Capua;[68] at least one of the Anician *proconsules Campaniae* in these years was a Christian;[69] the renowned Christian senator Petronius Probus was a *patronus originalis* at Capua itself;[70] and Campania boasted numerous saint's cults, one of whose future impresarios, Paulinus of Nola, was also a *consularis Campaniae* in the early 380s.[71] Despite this emerging Christian profile, it might have been possible for the emperors and the non-Christian Roman nobility to find a suitable 'neutral' ground in Campania, one not available in the spotlight of the turbulent Roman capital, but one where it was still tactful and prudent to omit the names of the emperors who had granted the privilege.[72]

Yet, less than four years after the *Feriale* was published at Capua by *iussio dominorum*, Theodosius began to issue the series of strongly anti-pagan laws later collected in book sixteen (10. 10–12) of the *Codex Theodosianus*. Overshadowed by these enactments, the festivals of the *Feriale Campanum*

[64] *Epist.* 1. 31–32. [65] *Epist.* 2. 26.

[66] *ILS* 8985; cf. Sym. *Epist.* 2. 60. See also M. T. W. Arnheim, *The Senatorial Aristocracy in the Later Roman Empire* (Oxford, 1972), 155–68.

[67] Symm. *Epist.* 4. 46, cf. 4. 35, and *CTh* 11. 28. 2.

[68] *Lib. Pont.* 34 (Silvester).

[69] Anicius Auchenius Bassus: *CIL* 14. 1875 (*ILS* 1292).

[70] Arnheim, *Aristocracy*, 156; *PLRE I*, 740, s.v. Probus 5.

[71] *PLRE I*, 681, s.v. Paulinus 21.

[72] On Rome's distinctive nature, see Salzman, 'Christianization'; and R. Lim, 'People as Power: Games, Munificence, and Contested Topography', in Harris (ed.), *Transformations*, 265–81.

appear as an interesting but inconsequential anomaly in the religious history of Capua. In a more broadly drawn context, however, the imperial *iussio* of 387 that sanctioned this *index feriarum* assumes greater significance. Against the background of a Milanese court in crisis, the erection of an imperially sanctioned calendar of decidedly non-Christian *feriae* in a region dominated by the political, social, and financial concerns of the Roman nobility, appears as a conciliatory gesture. The *Feriale* is thus better seen as a concession exacted against the grain of fourth-century imperial legislation gradually circumscribing pagan cultic activity than the magnanimous and voluntary attempt at civic consensus-building envisioned by Mommsen.

In the early 380s Gratian and then Valentinian II had rejected senatorial requests for the renewal of imperial support for traditional cult at Rome;[73] together with Theodosius, they had passed laws prohibiting divinatory sacrifice, although allowing certain temples to remain open for non-cultic use.[74] Then, in 387, in the midst of political turmoil, an imperial *iussio*, local but immediate in its force, established an annual cycle of traditional but provocative festivals at the Campanian provincial capital. Soon thereafter, amid the reconstruction in Italy after the defeat of Maximus, Theodosius's anti-pagan legislation became far more comprehensive and intrusive than before. The law issued at Milan in February 391, the year of Symmachus's consulship, and addresssed to Ceionius Rufius Albinus, then Urban Prefect and several decades later interlocutor in Macrobius's *Saturnalia*, virtually outlawed all approach to pagan temples.[75] A law issued at Constantinople in November of the following year pushed the prohibitions against sacrifice and the veneration of images explicitly into the private home and the countryside.[76] To be sure, these laws prohibited nothing explicitly enjoined by the text of the *Feriale*, but in 395 Honorius and Arcadius issued a law directly forbidding the inclusion of 'ceremonial days of pagan superstition' among the official holidays (*inter*

[73] Sym. *Rel.* 3. 1 for the embassy to Gratian, with A. Cameron, 'Gratian's Repudiation of the Pontifical Robe', *JRS* 58 (1968), 96–102.

[74] *CTh* 16. 7–9.

[75] *CTh* 16. 10. 10; on Albinus, see *PLRE I*, 37–8.

[76] *CTh* 16. 10. 12.

feriatos).[77] It is hard to see how the *Feriale Campanum*, despite its imperial imprimatur, could have withstood the cumulative force of this legislative barrage. It probably did not. But it remains an eloquent testimony to the inadequacy of the *Codex Theodosianus* as an unqualified legislative guide to the political, social, or religious complexity of this age.[78]

[77] *CTh* 2. 8. 22: July 395, reiterating an earlier (lost) law.

[78] The point is well made by D. Hunt, 'Christianising the Roman Empire: The Evidence of the Code', in J. Harries and I. Wood (eds.), *The Theodosian Code* (Ithaca, 1993), 143–58.

11

Imperial Honorifics and Senatorial Status in Late Roman Legal Documents

Ralph W. Mathisen

For most senators during the late Roman period, the reality of power and authority had been replaced by its mere appearance, which was manifested most clearly in the ranks and offices they held.[1] The quest for status was non-ending,[2] and the best kind of status was that bestowed by the emperor. It could be granted and manifested in many ways. During the course of the fourth century, for example, imperial office-holders came to be endowed with ranks that ranged from *inlustris* ('illustrious') for officials of the highest status, such as Praetorian and Urban Prefects, Masters of Soldiers, and members of the *comitatus* (the imperial court); to *spectabilis* ('respectable') for such middle-ranking officials as Proconsuls, Counts, Dukes, and Vicars; to *clarissimus* ('most distinguished'), the 'entry level' senatorial rank, for provincial governors and lesser officials of the *comitatus*.[3] As time

[1] An abbreviated version of this study was presented under the title 'Imperial Honorifics and Senatorial Status in Early Byzantine Documents' at the Byzantine Studies Conference at Princeton University on 4 November 1993.

[2] Much legislation dealt with who outranked whom: Ch. 6. 5 of the *Codex Theodosianus*, for example, was entitled 'Ut dignitatum ordo servetur' ('So that the Sequence of Ranks Might be Preserved'); the twelfth book of the *Codex Justinianus* dealt with the privileges of different ranks and officials; and *Nov. Val.* 11 was entitled 'De honoratis et quis in gradu praeferatur' ('On Officials and Who is Preferred in Rank'). For discussion, see e.g. R. W. Mathisen, 'Emperors, Consuls and Patricians: Some Problems of Personal Preference, Precedence and Protocol', *Byzantinische Forschungen*, 17 (1991), 173–90.

[3] See e.g. O. Hirschfield, 'Die Rangtitel der römischen Kaiserzeit', *Sitzungsberichte der königlichen preussischen Akademie der Wissenschaft*, 25 (1901), 579–610 = idem, *Kleine Schriften* (Berlin, 1913; repr. New York, 1975), 646–81; P. Koch, *Die*

went on, the titles associated with the most important offices became more and more extravagant, including *excellentissimus* ('most excellent'), *magnificentissimus* ('most magnificent'), *eminentissimus* ('most eminent'), *gloriosissimus* ('most glorious'), and so on.[4] These ranks could be gained in other ways, such as upon retirement from a government clerical post, or by purchase.[5] Generally speaking, the status associated with these titles has been well studied.[6]

Other kinds of Latin honorifics also were used by emperors to indicate status. These are what might be called '*tua*-epithets', which served as replacements for second-person pronouns when officials were either referred to or directly addressed in imperial legislation. As will be seen, these epithets made an addressee's level of status very clear indeed.

Late Roman imperial legal documents are striking for the majestic nomenclature that was used to characterize important persons. Emperors, for example, did not refer to themselves simply as 'I' or 'me'. They rather replaced the first person pronoun with terms such as 'nostra serenitas' ('Our Serenity'), 'nostra tranquilitas' ('Our Tranquility'), 'nostra maiestas' ('Our Majesty'), and 'nostra aeternitas' ('Our Eternity').[7] The highest-ranking imperial officials were

byzantinischen Beamtentitel von 400 bis 700 (Jena, 1903); H. Löhken, *Ordines dignitatum. Untersuchungen zur formalen Konstituierung der spätantiken Führungsschicht* (Cologne, 1982); and A. H. M. Jones, *The Later Roman Empire 284–602: A Social, Economic and Administrative Survey* (Norman, Okla., 1964), 134–5, 142–4, and passim.

[4] Note the titles of officials who attended the Council of Chalcedon in 451 (*ACO* 2. 3. 1. 27–8, cf. 2. 1. 19, 2. 1. 81–82): 'cum magnificentissimis principibus et gloriosissimis . . .'; 'gloriosissimis iudicibus'; and see *CJ* 12. 8. 4: 440–1 for a Master of Soldiers as *vir magnificentissimus*, and a Praetorian Prefect as *vir excellentissimus*.

[5] See R. W. Mathisen, 'Leo, Anthemius, Zeno, and Extraordinary Senatorial Status in the Late Fifth Century', *Byzantinische Forschungen*, 17 (1991), 191–222.

[6] See e.g. M. T. W. Arnheim, *The Senatorial Aristocracy in the Later Roman Empire* (Oxford, 1972); A. Chastagnol, 'L'Évolution de l'ordre sénatorial aux IIIe–IVe siècles de notre ère', *Revue historique*, 244 (1970), 305–14; M. E. Cosenza, *Official Positions after the Time of Constantine* (Lancaster, Penn., 1905); Jones, *LRE*, 104–5, 329–33, and passim; J. F. Matthews, *Western Aristocracies and Imperial Court, A.D. 364–425* (Oxford, 1975).

[7] Also 'nostra perennitas', 'nostra mansuetudo', 'nostra clementia', and 'nostra humanitas'. And note Ammianus (15. 1. 3) on Constantius II (337–61), 'confestim a iustitia declinavit ita intemperanter, ut 'Aeternitatem meam' aliquotiens subsereret ipse dictando, scribendoque propria manu orbis totius se dominum appellaret

accorded a similar kind of nomenclature, and were addressed by emperors, for example, as 'magnitudo tua' ('Your Magnitude'), or 'magnifica sinceritas tua' ('Your Magnificent Sincerity').[8] But the nature and significance of *tua*-honorifics applied to officials have been little studied.[9]

The *tua*-epithets appear in two different contexts. Documents that have survived in an essentially unabridged form almost always have a section that addresses the recipient in words such as, 'Dearest and Most Beloved Parent ('parens karissime et amantissime'): Your Illustrious and Magnificent Authority will see to it that . . .', and so on.[10] These full forms of address were ruthlessly edited out of the entries in the *Codex Theodosianus* ('Theodosian Code') (438)[11] and the *Codex*

. . .'. For terminology, see Hirschfeld, 'Rangtitel', 675; R. M. Honig, *Humanitas und Rhetorik in spätrömischen Kaisergesetzen* (Göttingen, 1960), 85–126; A. Magioncalda, *Lo sviluppo della titolatura imperiale da Augusta a Giustiniano* (Turin, 1991); G. Rösch, *Onoma basileias. Studien zum offiziellen Gebrauch der Kaisertitel in spätantiker und frühyzantinischer Zeit* (Vienna, 1978). For the literary style of late Roman imperial documents, see T. Honoré, *Law in the Crisis of Empire 379–455 AD: The Theodosian Dynasty and its Quaestors* (Oxford, 1998); R. MacMullen, 'Roman Bureaucratese', *Traditio*, 18 (1962), 364–78; G. Vidén, *The Roman Chancery Tradition: Studies in the Language of Codex Theodosianus and Cassiodorus' Variae* (Göteborg, 1984).

[8] *Tua* also can occur with non-honorific terms, as in 'officia tua' or 'potestas tua'. And other honorifics, such as 'dignatio tua', were used by the general public but not by emperors: see S. Lancel, 'Titres de rang et titres de courtoisie dans les actes de 411', in idem (ed.), *Actes de la conférence de Carthage en 411*, vol. 1, *SC* 194 (Paris, 1972), 328–31. Honorific terms occur occasionally in the third person. e.g. 'ab eius sublimitate' (*CTh* 10. 9. 3: 418).

[9] Honoré, *Law*, 266, for example, describes them merely as 'polite modes of address'. For some individual cases, see A. J. Fridh, *Terminologie et formules dans les Variae de Cassiodore. Étude sur le développement du style administratitif aux derniers siècles de l'antiquité* (Stockholm, 1956); Hirschfield, 'Rangtitel', 674–6; and Koch, *Beamtentitel*, 107–23; Lancel, 'Titres'. For other honorifics used in epistolography, see A. Engelbrecht, *Das Titelwesen bein den spälateinischen Epistolographen* (Vienna, 1893); L. Dinneen, *Titles of Address in Christian Greek Epistolography to 527 A.D.* (Washington, DC, 1929); M. B. O'Brien, *Titles of Address in Christian Latin Epistolography to 543 A.D.* (Washington, DC, 1930). Ecclesiastical titulature has been studied, for example, by E. Jerg, *Vir venerabilis. Untersuchungen zur Titulatur der Bischöfe in den ausserkirchlichen Texten* (Vienna, 1970); F. Lotter, 'Zu den Anredeformen und ehrenden Epitheta der Bischöfe in Spätantike und frühem Mittelalter', *Deutsches Archiv für Erforschung des Mittelalters*, 27 (1971), 514–17.

[10] Discussed by Honoré, *Law*, 266.

[11] T. Mommsen, P. M. Meyer, P. Krüger (eds.), *Theodosiani libri XVI cum constitutionibus sirmondianis et leges novellae ad Theodosianum pertinentes* (3 vols.; Berlin, 1905; repr. 1970–1); P. Krüger (ed.), *Codex Theodosianus, fasc. I, libri I–VI* (Berlin, 1923); see also O. Gradenwitz, *Heidelberger Index zu Codex Theodosianus*

Justinianus ('Code of Justinian') (533).[12] In general, they survive only in the documents preserved in collections such as the *Epistulae imperatores* ('Imperial Letters'),[13] the post-Theodosian Novels,[14] the Sirmondian Constitutiones,[15] the *Mosaicarum et Romanarum legum collatio* ('Collection of Mosaic and Roman Law'),[16] the *Consultatio veteris cuiusdam jurisconsulti* ('Deliberation of a Certain Ancient Jurisconsult'),[17] and the canons of church councils.[18] Nevertheless, even in the law codes honorifics survive embedded in the texts, either in the nominative, when an official is directly addressed in a manner such as, 'tua igitur sinceritas cognoscat' ('Therefore, Your Sincerity should understand that . . .'), or in oblique cases, for example, 'officium tuae sinceritatis' ('The bureau of Your Sincerity').

The following study proposes to ascertain whether there was any pattern in the way that these honorifics were applied to persons other than emperors. Were certain ones associated with particular officials or ranks? Did old ones go out of fashion as new ones came in? Did any come to be degraded through excessive or indiscriminate use? And one also might ask what kind of insights the *tua*-honorifics provide regard-

(Berlin, 1931). For the editing, note *CTh* 1. 1. 5: 26 March 429, 'The very words themselves of the constitutions . . . shall be preserved, but those words which were added not from the very necessity of sanctioning the law shall be omitted'; also *CTh* 1. 1. 6. 1: 20 Dec. 435, 'We grant to those men who are about to undertake this work the power to remove superfluous words . . .'. See Jones, *LRE*, 475, 'The codifiers were authorised to cut out the preambles and epilogues and other superfluous verbiage'.

[12] P. Krüger (ed.), *Corpus iuris civilis*, ii, *Codex Justinianus* (Berlin, 1954); see also R. Mayr, *Vocabularium codicis Justiniani* (Hildesheim, 1965); M. Amelotti (ed.), *Legis Iustiniani imperatoris vocabularium: Subsidia* (Milan, 1972–7).

[13] O. Guenther (ed.), *Epistulae imperatorum pontificum aliorum inde ab a.* CCCLXVII *usque ad a.* DLIII *datae avellana quae dicitur collectio*, *CSEL* 35. 1–2 (Vienna, 1895–8).

[14] Mommsen, Meyer and Krüger, *Theodosiani*, iii; see also M. Vianchi-Fossati Vanzetti, *Le Novelle di Valentiniano III. I Fonti* (Padua, 1988).

[15] Mommsen, Meyer and Krüger, *Theodosiani libri XVI*.

[16] M. Hyamson, *Mosaicarum et Romanarum legum collatio* (London, 1913).

[17] A. Vargas Valencia (ed.), *Consulta de un jurisconsulto antiguo* (Mexico City, 1991).

[18] Many other stray official documents in an unedited form are conveniently assembled in G. F. Hänel (ed.), *Corpus legum ab imperatoribus romanis ante Iustinianum latarum, quae extra constitutionum codices supersunt. Accedunt res ab imperatoribus gestae, quibus romani iuris historia et imperii status illustratur* (Leipzig, 1857–60; repr. Aalen, 1965).

ing the functioning of the late Roman system of senatorial status, and into the role of the emperor as the dispenser of rank and status.

In order to answer these questions, it proved useful to compile a catalogue of occurrences of the various epithets. A reasonably diligent search of extant late imperial documents unearthed 696 instances where honorifics were used as replacements for second-person pronouns.[19] The results of the survey are summarized in the accompanying Table 11.1: the 23 nominal epithets are listed on the left, and the 11 adjectival epithets used in addition to *tua* are listed across the top. For each combination the range of dates and number of observed occurrences is given. In the great majority of cases, a nominal epithet occurs alone with *tua*; in 98 cases a single adjectival epithet is added, and in 81 a double adjective. In addition, certain honorifics occur much more frequently than others. Specifically, the eight nominal terms *gravitas* ('gravity'), *sublimitas* ('exaltedness'), *sinceritas* ('sincerity'), *auctoritas* ('authority'), *celsitudo* ('highness'), *magnificentia* ('magnificence'), *magnitudo* ('magnitude'), and *culmen* ('highness') appeared 570 times in all; the remaining fifteen terms only 126 times.[20]

The earliest attested use of a *tua*-epithet comes from the year 293, when a *Rationalis* [*sc. rei summae*] ('Accountant [of the Revenues]')—the precursor of the *Comes sacrarum largitionum* ('Count of the Sacred Largesses')[21]—was addressed as 'gravitas tua' (*CJ* 10. 10. 1). A similar use had been around for some time. In the early third century, provincial governors

[19] Some documents have multiple epithets, and individual constitutions often were subdivided to make several entries in the law codes. As a result, the total number of original documents would be rather less than the total number of examples. In addition, many entries in the Theodosian Code appear again in the Code of Justinian; in such cases, usually only the Theodosian citation will be given here. And one must note the *de rigueur* caveat that the following discussion is based on the evidence at hand, which itself is dependent on the vagaries of survival.

[20] For a preference for substantives ending in *-tas*, *-tudo*, and *-tia* for imperial honorifics, see Honig, *Humanitas*, 103–25. Several of these terms had a long tradition in Roman rhetoric, note, e.g. Cicero, *De oratore* 1. 49, 'Si audierit hanc auctoritatem gravitatis . . . prudentia tamen rerum magnarum . . .'; ibid. 2. 56, 'Tanta in Domitio gravitas, tanta auctoritas'.

[21] The title had been changed by 340: see *CTh* 12. 1. 30: 340, and Cosenza, *Positions*, 71.

TABLE 11.1: Occurrences of Combinations of Nominal and Adjectival Honorifics Attested in Late Roman Legal Documents

Nominal Forms	Adjectival Forms			
	TUA alone	**Excellens**	**Miranda**	**Laudabilis**
Gravitas	(39) 293–403			
Devotio	(6) *c.*300–26			
Sollertia	(3) *c.*300–65			
Prudentia	(5) *c.*300–58+530*			(1) 358
Experientia	(6) 305–97			(3) 375–82
Dicatio	(4) 311–68			
Sublimitas	(128) 317–537	(1) 336	(1) 357	(1) 357
Sinceritas	(41) 319–99+535*			(3) 365–80
Auctoritas	(12) 327–96	(3) 363–97		(1) 384
Excellentia	(14) 335–460+535*			
Celsitudo	(45) 349–563			
Magnificentia	(39) 364–458+534*			
Laudabilitas	(4) 365–400			
Eminentia	(21) 365–538	(2) 386–98		
Amplitudo	(19) 366–524			
Culmen	(39) 368–529			
Magnitudo	(62) 369–570			
Praestantia	(6) 371–421			
Claritas	(4) 386–451+535*			
Spectabilitas	(7) 386–429			
Sollicitudo	(2) 410			
Eximietas	(1) 421			
Gloria	(5) 534–68			

Adjectival Forms			
Praecelsa	**Sublimis**	**Inlustris**	**Magnifica**
(3) 367			
(3) 367–82		(1) 365	(1) 364
(1) 392	(3) 360–94	(31) 364–458+535*	(3) 364–5
	(1) 440		
	(7) 391–465	(14) 380–458	
	(4) 389		
	(3) 393		
		(1) 369	

Table 11.1: (*cont'd*)

Nominal Forms	Adjectival Forms				
	Laudanda & Spectata	**Egregia**	**Spectata**	**Praecellens**	**Insignis**
Gravitas					
Devotio					
Sollertia					
Prudentia					
Experientia					
Dicatio					
Sublimitas		(1) 368			
Sinceritas	(1) 378–9		(2) 368–70		
Auctoritas				(1) 392	(2) 396–8
Excellentia					
Celsitudo					
Magnificentia					
Laudabilitas					
Eminentia					
Amplitudo					
Culmen					
Magnitudo					
Praestantia					
Claritas					
Spectabilitas					
Sollicitudo					
Eximietas					
Gloria					

Adjectival Forms			
Inlustris & Magnifica	**Sublimis & Magnifica**	**Inlustris & Praecelsa**	**Gloriosus & Eminentissimus**
(33) 438–582	(1) 441		(1) 542
(1) 385			
		(33) 420–73	
		(10) 419–52	

* In a few cases, two terminal dates are given, viz. the end of the first set of occurrences, followed by the short-lived revival in the 530s.
Numerals in brackets indicate number of occurrences.

were said to possess 'sua gravitas' ('their own gravity') or 'sua auctoritas' ('their own authority').[22] This kind of terminology appears to have evolved into epithets using *tua* that were applied directly to the officials themselves.[23]

Other *tua*-honorifics appear shortly thereafter. A constitution issued to the proconsul of Africa *c.*293/305 addressed him as 'sollertia tua' ('Your Sagacity'), 'prudentia tua' ('Your Prudence') and 'devotio tua' ('Your Devotion').[24] Other honorifics quickly materialize, the most common being 'sublimitas tua', 'sinceritas tua', and 'auctoritas tua', which are first attested in 317 (*CTh* 12. 1. 4), 319 (*CTh* 9. 40. 3), and 327 (*CTh* 1. 5. 2) respectively.[25] Also surfacing are 'experientia tua' ('Your Competence'), in 305 (*CJ* 3. 12. 1), and 'dicatio tua' ('Your Dedication') in 311.[26] One notes at once that some nominal epithets, such as 'sinceritas tua' and 'gravitas tua', refer to personal qualities, whereas others, like 'auctoritas tua' and 'sublimitas tua', allude to the prestige and sense of superiority bestowed by one's office. Indeed, these four epithets provide a convenient cross-section of the types of honorifics that were used, and had a very long shelf-life, eventually being utilized more than any others.[27]

Some terms served something of an all-purpose function. Before *c.*365, *gravitas* and *sinceritas* were applied indiscriminately to officials ranging from Praetorian Prefect,[28] of the highest rank, to *Praeses* ('Governor') and *Rationalis*;[29] and even,

[22] 'Gravitas sua': *CJ* 5. 62. 16: 244, 2. 26. 4 and 3. 34. 5: 246, 2. 26. 4: 286, and 2. 3. 18: 287; 'auctoritas sua': *CJ* 4. 37. 7: 222, 9. 42. 1: 287, and 8. 13. 10: 290.

[23] Occasionally, *vestra* was used, but only with Praetorian Prefects, e.g. 'celsitudinis vestrae' (*CTh* 1. 16. 5: 329, *CTh* 11. 25. 1: 393, *CJ* 1. 50. 2: 427); 'culminis vestri' (*CTh* 1. 29. 3: 368); 'gravitatis vestrae' (*CTh* 8. 5. 3: 326); 'magnificentia vestra' (*CJ* 1. 50. 2: 427); 'amplitudinis vestra' (*Nov. Val.* 35: 452); and 'magnitudo vestra' (*CTh* 16. 2. 42: 416).

[24] *Collat. Mos.* 15. 3. 1. *PLRE I*, 473–4, suggests a date of 300/3 based on the proconsular *fasti*. *Devotio* also appears in 311: S. Riccobono, J. Baviera, C. Ferrini, J. Furlani, V. Arangio-Ruiz (eds.), *Fontes iuris Romani antejustiniani. In usum scholarum*[2] (Florence, 1968–72), no. 93.

[25] Not to mention *celsitudo*, which appears in 329 with *vestra* rather than *tua* (*CTh* 1. 16. 5).

[26] Riccobono *et al.*, *Fontes*, no. 93.

[27] *Gravitas* is attested 39 times, *sinceritas* 53, *auctoritas* 90, and *sublimitas* 135.

[28] *Gravitas*: *CTh* 14. 8. 1: 315; *sinceritas*: *CJ* 12. 50. 3: 357.

[29] *Praeses*: *CTh* 2. 6. 2: 319 (*gravitas*); 9. 40. 3: 319 (*sinceritas*); *Rationalis summae*: *CJ* 10. 10. 1: 293, 3. 26. 7: 349; *Rationalis rei privatae* 10. 13. 1: 317 (*gravitas*).

in the case of *gravitas*, to the *ordo* (town council) of the city of Constantina.[30] *Sollertia*, too, was used for a Praetorian Prefect in 333 (*CTh* 8. 1. 3), along with the aforementioned Proconsul and a Vicar in 365 (*CTh* 11. 1. 13). It may have been felt that terms alluding to 'personal qualities' were not position or rank specific: *devotio* was used for officials ranging from a Praetorian Prefect (*CTh* 7. 20. 1: 318), to the Proconsul mentioned above, to a *Rationalis* (*CJ* 10. 13. 1: 317);[31] and *prudentia*, which reappeared *c.*350, was used for a Praetorian Prefect and a *Comes*.[32]

Other terms, however, seem to have been more office-specific. 'Auctoritas tua', for example, was reserved for Praetorian Prefects in its three occurrences prior to 360 (*CTh* 1. 5. 2: 327, 8. 5. 5: 354, 1. 5. 5: 355), as was 'excellentia tua', which first appears in 335,[33] and 'celsitudo tua', first seen in 349.[34] The introduction of these new terms, both of which clearly refer to the exalted nature of the position, surely were intended to put some distance between Praetorian Prefects and lower-ranking officials, who continued to be endowed with 'all-purpose' epithets such as 'gravitas tua' and 'sinceritas tua'. But even the lower-ranking offices did not go wanting, for other terms seem to have come to be associated with them. 'Dicatio tua' and 'experientia tua' seem to have been preferred for officials of lesser status,[35] and

[30] *CJ* 10. 32. 20: 340. *Gravitas* also was used in 325 (*CTh* 1. 15. 1) to refer to a *Magister Italiae* ('Master of Italy'), an otherwise unknown term that seems to be a synonym for a *Vicarius* ('Vicar') (see *PLRE I*, 685). And note also that the appellation 'serenitas tua' given in the *Consultatio veteris iuris consulti* to an Urban Prefect in 365 is surely an error for 'sinceritas tua'; cf. *CTh* 8. 5. 22: 365.

[31] The term last appears in 326, used for an indeterminate official (*CTh* 7. 22. 2). For discussion of its later manifestations, see P. M. Conti, *'Devotio' e 'viri devoti' in Italia da Diocleziano ai Carolingi* (Padua, 1971).

[32] *CTh* 9. 17. 2: 349; *CTh* 7. 1. 4 refers to 'Cretio v.c. comes' as 'prudentia tua', and is dated in the MSS to 350, but for *c.*357/61, see *PLRE I*, 231.

[33] *CTh* 12. 12. 10: 335, 9. 17. 2–3: 349, 7. 1. 3: 349, 11. 34. 2: 355. Hirsch, 'Rangtitel', 676, erroneously dates the inception of this title to 349.

[34] *CTh* 9. 17. 2: 349 (with *excellentia* and *celsitudo*), 11. 16. 8: 357; *celsitudo* had first appeared in 329, but with *vestra* (*CTh* 1. 16. 5).

[35] *Dicatio*: a *Corrector* in 313 (*CTh* 11. 30. 1), a Proconsul in 340 (*CTh* 11. 30. 21), and a *Comes rei privatae c.*368 (*CTh* 5. 14. 4), the last attested occurrence (and note that not until 372 did the *Comes rei privatae* even outrank proconsuls: *CTh* 6. 9. 1). *Experientia*: a *Praeses* in 305 (*CJ* 3. 12. 1); see also discussion below.

'sublimitas tua', which initially had been used occasionally for officials of middle rank—military Counts and Vicars[36]—after *c*.360 is attested only for the offices of Proconsul (the highest-ranking *spectabilis*) and higher. In general, the period before *c*.360 does not seem to exhibit a great deal of standardization or method in the use of epithets: some were specific, others were not.

Circa 360 and thereafter, however, there were further developments in the employment of honorifics, which no doubt were connected to the concurrent evolution of the status distinctions of *inlustris*, *spectabilis*, and *clarissimus*.[37] For one thing, one observes a vast increase in the number of occurrences. *Circa* 290–360, some 65 examples of the use of honorifics appear; but for the decade 360–9 alone, 73 are encountered.[38] The post-360 era also saw a great expansion in the variety of epithets used. Several new ones which went on to become very common appear, such as 'magnificentia tua', 'magnitudo tua', and 'culminis tui', first attested in 364 (*CTh* 1. 6. 2, 14. 22. 1, 12. 12. 3), 365 (*CTh* 12. 6. 5), and 368 (*CTh* 1. 29. 3) respectively. Curiously, *culmen* appears only in the genitive form (*culminis*), and was used only for civil officials, perhaps being an allusion to a judicial tribunal. And *magnificentia*, one might note, was a term that as recently as 320 had been used as an honorific to refer to the emperor himself.[39] A number of less common epithets also surface at this time: 'eminentia tua' ('Your Eminence') (*CTh* 10. 1. 9) and 'laudabilitas tua' ('Your Praiseworthiness') (*CTh* 10. 19. 3) by 365; and 'amplitudo tua' ('Your Amplitude') (*CTh* 8. 7. 9) by 366. And *sollertia*, not seen since *c*.300, makes its only other appearance at the same time (*CTh* 11. 1. 13: 365).

[36] Counts: *CTh* 12. 1. 4: 317 (*Comes Hispaniarum*), 12. 1. 33: 342 (*Comes Orientis*); Vicars: *CTh* 1. 15. 2: 348, 14. 1. 1: 357.

[37] See above, and note in particular the efforts of Valentinian I (364–75) to establish rules for determining precedence (*CTh* 6. 7. 1, 6. 9. 1, 6. 11. 1, 6. 22. 4, all sections of the same law of 372).

[38] The disparity cannot be accounted for simply by different survival rates: see the tables in O. Seeck, *Regesten der Kaiser und Päpste für die Jahre 311 bis 476 n. Chr.* (Stuttgart, 1919).

[39] *CTh* 12. 46. 1: 'Constantinus A. dixit, "iam tunc magnificentia mea . . ."'.

Many of these terms were more or less office-specific. *Magnificentia*,[40] *culmen*,[41] and *magnitudo*,[42] for example, are attested only for officials who held the highest-ranking offices. The same continued to be the case with *celsitudo*,[43] although *auctoritas* was occasionally used for officials of rather lesser rank, perhaps on occasions where special emphasis was given to the exercise of 'authority'.[44] *Eminentia* and *amplitudo* likewise are only attested for illustrious civil officials.[45] The introduction of these new honorifics may have been a response to a perceived banality or vulgarization of the existing terms, and an attempt to emphasize the especially exalted status of illustrious offices. But this does not mean that lower-ranking officials were neglected, for they too seem to have received their own idiosyncratic status designators. For example, *sollertia* and *laudabilitas*, terms alluding to personal qualities, seem to have been reserved for officials of *spectabilis* rank, being attested only for two Vicars and a *Comes metallorum* ('Count of the Mines').[46]

But for the least exalted of the senatorial officials there was no new terminology forthcoming. They made do with the occasional 'gravitas tua' or 'sinceritas tua'.[47] It would seem

[40] From 390 and earlier, for Praetorian Prefects (*CTh* 8. 4. 12: 372, 6. 29. 7: 390); Urban Prefects (*CTh* 1. 6. 2, 14. 22. 1: 364, 13. 3. 11: 376, 8. 9. 2: 382, 8. 7. 16: 385, 13. 3. 13: 387); and a *Comes rei privatae* (*CTh* 4. 22. 3: 389).

[41] From 390 and earlier, for the offices of Praetorian Prefect (*CTh* 1. 29. 3: 368, *CJ* 12. 17. 1: 387); and Urban Prefect (*CJ* 1. 43. 1: 385/9).

[42] For 390 and before, for the offices of Praetorian Prefect (*CJ* 11. 13. 1: 369; 11. 22. 3: 387); and Urban Prefect (*CTh* 8. 9. 2: 382; 15. 1. 27: 390).

[43] Attested for Praetorian Prefect (*CTh* 8. 8. 4: 386) and Urban Prefect (*CTh* 1. 6. 6: 365).

[44] A vicar in 377 (*CTh* 16. 6. 2) and a *Comes domorum* in 396 (*CTh* 10. 1. 15 = *CJ* 7. 38. 3). For its continued use with illustrious offices, note the offices of Praetorian Prefect (*CTh* 5. 13. 17: 364, 1. 29. 3: 368, 13. 13. 7: 371, *CJ* 11. 11. 3: 379?); Master of Soldiers (*CTh* 7. 1. 8: 365, 7. 1. 9: 367); Urban Prefect (*CJ* 2. 6. 7: 370, 1. 43. 1: 386).

[45] *Eminentia*: an Urban Prefect (*CTh* 10. 1. 9: 365) and a Praetorian Prefect (*CTh* 13. 5. 14: 371). Note also *CTh* 1. 16. 3, 'eminentissima praefectura', in 313, as well as the hybrid usage, in *CTh* 12. 12. 3 of 364 to a Praetorian Prefect, 'ad sedis tuae eminentiam'. *Amplitudo*: a Praetorian Prefect (*CTh* 8. 7. 9: 366).

[46] *Sollertia*: *CTh* 11. 1. 13: 365 (*Vicarius Africae* ('Vicar of Africa')). *Laudabilitas*: *CTh* 10. 19. 3: 365 (*Comes metallorum*), *CTh* 1. 15. 9: 378 (*Vicarius*). For the associated status designator 'vir laudabilis', see Hirschfeld, 'Rangtitel', 677–8.

[47] 'Gravitas tua': used for the offices of *Praefectus augustalis* (*CTh* 12. 1. 80: 380, still of *clarissimus* status: see *CJ* 1. 37. 1 of 386, but *spectabilis* by *c*.400: *Not. dig. or.*

that as far as the emperors were concerned, truly significant status accrued only to those who managed to rise above entry-level senatorial rank. If so, it would indicate that the emperors were well aware of the problem of 'rank inflation', and by their dispensing of honorifics distinguished those whose status was of an exceptional nature.

At the same time, adjectival forms—hitherto attested in only one instance[48]—began to be added rather frequently to the nominal epithets, presumably to endow the recipients with even greater lustre. Many of them were simply adjectival forms of honorifics already in use. *Laudabilis* (from *laudabilitas*) is encountered first in 357 (*CTh* 11. 30. 27), *sublimis* (from *sublimitas*) in 360 (*CTh* 16. 2. 15), *inlustris* (from *vir inlustris*) in 363 (*CTh* 11. 30. 31), *magnifica* (from *magnificentia*) in 364 (*CTh* 5. 13. 15),[49] and *praecelsa* ('very high') (from *celsitudo*) in 367 (*CTh* 10. 15. 4).

Spectata, which first appears in 368 (*Epist. imp.* 9), was of course derived from the designation *vir spectabilis*; its appearance anticipated that of the corresponding nominal epithet, 'spectabilitas tua', not encountered until 386 (*Sirm.* 8). A few rarely occurring adjectival epithets, such as *miranda* ('marvellous') and *egregia* ('outstanding') lacked corresponding nominal forms: each appears only a single time, in 357 (*CTh* 8. 5. 9) and 368 (*Epist. imp.* 8) respectively.[50] The first instance was early, and may not have caught on for the very reason that it did not have a matching nominal form. And *egregia*, if its use paralleled that of *spectata*, may have recalled the old rank-classification *vir egregius*.[51] But that term was a

57, and *CJ* 7. 62. 32: 440, where it ranks second after the proconsulate), *Consularis* (*CTh* 8. 5. 27: 365, *CJ* 1. 31. 1: 368), and *Praeses* (*CTh* 6. 31. 1: 365, *CJ* 12. 24. 1: 373, *CTh* 11. 23. 3: 396); and *Praefectus annonae* (*CTh* 13. 6. 5: 367, 14. 3. 21: 403, the last attested use of 'gravitas tua'), an official certainly of *spectabilis* rank by 397, although perhaps only recently so (*CTh* 12. 6. 24, where he ranks below vicars). 'Sinceritas tua': used for a *Consularis* (*CTh* 15. 1. 17: 365) and a *Praefectus annonae* (*CTh* 14. 17. 3: 365).

[48] In *Sirm.* 4: 335, a Praetorian Prefect was described as 'excellens sublimitas tua'.

[49] And locutions such as 'magnifica sedes tua' (*CTh* 8. 5. 19 and 12. 12. 4: 364) likewise first appear in the mid-360s.

[50] *Inlustris* also lacked a nominal form, but its use would have been based upon the existing status designator *vir inlustris*; and the unique adjectival form *praecellens* (*CTh* 9. 45. 1: 392) appears to be a hybrid of *praecelsa* and *excellens*.

[51] Jones, *LRE*, 525–6.

designation of mere equestrian status: perhaps someone realized that, and as a result the term was never used again.

In sum, the 40 years from the late 350s through the 390s were the great heyday of combination epithets. As seen in Table 11.1, there survive no less than thirty two combinations of eleven nominal forms (*auctoritas*, *celsitudo*, *eminentia*, *excellentia*, *experientia*, *magnificentia*, *magnitudo*, *praestantia*, *prudentia*, *sinceritas*, *sublimitas*) and eleven adjectival forms (*egregia*, *excellens*, *inlustris*, *insignis*, *laudabilis/laudanda*, *magnifica*, *miranda*, *praecellens*, *praecelsa*, *spectata*, *sublimis*). But only a relatively small number of nominal forms were heavily used with adjectives. In the entire sample, *auctoritas* appears 76 times with 10 different adjectives, *magnificentia* 53 times with 13, *magnitudo* 13 with 2, *sinceritas* 10 with 6, *sublimitas* 7 with 5, and *eminentia* 6 with 2. Five other nominal forms (*celsitudo*, *excellentia*, *experientia*, *praestantia*, *prudentia*) appear a total of 7 times with only a single adjective each, and the remaining 12 nominal forms are not attested with any adjectives besides *tua*. On the other hand, 5 of the adjectival forms (*egregia*, *insignis*, *miranda*, *praecellens*, *spectata*) appear a total of only 8 times, each with only one nominal form.

Like the nominal epithets, several adjectival terms were office or rank specific. Some of the applications are obvious. For example, *inlustris* appears only with illustrious offices,[52] and *spectata* with those of *spectabilis* rank: a Proconsul (*CJ* 11. 75. 2: 368/70) and a Vicar (*Epist. imp.* 9: 368; ibid. 13: 378/9). Likewise, the later nominal terms *spectabilitas* and *claritas*, both of which first appear in 386, would only be used for offices carrying those ranks.[53]

[52] e.g. a Praetorian Prefect (*CTh* 11. 30. 31: 363), an Urban Prefect (*Epist.imp.*10: 368/9), a Master of Soldiers (*CTh* 6. 24. 6: 395), a Master of Offices (*CTh* 6. 27. 23: 430), a *Comes rei privatae* (*Nov. Theo.* 5. 1: 438), a *Comes sacrarum largitionum* (*Nov. Val.* 7. 3: 447), and an undetermined financial Count in 444 (*Nov. Val.* 6. 3).

[53] *Spectabilitas*, e.g. for a Proconsul (*Sirm.* 8: 386); a *Comes rei privatae* (then of *spectabilis* status, having been *clarissimus* until 372 (*CTh* 6. 9. 1); both he and the *Comes sacrarum largitionum* became *illustres* shortly after 390: see Cosenza, *Positions*, 81; *CJ* 9. 27. 7: 390); a *Vicarius urbis Romae* ('Vicar of the City of Rome') (*CTh* 12. 1. 162: 399); and a *Castrensis* (Chamberlain) (*CTh* 6. 32. 1: 416). *Claritas*, e.g. for an Augustal Prefect (then of *clarissimus* status) (*CJ* 1. 37. 1: 386); and a *Consularis* (*ACO* 2. 3. 1. 21: 451).

Combinations of terms seem to have acquired special meaning. The employment of adjectival forms with *auctoritas*, for example, is instructive. They occur ten times between 363 and 397, all but once in the east.[54] Aside from its use with *inlustris*, different combinations tend to be used for different offices. Between 363 and 397, 'sublimis auctoritas tua' (*CTh* 16. 2. 15: 360, 8. 5. 35: 378, 12. 1. 139: 394) and 'excellens auctoritas tua' (*CTh* 8. 5. 16: 363, 7. 7. 1: 365/85, 16. 8. 2: 397) are used three times each and only for Praetorian Prefects; 'insignis auctoritas tua' appears twice for a *Magister militum* ('Master of Soldiers') (*CTh* 8. 5. 56: 396, 7. 7. 3: 398); and 'praecellens auctoritas tua' for a *Comes sacrarum largitionum* (*CTh* 9. 45. 1: 392). Only 'magnifica auctoritas tua' did double duty, being used for the offices of both Praetorian Prefect (*CTh* 5. 13. 15: 364, *CTh* 11. 16. 11: 365) and Master of Soldiers (*CTh* 7. 4. 12: 364). As the only exception, the term 'laudabilis auctoritas tua' was used in 384 for a *Praefectus augustalis* (Augustal Prefect) (*Sirm.* 3: 384), a clearly non-illustrious official. But in this instance the adjective *laudabilis* would have provided an indicator of the recipient's rank, given that, as seen above, the associated nominal form, *laudabilitas*, was customarily used for non-illustrious officials.[55] Indeed, the associated form, *laudanda*, was used in a similar manner in 378/9, when a Vicar of Rome was addressed as 'laudanda et spectata sinceritas tua' (*Epist. imp.* 13): if the *laudanda* did not make his *spectabilis* status sufficiently clear, the *spectata* certainly did.

Other examples likewise attest to some clustering of usages that suggest some differences between eastern and western preferences. For example, the terms *experientia* and *praestantia* ('pre-eminence'), which occur nine times between 371 and 414, appear nearly always in the east, with *experientia* being used exclusively for officials of *spectabilis* rank: Proconsuls, Dukes, and a *Comes rei privatae* ('Count of the Privy

[54] The exception being the Gallic poet Ausonius in 378 (*CTh* 8. 5. 35): 'sublimis auctoritas tua'.

[55] For the term *laudabilis* being applied to *spectabiles*, see also Symm. *Relat.* 23. 3. 4, 26. 3, for a 'v.c. et laudabilis vicarius'; for discussion, see Hirsch, 'Rantgitel', 677–8.

Purse').[56] The phrase 'sublimis magnitudo tua' occurs three times, all in 393 and all in the east (*CTh* 5. 13. 33, 8. 5. 52, 16. 8. 9); similarly, 'sublimis magnificentia tua' (*CTh* 7. 1. 13: 391; *CJ* 8. 11. 9: 393; *CTh* 10. 6. 1: 395) and 'inlustris magnificentia tua' (*CTh* 9. 27. 2: 380, 14. 17. 12: 393, 6. 4. 26: 393) occur three times each between 380 and 395;[57] and 'excellens eminentia tua' is found twice, in 396 and 398 (*CTh* 9. 38. 9: 396; 15. 1. 38: 398), all only in the east. Subsequently, however, between 405 and 458, 'sublimis magnificentia tua'[58] and 'inlustris magnificentia tua'[59] are attested ten times in the west, but only once, in 415, in the east.[60] What this pattern says, if anything, about east–west co-ordination, or the lack of it, is unclear.[61]

On the other hand, between 364 and 382 ten combinations of *sinceritas*, with *magnifica* (*CTh* 14. 2. 1: 364), *spectata* (*Epist. imp.* 9: 368; *CJ* 11. 75. 2: 368/70; *Epist. imp.* 13: 378/9) *laudabilis* (*CTh* 8. 5. 22: 365; *CTh* 14. 3. 17: 380), *praecelsa* (*CTh* 10. 15. 4: 367; *CTh* 14. 9. 1: 370; *CTh* 1. 6. 8: 382), and *inlustris* (*CTh* 1. 6. 6: 365), occur only in the west. Likewise, the compounds 'praecelsa sublimitas tua' (*Epist. imp.* 5–7: 367) and 'egregia sublimitas tua' (*Epist. imp.* 8: 368) are only attested being applied to Prefects of Rome—and only in the years 367–8. A related term, 'sublimis eminentia tua',

[56] *Experientia*, used for Proconsuls: K. G. Bruns (ed.), *Fontes* 97, 371; C. R. Zacharia, A. Lingenthal (eds.), *Ius Graecoromanum*. i: *Novellae et aureae bullae imperatorum post Justinianum* (Athens, 1931; repr. Aalen, 1962), 100: 375; and *CTh* 16. 5. 28: 395; *Duces*: *CTh* 16. 10. 8: 382, 8. 5. 57: 397; and the *Comes rei privatae*: *CTh* 10. 10. 16: 382. *Experientia* also had appeared once before, in 305, referring to a *Praeses* (*CJ* 3. 12. 1). The one western application was for a *Vicarius Romae* in 390 (*Collat. Mos.* 3. 1). *Praestantia*: Bruns, *Fontes*, 97, 371, and *CTh* 7. 18. 8: 383, Proconsuls; and *CTh* 11. 16. 12: 380, a *Comes rei privatae*. *Praestantia* also was used for higher-ranking officials, but usually accompanied by some qualifying word to make the status clear; e.g. in 369 a western Praetorian Prefect was referred to as 'illustris praestantia tua' (*CTh* 8. 7. 10). In the early fifth century, it was applied twice to Masters of Soldiers: *CTh* 7. 17. 1: 412, 1. 7. 4: 414.

[57] Interestingly, the latter two of these then occur six times between 405 and 412, only in the west.

[58] *Sirm.* 2: 405; 12: 407; and 11: 412; also *Nov. Sev.* 2: 465.

[59] *Sirm.* 9: 408, 16: 408, 14: 409, *Epist. Imp.* 21: 419, *Nov. Val.* 8. 1: 441, 8. 2: 441, 6. 2: 443, 15: 445, 28: 450, *Nov. Maj.* 4: 458.

[60] *CTh* 1. 7. 4 = *CJ* 1. 29. 2, to a Master of Soldiers.

[61] Honoré, *Law*, 41–106, 216–43, gives no indication that there were any correlations in style between east and west during this time, save for wondering (p. 238) whether there was 'a danger that western and eastern law may diverge'.

was applied four times, all in 382, to Urban Prefects, twice of Constantinople (*CTh* 14. 17. 9, 15. 1. 25) and twice of Rome (*CTh* 11. 30. 49, 14. 4. 5). Such patterns could reflect stylistic preferences of the clerk or *Quaestor sacri palatii* ('Quaestor of the Sacred Palace') responsible for drafting the legislation.[62]

Meanwhile, 'gravitas tua', which had been important before the 360s, appears to have been degraded in significance after the appearance of the new honorifics reserved for illustrious offices. Whereas it had been used to refer to a Praetorian or Urban Prefect five times before the mid-330s, it subsequently was used thus only once, in 364 (*CTh* 7. 4. 11: 364). Its later usage was limited to offices of middle to lower status, ranging from *Praeses*[63] and *Consularis* ('Governor') (*CTh* 8. 5. 27: 365; *CJ* 1. 31. 1: 368), up to *Praefectus annonae* ('Prefect of the Food Supply') (*CTh* 13. 6. 5: 367, 14. 3. 21: 403), *Vicarius* (*CTh* 1. 30. 29: 362), *Dux* ('Duke') (*CTh* 15. 1. 13: 364), and *Praefectus augustalis* (*CTh* 12. 1. 80: 380).

Yet another developmental stage appears beginning *c.*400, by which time the rank-classifications of *clarissimus*, *spectabilis*, and *inlustris* had become firmly established. *Tua*-honorifics now come to be applied only rarely to non-illustrious officials: between 400 and 429 only five examples survive; indeed, by this time few of the surviving constitutions were addressed to non-illustrious officials at all.[64] On the rare occasions when they did merit honorifics, specifically non-illustrious epithets were used—'spectabilitas tua' thrice and 'laudabilitas tua' once each for the offices of Proconsul and *Castrensis*,[65] both of *spectabilis* rank. And 'sollicitudo tua' was used to distinguish an official of mere *clarissimus* rank, a *Tribunus et notarius* ('Tribune and Notary'),

[62] Honoré, *Law*, 59, suggests that the author of all but the third of the laws of 382 was the *Quaestor* Nicomachus Flavianus: the *Quaestor* was the member of the *comitatus* who supervised the drafting of legislation.

[63] *CJ* 10. 26. 2: 364; *CTh* 6. 31. 1: 365; *CJ* 12. 24. 1: 373; *CTh* 11. 23. 3: 396.

[64] In the *CJ*, for example, nineteen instances, all to *spectabiles*, and none after 429; in the *CTh*, only twenty examples.

[65] Proconsuls, in 400 as 'laudabilitas tua' (*CTh* 12. 1. 166), and as 'spectabilitas tua' in 419 (*Epist. imp.* 35) and 429 (twice) (*CTh* 12. 1. 185–6); a *Castrensis* in 416 as 'spectabilitas tua' (*CTh* 6. 32. 1).

in 411.[66] On the other hand, the lone occurrence of 'eximietas tua', another newcomer, is found in 421 being used for an Urban Prefect (*Corp. leg.* no. 1174).

These observations suggest that by *c*.400 there was an increasing practice of applying honorifics only to the highest-ranking officials. In cases where honorifics certainly would have been found in the late fourth century, none are found in the fifth. For example, an unedited document addressed to a non-illustrious official—a *Consularis Tusciae Suburbicariae* ('Governor of Suburban Tuscany')—in 459 includes no honorifics at all, only the directive, 'Unde, Rogatiane karissime . . .' ('Whence, dearest Rogatianus . . .') (*Nov. Maj.* 9).

Related to this phenomenon, it seems, is the disappearance of honorifics that in the past had been used to refer to non-illustrious officials. 'Experientia tua', 'sinceritas tua', 'laudabilitas tua', and 'gravitas tua' are old-timers that are last seen, in any combination, in 397 (*CTh* 8. 5. 57), 399 (*CTh* 13. 1. 16), 400 (*CTh* 12. 1. 166), and 403 (*CTh* 14. 3. 21) respectively.[67] 'Praestantia tua' is not found after 414 (*CTh* 1. 7. 4). And 'auctoritas tua' by itself disappears after 396 (*CTh* 10. 1. 15 = *CJ* 7. 38. 3), although, as will be seen below, it enjoyed continued life coupled with adjectival epithets. It is quite likely that these epithets fell out of use at least in part because of their association with non-illustrious offices. This kind of marginalization of senators without illustrious status culminated at some time in the mid-fifth century, when such persons lost the opportunity to serve as members of the Senates of Rome and Constantinople, a privilege that henceforward was open only to those of illustrious rank.[68]

[66] *Corp. leg.* no. 1163. The only other appearance of this term is in *Consultatio* 7. 1, in an unattributed ruling addressed to an unnamed official: 'adde dum sollicitudinis tuae cura tractavit'. It perhaps dates to the late fourth century.

[67] See below for an archaizing reuse of 'sinceritas tua' in the 530s.

[68] See Jones, *LRE*, 529. A constitution of Marcian of 450 noted, 'Nemo ex clarissimis et spectabilibus qui in provinciis degunt ad praeturam postea devocetur' ('No one from among the *clarissimi* and *spectabiles* who lives in the provinces may be summoned later to the praetorship'): this effectively prevented those of non-illustrious ranks from becoming members of the Senate. By the time the *Corpus iuris civilis* was issued in 533, this practice had become institutionalized, as attested by an interpolation in Ulpian in the *Digest*: 'Senatores autem accipiendum est eos, qui a patriciis et consulibus usque ad omnes illustres viros descendunt, quia et hi

One can only speculate as to what officials of lower rank thought about being excluded from the receipt of *tua*-honorifics in documents emanating from the imperial chanceries. Perhaps a hint of their sentiments can be inferred from the participation of the *Tribunus et notarius* Marcellinus in the Council of Carthage of 411, where he twice referred to himself as 'dicatio mea',[69] using an honorific that is last attested in an imperial document *c.*368 (*CTh* 5. 14. 4). In addition, these terms continued to be used outside secular officialdom to grant additional resplendence to officials who would not otherwise have merited them. On the same occasion, Marcellinus was addressed by the African bishop Petilianus as 'magnificentia tua', a flattering appellation that no emperor would have accorded him.[70] Similar adulatory employment was made at this time of the honorifics 'sinceritas tua', 'praestantia tua', and 'prudentia tua'.[71] As a result, honorifics that were no longer utilized in official parlance retained something of their glamour by being reprised in other situations. And their continued use in this manner demonstrates how well that not only secular but also ecclesiastical dignitaries understood exactly what their significance was.

The fifth century also saw a tightening of the procedures regarding compound epithets. The great days of mixing and matching were over. For the 180 years after 400 CE, seventy five of the seventy six surviving examples of compounds represent only seven combinations utilizing only three nominal usages (*auctoritas*, *magnificentia*, and *magnitudo*) and three adjectival forms (*inlustris*, *magnifica*, and *sublimis*).[72] Furthermore, different combinations of the surviving *tua*-epithets came into favour in the east and west.[73] Between 420 and 445, for example, 'sublimitas tua' is found twenty five times, all

soli in senatu sententiam dicere possunt' ('It must be accepted, moreover, that the senators are those who are descended from patricians and consuls, as well as all the illustrious men, because these alone are able to speak their opinion in the Senate').

[69] *Conc. Carth. a. 411* 1. 10 ('qui dicationi meae . . . praestantur'), 1. 17 ('qui dicationi meae . . . rescribentes'): *SC* 195. 582, 602.

[70] *Conc. Carth. a. 411* 1. 165: *SC* 195. 810; see Lancel, 'Titres', 329.

[71] Lancel, 'Titres', 330.

[72] The exception being 'sublimis excellentia tua' in 440 (*Nov. Val.* 7. 1).

[73] It is difficult to make comparisons after *c.*460, because by this time nearly all the surviving documents are eastern.

but two of them in the east.[74] 'Tui culminis' occurs nineteen times between 412 and 467, again all but once (*Nov. Val.* 33: 451) in the east. And 'magnitudo tua' survives twenty seven times for the period 396–474—all but three times from the east.[75] The atypical western usage of these eastern terms is focused in the 440s, and one wonders whether there might have been some 'easternizing' tendency in the western chancery at this time.[76]

The most striking illustration of the contrasts between eastern and western practices is provided by variants of the terms *magnificentia/magnifica*, which may have been particularly valued in part because, as already noted, this had been an honorific applied to the emperor himself. The simple 'magnificentia tua', in the text of documents, continued to be used in both east and west. But different combinations came to be preferred for the formal concluding address. Between the years 438 and 468, for example, the phrase 'illustris et magnifica auctoritas tua' occurs twenty nine times, all in the east.[77] On the other hand, between 420 and 473, 'illustris et praecelsa magnificentia tua' is found thirty times—all in the west.[78] Likewise, 'inlustris magnificentia tua' and 'sublimis magnificentia tua' occur fourteen times between 405 and 458, all in the west.[79]

Furthermore, by the 440s, in the west at least (where the evidence, in the form of unedited documents, is best), only the highest ranking *inlustres*—Prefects and Masters of Soldiers—received the aforementioned 'full treatment' in the

[74] Until *c.*400, it had been used approximately equally in east and west. Between 400 and 420, it appears ten times in the west and four in the east. Thereafter, it virtually disappears for a time from the west, resurfacing briefly in 429 (*CTh* 12. 6. 32) and 431 (*CTh* 11. 1. 36). It then reappears in the west in 445 (*Nov. Val.* 18; cf. *Nov. Val.* 27: 449).

[75] The exceptions being *Nov. Val.* 7. 1: 440, 18: 445, and 28: 450.

[76] Honoré, *Law*, 271, suggests that the *Quaestor sacri palatii* of 446–7, who would have been responsible for drafting the laws, 'shared the impulses towards modernization that prevailed in the east'. For differences in eastern and western usages, see also Vidén, *Tradition*, 25–31, 77–80, 153–5.

[77] The variant 'sublimis et magnifica auctoritas tua' is attested once (*Nov. Theo.* 5. 3: 441).

[78] A pattern also noticed by Honoré, *Law*, 265–6, who notes that two-thirds of western laws during this period use this formula.

[79] Curiously, as already seen, between 380 and 395 the same phrases were used only in the east.

formal address. Others had to settle for less. Urban Prefects, for example, were merely 'inlustris magnificentia tua',[80] and the *Magister officiorum* ('Master of Offices'), *Comes sacrarum largitionum*, and *Comes rei privatae* were styled 'inlustris auctoritas tua'.[81] Lower-ranking officials, as already noted above, were left out altogether, save for a continued occasional use of 'claritas tua', attested in 451 for an eastern *consularis* (*ACO* 2. 3. 1. 21), and in 535 for a *praeses* (*Nov. Just.* 34)—and even this modest appellation was no more than an acknowledgement of the titular rank of *clarissimus*.

The divergence of practices between east and west fundamentally, of course, would represent one more example of the increasing general administrative gap between east and west after the death of Theodosius I in 395.[82] But whether the dissimilarities arose out of conscious efforts to be different, or merely as a result of the evolution of different practices at the two courts in isolation from each other, is, again, difficult to determine.

After the disappearance of the western imperial court in the 470s, practices involving honorifics in the eastern empire continued as before. For example, 'inlustris et magnifica auctoritas tua' remained the standard form of direct address until the last extant Latin example in 582.[83] Other 'superiority' terms, such as 'culminis tui', 'excellentia tua', 'sublimitas tua', 'eminentia tua', 'celsitudo tua', and 'magnitudo tua' also continued in use, being last attested in 529,[84] 535 (*Nov.*

[80] *Nov. Val.* 8. 1 and 8. 2: 441, 15: 445, 28: 450, *Nov. Maj.* 4: 458; cf. *Epist. imp.* 21: 419. In a single case, a Praetorian Prefect received the appellation, in 443: *Nov. Val.* 6. 2.

[81] *Nov. Val.* 27: 449 (*Magister officiorum*); *Nov. Maj.* 5: 458 (*Comes rei privatae*); *Nov. Val.* 7. 3 and 23: 447 (*Comes sacrarum largitionum*). Also used in 444 for an official addressed 'Hisiodoro comiti', a *Comes* of indeterminate status (*Nov. Val.* 6. 3): J. R. Martindale, *PLRE II*, 628, s.v. 'Isidorus 4', suggests that he also was a *Comes sacrarum largitionum* because he is *inlustris* and is 'styled "frater amantissime", a form of address used in the *novellae* at this period to *magistri officiorum*, *comites sacrarum largitionum* and *comites rei privatae* only.' This is consistent with the titulature, although it also would admit of his having been *Comes rei privatae*.

[82] See e.g. Jones, *LRE*, 342–3, 366–7, 389 ('there was naturally less interchange between East and West').

[83] *Ius Graecoromanum*, no. 13. The use of honorifics continued, of course, in the later Greek documents, but they are beyond the scope of this study.

[84] *De Iustiniano codice confirmando* 3.

Just. 35), 537 (*Nov. Just*. 80), 538 (*Nov. Just*. 68), 563 (*Nov. Just*. 143), and 578 (*Ius Graecoromanum* no. 6) respectively. And, as with *magnificentia* in the past, the popularity of such terms as *culmen* and *celsitudo* could have been a result of their being applied to the emperor.[85] Furthermore, the occasional ascription of *tua*-honorifics to officials of lower rank continued to be restricted to the rank-specific term 'claritas tua', as applied to a *Praeses* in 535.[86]

There are, morever, two intriguing anomalies. Two documents of the 530s revived honorifics that long since had fallen into desuetude. For example, *CJ* 1. 17. 1, issued in 530 to the *Quaestor sacri palatii* Tribonian, and authorizing the issuance of the *Corpus iuris civilis*, rejuvenated the honorifics 'prudentia tua', last used in 357 (*CJ* 12. 50. 3), and 'sinceritas tua', last seen in 399 (*CTh* 13. 1. 16). Is it too much to suggest that the legal staff's rummaging through the archives prior to the publication of the *Codex Justinianus* resulted in the sentimental resurrection of archaic honorifics? 'Prudentia tua', for example, had a long history of application to skilled rhetors;[87] it also was used elsewhere to describe Tribonian.[88]

A similar case is seen in *CJ* 1. 27. 1, issued in 534 and re-establishing the prefecture of Africa. It revived the honorifics 'magnificentia tua' and 'excellentia tua', which are last seen in 458 (*Nov. Maj*. 2) and 460 (*CJ* 2. 7. 11) respectively. This, too, may have been a case of deliberate archaizing, in this case in recognition of the recovery of one of the empire's lost possessions. However that may be, such revivals were

[85] *CJ* 12. 3. 5: 531/3, 'imperatoriam autem celsitudinem'; *CJ* 3. 1. 8: 531, 'ab imperiali culmine'. And 'celsitudo tua' had been rather used, perhaps rather impertinently, by Symmachus in a letter to the emperor Theodosius I, 'desideravi tamen in litteris celsitudinis tuae copiam . . .' ('I longed for the fulsomeness of Your Highness in a letter'). (*Epist*. 10. 1).

[86] *Nov. Just*. 34; also applied to a *consularis*: *Nov. Just*. 166: 564.

[87] e.g. 'Illam disputandi prudentiam' (Cicero, *Partit. orat*. 81); and note also *Nov. Just*. 35, which refers to a deceased Quaestor as a 'prudentissimae memoriae virum' ('a man of most prudent memory'). For rhetors and the law, see Greatrex in this volume.

[88] *CJ* 1. 17. 2, 'prudentissimum magistrum ex quaestore et ex comite Tribonianum' ('the Most Prudent Master [of Offices] Tribonian, an Ex-Quaestor and Ex-Count').

very fleeting. The idea never took hold, and these are the only extant examples of the reuse of obsolete honorifics.[89]

At the same time, in 534, one last new honorific term emerged: 'gloria tua'. A look at *CJ* 1. 27. 2 might help to explain why. Here, the Master of Soldiers Belisarius is referred to as 'magnitudo tua' no less than eleven times in succession. By the end of the document, the bloom must have been off the rose, and perhaps this helps to explain why he then was addressed as 'gloria tua'—another honorific that was associated with the emperor.[90] But even this innovation seems modest compared to some of the extravagances of earlier times: the only variation was the unique use of an adjectival form in the appellation 'gloriosus et eminentissimus auctoritas tua' in 542 (*Nov. Just.* 117). Otherwise, the late sixth century marked the end of the use of Latin honorifics by the imperial chancery. Subsequently, in the seventh century and later, the use of honorifics continued in the Byzantine court, but in Greek.[91]

This overview of the use of *tua*-honorifics by the imperial chanceries during the period *c.*293–578 documents the evolution of a truly 'late Roman' form of according status. Initially granted in a more-or-less haphazard manner to all officials with ranks of *clarissimus* and above, the practice became increasingly structured. In the last half of the fourth century, certain combinations of nominal and adjectival forms became associated with particular ranks and even offices, and differences in eastern and western practices began to emerge. After *c.*400 there was a further systematization of the use of honorifics that remained very stable until the late sixth century.

Indeed, the construction of a chart (Table 11.2) documenting the occurrence of different nominal epithets with

[89] Note also the use of 'nostra auctoritas' in 533 (*CJ* 1. 17. 2), a possible indication that the term had lost its association with imperial officials, being last attested in 396 (*CTh* 10. 1. 15 = *CJ* 7. 38. 3), and now could be used to refer to the emperor.

[90] Note *CJ* 1. 14. 8: 446, 'Id ad beatitudinem nostri imperii et ad nostram gloriam redundare' ('This redounds to the beatitude of Our Power and to Our Glory'). It was used again in 536, in *Nov. Just.* 105, to the *Comes sacrarum largitionum*; and in 540, in *Nov. Just.* 123, where the *Praefectus praetorio Illyrici* ('Praetorian Prefect of Illyricum') was referred to as 'celsitudo tua' three times.

[91] For Greek equivalents of some Latin terms, see Koch, *Beamtentitel*, 127.

TABLE 11.2: Honorifics Attested for Different Offices

	Inlustres						
'Superiority' Terms							
Gloria	PPO 540	MVM 534	PU 568	MagOff 546		CSL 536	
Eximietas			PU 421				
Culmen	PPO 368–529		PU 385–524	MagOff 441–527			PSC 442
Celsitudo	PPO 349–563	MVM 451–518	PU 365–538	MagOff 441–518		CSL 400–536	
Eminentia	PPO 371–538		PU 365–89	MagOff 503–35		CSL 399–535	
Magnificentia	PPO 364–534	MVM 391–445	PU 364–458	MagOff 405–15			CRP 389
Excellentia	PPO 335–534	MVM 365			QSP 535		
Amplitudo	PPO 366–472		PU 441–524	MagOff 450–91		CSL 426	CRP 458
Praestantia	PPO 369	MVM 412–14	PU 421				CRP 380
Magnitudo	PPO 365–570	MVM 473–534	PU 382–474	MagOff 444–527	QSP 526	CSL 426–7	PSC 554
Sublimitas	PPO 331–537	MVM 393–492	PU 321–439	MagOff 395–527	QSP 424–537	CSL 395–450	CRP 345–531
Auctoritas	PPO 327–582	MVM 364–441	PU 368–452	MagOff 438–52	QSP 535	CSL 392–447	
'Personal Quality' Terms							
Prudentia	PPO 349–57				QSP 530		
Sollertia	PPO 333						
Sinceritas	PPO 357–87*	MVM 373	PU 365–99		QSP 535		CRP 365–85
Devotio	PPO 318	MVM 311					
Gravitas	PPO 315–64		PU 326				
Dicatio		MVM 311					CRP 368
Spectabilitas							CRP 398
Experientia							CRP 382
Laudabilitas							
Claritas							
Sollicitudo							

TABLE 11.2: (*cont'd*)

Spectabiles

'Superiority' Terms							
Gloria							
Eximietas							
Culmen							
Celsitudo							
Eminentia							
Magnificentia							
Excellentia	Procos 354						
Amplitudo	Procos 400–401						
Praestantia	Procos 383						
Magnitudo		PrfAug 468					
Sublimitas	Procos 395–6		Comes 317–42		Vicar 348–57		
Auctoritas		PrfAug 384	Comes 396		Vicar 377		
'Personal Quality' Terms							
Prudentia	Procos 297		Comes 350				
Sollertia	Procos 300				Vicar 365		
Sinceritas	Procos 370–71				Vicar 324–88	PrfAnn 365	
Devotio	Procos 297						
Gravitas		PrfAug 380		Dux 349–97	Vicar 321–62	PrfAnn 367–403	PrfVig 314
Dicatio	Procos 340						
Spectabilitas	Procos 386–429	Castren 416			Vicar 399		
Experientia	Procos 371–95			Dux 382			
Laudabilitas	Procos 400		Comes 365	Dux 397	Vicar 378		
Claritas		PrfAug 386					
Sollicitudo							

Clarissimi

Cons 365	Praes 319			
		Rat'is 317		
Cons 300	Praes 319–538	Rat'is 293–349		
			Correc 313	
	Praes 305			
Cons 451	Praes 535			
				Tr&Not 410

Abbreviations of offices: Castr (*Castrensis*), Cons (*Consularis*), Correc (*Corrector*), CRP (*Comes rei privatae*), CSL (*Comes sacrarum largitionum*), MagOff (*Magister officiorum*), MVM (*Magister utriusque militiae*), Praes (*Praeses*), PrfAnn (*Praefectus annonae*), Prf Aug (*Praefectus augustalis*), PrfVig (*Praefectus vigilum*), Procos (*Proconsul*), PPO (*Praefectus praetorio*), PSC (*Praepositus sacri cubiculi*), PU (*Praefectus urbi*), QSP (*Quaestor sacri palatii*), Rat'is (*Rationalis*), Tr&Not (*Tribunus et notarius*). Note that the status designators *inlustris*, *spectabilis*, and *clarissimus* are those assigned circa the 390s.

different offices reveals a significant pattern. Epithets associated with the highest-ranking offices, and especially those of illustrious status, generally referred to the excellence or exaltedness of the office. These include *amplitudo*, *auctoritas*, *celsitudo*, *culmen*, *eminentia*, *excellentia*, *eximietas*, *gloria*, *magnificentia*, *magnitudo*, *praestantia*, and *sublimitas*, and might be categorized as 'superiority' epithets. Terms associated with lower-ranking offices, however, almost always related to the 'personal qualities' of the office-holders: to particular skills, their character, or even the rank assigned to their office. These include *claritas*, *devotio*, *dicatio*, *experientia*, *gravitas*, *laudabilitas*, *prudentia*, *sinceritas*, *sollertia*, *sollicitudo*, and *spectabilitas*. One notes, for example, that offices that eventually had *clarissimus* status only were accorded the 'personal quality' epithets. This twofold categorization of honorifics not only would have made the intent that lay behind each appellation quite clear, but also would have provided a guideline for the introduction of new epithets, or for the occasional times when members of the chancery exercised their imagination and created honorifics that are not otherwise attested.

The same general rule applied to the use of adjectival forms. A look at Table 11.1 shows that they were almost always combined with corresponding nominal forms, that is, 'superior' adjectival epithets with 'superior' nominal ones, and conversely. The only exception is 'sinceritas tua', a 'personal character' nominal form that occurs a total of seven times with four different 'superior' epithets. *Sinceritas*, however, was an all-purpose epithet with a long history of use with illustrious offices, and perhaps this accounted for these combinations.

Finally, the epithets used to refer to the highest state officials changed very little—for example, 'inlustris et magnifica auctoritas tua' remained the standard way to address Praetorian Prefects in the east from the early fifth to the late sixth century. On the other hand, the according of *tua*-honorifics to officials of less than illustrious rank virtually ceased. These observations somewhat contradict the conventional portrayal of this as a period of rank inflation,[92] and of the continual

[92] See Jones, *LRE*, 547–8 and passim.

introduction of increasingly grandiose titles and offices. Yes, high ranks might have been granted to increasingly large numbers of individuals, but the second-person honorifics used to refer to the individuals who actually held office were sparingly given and only to officials of the highest rank, and would have provided a graphic indicator of who, in the imperial scheme or rank and status, counted, and who did not.

12

Why Not Marry a Jew? Jewish–Christian Marital Frontiers in Late Antiquity

Hagith S. Sivan

In 388 CE the emperor Theodosius I (379–95) issued a general ban on marriage between Christians and Jews (*CTh* 3. 7. 2 = 9. 7. 5 = *CJ* 1. 9. 6) addressed to Cynegius, the Praetorian Prefect of the East (whose domain included Palestine). This brief constitution was destined to play a critical role in Jewish–Christian community relations throughout the Middle Ages and the early Modern era.[1] It also represents the culmination of a debate on intermarriage that had taken place among rabbis on the one hand and in Christian episcopal circles on the other.[2] And while both Jewish rabbinic and Christian ecclesiastical authorities banned marriage outside the faith, neither had the power to invalidate such unions.[3] They could, of course, exercise considerable informal pressure on the couple and on their families. But so long as disparity of cult (*disparitas cultus*) and ethnicity were not recognized as marital barriers in civil (Roman) law, marriage between Jews and Christians was, to all intents and purposes, valid. The following study will discuss the contents

[1] For medieval development, see J. A. Brundage, 'Intermarriage between Christians and Jews in Medieval Canon Law', *Jewish History*, 3 (1988), 25–40; W. Pakter, *Medieval Canon Law and the Jews* (Ebelsbath, 1988); and L. I. Newman, 'Intermarriage between Jews and Christians during the Middle Ages', *Jewish Institute Quarterly*, 2 (1926), 2–8, 21–8.

[2] See my 'Rabbinics and Roman Law: Jewish–Gentile Marriage in Late Antiquity: Rabbinic, Episcopal and Roman Perspectives', *Revue des études juives*, 156 (1997), which expands on some of the ideas presented here. I am grateful to the editor, Professor Mimouni, for permitting me to reprise portions of that article here.

[3] For mixed marriages in the Sasanian Empire, see Erhart in this volume.

and context of Roman legal perspectives on Christian–Jewish intermarriage in the fourth century.

The Theodosian ban reads thus:

Let no Jew accept a Christian woman in marriage, nor a Christian man contract marriage with a Jewish woman. For if anyone should commit something of this sort, the crime of adultery will be considered to have taken place, and the freedom of accusing will be granted also to members of the public.

Ne quis Christianam mulierem in matrimonio Iudaeus accipiat, neque Iudaeae Christianus coniugium sortitiatur. nam si quis aliquid huiusmodi admiserit, adulterii vicem commissi huius crimen obtinebit, libertate in accusandum publicis quoque vocibus relaxata (*CTh* 3. 7. 2 = 9. 7. 5 = *CJ* 1. 9. 6).

Ancient editors of this law elected to insert the text in two different places in the Code, one relating to the general issue, the other to the penalties imposed on transgressors. It thus appears both in a section (3. 7) devoted to marriage ('De nuptiis') and in one (9. 7) concerning the Augustan legislation on adultery ('Ad legem Juliam de adulteriis'). Modern interpreters of this ban have regarded it as an attempt to curtail proselytism and as an expression of a desire to avoid the application of Jewish institutions, like polygamy, because it contradicted the marital impediments imposed by Roman law.[4] It has also been asserted that this law represents a drive toward religious and political unity of the empire through an assertion of Christian matrimonial unity (*concordia fidei*).[5] All three hypotheses are reasonable, but only up to a point. There are enough Roman laws specifically dealing with proselytism without the need to resort to the bedroom to add yet another deterrent. The relevance of the ban to the issue of proselytism is, therefore, doubtful. There also is a specific law banning polygamy (which had already been banned by

[4] Gothofredus for the first. G. L. Falchi, 'La legislazione imperiale circa i matrimoni misti fra Cristiani ed Ebrei nel IV S.', *Atti dell'Accademia Romanistica Constantiniana*, 2 (1988), 203–11, esp. 207. See also A. M. Rabello, 'Il problema dei matrimoni fra ebrei e Cristiani nella legislazione imperiale e in quella della chiesa (IV–VIs.)', *Atti dell' Accademia Romanistica Constantiniana*, 2 (1988), 213–24.

[5] M. Bianchini, 'Disparita di culto e matrimonio orientamenti del pensiero cristiano e della legislazione imperiale nel IV. S.', *Serta historica antiqua*, (1986), 233–46, esp. 245.

Diocletian in 285: *CJ* 5. 5. 2), as well as laws which repeatedly insist that internal matters ought to be handled by the Jewish authorities and not by Roman judicial bodies. As part of the Roman–Christian rhetoric on family values and marriage the 388 ban on Jewish–Christian intermarriage is unique and requires a different explanation.

In the first place, *CTh* 3. 7. 2 is not the first imperial law on intimate relations between Jews and Christians. A much truncated law issued in 339 deals with a specific group of Jewish men who, for reasons not disclosed in the law, married (Christian?) weavers.[6]

With regard to women formerly employed in our weaving establishment and whom the Jews associated in their turpitude [or 'lewd wedlock'], it is our pleasure that these women shall be restored to the weaving establishment, and that for the rest it must be observed that Jews may not unite in disgrace with Christian women, and if they do, they shall be subject to capital punishment.

Quod ad mulieres pertinet, quas Iudaei in turpitudinis suae duxere consortium in gynaeceo nostro ante versatas, placet easdem restitui gynaeceo ideque in reliquum observari, ne Christianas mulieres suis iungant flagitiis vel, si hoc fecerint, capitali periculo subiugentur (*CTh* 16. 8. 6).

The law envisages two situations, an existing marriage between Jews and weavers, and future marriages between Jewish men and Christian women.[7] In the first case, the emperor merely wanted the women to return to their jobs; in the second, dire penalties were imposed on the Jewish husbands. Yet, why Jewish men would 'hang around' imperial workshops is not explained. Moreover, to judge by the use of the singular (*gynaeceum*), which describes the troublesome location where Jewish men associated with weavers, the first civil prohibition on mixed religious marriage owed its

[6] The date of this law has been debated: see A. Linder, *The Jews in the Legal Sources of the Early Middle Ages* (Detroit, 1997), no. 11, p. 146, versus *PLRE I*, 284–5 (Evagrius 2).

[7] Both Antti Arjava and Judith Evans Grubbs (q.v. elsewhere in this volume) questioned my interpretation of this constitution as one dealing with sexual ('marital') relations. But a conversation with Lellia Cracco Ruggini confirmed that the terminology clearly points to intimate relations based not on a labour association but on a type of marriage.

existence to specific local circumstances that no longer can be recovered.[8] Perhaps the law had been prompted by cases of women who left an imperial *gynaeceum* to marry Jews.[9] While it is not clear how marriage was related to the economics of the job market, or whether and why marriage prevented these women from continuing to work in the imperial *gynaeceum*, the law implies that the women no longer were there. Flight of labourers from their workshops was by far the most worrisome aspect of the management of such establishments, and several laws impose dire financial penalties on those who harbour fugitive weavers.[10]

The social status of neither the Jewish men who sought to marry weavers nor of their chosen brides is designated. Yet, it is vital for an understanding of the ban to gauge whether the couples involved were both free, both servile, or of disparate status. If both were slaves, a law like the one under discussion was unnecessary. The fate of a union of such people was in the hands of their masters and did not require the intervention of the imperial bureaucracy. Even if the women were slaves, the servile status of their Jewish suitors is not indicated in the law and is an unlikely assumption.

If, as has been assumed, most of the women who worked in the imperial *gynaeceum* were free, the law may indeed be dealing with *iustum matrimonium*.[11] But the evidence concerning members of *gynaecea* shows considerable varieties of

[8] On the *gynaecea*, see Jones, *LRE*, 836–7; J. P. Wild, 'The Gynaeceum at Venta and its Context,' *Latomus*, 26 (1967), 648–76; and idem, 'The Gynaecea', in R. Goodburn, P. Bartholomew (eds.), *Aspects of the Notitia Dignitatum* (*BAR 15*, Supp. 15) (Oxford 1976), 57–98. See also the *Oxford Dictionary of Byzantium* where *gynaecarii* are identified as men and not women. For a reading of this law as a check on vigorous proselytising efforts of Jews, B. S. Bachrach, 'The Jewish Community in the Later Roman Empire as Seen in the Codex Theodosianus', in J. Neusner, E. S. Frerichs (eds.), *'To See Ourselves as Others See Us': Christians, Jews and 'Others' in Late Antiquity* (Chico, Calif, 1985), 399–421, esp. 408 ff. on this constitution.

[9] Suggested by M. Avi-Yonah, *The Jews under Roman and Byzantine Rule* (Jerusalem, 1984), 175.

[10] *CTh* 10. 20. 2: 357/8; 6 and 7: 372; 8: 374; 9: 380. Wild, 'Gynaeceum', 658, believes that local landowners actually enticed workers in order to gain their help in furnishing the quota of clothing to which they were liable.

[11] F. Millar, 'Condemnation to Hard Labour', *Papers of the British School at Rome* (1984), 144, believes that the bulk were free but tied to their occupation. He does not use this law to substantiate this assertion, nor does he deal with gender distinctions. Wild, 'Gynaeceum', 654, brings evidence on a type of textile home industry which had to maintain a fixed annual output.

status. *CTh* 10. 20. 3, of 365, applies to marriage between freeborn women and fiscal slaves in the imperial weaving mills and mints.[12] It reminds potential transgressors that this kind of marriage is tantamount to *contubernium*, a union between slaves, in which the children follow the status of the unfree partner. *Consortium*, the term used to describe the union between Jewish men and their weaving brides, is used in classical Latin for the sharing of property, or a community of life, and becomes common in the context of marriage in Christian writings.[13] While the latter appears to be the case in *CTh* 16. 8. 8, it is not unlikely that the type of liaison that the law describes is not *iustum matrimonium* but an informal union.[14] It may imply that these women, like their husbands, were free. Yet, if this is the case, it is difficult to see by what means the emperors proposed to implement their law and to force the return of these women to their jobs and, by implication, to annul their marriage.

Furthermore, *CTh* 16. 8. 6 traditionally has been associated with another constitution, promulgated on the same day, which deals with the purchase and circumcision of slaves, especially Christian ones:

If any Jew should suppose that he should purchase a slave of another sect or people, such slave shall be immediately vindicated to the fisc. If, having bought a slave, [a Jew] proceeded to circumcise him, he shall be penalized not only with the loss of the slave, but also with capital punishment. But if a Jew should not hesitate to purchase slaves who are adherents of the venerable faith, he shall immediately be deprived of all such slaves found in his possession without delay since (a Jew) ought not to own Christian men.

Si aliquis Iudaeorum mancipium sectae alterius seu nationis crediderit conparandum, mancipium fisco protinus vindicetur: si vero emptum circumciderit, non solum mancipii damno multetur, verum etiam capitali sententia puniatur. quod si venerandae fidei conscia mancipia Iudaeus mercari non dubitet, omnia, quae aput

[12] See J. Evans Grubbs, *Law and Family in Late Antiquity: The Emperor Constantine's Marriage Legislation* (Oxford, 1995), 268–9.

[13] *Digest* 23. 2. 1; Linder, *Jews*, 150, draws attention to many other uses of the term in the Theodosian Code (including marriage).

[14] I owe this observation to Judith Evans Grubbs, who believes that *CTh* 16. 8. 8 does not deal with marriage, but with a business arrangement that harmed the output of the *gynaeceum* and caused its supervisor to complain.

eum repperiuntur, protinus auferantur nec interponatur quicquam morae, quin eorum hominum qui Christiani sunt possessione careat (*CTh* 16. 9. 2).

If this association of *CTh* 16. 8. 6 with 16. 9. 2 indeed represents the original law, the clear inference is that both parts dealt with persons of servile status. In fact, there is a clear parallel in the ascending rhetoric of each part of the constitution. Both begin with 'restoration', the male slaves being appropriated by the imperial treasury while the female weavers are to be returned to their *gynaeceum*. In neither case, straightforward purchase or 'marriage', is the Jewish purchaser, owner, or 'husband' punished. But then comes an escalation, with capital punishment meted out to Jews for both circumcising Christian slaves and for marrying Christian women.

Now, if free men, as the Jewish husbands must have been, married servile women, as the weavers presumably had been, this was not a valid marriage (*iustum matrimonium*) by law. Yet, careful as this law appears as far as correct terminology is concerned, there is sufficient evidence of confusion in the laws to susbtantiate the assumption that the formulators (or editors) of the laws allowed their convictions to determine the style at the expense of precision.[15] Contemporary laws regulating marital alliances of curials, such as *CTh* 12. 1. 6, provide suggestive parallels with *CTh* 16. 8. 6. Both discuss unions that the state regarded as detrimental to its well-being. Each relates to relations between free men and bonded women. In both cases the violating woman becomes the property of the state and the man is capitally punished. These resemblances imply that the marriages which the legislator of *CTh* 16. 8. 6 so deplored likewise violated imperial regulations on marriage between free and bonded. The indignation so evident in the harsh rhetoric of the ban was largely due to the fact that as a result of the liaison between Jewish men and weavers imperial textile factories lost their trained and servile workforce.

The issue of Christian–Jewish religious disparity is only introduced in the second part of each section of the original

[15] A good example is *CTh* 12. 1. 6; see also Evans Grubbs, *Law and Family*, 278.

law (*CTh* 16. 9. 2 and 16. 8. 6), with a general ban on circumcision of slaves on the one hand, and on marriage between Jewish males and bonded Christian women on the other. To be precise, the religious affiliation of the weavers of the *gynaeceum* which had prompted the law in the first place is not stated. They could have been of 'any sect or nation', to quote the part relating to male slaves. That the original law was largely concerned with keeping these weavers at their workplace is evident. It also leads to the conclusion that the general ban on mixed marriage in which religion is introduced related only to marriage between Jews and women belonging to imperial workshops who also happened to have been Christian. Religious disparity, then, was introduced, it seems, not as a marital impediment *per se*, but to emphasize imperial displeasure at relations of power between Jews and Christians.

If *consortium*, the term employed to characterize the relations between weavers and Jewish men can denote marriage, *flagitia*, the word by which the law describes the unions between Christian women and Jewish males is more problematic. The question is whether marriage indeed lurks behind the rhetorical garb of the law. *Flagitium* can mean an act done in the heat of passion, a burning shame, and an infamous act.[16] In Tacitus (*Ann.* 15. 44) the word was applied to the way in which Christian activities were perceived in the popular mind, while both Cicero and Tacitus used it in conjunction with *adulterium* and *stuprum*, illicit sexual liaisons.[17] Although *flagitium* does not describe marriage, legitimate or illegitimate, it is difficult to see what else the legislator had in mind when referring to men and women whose association was here condemned.

Because these bans were essentially a repetition of previous laws on Christian slaves in Jewish households and on unions between free (Jewish) men and servile (Christian) women, the editors of the Theodosian Code divided it into

[16] P. G. W. Glare, *Oxford Latin Dictionary* (Oxford, 1982), and C. T. Lewis, C. Short, *A Latin Dictionary* (Oxford, 1989).

[17] Cicero, *De Senectute* 12. 40; Tacitus, *Ann.* 14. 51. The word does not appear in A. Blaise, *Dictionnaire Latin–Français des auteurs chrétiens* (Paris, 1954, repr. 1993).

two parts, on the basis of gender and a different frame of reference. *CTh* 16. 9. 2 ended up in a section wholly devoted to slaves in Jewish households, while *CTh* 16. 8. 6 was grouped in a section vaguely entitled 'On Jews, Caecoli, and Samaritans'. In fact, it is clear that the compilers no longer understood the purpose of the original law and, relying on the clause prohibiting mixed marriage between Jewish men and Christian women, assigned it to the section that dealt in general with Jewish affairs.[18] A century later, when the editors of the Code of Justinian re-examined the Theodosian collection of imperial constitutions, the provision on unions between weavers and Jews no longer made sense. The seemingly general prohibition of 339 did not require repetition, for in 388 the emperor Theodosius I issued a clear-cut ban on Jewish–Christian marriage. As a result, *CTh* 16. 8. 6 was omitted from the Code of Justinian.

Because of its self-imposed limitations, *CTh* 16. 8. 6 hardly answered larger contemporary objections, such as those expressed by rabbis and bishops, to marriage outside the faith. Already at the turn of the fourth century, the canons of the Council of Elvira, in Spain, penalized catholic parents who countenanced the marriage of their daughters to a Jew (or a heretic).[19] It took the court nearly a century to respond to episcopal efforts to erect marital boundaries throughout the empire and half a century since *CTh* 16. 8. 6 to consolidate its approach to intermarriage.

Both *CTh* 16. 8. 6 and 3. 7. 2 = 9. 7. 5 belong to a series of imperial laws which dealt with Jewish affairs in Late Antiquity.[20] While the quantity of 'Jewish' laws dating to the fourth and the fifth century implies sustained imperial efforts to define the status of the Jewish community in the Roman empire, mixed marriages constituted only one among several issues that required imperial intervention. In addition, matters such as voluntary apostasy and proselytism, circumcision of Christian slaves, and internal jurisdiction of

[18] In addition, the status of women working in the *gynaecea* may have changed, making the law irrelevant.

[19] 'neque Judaeis neque haereticis dare placuit' (*Conc. Eliber.* can. 16: *PL* 84. 304).

[20] Linder, *Jews*.

Jewish courts, to mention a few, also drew the attention of Roman legislators.

CTh 3. 7. 2 = 9. 7. 5 introduced two novelties into existing imperial legislation on mixed marriages. One is the application of the ban to all mixed marriages (here clearly defined as *matrimonium iustum*) between Jews and Christians, regardless of gender, class, and rank. The second is the equation of such marriages with adultery. The former signalled the conclusion of a long process of rabbinic and episcopal reflections on the subject. The latter enabled such marriages to be dissolved, because Roman law never provided for a divorce on the ground of the disparity of cult.

Indeed, *disparitas cultus*, or the disparity of cult as a matrimonial impediment in civil law, represents a wholly new legal concept. It can be compared to another ban that likewise forms a departure from the norms of both classical and late classical law, namely the ban on 'Roman–barbarian' marriage issued in 373 by Valentinian I.[21] In brief, *CTh* 3. 14. 1 was issued to Theodosius (the father of Theodosius I), who was serving as the highest military authority in Mauretania in the midst of a difficult campaign against the rebel Firmus, a member of a royal native clan. Neither Firmus nor the Moorish peoples that supported him were 'barbarians', in the sense of outsiders or foreigners. They had lived for centuries within the Roman *limes* of Africa, had served in the Roman army, and Firmus's family even underwent a precocious conversion to Christianity at the beginning of the fourth century. The African society in which the rebellion took place was multi-layered with a significant degree of interaction between 'Roman' provincials and their Moorish neighbours. In time of trouble, however, the government attempted to drive a wedge into the socio-economic structures that were perceived to be potentially dangerous to the Roman war-effort in the area. Hence, the general ban on mixed

[21] 'Nulli provincialium, cuiuscumque ordinis out loci fuerit, cum barbara sit uxore coniugium, nec ulli gentilium provincialis femina copuletur. quod si quae inter provinciales atque gentiles affinitates ex huiusmodi nuptiis extiterint, quod in iis susceptum vel noxium detegitur, capitaliter expietur' (*CTh* 3. 14. 1). For discussion, see H. S. Sivan, 'Why not Marry a Barbarian: Marital Frontiers in Late Antiquity', in R. W. Mathisen, H. Sivan (eds.), *Shifting Frontiers in Late Antiquity* (London, 1996), 136–45.

Roman–barbarian marriage, and the capital punishment, but only if such unions appeared suspicious to the authorities.

By introducing an ethnic dimension into marital impediments, *CTh* 3. 14. 1 paved the way for the use of religion as another marital barrier. And while it seems, at present, impossible to recover the precise circumstances that had prompted the ban on Jewish–Christian marriage in 388, it is likely that both Christian and Jewish ideologies had exercised some influence in its formulation. Particularly striking is the introduction of the issue of adultery as a component of the ban. Jewish, imperial, and ecclesiastical strictures on adultery have a long history.[22] Imperial legislation on adultery from Augustus (27 BCE–14 CE) onward aimed to preserve the integrity of the family by penalizing extra-marital affairs of married women and by making adultery a public offence.[23] Under Constantine (306–37), the public was excluded from the circle of potential accusers, but the right of the husband to accuse a woman on the basis of suspicion alone was reinforced. The emperor even encouraged male relatives of a suspected adultress to bring an accusation against her and granted them the right to withdraw their suit if they could not prove it at court.[24]

Adultery also became, under Constantine, one of three lawful bases for divorce, alongside prostitution and magic. If a husband was able to divorce his wife on any of these grounds, he was also entitled to her dowry as well as to a tranquil successive marriage.[25] The penalties for adultery ranged from exile and confiscation of property to death, depending on the rank of the offender and the presence of other serious crimes.[26] Moreover, although women were by legal definition culpable of adultery, their partners, as well as male adulterers, were occasionally punished, and at times as severely

[22] For adultery in Roman law, see Evans Grubbs, *Law and Family*, and A. Arjava, *Women and Law in Late Antiquity* (Oxford, 1996), each with comprehensive bibliography. On the adulterous wife in Judaism, A. Desoto, *The Law of Jealousy: Anthropology of Sotah* (Atlanta, 1989).

[23] *CJ* 9. 9. 2 (Antonine); 9. 9. 19 (Diocletianic).

[24] See my 'The Body of a Sinner, the Price of Piety: The Politics of Adultery in Late Antiquity', forthcoming in *Annales*.

[25] *CTh* 9. 40. 1 and 11. 36. 1: 313/4; 9. 38. 1: 322.

[26] Evans Grubbs, *Law and Family*, 221.

as wayward women.[27] Declaring as adulterous legal marital alliances between Christians and Jews provided their families and even the public with the means to undermine the validity of the marriage. Specifically, the equation of such marriage with adultery did not nullify it. But it put it within a category that had been repeatedly denounced by emperors, bishops, and rabbis, and it facilitated divorce.

Whether or not this ban can be also seen as an expression of anti-Jewish policies is another question. It is possible that Ambrose, bishop of Milan, had some influence on its formulation.[28] But Ambrose, as well as other theologians, was opposed to all mixed marriages, religious or ethnic, on principle, including Jewish–Christian unions. Pressure on the court to issue this ban may have come from various circles, not the least from the prefect who received the law, and who himself was known for his fanatical Christianity.[29] Cynegius had far better relations with the emperor than Ambrose. In the year when the ban was issued, Cynegius was the recipient of several constitutions against heresy (*CTh* 16. 5. 14–16), a reminder that the arrows of imperial legislation were not aimed exclusively at Jews. Nor can pressure from Jewish leadership circles be wholly discounted. In 392 complaints were sent, possibly from Palestinian rabbinical circles, against Jews who disregarded their sentences of excommunication.[30] The emperor sided with the complainers and ordered the recalcitrant members of their communities to obey the rabbis' commands.

Regardless of the reasons for its issuance, the ban on mixed marriage undermined the legal validity of such marriages. It also made these unions into a dangerous proposition. Yet, the efficacy of the law remains an open question. It was

[27] Ammianus 28. 1.

[28] Ambrose, *De Abrahamo* 1. 9. 84; Epiphanius, *Haeres.* 61. 1 and 5; see Linder, *Jews*, 178, for Ambrosian influence. Bianchini, 'Disparita', and Rabello, 'Problema', concur with regard to the strong religious flavour of this ban. C. Vogler, 'Les Juifs dans le Code Theodosien', *Le Point Theologique*, 33 (1979), 52, suggests that this law reinforced legal barriers of status on marriage between curials, but this is implausible.

[29] J. Matthews, 'A Pious Supporter of Theodosius I: Maternus Cynegius and his Family', *JThS* 18 (1967), 438–46.

[30] *CTh* 16. 8. 8 (Linder, *Jews*, no. 20).

retained both by the editors of the *Breviarium Alaricianum* ('Breviary of Alaric') of 506, with significant modifications, and by the compilers of the Code of Justinian.[31] But any cases that illustrate the operation of the law do not survive.[32] So we cannot tell whether rabbinic, episcopal, and imperial strictures against marriage outside the faith were able to prevent such mesalliances.

In sum, so long as an option of civil marriage was available to anyone who could not marry according to the Law of Moses and Israel or according to Christian marriage formulae, the pressure of communal authorities, whether Jewish or Christians, operated within the limits of the law. Only when ethnic and religious disparities constituted marital impediments in civil law did marriage outside the faith become illegal. The introduction of a civil ban on Jewish–Christian intermarriage probably had its roots in changing attitudes by the government on the one hand, and the growing influence of religious leaders who desired clear-cut boundaries around their communities of faith on the other. It reflects a far-reaching novelty in concepts of marriage. Banned marital unions were no longer based only on class, rank, or civic disparities. Ethnicity and religious affiliation were added to a list of prohibitions that determined the suitability (or lack of it) of prospective spouses.

The 388 ban on Jewish–Christian marriage, then, introduced several novelties. It pronounced a legally married couple as adulterous; it made their marriage a public criminal offence; and it clearly made disparity of cult a weighty consideration in marital arrangements. Mixed religious marriage became a moral offence, precisely the same stigma that both rabbis and bishops had attached to it. By opening the case to public accusations of adultery the state made such marriages into an affair that could be prosecuted in court. Mixed religious marriages were then taken out of their intimate and private familial context and brought to the harsh limelight of the public arena.

[31] *Breviarium* 3. 7. 2 and 9. 4. 4; see F. Arvizu, 'La Femme dans le Code d'Euric', *RHDFE* 62 (1984), 391–405; and *CJ* 1. 9. 6.

[32] But the danger of exposing adultery to the public by opening a law suit is well represented by Jerome, *Epist.* 1.

13

Virgins and Widows, Show-Girls and Whores: Late Roman Legislation on Women and Christianity

Judith Evans Grubbs

Much has been written in the past fifteen years about the role of women in late antique Christianity,[1] and more recently, on women in late Roman law.[2] Less has been done on the intersection between the two: that is, late Roman legislation directed explicitly toward the relationship between women and the Christian church. Yet, this is a topic for which there exists interesting and abundant evidence, in both the legal sources and contemporary Christian writings. This study will discuss legislation on women and Christianity in the Theodosian Code and the post-Theodosian *novellae*. What issues involving Christian women particularly concerned the imperial government? What events or individuals prompted legislation aimed at women and the church? Did imperial policy change between the mid-fourth century, when legislation concerning Christian women first appeared, and the later fifth century, when 'the Church' had become firmly entrenched in imperial society?

[1] See e.g. E. A. Clark, *Ascetic Piety and Women's Faith* (New York, 1986); G. Clark, *Women in Late Antiquity: Pagan and Christian Lifestyles* (Oxford, 1993); G. Cloke, *This Female Man of God: Women and Spiritual Power in the Patristic Age, AD 350–450* (London, 1995); and S. Elm, *'Virgins of God': the Making of Asceticism in Late Antiquity* (Oxford, 1994).

[2] See A. Arjava, *Women and Law in Late Antiquity* (Oxford, 1996); J. Beaucamp, *Le Statut de la femme à Byzance* (4ᵉ–7ᵉ siècle). i. *Le Droit impérial* (Paris, 1990); and J. Evans Grubbs, *Law and Family in Late Antiquity: The Emperor Constantine's Marriage Legislation* (Oxford, 1995).

Roman law, like Roman society, was acutely status conscious, and expectations and ideals of female behaviour varied according to the social and legal status of the woman involved. The law determined, according to status, the sexual relationships and roles open to a woman, and the amount of protection from violence or exploitation she could expect. There was one standard for respectable women, who were expected to marry and ensure the continuity of family and state by child-bearing, and another quite different standard for lowborn women whose purpose was to provide entertainment for the people and sexual recreation for men.[3] These expectations of gender and status were codified by the first emperor Augustus (27 BCE–14 CE), whose laws on marriage and adultery encouraged marriage and child-bearing and harshly punished extramarital relations by or with a married woman of respectable class. Imperial legislation after Augustus continued to distinguish between 'respectable' women, who were legally protected from abuse and deception but punished severely if they committed adultery, and women of low or slave birth, who could engage in dishonorable occupations like prostitution without fear of prosecution for adultery, but who were barred from legal marriage with men of respectable status.[4]

During Late Antiquity, however, another type of woman emerged in the legal sources: women whose social and legal situation was in some way affected by their adoption of Christianity or of Christian asceticism. Two kinds of Christian women especially attracted the attention of imperial lawmakers: on the one hand, celibate widows and virgins of respectable birth; and on the other, women of low birth who were employed as showgirls (*scaenicae* and *mimae*) or prostitutes. Respectable women were of interest because of their wealth and family connections, lowborn women because they rendered services in demand by the general (male) public. In

[3] See J. Gardner, *Women in Roman Law and Society* (London, 1984), for classical law, and, for the later period, Arjava, *Women and Law*, passim; and Evans Grubbs, *Law*, 321–36.

[4] For the Augustan legislation, see S. Treggiari, *Roman Marriage: Iusti Coniuges from the Time of Cicero to the Time of Ulpian* (Oxford, 1991), 60–80.

both cases, their Christian beliefs led these women to deny the traditional roles assigned them by the Roman hierarchies of gender and status, thus creating a potential for social dislocation to which the late Roman government felt compelled to respond.

Constantine I (306–37), the first Christian emperor, did not legislate explicitly on the behaviour or lifestyles of Christian women, but two of his laws were of great significance to Christian women, particularly wealthy ones: his repeal in 320 of the Augustan penalties on inheritance by the unmarried and childless (*CTh* 8. 16. 1), and his law of 321 enabling Christians to leave legacies directly to the Christian church (*CTh* 16. 2. 4). During the following century, aristocratic euergetism in founding and endowing churches and Christian institutions surged, especially in the west.[5] The Constantinian laws enabled wealthy Christian women, especially widows, to leave substantial legacies to churches and indeed to individual clergy—legacies which were to become the subject of controversial legislation.

The earliest reference to Christian women in the Theodosian Code is anomalous, and clearly pertained to a specific incident involving imperial workers who happened to be Christian. A law of Constantine II enacted in 339 commanded that the women formerly employed in the imperial weaving factory (*gynaeceum*) who had been led away by Jews into the 'association of their turpitude' were to be returned to their jobs. In the future, Jews were not to 'join Christian women to their crimes' upon pain of a capital penalty (*CTh* 16. 8. 6).[6] Although sometimes interpreted as referring to marriage between Jewish men and Christian women, this law in reality concerns defection from their jobs by female weavers, under Jewish instigation. That the women were Christian (and perhaps had also been converted to Judaism) no doubt aggravated the offence, but the real issue, as far as the

[5] See C. Pietri, *Roma Christiana* (Rome, 1976), 1. 558–73; and J. Harries, '"Treasure in Heaven": Property and Inheritance among Senators of Late Rome', in E. Craik (ed.), *Marriage and Property* (Aberdeen, 1984), 54–70.

[6] For discussion of this law, see Sivan in this volume.

government was concerned, was the abandonment of their jobs by imperial workers.[7]

A larger group of laws dealt with Christian women who were following a celibate lifestyle. The earliest appearance of such women in imperial legislation is found in a law of Constantius II (337–61) addressed to the prefect of Rome in 354. It declared that those who abducted widows were to be punished with the same severity as those who made attempts on the 'modesty (*pudor*) of sacrosanct virgins', and it further noted that the abducted woman's consent after the fact would not do her abductor any good (*CTh* 9. 25. 1: 354). Constantius' father Constantine also had legislated against abduction (*raptus*), but his law (*CTh* 9. 24. 1: 326) involved only virgins destined for marriage. At that time, 'sacrosanct' virgins and widows, those who had devoted themselves to a life of holy celibacy were not numerous or visible enough to warrant imperial legislation.[8] Constantius' law indicates that by the mid-fourth century, dedicated celibate women did form a recognizable and distinct group in Rome. They were expected to lead lives of pious seclusion in their own or their parents' home, or perhaps in the company of other celibate women of similar class and background.[9] Evidently their single status, and probably also their wealth, made them tempting targets for male predators. The law raises the possibility that a woman might subsequently consent to marry her abductor (even though this was strictly forbidden under the law), which suggests that some women who dedicated themselves to celibacy later may have regretted their decision.

Ten years later, in 364, an enactment of the emperor Jovian (363–4) declared, 'If anyone has dared, I will not say

[7] Part of a longer law which also dealt with the purchase and circumcision of Christian male slaves by Jews (*CTh* 16. 9. 2). See A. Linder, *The Jews in Roman Imperial Legislation* (Detroit, 1987), 144–51; and B. S. Bachrach, 'The Jewish Community of the Later Roman Empire as Seen in the Codex Theodosianus', in J. Neusner, E. S. Frerichs (eds.), *'To See Ourselves as Others See Us': Christians, Jews, 'Others' in Late Antiquity* (Chico Calif., 1984), 399–421, esp. 408–12.

[8] See J. Evans Grubbs, 'Abduction Marriage in Antiquity: A Law of Constantine and its Social Context', *JRS* 79 (1989), 59–83: Constantine's law legislated against bride theft, or abduction marriage.

[9] G. D. Gordini, 'Origine e sviluppo del monachesimo a Roma', *Gregorianum*, 37 (1956), 220–60, esp. 230–2; Pietri, *Roma*, 1. 120–1.

to abduct, but even to make an attempt on consecrated virgins or widows for the sake of marriage, he shall be afflicted with a capital sentence'.[10] Sozomen (*HE* 6. 3) supposed that Jovian made this law in reaction to the easy-going attitude to such cases taken by his predecessor Julian (361–3), who had refused to attach the same importance to the abduction of holy virgins and widows that Christian emperors had. Here, not only the actual act of abduction is punishable, but even the solicitation of the hand of a consecrated woman in marriage. The woman herself, however, does not seem to have been penalized, even if she consented to such a solicitation.[11]

Fifth-century western emperors continued to condemn the abduction of dedicated virgins. A law of Honorius (395–423) dated 420 appears not only in excerpted form under the relevant title in the Theodosian Code (9. 25. 3), but also in full as the tenth Sirmondian Constitution. The complete version indicates that the emperor was actually more concerned about another problem involving women and Christian celibates. Clerics, Honorius said, were not to have women living with them who were not closely related by blood, or women who were misleadingly called 'sisters' even though they were really nothing of the kind. Only a cleric's mother, daughter, or real sister could live with him, or the wife he had married before he decided to enter the church, with whom he was now expected to live in a celibate union. The law was aimed at the so-called *subintroductae* (Greek *syneisaktes*), celibate women who cohabited with celibate men as an alternative to single-sex monasticism. This practice went back at least

[10] *CTh* 9. 25. 2. The law is said to have been 'Given' ('Dat.') at Antioch on 19 February 364, but Jovian died on 17 February at Dadastana, between Bithynia and Galatia (Ammianus 25. 10. 12). O. Seeck, *Regesten der Kaiser und Päpste für die Jahre 311 bis 476 n. Chr.* (Stuttgart, 1919), 214, changed 'Dat.' to 'Pp.' ('Posted') to explain the apparently posthumously-made law. Alternatively, the law could have been issued in Jovian's name after his death, as occurred in the case of *CJ* 5. 17. 7, which was promulgated after Constantine's death (see Evans-Grubbs, *Law*, 232). Ammianus does report (26. 1. 5) that for ten days after Jovian's death, no one was in charge.

[11] See L. Desanti, 'Sul matrimonio di donne consacrate a Dio nel diritto romano cristiano', *Studia et documenta historiae iuris*, 53 (1987), 270–96, who discusses variations in the manuscript versions of this law, and its adaptation in the *Breviarium* of Alaric II and the *Lex Romana Burgundionum*; for these law codes see also Arjava and Matthews in this volume.

to the early third century, but was strongly condemned by Christian leaders and church councils in both west and east.[12]

The compilers of the Theodosian Code did a 'cut-and-paste' job with Honorius' law, putting various pieces into quite different sections. The part dealing with clerics who lived with 'extraneous women' appears in book 16 (*CTh* 16. 2. 44), which is devoted to religious matters, whereas the part concerning abduction of consecrated virgins and widows was put in book 9 (*CTh* 9. 25. 3), devoted to criminal law. Neither of the extracts in the Code preserves the law's preamble, but the Sirmondian Constitution does.[13] Here, Honorius states that he was acting on a recommendation (*suggestio*) from a priest who was concerned about the disrepute and scandal the clergy was bringing upon itself. The priest also called for penalties against abductors of consecrated women, but his main concern was the *subintroductae*. Perhaps the two earlier laws against the abduction of consecrated women were also enacted at the suggestion of church officials, but without their preambles we have no way of knowing. The abduction of holy virgins was again condemned in 458 by the western emperor Majorian (457–61), though his law is rather anti-ecclesiastical in tone.[14] Ultimately, Justinian (527–65) legislated against the *raptus* of women of all marital and social statuses.[15]

A different kind of predator upon holy women was attacked in a law (*CTh* 16. 2. 20: 370; cf. 6. 2. 22: 372) of the emperor Valentinian I (364–75), which was addressed to Damasus (366–84), the flamboyant bishop of Rome, and read aloud in the churches of Rome. It decreed that clerics and 'those who wish to be called by the name of continents' were not to approach the homes of widows or female minors and were to be expelled from Rome if the relatives of such women reported them. According to Valentinian, ecclesiastics were attaching themselves to Christian women 'under

[12] Cyprian, *Epist.* 4; Council of Elvira, Can. 27; Council of Ancyra, Can. 19; Council of Nicaea, Can. 3; see also E. A. Clark, 'John Chrysostom and the *Subintroductae*', in eadem, *Ascetic Piety*, 265–90; and Elm, '*Virgins*', 48–51.

[13] For the editing done in the law codes, and the extant full forms of laws, see Mathisen in this volume.

[14] *Nov. Maj.* 6: see below for discussion.

[15] *Nov.* 6. 4, on which see below; it presumably was not recommended by an ecclesiastic; see Evans Grubbs, 'Abduction', 77–9.

the pretext of religion' and receiving gifts or legacies from the devout ladies, to the detriment of the women's families. All such legacies were null and void and henceforth anything left by women to ecclesiastics was to be confiscated by the imperial treasury.[16]

Valentinian was attempting to check what he saw as pernicious meddling by some ecclesiastics into the financial affairs of wealthy Romans. He was not opposed to Christian women adopting an ascetic lifestyle, for in other legislation he released widows and women 'living in perpetual virginity' from payment of the head tax (*CTh* 13. 10. 4: 368; 13. 10. 6: 370). The law forbidding wealthy celibate women to leave legacies to clerics should be considered along with another law of the following year, addressed to the Senate of Rome, which concerned family conflicts regarding the choice of a husband for widows under 25 (*CTh* 3. 7. 1: 371). Both laws concern under-age widows of property, and both refer to male relatives (*propinqui*) as parties interested in the fate of that property. Both laws are probably imperial responses to complaints from the Roman senatorial class about designs on unmarried and allegedly impressionable young heiresses by outside parties, either over-attentive clerics interested in increasing the coffers of their church or parvenu fortune-hunters seeking a wealthy wife.[17]

There are many stories from this period of wealthy aristocratic Christian women who renounced secular society and used the fortunes they had inherited to found monastic institutions, endow churches, and perform works of Christian charity. A standard topos of these biographies is that the devout woman was subjected to pressure from her family to marry (or remarry) and have children to whom she could pass on her considerable wealth.[18] The seriousness of such

[16] *CTh* 16. 2. 20: 370; cf. 16. 2. 22: 372. Interestingly, this had been the fate of illegal legacies to the unmarried and childless before Constantine's repeal of the Augustan marriage legislation.

[17] I owe to Antti Arjava (q.v. in this volume) the suggestion that *CTh* 3. 7. 1 was enacted in response to a request from the Senate of Rome. See also Arjava, *Women and Law*, 159–61. On the impetration of imperial legislation by means of a *suggestio*, see J. Harries, 'Introduction: The Background of the Code', in J. Harries, I. Wood (eds.), *The Theodosian Code: Studies in the Imperial Law of Late Antiquity* (London, 1993), 1–18 at 12.

[18] The bibliography is vast; see most recently Cloke, *Female Man*, esp. 33–56.

family opposition, however, has been questioned, on the assumption that under a Christian emperor conversion to the imperial faith carried political and social advantages, and that in senatorial families which still included many prominent male pagans, the presence of one or two dedicated Christian virgins was politically sensible.[19] Nevertheless, Valentinian's law suggests that aristocratic women who adopted asceticism did face family opposition, but its emphasis on gifts and legacies given to clerics by such women suggests that objections arose primarily from financial rather than religious considerations.

It also is likely that the law's distrust of clerics who preyed on wealthy unmarried women had some foundation. Its addressee, pope Damasus, was a highly controversial figure whose enemies called him 'the matrons' ear-tickler' (*matronarum auriscalpius*) because Christian ladies were so fond of him.[20] According to Damasus' secretary Jerome (*Epist.* 52. 6), the law was circumvented by the practice of leaving trusts (*fideicommissa*)—a well-known dodge used 400 years earlier by wealthy Romans who had wanted to evade the Augustan marriage laws.[21] Although Jerome also condemned clerics who devoted their time to 'learning the names, homes, and habits of matrons' (*Epist.* 22. 28), his own intimate friendship with the high-born widow Paula and other aristocratic women left him open to the same criticism. It may be that Jerome himself, who in 385 had to leave Rome in a hurry after Damasus' death, was prosecuted or threatened with prosecution because of his attentions to wealthy widows and minors. Jerome's own statements indicate that legal proceedings of some sort were brought against him, although it usually had been thought that he was referring to a hearing before ecclesiastical rather than civil authorities.[22]

[19] As argued by H. S. Sivan, 'On Hymens and Holiness in Late Antiquity', *JAC* 36 (1993), 81–93.

[20] *Collectio Avellana*, *Epist.* 1. 9: *CSEL* 35. 1. On Damasus, see J. N. D. Kelly, *Jerome: His Life, Writings, and Controversies* (New York, 1975), esp. 80–90.

[21] A *fideicommissum* was a trust by which the testator charged his (or her) heir to hand over all or part of the estate to another person; see R. Saller, *Patriarchy, Property, and Death in the Roman Family* (Cambridge, 1994), 167–80; and Sirks in this volume.

[22] Jerome, *Epist.* 45; see Kelly, *Jerome*, 111–14. Criticism of the law also in Ambrose, *Epist.* 73. 13–14: *CSEL* 82. 3 = *Epist.* 18: *PL* 16. Because bishops had jurisdiction in civil cases (granted by Constantine: see *CTh* 1. 27. 1: 318; *Sirm.* 1: 333; and

In 390, the issue surfaced again in a law of Theodosius I (379–95) (*CTh* 16. 2. 27). The law began by setting out rules for the consecration of deaconesses: 'according to the precept of the apostle' (I Timothy 5: 9), a woman could not become a deaconess until she was 60 years old and 'had the longed-for offspring at home'. If she met those qualifications, she was to appoint a guardian (*curator*) for any children still under the legal age of 25 and to entrust her possessions to 'suitable [persons] for administering with careful piety'. She was then to retain only the revenues from her estates, which she could dispose of as she liked. Moreover, the law continued,

> She is to squander nothing from her necklaces, bedding, nothing from her gold, silver, and other distinctions of a famous house, under the defence of religion but is to make over everything intact to her children and next-of-kin or any others whatever in the opinion of her own judgment and when she dies, she is to make heir no church, no cleric, [and] no pauper.[23]

Deaconesses' wills made in violation of this prohibition were null and void. If clerics attempted to extort bequests by means of *fideicommissa*, 'they are to be exiles from all the goods at which they had gaped' and the deaconess' property was to go to any legitimate heirs who could prove their claim.

The law also forbade women to cut off their hair 'against divine and human laws at the bidding of an induced belief' ('instinctu persuasae professionis'). A bishop who allowed a woman 'with shorn head' to enter the church or take communion was to be deposed. This particular provision seems to have been aimed at women who followed the more extreme style of ascetic deportment, those who, in addition to the usual sexual renunciation and fasting, cut off their hair and sometimes also wore men's clothing in an attempt to eradicate

Dossey and Lenski in this volume), Jerome could have been tried in an ecclesiastical court for violation of *CTh* 16. 2. 20; see J. C. Lamoreaux, 'Episcopal Courts in Late Antiquity', *JECS* 3 (1995), 143–67.

[23] 'Nihil de monilibus et superlectili, nihil de auro argento ceterisque clarae domus insignibus sub religionis defensione consumat, sed universa integra in liberos proximosve vel in quoscumque alios arbitrii sui existimatione transcribat ac is quando diem obierit, nullam ecclesiam, nullum clericum, nullum pauperem scribat heredes.'

all signs of gender difference. Mainstream Christian leaders disapproved of such behaviour; about forty years earlier, the Council of Gangra in Paphlagonia had condemned the female followers of Eustathius of Sebaste for cutting off their hair and wearing male clothes.[24]

The law was issued on 21 June 390, while Theodosius was at Milan, but it was addressed to the eastern praetorian prefect Tatianus, a pagan, and was directed at the eastern church, for the western church did not have an office of deaconess.[25] This ban on Christian clerics inheriting from wealthy women is similar to Valentinian's law of twenty years earlier, which had been directed to the churches of Rome. But Theodosius' ruling did not stand for long. On 23 August 390, exactly two months and two days later, while still in Italy, at Verona, Theodosius issued an order (*CTh* 16. 2. 28) to Tatianus that the law which had forbidden a member of the clergy to 'invade' the property of a deaconess or widow 'like a despoiler of the infirm sex' was to be removed from the registers and not thereafter applied. The second part of the original law, refusing communion to women with shorn heads, was apparently not rescinded.

The Theodosian Code's truncated versions of both of these laws give no clue as to why Theodosius first enacted sanctions against Christian clerics who benefited from wealthy women, but then so swiftly yet grudgingly (as inferred from the language) changed his mind. Sozomen suggested there was a link with a recent scandal in Constantinople, where a Christian woman claimed that she was raped by a deacon while she was doing penance in church.[26]

Perhaps more relevant is the case of Olympias of Constantinople, friend and benefactress of John Chrysostom.

[24] S. A. H. Kennell, 'Women's Hair and the Law: Two Cases from Late Antiquity', *Klio*, 73 (1991), 526–36. On Eustathius' followers: Council of Gangra, Cans. 13, 17, in C. J. Hefele, H. Leclercq, *Histoire des conciles d'après les documents originaux*, vol.1, pt.2 (Paris, 1907), 1038, 1040; Sozomen *HE* 3. 14; and Elm, '*Virgins*', 106–11, 218–19.

[25] Tatianus: see J. Matthews, *Western Aristocracies and Imperial Court* (Oxford, 1975), 114, 224. Deaconesses: Cloke, *Female Man*, 205–11; Elm, '*Virgins*', 170–82; A. G. Martimort, *Diaconesses: Essai historique* (Rome, 1982); trans. K. D. Whitehead as *Deaconesses: An Historical Study* (San Francisco, 1986).

[26] *HE* 7. 16. See G. Clark, *Women*, 53–5.

According to her anonymous biographer, the widowed Olympias wished to devote herself to ascetic celibacy and give her enormous wealth to Christian charity. However, Theodosius (who was related to Olympias by marriage) heard that she was squandering her wealth and tried to press her into a second marriage with one of his kinsmen. When Olympias steadfastly refused to remarry, Theodosius told the prefect of Constantinople not to allow her control over her property until she turned 30. Nevertheless, when Theodosius returned to the east in 391, he relented and granted Olympias control of her wealth. She was then ordained deaconess by Nectarius, bishop of Constantinople, when she was probably still under 30 and certainly well below the age of 60 prescribed by Theodosius' law, and began making generous donations to a number of clerics. So lavish was her munificence that even her good friend Chrysostom reproached her for her lack of discrimination.[27]

Theodosius' first law may have been intended to exert pressure on Olympias to force her to remarry, and when that tactic failed, Theodosius saw no point in alienating other powerful church officials and rescinded the law altogether. Thirteen years later, Olympias was among those implicated in the burning of Chrysostom's church in Constantinople after he was exiled, and went into exile herself.[28]

A colourful account of the application of Theodosius' first law to an individual cleric is found in a fascinating but little-known work, the *Miracles of St Thekla*, written in the mid-fifth century by a priest of the shrine of St Thekla near Seleucia in southern Turkey. One of Thekla's miracles involved Menodorus, a former priest of the church of Saint Thekla who had become bishop of Aigeai. A wealthy and devout woman had made Menodorus her heir, knowing (according to the author of the *Miracles*) that he would use the inheritance for the good of the church and not for his personal enrich-

[27] *Life of Olympias* 4–6, in A.-M. Malingrey (ed.), *Vie de Olympias*, *SC* 13 (bis) (Paris, 1968), 412–20; Sozomen, *HE* 8. 9, trans. E. A. Clark in *Jerome, Chrysostom, and Friends: Essays and Translations* (New York, 1979), 107–44; see also G. Dagron, *Naissance d'une Capitale: Constantinople et ses institutions de 330 à 451* (Paris, 1974), 500–6.

[28] See *CTh* 16. 2. 37: 404; Sozomen, *HE* 8. 24; E. Clark, *Jerome*, 116.

ment. But the wicked, greedy eunuch Eutropius, a powerful minister at the imperial court in Constantinople, heard about Menodorus' windfall and determined to have it for himself.[29] Eutropius prevailed upon the emperor to pass a law that no cleric could be the heir of a woman unless he was related to her—an apparent reference to *CTh* 16. 2. 27, discussed above, of 390. The law had general application, but, the author says, Menodorus was the real target.

Menodorus was arrested and brought under imperial guard to Constantinople to stand trial. In despair he prayed to Christ, and then to Thekla. The saint appeared to him in a dream and told him he would never get out of this fix without a good lawyer. She knew just the man, a rhetor named Atalantius, who would appear at the doors of the church the next morning. Menodorus rushed to the church the next day, and sure enough, there was a man meeting the saint's description. In court, Atalantius argued that although it was true that a cleric could not be heir to an unrelated woman, Menodorus as bishop was not a cleric but a leader of clerics—therefore, the law did not apply to him. Surprisingly, this rather sophistic argument worked, and the once high and mighty Eutropius was defeated 'as easily as a spider'.[30]

Unfortunately, this interesting story runs into a chronological problem, for Eutropius[31] served under neither Theodosius I (379–95) nor Theodosius II (402–450) but *c.*395–9, under Arcadius (383–408), the son of Theodosius I. Perhaps the author of the *Miracles* attributed to the notorious Eutropius, the subject of a famous attack by the poet Claudian, actions that really belonged to someone else—maybe to Tatianus, the law's actual addressee, who as a pagan may have had no desire to see the enrichment of Christian clergy. Or perhaps Eutropius attempted to apply the law of 390, but failed (perhaps because the clever lawyer in fact pointed out that the law had been annulled). Or perhaps the

[29] For Eutropius, see also J. Long, *Claudian's* In Eutropium, *or, How, When, and Why to Slander a Eunuch* (Chapel Hill, 1996).

[30] Miracle 9, in G. Dagron (ed.), *Vie et miracles de Ste Thecle* (Brussels, 1978), 304–9; see also 132–3.

[31] J. R. Martindale (ed.), *The Prosopography of the Later Roman Empire, Volume II. A.D. 395–527* (Cambridge, 1980), 440–4.

author of the *Miracles*, writing several decades after both Theodosius and Eutropius, got some other legal incident involving the imperial court confused with Theodosius' law of 390. Or perhaps Eutropius did in fact impetrate such a law, which has not survived.

Fifth-century policy in the eastern Empire indicates a progressive softening of official resistance to the church and its clerics as beneficiaries. In 434, Theodosius II decreed that if any 'religious' man or woman (deaconesses are explicitly mentioned) died intestate, and there were no relatives or civic obligations with any claim upon the deceased's property, it went to his or her church or monastery (*CTh* 5. 3. 1). In 455, the eastern emperor Marcian (450–7) explicitly repealed both Valentinian's law of 370 and Theodosius' already revoked law of 390 (*Nov. Marc.* 5). Marcian declared that any religious woman (a dedicated widow or virgin, or a deaconess) could leave as much as she liked in whatever way she liked to churches, clerics, monks (male or female) or to the poor. Because this law is preserved outside of the Theodosian Code, we have its full text, which shows that Marcian's decision was prompted by a particular case which, like the case of Menodorus, involved a cleric named in a wealthy woman's will. The lady Hypatia had made the priest Anatolius her heir and the will's validity had been questioned, on the basis not only of Theodosius' law (which apparently was known to have been repealed[32]), but also of the 85-year-old law of Valentinian I. Examination of the full text of Hypatia's will had convinced the emperor that she was of sound mind. He further declared that his decision applied not only to Hypatia's institution of Anatolius as heir, but to all similar cases.

In the west, however, celibate women and the disposition of their property continued to trouble secular authorities. In 458, a lengthy novel of the western emperor Majorian, the colleague of Marcian, attacked what was seen as a failure by western Romans to follow what ought to be their natural

[32] Marcian's law has a lacuna just after the mention of Valentinian's law (*CTh* 16. 2. 20) and some legislation of Theodosius. It appears that the lacuna contained references to *CTh* 16. 2. 27–8, and an explanation that *CTh* 16. 2. 28 had repealed the previous legislation.

inclination and civic duty to marry and procreate.[33] Perhaps he was concerned about a possible decline in the birth rate,[34] and (in a measure reminiscent of Augustus' laws of almost 500 years earlier) as a result ordered that childless widows should remarry within five years or hand over their property either to their relatives or (in the absence of relatives) to the imperial *fisc* (*Nov. Maj.* 6. 5). Even more distressing to Majorian was the increasingly popular practice of parents consigning their young daughters to perpetual virginity in a monastery: the result was that 'virginal desire, suppressed by paternal power' was called away from legitimate marriage only to fall into 'illicit allurements'.[35] Therefore no virgin was to become officially consecrated until after she had reached her fortieth year, by which time it could be assumed that she was no longer 'burning with other desires of her adult sex'.[36] Parents, deacons and orphaned girls who did not observe this delay were to be fined a third of their property, and daughters who were disinherited because they had married in defiance of parental wishes were to receive their due inheritance. The same law also denounced the abductors of consecrated virgins;[37] parents of marriageable girls who extorted a large bride gift (*donatio ante nuptias*) from ardent suitors and did not provide an equivalent dowry;[38] and inheritance hunters (*captatores*) (*Nov. Maj.* 6. 11).

Five years later, in 463, Majorian's successor Severus (461–5) annulled most of the provisions of Majorian's law in a novel entitled 'Abrogatis capitibus iniustis legis divi

[33] 'Susceptis regendi imperii gubernaculis cogitare debemus, quemadmodum nostra res publica et armis et legibus et integra religionis reverentia conservatur atque proficiat: cui plurimum sub hac emendatione confertur, si nobilium feminarum amplectenda generositas procreatis liberis multiplicata subcrescat, si piae necessitudines inter parentes et filios nullis insidiarum vitiis immutentur et verum dei cultum mens non invita suscipiat . . .' (*Nov. Maj.* 6, praef.).

[34] 'Et qua studiose tractatur a nobis utilitas filiorum, quos et numerosius procreari pro Romani nominis optamus augmento et procreatis conpetentia commoda perire non patimur, noc necessario putavimus praecavendum, ut marem feminamque iugendos copula nuptiali par condicio utriusque constringat' (*Nov. Maj.* 6. 9).

[35] 'Cupiditas virginalis patria potestate conpressa subdolam voluntatem nubendi, alte concipiat et a legitimo revocata consortio ad inlicitas trahatur inlecebras' (*Nov. Maj.* 6. 1). For a discussion of 'paternal power', see Arjava in this volume.

[36] 'Aliis adulti sexus sui votis calentem' (*Nov. Maj.* 6. 2).

[37] *Nov. Maj.* 6. 4; see above for further discussion of abduction.

[38] *Nov. Maj.* 6. 9–10; for the bride-gift, see Arjava in this volume.

Majoriani Augusti' ('On the Abrogation of the Unjust Chapters of the Law of the Divine Emperor Majorian') (*Nov. Sev.* 1). Severus' law retained only those provisions 'that the authority of ancient laws commends', namely the rule that widowed mothers had only the usufruct of their bride gifts and could not alienate them from their children. The law does not indicate, however, why Majorian's rulings were considered objectionable or why they were being rescinded; presumably, there had been objections by those who would have been the most affected, senatorial aristocrats.[39]

These laws suggest that, beginning in the fourth century, imperial legislators regarded Christian women of respectable birth who adopted a celibate lifestyle in the same light as other women of respectable status. Such women were considered impressionable and in need of protection not only from violence, but also from greedy clerics who might worm their way into the women's homes and pocketbooks. The wishes of the women themselves were not material; the emperors were more concerned to keep powerful families happy by stopping the flow of women's inheritances to unrelated clerics, and this attitude only changed in the mid-fifth century, as the interests of church and state were merging.

One now can turn to the least privileged ranks of Roman society, where imperial law also addressed women who turned to Christianity: prostitutes and show-girls (who were often prostitutes as well). These women followed professions that had always been considered dishonourable and degrading, but quite legal and indeed socially rather useful. The emperor Caligula (37–41) had instituted a tax on the activities of prostitutes in the mid-first century, and Constantine had made prostitutes subject to his *collatio lustralis*, a new tax on merchants and tradespeople.[40] But Christian leaders considered such occupations sinful, and prostitutes or actresses who converted to Christianity were obliged to renounce their profession before receiving baptism. A whole genre of early saints' lives was devoted to the 'penitent harlot' who was inspired by a holy man to forsake the brothel or the stage, and did

[39] For discussion, see H. Wieling, 'Iniusta lex Maioriani', *RIDA*, 38 (1991), 385–420.

[40] See T. A. J. McGinn, 'The Taxation of Roman Prostitutes', *Helios*, 16 (1989), 79–110. Constantine's taxing of prostitutes: Zosimus, *Historia nova* 2. 38.

penance unceasingly until she died (which she generally did soon after repenting).[41] The rulings of late antique church councils and late Roman emperors suggest that these are not merely hagiographic topoi.

Constantius II (337–61) was the first emperor attested to have addressed the conversion of prostitutes to Christianity. In 343 he declared that if women 'who are discovered to have dedicated themselves to the veneration of the Christian law' had been sold to brothels 'to fulfil the vile service of prostituted modesty', they could not be sold again to anyone other than 'ecclesiastics' or 'Christian men' (*CTh* 15. 8. 1). Presumably these Christian men would buy the women in order to free them from a life of shame and sin.

Constantius did not put a stop to prostitution; indeed, he was quite uninterested in the prostitution of women who were not Christian. Nor did his law prevent the current owners of Christian women from prostituting them; it merely forbade their resale as prostitutes—a policy with precedents in classical law.[42] Moreover, the law specified that the ecclesiastic or other Christian who bought such a woman must pay 'a suitable price' ('competenti pretio')—her pimp had to be compensated.

There was no further legislation dealing with female prostitution for almost another century, although male prostitution was attacked in 390 by Theodosius I (*Collatio Mos. et Rom. Leg.* 5. 3). Then, in 428, the eastern emperor Theodosius II addressed a law (*CTh* 15. 8. 2) to the praetorian prefect Florentius, condemning the prostitution of daughters by their fathers and of slavegirls by their masters. These fathers and masters were to be deprived of their *potestas* over the women they had prostituted—and therefore also of the income provided by their occupation.[43] Those forced into prostitution (not only daughters and slaves, but others forced by poverty to sell themselves) were encouraged to seek the help of 'bishops, judges, and even *defensores* [*civitatum*]'. Fathers and masters who continued to pimp were not only

[41] e.g. Thais, Pelagia, Mary. See Cloke, *Female Man*, 198–201.

[42] See T. A. J. McGinn, '*Ne serva prostituatur*: Restrictive Covenants in the Sale of Slaves', *ZSS RA* 100 (1990), 315–53.

[43] Beaucamp, *Le Statut*, 125.

deprived of their power, but sent to the mines. This, the law said, 'is a lesser penalty than that [suffered] if someone were forced, at the command of a pimp, to bear the filth of a coition that she does not want'.[44] The law speaks of prostituted daughters and slaves without making a distinction according to status (or religion, unlike Constantius' law) regarding the shame and injustice they had suffered. This is remarkable in view of Roman law's traditional preoccupation with status.

The edited version of this law in the Theodosian Code gives no indication of what prompted it. But Theodosius II enacted another law in 439, which is preserved in full outside of the Code (*Nov.* 18). Addressed to the praetorian prefect Cyrus, it recalled the great benefaction performed by Florentius, Cyrus' predecessor and the addressee of Theodosius' first law against prostitution eleven years earlier. For, the law says, it was Florentius himself who informed the emperor of the shocking disgrace of prostitution and thereby freed the state from 'the stain of shameful turpitude and ignominy'. And when Florentius learned that pimps were allowed to operate because the imperial treasury reaped a lucrative lustral tax payment from their activities, he had offered to make up the loss to the imperial coffers from his own property. Therefore, the emperor concluded, the law enacted eleven years earlier at the urging of Florentius must continue to be observed under Cyrus' administration. Pimps in Constantinople who were still practising were to be flogged and driven from the city and if Cyrus' office disregarded the law, it would incur a fine of twenty pounds of gold.

Given that the law would have continued in force under any circumstances, the last sentence implies that Cyrus had failed to enforce his predecessor's law, and that his negligence had prompted the repetition. But the reissue of the ban on forced prostitution was probably no more effective than the original. Indeed, prostitution of slaves and free women against their will was banned again in the east by the emperors Leo (457–74) and Justinian,[45] demonstrating the general ineffectiveness of such legislation.

[44] '. . . quae minor poena est, quam si praecepto lenonis cogatur quispiam coitionis sordes ferre, quas nolit' (*CTh* 15. 8. 2).

[45] Leo: *CJ* 1. 4. 14, 11. 41. 7 (undated). Justinian: *Nov. Just.* 14. 1 (535). See Beaucamp, *Le statut*, 126–9. These laws explicitly concerned Constantinople.

Another group of lowborn women often linked with prostitutes in law and in public perception was also the target of late imperial legislation: *scaenicae* or *mimae*, actresses in the vulgar and popular mime shows. There were many of these women in the major cities of the Empire, east and west; the laws attest to their presence in Rome, Gaul, Carthage, and Constantinople. Ammianus Marcellinus reported that during a food shortage in Rome in 383, foreigners were expelled from the city, but three thousand dancing girls (*saltatrices*) were allowed to stay—greatly to the disgust of Ammianus, who may have been one of the foreigners asked to leave.[46]

The conversion of such persons to Christianity caused considerable concern to imperial lawmakers. Dancing girls and mime actresses were essential for the production of public entertainments, and as important for maintaining public order as the staff of imperial bakeries and weaving mills. But unlike bakers or weavers, actors who had been baptized could not remain in their profession. Thus Christian emperors were forced to agree, albeit reluctantly, to their removal from the stage.

In 371, a law of Valentinian I addressed to the praetorian prefect of Gaul declared that actors and actresses who on their deathbed 'hastened to the sacraments of the greatest god' (that is, were baptized) and then recovered, could not be recalled to the theatre (*CTh* 15. 7. 1). Therefore, the emperor continued, extreme care had to be taken to baptize only those stage people who actually were dying. A few months later, still in 371, a second law (*CTh* 15. 7. 2), addressed to the proconsul of Africa, added that daughters of actors who conducted themselves in a proper and respectable manner were to be protected from attempts to force them into their parents' profession. Only those women who could be shown by their behaviour and morals to have followed a 'vulgaris vita' were to be permitted on the stage.

Valentinian's policy was reiterated a decade later by his successor in the west, Gratian (367–83), in laws directed to Rome and Carthage. A rather unpleasant law of 381, directed to Valerianus, prefect of Rome, declared that a 'woman of

[46] Amm. 16. 6. 19. On mimers, see C. Roueché, *Performers and Partisans at Aphrodisias in the Roman and Late Roman Periods* (London, 1993), esp. 23–30.

the stage' who returned to 'shameful embraces' was to be dragged back to the stage 'without hope of any absolution and remain there continuously until a ridiculous old woman, deformed by old age . . . when she could be anything but chaste' (*CTh* 15. 7. 8).[47] This stereotype of old women, repulsive but still sexually voracious, recalls classical invective against women, and betrays the rhetorical and literary training of the law's drafter.[48] Evidently, the lawmaker's concern was to retain as many *scaenicae* as possible in order to keep the public entertainments staffed. Thus, those who had left the stage because they had converted to Christianity but did not maintain a properly Christian lifestyle were to be compelled to return to their old profession. The 'shameful embraces' either might refer to prostitution, or may simply be a rhetorical way of describing behaviour thought to be inappropriate for a baptized Christian.

The laws also reveal that wealthy individuals were kidnapping actresses and carrying them off to their homes to provide private entertainment (*CTh* 15. 7. 5: 380), and were purchasing female lyre players for the fulfilment of their own 'desire for delectation' (*CTh* 15. 7. 10: 385). Such private entertainments were forbidden, but no penalties were prescribed for those who flouted the laws.

Two laws of Theodosius I, addressed to the eastern praetorian prefect Rufinus, involved the dress and deportment of show-girls. They were not to wear gems or silks decorated with figures or gilded clothing, and certainly not purple, a colour suitable only for the highest ranks (*CTh* 15. 7. 11: 393). Nor were mimes 'who earn their living by the wantoness of their body in public' to dress like 'virgins who have dedicated themselves to God' (*CTh* 15. 7. 12: 394). This reference to mime actresses dressing like virgins raises interesting questions. Was this some new type of mime devised along the lines of the old adultery mime, depicting the debauchery of Christian virgins as a comic farce? Or were these mimes dressed as virgins really Christian converts

[47] To be joined with *CTh* 15. 7. 7. See also *CTh* 15. 7. 4: 380, to Paulinus, Urban Prefect of Rome; repeated in 15. 7. 9: 381, to Herasius, Proconsul of Africa.

[48] See A. Richlin, 'Invective against Women in Roman Satire', *Arethusa*, 17 (1984), 67–80. Rhetorical training: Evans Grubbs, *Law*, 50–3.

who were trying to abandon their old profession for a life of penitent celibacy?

The series of laws found under the title 'On Stage People' (*De scaenicis*) in the Theodosian Code ends with a law of the western emperor Honorius addressed to the 'Tribune of Pleasures' (*Tribunus voluptatum*) at Carthage, demanding that all female mimes who had previously been released from their obligations by imperial rescript be recalled to the stage. The law as we have it says nothing about actresses who had abandoned the stage after baptism, so it is not clear if they too were included in this general recall (*CTh* 15. 7. 13: 413).

Evidently stage-girls, like so many others in the late Empire, were attempting to escape their occupational obligations, and conversion to Christianity presented an attractive alternative to a degrading and wearying life on the stage. Although the preambles to these laws do not survive to tell us what prompted them, it is likely that they were imperial responses to two quite different special-interest groups: Christian leaders demanding that women of the stage be allowed to renounce their sinful life and receive baptism, and officials like the 'tribune of pleasures' complaining that the supply of entertainers was being jeopardized by such conversions. Emperors of the late fourth and early fifth centuries seem to have been quite unmoved by the plight of the women themselves. Only in the mid-fifth century in the east did this change, with the legislation first of Leo and then, in the sixth century, of Justinian. By then, stage-girls and prostitutes had come to be equated in law and both were protected from the exploitation of their bodies for public pleaure. In Justinian's case, influence may plausibly be attributed to his wife Theodora, a former stage-girl whose salacious performances are described in the *Secret History* of Procopius.[49]

Examination of late imperial legislation on women points up the tensions inherent in any attempt to 'Christianize' Roman law, and illustrates how conflicts could arise between the perceived needs of the state and the demands of the church.

[49] Leo's law (see above) concerned stage-people as well as prostitutes. On Justinian's legislation, see Beaucamp, *Le Statut*, 130–2.

The state depended on a supply of women of high status to bear future subjects and maintain their ancestral lineage, and on a supply of low-status women to provide commercial sex and public entertainment. But Christian ideology extolled celibacy and condemned the exploitation of women's bodies for pleasure. Christian writers glorified women who ostentatiously refused marriage and left their massive fortunes to the church, and praised 'penitent harlots' who had renounced their shameful ways. But Christian emperors were less enthusiastic about women who abandoned their allotted roles, for by so doing they disrupted the social order. Well-born women who refused advantageous marriages could disaffect powerful families annoyed at the loss of inheritances and future heirs. Mimes and dancing-girls who abandoned the stage might trigger discontent among the populace annoyed at the loss of their traditional entertainments. And prostitutes who forsook their trade for a life of Christian virtue were a financial liability to the state, for they deprived the imperial treasury of much-needed revenues.

While declaring that women truly devoted to Christianity were not to be forced into roles they did not want (whether marriage or the stage), imperial law made little attempt to dismantle traditional gender roles or moral values based on the status hierarchy. Emperors had no objection to legislating on the private behaviour of clerics and celibate women when asked to do so by church officials, as in the law of Honorius enacted in response to a priest's recommendation. But when workers in state industries or the interests of powerful aristocratic families were involved, the imperial response was more muted. Only two of the laws discussed above seem to have been issued in response to Christian concerns which ran counter to the interests of secular society: the law of Theodosius II on prostitution, enacted at the suggestion of the zealous and generous Florentius, and the law of Marcian rescinding earlier bans on legacies to clerics by wealthy women. Both these laws date to the mid-fifth century and both are from the eastern Empire. Moreover, as so often in Roman law, Theodosius and Marcian were reacting rather than initiating, in that they were responding to specific requests by officials like Florentius or individual clerics like

Anatolius. At the same time in the west, Majorian attempted to turn the clock back to an era when marriage and procreation were mandated by the state. In general, fourth- and fifth-century legislation on Christian women reveals a society in which interests of church and state more often collided than coincided.

14

Canonists Construct the Nun?: Church Law and Women's Monastic Practice in Merovingian France

Catherine R. Peyroux

'In episcopo ecclesia est.'[1] So goes the venerable adage, surely never more appropriate than when bishops were gathered in solemn council to manifest the authority of the church in the production of the body of decrees and statutes governing the faith, and the faithful, that we identify as early medieval canon law. The role and prerogative of this church in the governance of religious women in the christianized barbarian kingdoms of the west has long been a matter of speculation and dispute. In recent years, two dominant interpretations have emerged. One sees the Merovingian period as a time characterized by the comparative autonomy, and equality of spiritual potential, of consecrated women, whose religious authority would later be eclipsed in the Carolingian age by the rise of an organized church that 'reflected the prejudices of the patriarchal societies where Christianity was born and propagated'.[2] A second, revisionist account sees the sixth century as a time when reforming bishops like Caesarius of Arles reinvented female monasticism, and in the process constrained nuns ever more tightly by canonical legislation and monastic rules that emphasized strict claus-

[1] R. Foreville, Preface to O. Pontal, *Die Synoden im Merovingerreich* (Paderborn, 1986), p. ix.

[2] S. Wemple, *Women in Frankish Society: Marriage and the Cloister, 500–900* (Philadelphia, 1981).

tration and separation from the world.[3] Because clerical disapproval regarding the physical proximity of monks and nuns is taken by both accounts as a sign of episcopal denial of women's capacity to transcend their biological sex in monasticism, special attention will be given below to legislation on the licit and illicit proximity between nuns and male religious, both monks and clergy.

In principle as well as practice, the preferred source of legislative authority for an early medieval bishop was a group of other bishops, met in solemn council. Ideally the clergy met on a regular basis. 'How long', wrote bishop Avitus of Vienne in his invitation to the Council of Epaon in 517, 'either from forgetfulness or from busyness, we have delayed that thing so necessary and not without divine inspiration instituted by the Fathers'.[4] Avitus was writing only six years after the well-attended Frankish Council of Orléans (511), where thirty-two bishops had subscribed to the *acta*, and just eleven years after the similarly well-attended Council of Agde (506), which united some thirty-four bishops or their representatives from the Visigothic territories in Gaul. Despite their regional affiliations, these two councils did not represent wholly separate groups. The regional clergies in the sixth century were created by historical accidents of changing political boundaries: eight of the men who had sat at the Visigothic Council of Agde also attended the Frankish Council of Orléans five years later.[5] More importantly, bishops of the post-Roman kingdoms were connected through common cause and purpose: although the Burgundian clergy assembled by Avitus had not been in attendance at the Council of Orléans, they proceeded to work from the Orléans legislation in a way that shows the contiguity between the Frankish and Burgundian churches.[6]

Once met in the drama of assembly and deliberation, the clergy turned to the business of consensus. Negotiated

[3] D. Hochstetler, *A Conflict of Traditions: Women in Religion in the Early Middle Ages, 500–840* (Lanham, Md., 1992).

[4] C. de Clercq (ed.), *Concilia Galliae a. 511–a. 695*, *CCL* (Turnhout, 1963), 22.

[5] Compare the subscription lists in C. Munier (ed.), *Concilia Galliae, a. 314–a. 506*, *CCL* 148 (Turnhout, 1963), 213–14, and *CCL* 148A. 13–14.

[6] Cf. Orléans cans. 11, 13, 19, 22, 23, 29, with Épaon cans. 23, 32, 29, 10, 18, 20 (*CCL* 148A. 78–88, 106–16).

agreement was the delicate balancing of concerns that made the conciliar system work and gave the decisions their authority. This agreement had two dimensions: the bishops were eager to reach an accord, and they were simultaneously constrained to keep to the path trodden by their predecessors.[7] The documents of former councils were mined for information and instruction regarding contemporary difficulties; in many instances the re-use of canons by later councils may be identified. Furthermore, conciliar legislation in fifth- and sixth-century Gaul was overwhelmingly the province of the episcopal clergy; abbots rarely appear in the subscription lists.[8] Thus the church in council was a relatively closed group of ecclesiastics who were tempered by the nature of the exercise to look to one another and to the earlier decisions of men much like themselves in training and experience for answers to the dilemmas that confronted them. This was certainly the bishops' practice in their conciliar response to female monasticism, of which the problem of proximate male and female monastic communities formed a part.

In the autumn of 506 the Catholic clergy of the kingdom of Toulouse, the Visigothic territories in Gaul, joined 'in the name of God' in the basilica of St Andrew at Agde, 'intending to consider the discipline and ordination of clerics and also the higher priesthood, or else matters beneficial to the church'.[9] Among those matters, for the first time, bishops in council discussed monasteries of virgins. Thus began the effort to articulate a collective episcopal policy toward communities of professed women. It may well have been prompted by the particular interests of the bishop who presided over the session, Caesarius (502–42), the metropolitan bishop of Arles. Caesarius was then a young and very recent bishop (he had been elected in 503) who had begun his religious career as a zealous monk at the monastery of Lérins.[10] Long after departing Lérins, indeed, throughout his prolonged and influential career in the secular clergy, Caesarius retained a fervent interest in the monastic life which included the

[7] J. M. Wallace-Hadrill, *The Frankish Church* (Oxford, 1983), 95.
[8] Wallace-Hadrill, *Frankish Church*, 94. [9] *CCL* 148. 192.
[10] Caesarius' exemplary monastic origins are emphasized in the *Vit. Caes.* 1. 4–7: G. Morin (ed.), *Caesarii sancti episcopi Arelatensis, Opera omnia* (Maredsous, 1942), 2. 297–323.

supervision of female monasticism. Within two years after Agde he would lay the foundations just outside the city walls of Arles for his first monastic community for women, never finished, which was to have housed his sister Caesaria.[11] By 512 he established a women's monastery within the city's walls that was dedicated to St John the Baptist; Caesaria was the abbess, and the women there lived under the rule which had been written especially for them by Caesarius.[12] Thus, some part of the attention given by the bishops assembled at Agde to diocesan control over monastic communities, particularly the attention paid to communities for women, is probably to be attributed to Caesarius' influence over the proceedings.

Previously, the episcopal councils of Gaul and Spain had produced comparatively few pronouncements regarding the subject of female religious. Fourth- and fifth-century conciliar discussion of women in the church addressed itself mainly to the governance of women associated with the clergy.[13] Not until the last quarter of the fifth century did an unofficial Gallic collection known as the *Statuta ecclesiae antiqua* advise that the (male) secular agent for religious women should be approved by the local bishop.[14]

The record of conciliar legislation in the fourth and fifth centuries reflects the bishops' perception that single women vowed to God were on the whole following individual paths of holiness among the Christian faithful, with the emphasis here on 'among'. After her ceremony of consecration, a woman who had promised herself to God might return to the family home to live out her life,[15] or she might enter

[11] This foundation, outside the city walls, was destroyed in the Burgundian–Ostrogothic conflict of *c.*508 (*Vita Caesarii* 1. 28).

[12] W. Klingshirn, *Caesarius of Arles: The Making of a Christian Community in Late Antique Gaul* (Cambridge, 1994), 104–8, 117–20.

[13] Several councils regulated which women could live with deacons, priests, or bishops: note Arles II (*c.*500), can. 3 (*CCL* 148. 114), with R. Mathisen, 'The "Second Council of Arles" and the Spirit of Compilation and Codification in Late Roman Gaul', *Journal of Early Christian Studies*, 5 (1997), 511–54; Angers (453), can. 4 (*CCL* 148. 137). For the problem of clerics' relations with women not of their own family, note Angers (ibid.) and Tours (461), can. 3 (*CCL* 148. 145); as well as *Stat. eccl. ant.* 27 (*CCL* 148. 171).

[14] *CCL* 148. 173.

[15] A practice common in the fourth century; see R. Metz, 'Les Vierges chrétiennes au IVe siècle', in *Saint Martin et son temps*, Studia Anselmiana, 46 (Rome, 1961), 109–32.

or found one of the many small, urban, domestic clusters of religious women that seem to have been the predominant type at this time.[16] Collective episcopal anxiety about setting professed women visibly apart from their peers surfaced rather late: an opinion that consecrated women in Gaul should wear clothing 'appropriate to [their] profession and chastity'[17] appeared only toward the end of the fifth century.

The church councils of the fourth and fifth centuries had been content to address the individual rather than the corporate devotional lives of female religious. At Agde, the bishops assumed a collective responsibility for overseeing the latter. The twenty-eighth canon admonished that 'monasteries of virgins should be placed far from monasteries of monks, either on account of the devil's treacheries or the adverse talk of men'.[18] Significantly, this first conciliar pronouncement that directly mentioned cenobitic female monasticism did so in the context of denouncing proximate male and female communities and the dangers inherent in them. The reasons given for separating men's and women's monasteries—either sexual temptation (the devil's treacheries) or adverse gossip—suggest that opportunities for mutual access between monks and professed women were considered to be a refinement of the general problem of monastic chastity, whereby the sexual purity of the professed person was implicitly threatened by physical exposure to members of the other sex. For this, the conciliar solution was physical separation of the sexes through physical separation of the communities; in the eyes of the bishops, even between two religious, monastic vows did not constitute a sufficient safeguard for perpetual chastity.

Anxiety about ensuring a chaste environment was of course associated with both male and female monasteries, over both of which bishops repeatedly asserted their supervisory

[16] J.-M. Guillaume, 'Les Abbayes de femmes en Pays Franc, des origines à la fin du viie siècle', in M. Parisse (ed.), *Rémiremont: L'Abbaye et la ville* (Nancy, 1980), 24–46.

[17] *Stat. eccl. ant.* 99: *CCL* 148. 184. Canon 19 of the Council of Agde (*CCL* 148. 202) restricted the veiling of professed virgins to those aged 40 years or older, a technicality conspicuous by its absence in hagiographical accounts: Metz, 'Vierges', 124.

[18] 'Monasteria puellarum longius a monasteriis monachorum, aut propter insidiis diaboli, aut propter oblocutiones hominum collocentur' (*CCL* 148. 205).

role.[19] In the case of male houses, sixth-century councils attended to the requirements of monastic chastity as a straightforward management problem, the habitual conciliar approach, by summarily declaring the male communities closed to women: 'A woman shall not be allowed to enter at all within the monastery's walls.'[20] But, unlike male monastics, professed women depended on a member of the opposite sex to administer the sacraments, and thus their space could not be completely closed to male religious. Instead it was necessary to regulate more closely which male religious were to be admitted to women's houses. Well over half of the sixth-century conciliar legislation regarding women's communities addressed the task of defining licit male access to female monasteries.[21]

For example, rulings promulgated at Agde increased direct episcopal authority over the distribution of the sacraments in monasteries, and that included the religious services required by communities of professed women. Other councils narrowed the categories of those who were to be granted admission to women's monasteries. Even ordained clergy were not allowed wholly unrestricted access. The Council of Epaon authorized entry into a monastery of virgins for 'those men of approved life and advanced age'; clerics who had entered for the purpose of celebrating the mass were advised to depart swiftly upon its completion. Among those explicitly prohibited access were 'any other cleric or any young monk'.[22] Episcopal entry was, however,

[19] Agde, can. 27, required episcopal approval of all new monasteries; 'Monasterium novum nisi episcopo aut permittente aut probante nullus incipere aut fundare praesumat', *CCL* 148. 205; see also Épaon (517), can. 10 (*CCL* 148A. 26); Orléans, can. 22 (*CCL* 148A. 11); and Arles (554), can. 2 (*CCL* 148A. 171).

[20] Tours (567), can. 17 (*CCL* 148A. 182); Auxerre (561/605), can. 26 (*CCL* 148A. 268). In legislation, bishops relied on the walls of the monastery to define boundaries, but a canon issued at an unknown location in the early seventh century that sought to restrict secular activities within male (or female) enclosures shows how 'un-walled' the monastery remained in the expectations of the surrounding community: 'Ut intra septa monastyrii non baptizetur nec missae defunctorum saecularium in monastyrio celebrentur nec saecularium corpora ibidem sepeliantur forsitan permiso ponteficis' (can. 6: *CCL* 148A. 287).

[21] The exceptions are Orange V (549), can. 19; Mâcon I (581/3), can. 12; and Lyon III (583), can. 3 (*CCL* 148A. 155, 226, 232); these address the related issues of the illicit marriage of consecrated virgins and the breaking of monastic cloister.

[22] *CCL* 148A. 34; note also the more restrictive version of this canon enacted at Mâcon (581/3), can. 2 (*CCL* 148A. 223).

guaranteed. At Arles in 554, the care of a women's community was reserved to the bishop of the city in which it was established, and the bishop was directed to see that the abbess lived according to the monastic rule.[23]

By the middle of the sixth century, then, western conciliar legislation had called for the separation of communities of professed male and female religious; enjoined stricter attention to the women's community on the part of the local clergy; and commended female houses to the charge of the local bishop. The theory of chastity underlying this legislation emphasized the management of the physical environment of the professed religious as a means of safeguarding spiritual purity.

It is not known whether the council of Arles in 554 had a specific rule in mind when it framed the canon requiring episcopal supervision over the regular life of a women's monastery. The candidate most likely to have been favoured by the Gaulish bishops, however, was Caesarius of Arles' *Regula ad virgines* ('Rule for Virgins'), written sometime between 512 and 534 for the monastery dedicated to John the Baptist that was ruled by his sister Caesaria.[24] This monastic rule for women had a significant influence on the regular life of professed women in sixth-century Francia. It formed the direct basis for two of the other three extant nuns' rules known to have circulated in Merovingian Gaul and may have indirectly informed the third.[25] It is a rule known to have been esteemed by bishops with an interest in female monasticism. Syagrius of Autun adopted it for the monastery of Notre Dame at Autun.[26] Gregory of Tours preserved an episcopal evaluation of the *Regula* in a letter that

[23] *CCL* 148A. 171–2.

[24] H. Mayo, 'The Sources of Female Monasticism in Merovingian Gaul', *Studia Patristica*, 16. 2 (1985), 32–7, at 32. For the text, see A. de Vogüé. J. Courreau (eds.), *Césaire d'Arles, Œuvres monastiques*. i. *Œuvres pour les moniales*, *SC* 345 (Paris, 1988).

[25] Mayo, 'Monasticism', 35, notes that Caesarius' rule was a 'major source' for those of Aurelian and Donatus, and through Donatus perhaps influenced a third, the *Regula cuiusdam patris ad virgines* ('Rule of a Certain Father to the Virgins').

[26] C. Lambot, 'Le Prototype des monastères cloîtrés de femmes', *Revue liturgique et monastique*, 23 (1956), 169–74, at 173–4.

had been written by his predecessor and six other bishops to Radegund concerning her monastery of the Holy Cross at Poitiers, where the community followed Caesarius' precepts.[27] In it the bishops specifically commended the provisions for the cloistering of nuns with the words 'sicut continet regula' ('just as the rule specifies') (*Hist.* 9. 39). In addition they commanded all their episcopal successors to enforce the sanctions that they had prescribed against nuns who broke Caesarius' prohibitions against leaving the monastery (*Hist.* 9. 39).

It is fitting that the *Regula* should have met with broad approval; from the point of view of the episcopal governance of female religious it offered a programme of regular prescriptions that closely paralleled the sixth-century conciliar proscriptions.[28] The hallmark of the rule, much emphasized in the bishops' letter to Radegund, was its insistence on the nun's strict observance of physical cloister.[29] This injunction begins the rule (*Regula ad virgines* 1), and is repeated with special emphasis toward the end:

> Indeed, we wish this especially to be observed by you without any relaxation, that no one of you up to the time of her death leave the monastery, or go into that basilica into which you have a door, or presume on her own to go out.[30]

[27] Gregory of Tours, *Historiae* (henceforth *Hist.*) 9. 39, 10. 40. The letter that Gregory thought had been written at the time that Radegund founded the monastery must have been composed at least a decade later: see Y. Labande-Mailfert, 'Les Débuts de Sainte-Croix', in *Histoire de l'Abbaye Sainte-Croix de Poitiers* (Poitiers, 1986), 21–116, at 35–8, 42–5.

[28] Indeed, the rule contains a subscription list remarkably similar to a conciliar document, signed by seven bishops (*Regula ad virgines* 124), four of whom attended Arles IV (524) (*CCL* 148A. 45).

[29] Caesarius's provisions for unbroken claustration are analysed by J. Tibbetts Schulenberg, 'Strict Active Enclosure and Its Effects on the Female Monastic Experience (ca. 500–1100),' in J. Nichols, L. Thomas Shank (eds.), *Medieval Religious Women*, i. *Distant Echoes* (Kalamazoo, 1984), 51–86; and D. Hochstettler, 'The Meaning of Monastic Cloister for Women according to Caesarius of Arles', in T. F. X. Noble, J. J. Contreni (eds.), *Religion, Culture and Society in the Early Middle Ages* (Kalamazoo, 1987), 27–40.

[30] 'Hoc enim est quod specialiter absque ulla dimunitione a vobis volumus observari, ut nulla ex vobis usque ad mortem suam de monasterio egredi, vel in ipsam basilicam, in qua ianuam habetis, aut permittatur, aut per seipsam praesumat exire' (*Regula ad virgines* 50).

Equally, the cloister was not to be broken from the outside by the female lay relatives of the nuns or by any men at all except those needed for the mass.[31]

These instructions enjoining claustration, noticeably more strict than those in Caesarius' counterpart rule for monks, were reinforced physically by Caesarius at the women's monastery of John the Baptist in Arles through the simple expedient of blocking off the external doors to the monastery.[32] Caesarius' hagiographers also promoted the monastery's reputation for strict enclosure. They reported that the nuns followed Caesarius' regulations about cloister even at peril to their lives in a tale about a fire that started near the monastery and approached so that there was no doubt that everything would be burned. Although the nuns were 'disturbed (*turbatae*) because they were not allowed to leave', they remained within the confines of the monastery, to be rescued only by Caesarius' timely and miraculous quelling of the flames (*Vita Caesarii* 2. 26). Cloister in Caesarius' rule represents, therefore, a rigidly literal interpretation of strict and unbroken physical separation of the female religious from laypersons or male monastics, separation, in fact, from every outside contact except that required for the mass: the conciliar ideal in action.

Having considered the question of what bishops wanted to see, we need now to place some degree of context around the conciliar legislation. To this end, we may briefly compare the prescriptive and proscriptive material generated by Caesarius' rule and church councils to the descriptive account provided by Gregory of Tours of two contemporary women's communities. As noted, Radegund's monastery at Poitiers followed the *Regula ad virgines*. This was broken egregiously during a revolt against the successor of Radegund by some members of the monastery in 589, which began when a group of some forty nuns walked out of the monastery (*Hist.* 9. 39–43, 10. 15–17). To resolve the many disputes connected

[31] *Regula ad virgines* 36 (secular clergy), 37 (laywomen), 38 (abbots might be allowed to pray in the oratory upon request), and 39 (abbots and monks are not to be invited to meals).

[32] *Regula ad virgines* 37, speaking of permanently closed doors to the outside in the old baptistery, the *scola* ('gallery'), the weaving room, and a tower door.

with the incident the participants were eventually called, under duress exerted by the Frankish kings Childebert II (575–95) and Guntram (561–92), before a tribunal of bishops. In this familiar story, it is the circumstances surrounding episcopal governance of the monastery that concern us.

The first point to be noted is that the bishops' intervention in the matter was rarely taken on their own initiative, but rather was more often impelled by the royal relatives of the rebellious nuns. After the dissident nuns first left the monastery, alleging bad behaviour on the part of their abbess, their leader, Clotild, sought the aid of her relative, king Guntram. She then rejoined her companions at Tours to await the bishops whom the king ordered to investigate the matter. The nuns waited in vain (*Hist.* 9. 40); eventually they returned to Poitiers and based themselves in the church of St Hilary, where they gathered a band of male supporters and began a direct offensive against the abbess at Holy Cross. During the early stages of the altercation, bishop Maroveus of Poitiers had been less than assiduous in his role as shepherd of the monastic flock. Gregory thought Maroveus nursed a grudge against the community that had been left over from an earlier quarrel with Radegund (*Hist.* 9. 40). But even if he had decided to intervene in the governance of the nuns, in practice the scope of his jurisdiction was unclear, for Radegund herself had undermined relations between Holy Cross and the bishop of Poitiers by pointedly bypassing the latter's authority for the protection of the bishop of Tours, preferring to associate her convent with the aura of St Martin.[33] By the time Maroveus made an active attempt to quell the violence it had grown well beyond his control (*Hist.* 9. 15). Gregory, who was among those appointed to the tribunal inquiry, refused even to enter the city until the revolt could be put down by secular force (*Hist.* 10. 15).

In this instance, the bishops' canonical sanctions were simply not effective without the backing of secular authority. After the mutinous nuns returned to St Hilary's church at Poitiers, the metropolitan bishop of Bourges, accompanied

[33] See B. Rosenwein, *Negotiating Space: Power, Restraint, and the Privileges of Immunity in Early Medieval Europe* (Ithaca, NY, 1998), 57.

by Maroveus and others, championed an effort to persuade the women to return obediently to their monastery. Upon receiving the nuns' refusal, the bishops imposed their final sanction, excommunication. This had two results. The immediate response of the rebels was to set their band of supporters to a violent attack upon the episcopal deputation. After this the bishops took no further direct action, but exchanged letters exhorting unceasing prayer for divine intervention (*Hist.* 9. 41–2). The second effect of the excommunication was to provide Clotild with an excuse for disobeying all further ecclesiastical emissaries: summoned to appear before the priest Theuthar, who had been sent by king Childebert, the nuns refused, saying 'We will not come, because we are suspended from communion. If we are allowed to reconcile, then we will not delay to come to an audience' (*Hist.* 9. 43). The rebels were only compelled to answer to the bishops at the tribunal after the local count, backed by written orders from the kings, suppressed the nuns' revolt by means of brutal force (*Hist.* 10. 15).

Gregory's account of the fractious events at the monastery at Poitiers offers a vivid historical corrective to the hagiographical ideal of nun's cloister set forth by Caesarius' hagiographers. Equally, his description of the bishops' response to the revolt provides a useful insight into the practical limitations to the scope of the episcopal authority that was proclaimed so unequivocally at church councils. It is true that, when pushed, the tribunal of bishops sought to enforce the rule governing the women religious at Poitiers. According to the proceedings reported by Gregory, the first question that the bishops asked of the chief malcontents was, 'Why had they departed so rashly against [the precepts of] their rule, leaving the gates of the monastery broken?' (*Hist.* 10. 16). The bishops likewise insisted upon the canonical basis of their authority as judges.[34] Nonetheless, it required secular might and urging to bring the bishops to a formal adjudication of the matter.[35] Moreover, as this case illustrates, the authority of the councils was limited in its potency not

[34] e.g. 'Reseratis a nobis et recensitis canonibus'; 'Haec nos pro vestra iussione, quod ecclesiasticum pertenuit ordinem, circumspectis canonibus' (*Hist.* 10. 16).

[35] For episcopal adjudication, see also Erhart, Harries, Lenski, and Dossey in this volume.

simply by the ability of bishops to enforce it, but also by their inclination. It was not Maroveus or Gregory but Guntram who sought to quell the nuns' dissent in the early stages of its course by calling in a group of bishops to investigate.

This tale helps to show the limitations governing the actual application of conciliar pronouncements on women's monasticism, even in circumstances where bishops clearly perceived a violation of canon law. To conclude this survey of the official ecclesiastical stance regarding formal relations between male and female monasteries, we might consider a more puzzling case wherein a bishop well-versed and assiduously attentive to the rulings of councils did not perceive a contravention of conciliar legislation regarding proximately situated male and female communities. The bishop was Gregory himself and the communities were the religious domiciles associated with and established in the precincts of the church of St Martin at Tours.

Sometime between 573 and 576, the noblewoman Ingetrude, another pious female relative of Guntram, founded a women's monastery at Tours. Like Radegund's foundation at Poitiers, Ingetrude's monastery not only housed a number of royal and aristocratic women, but also experienced a rebellion, in this case, by Ingetrude's daughter, a sometime resident there. Situated as it was in the forecourt of the basilical church of Gregory's own city, Gregory knew it well and chronicled the difficulties there in some detail.[36] Because canonical legislation designed to manage women religious relied so heavily on controlling physical access between nuns and the outside world, we are concerned here to understand both the built environment as well as the monastic discipline.

Gregory informs us more than once that Ingetrude's nunnery was established 'in the atrium of [the church of] St Martin' (*Hist.* 9. 33, 10. 12). This was a busy and public place, designed both to house the many pilgrims who visited and to allow them clear visual access to the saint's tomb.[37] But

[36] *Hist.* 9. 33, 10. 12; also 5. 21, 7. 36.

[37] See W. Jacobsen, 'Saints' Tombs in Frankish Church Architecture', *Speculum*, 72 (1977), 1107–43, at 1109 and 1111 (with a sketch depicting the view of the altar and tomb). For the polyvalent religious functions of the early medieval atrium, see J. Guyon, 'L'Architecture religeuse chez Grégoire de Tours', in N. Gauthier, H. Galinié (eds.), *Grégoire de Tours et l'espace gaulois* (Tours, 1997), 197–207, at 205–6.

Ingetrude's monastery was not in fact situated in this open area, but rather in a bounded space to which Ingetrude could forbid access, a space that after her death could be stripped of all furniture leaving only bare walls (*Hist.* 10. 12). Gregory may have placed the monastery 'in the atrium' because it abutted upon or opened into this central meeting point of Martin's worship. It would have been deliberately situated there to connect Ingetrude's establishment closely with the active cult of the saint. Gregory discloses only indirectly that the community shared this situation with a number of male religious habitations, variously attached to the church.[38]

Besides the professed women of Ingetrude's 'monasterium puellarum' (*Hist.* 10. 12), the Breton priest Winnocus also dwelt in the church,[39] as did the basilical 'abbot', a dignitary who had charge over the martyrium of the church.[40] In addition to the pilgrims camped in the atrium, those seeking asylum as well as the poor who were the church's dependants were housed in multiple cells located around the church.[41] With regard to Ingetrude's monastic discipline, Gregory does not specify which, if any, rule she followed, but the practice of her monastery does not seem to have included the radical physical separation from all men but the bearers of the sacraments that the canonical legislation demanded. For example, Ingetrude habitually collected the water for washing Martin's tomb, and Gregory expressed no surprise or disapproval when he reported that the priest Winnocus was standing nearby during the process.[42] The precise location of this activity is unspecified; if it took place inside the monastery quarters, it seems doubtful that Winnocus was administering the sacraments, and if in the atrium or church, it seems more doubtful still that he would have been the only male present.

[38] For the location of Ingetrude's house and the surrounding *cellulae*, see L. Pietri, 'Bâtiments et sanctuaires annexes de la Basilique Saint-Martin de Tours, à la fin du VIe siècle', *RHEF* 62 (1975), 223–34; and eadem, 'Les Abbés de basilique dans la Gaule de VIe siècle', *RHEF* 69 (1983), 5–28.

[39] Pietri, 'Bâtiments', 227.

[40] Pietri, 'Abbés', 10–11, demonstrates that this 'abbot' had no monastic responsibilities.

[41] Pietri, 'Bâtiments', 227–8.

[42] *Hist.* 5. 21; this example was suggested by Ralph Mathisen.

From the perspective of the bishops' imagination of the proper order for monastic women, as articulated in canon law, Ingetrude's foundation would seem thoroughly to have contravened the spirit if not the absolute letter of canon twenty-eight of the Council of Agde, which prohibited monasteries of virgins and monks from close habitation on account of sexual temptation or gossip. Should we understand that priests, church associates, claimants of sanctuary, and the destitute were held by Gregory to be immune from the sexual temptations that beset monks? Or does this tell us something quite different about the governing of female monastics in the sixth century: that these canons must be interpreted as a sort of episcopal cosmology of the ordered Christian community rather than a blueprint for episcopal interventions. When push came to shove, as in the case of the bishops' unenthusiastic reaction to events at the monastery at Poitiers, canonical utterance provided guidance for action. Then, if ever, the *ecclesia* resided in the bishop. But so much more often, as in the placement of Ingetrude's foundation, it would seem that push never came to shove, and that Merovingian women's monasticism grew up between the laws, in the interstices of sixth-century orthodoxy.

15

The Farmer, the Landlord, and the Law in the Fifth Century

Boudewijn Sirks

Sometime about the beginning of the fifth century CE a landowner—let us call him Possessor—in North Africa, in present day Tunisia, wrote an elegant and literary letter to another landowner, Salvius, who lived in the town of Mactaris.[1] After an introduction, Possessor reminded Salvius of the time they had spent together as law students and barristers in Rome, and then said:

I do not know at all why you want to scare poor farmers, and I cannot understand why you want to press upon my farmers the fear of a production in court. As if I could not comfort them, release them from fear, tell them there is less to fear than you claim. I concede I was often frightened by the weapons of your eloquence in the days when we fought each other in the courts, but often I returned the blows. Indeed, together with you I have learned by which right (*quo iure*) and according to which procedure (*quove ordine*)[2] *coloni* are reclaimed, who is entitled to bring an action, and who is not entitled to the result of an action. You say that you want to recall the 'Volusians' and you assiduously and angrily proclaim that you will fetch the peasants with force from my turret.[3] And

[1] Ps.-Sulpicius Severus, *Epistula ad Salvium*: ed. C. Halm, *CSEL* 1 (Vienna, 1866), 251–6; discussed by C. Lepelley, 'Trois documents méconnus retrouvés parmi les spuria de Sulpice Sévère', *Antiquités Africaines*, 25 (1989), 235–62. The text is preserved only in the ninth-century *codex Vaticanus Palatinus Latinus* 829.

[2] *Iure*: the legal basis of the claim; *ordine*: the formulaic procedure of the *cognitio extra ordinem*.

[3] *Turricula*: Lepelley, 'Documents', 245, explains this as a reference, first to the towers we often see on the depictions of African estates as a metaphor for such an estate, and also to dovecotes. This would mean that the *coloni* were being equated with pigeons. Although Lepelley's explanation may be sound, the use of *turricula* in this sense is not attested elsewhere.

you recklessly threaten that you, who, as I hope and desire, are linked to me by a former relationship, will drag my people into court without a summons.[4] I am asking Your Outstanding Prudence[5] whether advocates use one law and retired advocates another, whether there is one kind of equity in Rome and another in Mactaris.[6]

Here, farmers have left an estate called the *fundus Volusianus* ('Volusian field') and reside now on the farmstead of Possessor. Salvius claims to be the owner of the *fundus Volusianus* and on that account wants to recall them. He threatens not only these individuals but also the farmers of Possessor, as is clear from the subsequent text. He even threatens the *actores*, Possessor's farm managers. He proposes to have all of them, without exception, brought into court without a summons. It now is Possessor's duty to stand up for his people and restrain Salvius. His position as patron and landowner obliges him to act thus. He says that he very well knows what requirements the law sets out for a claim like Salvius' and he suggests that Salvius does not meet them.

Salvius probably claimed that these farmers were under a lien to him as a consequence of his ownership of the *fundus Volusianus* (othewise there would have been no case). If they were, he could, with the assistance of the law, recall them to the land from which they had originated. This kind of lien was embodied in the late Roman institution known as the colonate, as a consequence of which people (referred to as 'coloni censiti') were registered in the census to a particular piece of land and, in case of the 'adscripticiate colonate', were subjected to the powers of the landlord of that land.[7]

This account serves to introduce the broader question of why a farmer, or anyone active in a trade on an estate, would

[4] *Conventione neglecta*: Lepelley, 'Documents', 245, interprets this as referring to an agreement between Dionysius and Salvius. However, *conventio* can also mean summons: see H. Heumann, E. Seckel (eds.), *Handlexikon zu den Quellen des romischen Rechts* (Jena, 1907) s.v.: 'gerichtliche Belangung'; and M. Kaser, *Das römische Zivilprozessrecht* (Munich, 1966), 458, 461: 'Ladung'. The context of an *exhibitio*, namely by an *interdictum*, makes the latter meaning more probable. The writer is arguing that such a seizure of the *coloni* by Salvius would be illegal.

[5] 'de insigni prudentia tua': for these '*tua*-epithets', see Mathisen in this volume.

[6] Quoted in the Appendix below.

[7] See A. J. B. Sirks, 'Reconsidering the Roman Colonate', *ZSS RA*, 110 (1993), 331–69. This study will not deal with the other kind of *coloni*, the *coloni liberi* (see Sirks, 'Reconsidering').

wish to tie himself and his family to the power of an estate owner, and just what the role of the imperial government was in such an arrangement. Some sense of the constraints affecting the poor is gained from Salvian of Marseille, who said *c*.440:

> And therefore, when they are not capable of doing what they would prefer, they do the only thing they are capable of: they render themselves to the powerful in order to be protected and shielded, they turn themselves into rich peoples' conquests and pass into their property and power of disposition'.[8]

Further on, Salvian compared such persons to Odysseus' men whom Circe changed into pigs, 'because they [the rich] start to treat them, whom they have accepted as outsiders and strangers, as their property, and they change into slaves those who certainly are freeborn men'.[9]

Times were sometimes so hard that people placed themselves or their children into slavery or debt-slavery. An enactment of 293 declared illegal the pledge of free men for debts (*CJ* 8. 16. 6; quoted in Appendix). From 315 farm equipment also was declared unpledgeable, a ruling that was meant to safeguard the uninterrupted tilling of the soil, but which cut farmers off from access to credit (*CTh* 2. 30. 1). This resulted in less savoury means of raising capital such as the sale of children for those in dire financial straits.[10] It will be suggested here that the colonate might have been a solution to the need of destitute farmers for credit: it would have embodied a permanent obligation that was even stronger than one based on a private law contract.

For property owners, the colonate would have had the same advantage that debt-slavery had over a labour contract in which merely food and lodgings were provided. A labour contract involved only the contracting parties, but in debt-slavery the debtor-slave could be transferred to another person. The colonate operated in a similar manner. Registered farmers were

[8] 'ergo quia hoc non valent, quod forte mallent, faciunt quod unum valent. tradunt se ad tuendum protegendumque maioribus, dediticios se divitum faciunt et quasi in ius eorum dicionemque trascendunt' (*De Gub*. 5. 38)

[9] 'nam quos suscipiunt ut extraneos et alienos, incipiunt habere quasi proprios: quos esse constat ingenuos, vertuntur in servos' (*De Gub*. 5. 45).

[10] *CJ* 4. 43. 2: 329.

tied to the land and would be transferred with the land. Thus one could sell land with the manpower to till it. But it remains to be seen just what the particular terms of the colonate were in this regard, and how it was different from debt-slavery.

Taxes were one important consideration. A western law of 371 dealt with registered farmers (individuals 'cum emolumentis tributariis', that is, for whom taxes were owed) who had fled (*CJ* 11. 48. 8; quoted in Appendix). If they were found with a landowner who knew they were fugitives, and consequently did not pay them for the labour that they had given in exchange for his guarantee, then he was required to pay the taxes that were due. The labour that they performed at the discretion of the landowner would have taken merely a part of their time; if they had been free, they would have received some recompense, even if only food and lodgings, in exchange for it. On the other hand, if the registered fugitives had kept their status secret, claimed that they were free to engage themselves ('quasi sui arbitrii ac liberi'), and become tenants or share-croppers, retaining after the payment of the rent something for themselves ('excolentes terras partem fructuum pro solo debitam dominis praestiterunt cetera proprio peculio[11] reservantes'), then the fugitives had to pay their taxes themselves, 'because this is clearly a private contract' ('nam manifestum est privatus contractus'). In this case the authorities did not consider they were a party to the agreement. And this suggests that in the other kind of agreement (which likewise implies the existence of a different kind of contract), where the taxes were due from the landlord, the government did have an interest.

The constitution ends with the very significant ruling that if a fugitive was a debtor 'as is usually the case, as a result of any sort of dealings of this type' ('ut solet ex quibuscumque commerciis huiusmodi'), the judge must insist that the fugitive repay the debt before he was returned to his original place of residence. Here the veil over the late antique agricultural credit system on estates is lifted for a moment, and to this we shall return later on. For now, it suffices to say that, from

[11] The significance of this term will be discussed in detail below.

the perspective of the government, the colonate was related to the obligation of the landlord to pay the taxes of his registered farmers.[12]

One debt, therefore, always would be secured: the taxes due to the fisc for the registered person. One might suggest therefore that the colonate was an agreement between a landlord and a farmer, broadly defined, that was upheld by public law if the debt to the fisc, in the wide sense, also was secured. The claims of the fisc, therefore, were the most important ones. This agreement would imply a certain amount of labour or services on the part of the *colonus*, performed at the wish of the landowner, gratuitously or for a subnormal remuneration.

Among the first to have entered such an agreement and become registered would have been those who had nothing to offer as security but themselves, or rather, their labour. This could include not only tenants (such as the tenant of an orchard)[13] and farmhands, but also others, as long as there was some kind of labour they could perform on an estate for at least part of the year. They also could continue their trades. In this regard one encounters a field-guard and, perhaps, goldsmiths.[14] For our purposes, therefore, the term 'farmer' in this context does not refer just to a tiller of the soil *per se* (as is generally assumed[15]) but more to the nature of the obligations that were assumed when someone entered the colonate. As such, it could encompass many different occupations.

It is important to stress, moreover, that registered farmers were not slaves. In 530, the emperor Justinian (527–65) stated clearly in the Byzantine Empire that even though their situations seemed similar, *coloni adscripticii* (the preferred term in the east) were free men and not slaves (*CJ* 11. 48. 21, quoted in Appendix). In Africa and Gaul in the fifth century the legal distinction between *coloni originarii* (or simply *originarii*,

[12] For the interrelationship between labour and credit by the employer, see D. Rathbone, *Economic Rationalism and Rural Society in Third-Century Egypt: The Heroninos Archive and the Appianus Estate* (Cambridge, 1991).

[13] *P. Oxy.* 2478, which may, however, refer only to the caretaker of the orchard.

[14] Field-guards: *P. Oxy.* 1979; *P. Lond.* 3. 778. Goldsmiths: *P. Oxy.* 2420.

[15] See Sirks, 'Reconsidering', 333–4.

as they were called in the west),[16] was the same. Salvian's wording above shows his own sensitivity to the difference between *coloni* and *servi*. But after the publication of the *Codex Theodosianus* ('Theodosian Code') (*CTh*) in 438, several Novels limited the extent to which *coloni* could exercise their free status: for example, if they fled and stayed with another landlord for thirty years, they automatically became his registered farmers (*Nov.Val.* 27: 449).

The question now arises of what happened to the colonate in the barbarian successor states after the disappearance of Roman authority. In the Visigothic kingdom, the colonate was not at once abolished nor did it fade into oblivion. Laws specific to the colonate from both the *Codex Theodosianus* and the Novels were incorporated into the *Breviarium Alaricianum* ('Breviary of Alaric') of 506.[17] The same goes, to a rather lesser extent, for the contemporaneous *Lex Romana Burgundionum* ('Roman Law of the Burgundians') (*LRB*) (of 516) of the Burgundian kingdom.[18] In addition, the *Edictum Theodorici* ('Edict of Theoderic') often refers to the colonate, demonstrating its continued existence in the first quarter of the sixth century in the Italy of Theoderic the Great.[19] The continued viability of the colonate in barbarian Europe would suggest that it continued to provide the same kind of financial guarantee that it had during imperial times. It would seem unlikely, for example, that the capitation had been abolished, as had been done in Thrace in 393, necessitating thereby

[16] But not every *originarius* was a *colonus*: see *Edict. Theod.* 142, where slaves are *originarii*. Used in a generic sense, the adjective denotes an *origo*, or place of origin; thus a decurion can be *originalis* (*CTh* 12. 1. 96). In the technical sense, as here, it indicates an attachment, by census registration, to a particular piece of land.

[17] *CTh* 5. 17. 1–2; 5. 9. 1–2, 5. 18. 1; 5. 10. 1, 5. 19. 1; 5. 11. 1; *Nov. Val.* 8, 9, 12, 27, 31, 35; *Nov. Maj.* 1, 7.

[18] *LRB* 6. 2 is an otherwise unattested citation from *CTh* 5. 9, which is headed, 'De fugitivis colonis, inquilinis, et servis' ('On Fugitive *Coloni*, *Inquilini*, and Slaves'); and *LRB* 14. 2 (discussed below) came from the *Codex Hermogenianus* and survives as *CJ* 8. 13. 20.

[19] *Edict.Theod.* 21, 48, 56, 63–67, 68, 80, 97, 98, 104, 109, 121, 128, 134, 148. For the suggestion that this document originated in the Visigothic kingdom in the late fifth century, see G. Vismara, *Edictum Theodorici* (Milan, 1967); and H-.J. Becker, s.v. 'Edictum Theoderici', in *Handbuch der Deutschen Rechtsgeschichte* (*HRG*), i (Berlin, 1971). For contra, see R. Lambertini, *Introduzione allo studio esegetico del diritto romano* (Bologna, 1993), 92.

the imposition of the so-called free colonate (*CJ* 11. 52. 1; quoted in Appendix). Nor does it seem that any new financial reason had arisen that would have justified the colonate on any other ground.

Several paragraphs in the *Edictum Theoderici* provide some insight into the status of *originarii*, who were equated with slaves.[20] This, however, is only an indication of their low social status, and does not mean that they were legally of the same status as slaves. Only with cattle theft or rape (*Edict. Theod.* 56 and 109) might the master of an *originarius* pay the fine for him or hand him over to the judge for punishment. This appears like a noxal liability (in *Edict. Theod.* 109 the word *noxia* is indeed used) and it may indeed have been such, because noxal liability was, originally at least, the consequence of having authority (*manus*, *mancipium*, *potestas*, or *dominium*) over someone.[21]

Another indication of the low status of a *colonus* in barbarian Europe is that he could not dispose of his *peculium* (that is, his property, probably referring to movables) without his landlord's consent.[22] This is seen in the *Breviarium*, which incorporated *CTh* 5. 19. 1: 'A *colonus* is not permitted to alienate his *peculium* without the knowledge of his master or to bring a civil case' ('Ne colonus inscio domino suum alienet peculium vel litem inferat civilem'). The same restriction appears in *LRB* 14. 6 (quoted in Appendix), which stated, 'Nor is a slave or a *colonus* permitted to alienate his *peculium*; in addition, anyone selling [it] is liable to an action for theft (*furti actione*)'. It drew authority from two Roman rulings, one from the *Codex Hermogenianus*, where it figured under the title 'De eorum contractibus qui alieno iuri subiecti sunt' ('On the Contracts of Those who are Subjected to Another's Authority'), and the other a constitution from the Theodosian Code 5. 19 which is not transmitted in the surviving manuscripts.[23]

[20] *Edict. Theod.* 21, 56, 63, 64, 80, 84, 97, 98, 104, 109.

[21] This was the liability of the master of a slave or the father of a son *in potestate* for delicts committed by the slave or son: see M. Kaser, *Das römische Privatrecht*, i. (Munich, 1971), 164, 631, and ii. (Munich, 1975), 430. Its presence here would imply that a *colonus originarius* was under the *potestas* of the landowner.

[22] For the *peculium*, see also Arjava in this volume.

[23] *CTh* 5. 19. 2. Mommsen, in his edition of the Theodosian Code, presumes that this law could be or is related to *CJ* 11. 50. 2 (see Appendix).

This is a remarkable ruling, because a fundamental concept of the Roman *peculium* was that a slave or a *filius familias* (who is not mentioned here) could carry on a trade with, and thus sell, the *peculium* without much ado, the consent of the *pater familias* being assumed (some form of consent always having had to be present).[24] Therefore, *LRB* 14. 6 must concern sales of the *peculium* made without consent of the landlord, a conclusion consistent with *LRB* 14. 4 and 5. 17.

Further insight into the significance of this ruling may be gleaned from its context within the code. *LRB* 14. 6 falls under the title 'De ablatis pigneribus et fideiussoribus' ('On Pledges Taken Away and on Those who Secure Loans'). In this section, nos. 1–3 deal specifically with *pignora* (pledges), and nos. 7–8 with *fideiussores* (those who secured loans), in conformation with the rubric. The place of nos. 4–6, however, is not so clear, although it would seem that they, too, were intended somehow to be grouped together, and to relate in some way to *pignora* and *fideiussores*. Number 4 forbade a *filius familias* (as well as a *colonus* or slave) from making a contract on his own authority: he could only do so under the *mandatum* (authority) of his mother or father. This was an expansion upon *CJ* 4. 1. 7: 293, which prohibited a *filius* from litigating or oath-taking. Number 5 qualified no. 4 by permitting a *filius* to make contracts if his *pater* was 'apud hostes' ('in the presence of enemies'). Number 6 then returned to slaves and *coloni*, who had been forbidden to contract by no. 4. This could suggest that no. 6 was intended to be read in parallel with no. 4, indicating that it too involved action that was permitted only with the *iussum* or *mandatum* of the landlord, and that both *filii* and *coloni* were forbidden to sell without permission. An argument for this is the rubric *CTh* 5. 11 (cited in *LRB* 14. 6), which implies that alienation was allowed if the landowner knew of it (and, presumably, approved). Whatever a *filius* acquired, he acquired for his father (no. 4); likewise, whatever a *colonus* acquired was acquired for his master (no. 6 does not say this but *CJ* 11. 50. 2. 3 (quoted in Appendix), the text upon which no. 6 appears to be based, does). The *filius* may not enter into contracts without the mandate of his father or

[24] See Kaser, *Privatrecht*, 1. 341 ff.

mother,[25] and the *colonus* may not alienate his *peculium* (no. 6, with *CJ* 11. 50. 2. 3).

So, if they were not slaves-qua-slaves, why were *coloni* restricted in this respect? The beginning of *CJ* 11. 50. 2 provides some clarification of their subjected position, noting:

The *coloni* who are merely *adscripti*, just as they are free from those to whom the taxes do not make them subjected, are in a like manner considered to be surrendered in little more than a sort of servitude to those to whom they are obligated on account of the yearly payments and the requirements of their status.

This phrase, cryptic as it may seem, nevertheless clearly defines the status of *coloni censibus adscripti*.[26] On account of the regular taxes, they were subjected to certain persons in a manner that almost made them slaves.[27] Only in certain restricted instances, as when a master attempted to exact more than was customary, were they able to take their masters to court in civil law.[28]

This kind of subjectedness was strictly with regard to their landlords. They were free from those to whom they were not obligated on account of the regular taxes. This means that these *coloni* were not slaves; nor was the colonate a civil status halfway between freedom and slavery: one cannot be almost a slave to one person and a free citizen to another. *Coloni*,

[25] The mention of his mother may refer to the case of a son acting for his mother as procurator. Because a *filius familias* could enter a contract, even though it could only be executed when he was *sui iuris* (see Kaser, *Privatrecht*, 1. 341), the law concentrates here on the *peculium*.

[26] That is, the *coloni adscripticii*, as contrasted to the *coloni liberi* as defined in *CJ* 11. 52. 1 (see Appendix).

[27] See *Edict. Theod.* 48, which applied to 'libertos orginarios vel servos', which does not mean that *originarii* were *liberti*, but that they were subjected to the same restraint as *servi*. When such requirements were abolished, as when the *capitatio* was eliminated in Thrace in 393 (*CJ* 11. 52. 1: see Appendix), the *coloni* became *ipso iure* free from this bond.

[28] This is the subject of title *CJ* 11. 50, 'In quibus causis coloni censiti dominos accusare possunt' ('Under which conditions coloni registered in the census are able to take their masters to court'). Note in particular *CJ* 11. 50. 1, issued under Constantine (306–337): 'Quisquis colonus plus a domino exigitur, quam ante consueverat et quam in anterioribus temporibus exactus est, adeat iudicem, cuius primum poterit habere praesentiam, et facinus comprobet, ut ille, qui convincitur amplius postulare, quam accipere consueverat, hoc facere in posterum prohibeatur, prius reddito quod superexactione perpetrata noscitur extorsisse'.

therefore, might be compared to freedmen regarding their processual capacities and to *filii familias* regarding their contractual and possessory capacities: restricted with regard to the *manumissor*-cum-*pater familias*, unrestricted regarding all other people.

The census registration that established the bond between a *colonus* and a landlord most probably treated the *colonus*, and his family, legally as if they were under the *potestas* of the owner of the land that was registered in the census. We may think of a registration as being 'in mancipio', as if the *coloni* were slaves (or probably better, debtor-slaves). The personal registration of a *colonus* presumably implied a lien on his property, which would serve as security.[29] This would account for the *colonus*' property being referred to as *peculium* and, in particular, for the prohibition of alienation without permission, which would not make sense unless the 'peculium' was serving as a pledge. The practice of registration under another's name was well known as a means to escape public obligations, and may well have been used in this case too.[30] The property in question, it seems, consisted of movables, for *CTh* 11. 1. 14 stated that as soon as a *colonus* possessed his own land he was no longer registered as such. Any property that was acquired by the *colonus* would be brought under the lien immediately, and so a *colonus* would continue to 'acquire' for his master (although, unlike the case of a slave, the acquisition did not become the property of the master).

A further argument for this assumption is that in *LRB* 14. 6 there is no doubt regarding the master's right to approve alienation. Any sale without consent is forbidden. *Peculium* thus was used metaphorically and not in its original strict legal sense.[31] Other possibilities do not seem likely. For if the *colonus* had given his property in pledge, the creditor-

[29] But because there is no mention in *LRB* 14. 4 above of *fideiussio*, some other kind of equivalent pledge must have been involved.

[30] See *CTh* 13. 7. 2, which prohibited this practice with respect to shipping: 'multi naves suas diversorum nominibus et titulis tuentur . . . ad evitationem publicae necessitatis'.

[31] Unfortunately, we know hardly anything about the status *in mancipio*. What if such a person had possessions? Did they become property of the master? Or could they serve as security? Was the term *peculium* then analogously used?

pledgee (presumably the landowner on whose land he was registered) could have used the *actio Serviana* ('Servian Action') to recover the pledged possessions if the *colonus* attempted to alienate them to someone else. If, for example, the *colonus* had sold them after pledging them to the landlord. His right to alienate had remained unimpaired on the grounds of the fundamental rule of pledge law, but the *actio Serviana* could be brought against any third party. A prohibition for the *colonus* not to sell would be superfluous here.

Another less likely possibility is that the goods of the *colonus* were in reality those of his landowner, given to him *in precario* (that is, the ownership was transferred, but the landowner retained the right to claim a transfer back at any moment). Because the *colonus* would be bound to return them on demand, selling them would be *furtum* ('theft'), and he would not be authorized to sell. But if this were so, it would be strange why no. 6 was placed under a title concerning *pignora* and *fideiussores*, because the goods would not constitute a pledge (or function as such) and the landowner would not be a *fideiussor*. A property transfer *in fiducia* of the *colonus*' assets to his landowner would have been possible, and the landowner would have been the owner of the goods. If these were with the *colonus*, we must assume that he held them *in precario*, in lease or on account of another agreement, or else a sale would be allowed (the *colonus* merely could not deliver). Yet, for this the reference to the goods as *peculium* is a counter-argument.[32]

A sale without permission would then imply *furtum*, and the buyer also was liable to the penal *actio furti* because he committed receipt of stolen goods. Normally only the owner and those with a legal interest that a thing remained intact, such as those liable for *custodia* and pledgees in possession

[32] It also is assumed that in the fifth century *fiducia* was no longer used: see G. Noordraven, *Fiducia in het Romeinse recht* (Arnhem, 1988), 11–12. The text of the *Codex Hermogenianus* would have fitted *fiducia*, being from at the latest 290, but its application in the sixth century would then have to be based on a misinterpretation, namely that it concerned a non-possessory pledge or hypothec. In that case, however, the above objections prevail. It also is not impossible that 'vel colonum' is an interpolation.

of the pledge, or *fiduciarii*, could avail themselves of this action to punish the thief or *fraudator*.[33]

In case the landowner had merely promised to loan money or give credit, or to be surety for a future debt (as a *fideiussor*, through a *stipulatio*), the prohibition of alienation was very useful and provided an advantage over the *actio Serviana*, which could be exercised only if there was an actual debt present; it did not apply to a pledge for future debts. A party in need of credit could agree not to sell his property in the future, but in private law, under the *actio Serviana*, this was an agreement without real effect. He would remain authorized to alienate his property and the sale could not be reversed. The future creditor could sue him for breach of contract, but this would avail little, because the property was gone and could not be recovered.

But a reinforcement of such an agreement that was effected through public law, by means of the census registration, would have effect, and would make agreements of this nature much more attractive to landlords. In this case, a sale by the *colonus* would be in defiance of the law and thus invalid or reversible. This would assure the landowner that the *colonus* would fulfill his obligations.[34] The very act of registration would enable a buyer to discover that a prospective purchase involved a *colonus adscripticius*, whose property therefore already was encumbered, and if this did not suffice to prevent a private law agreement from being made, it would at least make it *mala fide* ('in bad faith') and thus constitute *furtum*.

The preceding discussion, and especially the analysis of *CJ* 11. 48. 8, therefore suggests that there was a link between the colonate and the credit system of rural estates. This would be consistent with the idea of the colonate as an agreement for surety against debts in exchange for the rendering of services. It would also explain the laws of *CTh* 2. 31. 1 of

[33] 'Cuius interest rem salvam esse, rem non perire' (Gaius 3. 203). See Kaser, *Privatrecht*, 1. 616–17.

[34] Just as the incapacity of a *filius familias* to make a contract was related to the desire that a father or mother would not be bound by a disadvantageous contract, likewise here a fear that such a sale would be disadvantageous to the landlord is another argument for the hypothesis that the goods served as a kind of security.

422 (a constitution split into several parts), in which it is stated that loans to *coloni* without their landlord's assent do not bind the landlord.[35] Normally this would have been too obvious to state, as the law also says, and perhaps we may indeed see no more than this in the text, but it suggests that otherwise the landowner would indeed have been bound.

Another argument for a connection with a credit system and security is *CTh* 2. 32. 1 of 422 (which probably included *CTh* 2. 31. 1 as part of the original constitution). It states that if someone gives a loan to a *colonus* without his master's knowing, the *colonus* has to repay out of his own *peculium*.[36] The *interpretatio* to the Theodosian text qualifies this with the words, 'If his accounts are without debts to his master' ('si nihil de rationibus sius domino debuerit'). Likewise, *Edict. Theod.* 121, which combines *CTh* 2. 31. 1 and 2. 32. 1, adds the words, 'After deduction of what is owed to the master' ('considerata vel servata prius indemnitate domini'). A *peculium* did not have to consist merely of an account, as seen above, when there was a question of selling goods. Here, however, the stress is on the debts to the landowner. In addition, the reservation regarding the master's claims is not normal: it not only gives him a right of priority, similar to that of a pledgee, but it also implies that the *colonus* probably owed him money. On the other hand, the power of the landowner-patron was not unrestricted. A proper *peculium* could be recalled at any time, but the texts do not indicate such a power at all. On the contrary, as soon as the *potestas* ended, the *colonus* could unrestrictedly and fully dispose of his goods (*CJ* 11. 48. 19, 11. 53. 1. 1).

We may assume that the *peculium* comprised of goods belonging to the *colonus*, such as (agricultural) instruments and money,[37] which served as security for the master of the

[35] '. . . igitur in perpetuum edictali lege sancimus, ut, qui servo, colono, conductori, procuratori actorive possessionis pecuniam commodat, sciat, dominos possessionnum cultoresve terrarum obligari non posse'. On this text, one fragment of a large law dealing with the agrarian credit system, see S.-A. Fusco, *Pecuniam Commodare. Aspetti economiche e sociale della disciplina giuridica dei rapporti di credito nel V secolo d.C.* (Perugia, 1980).

[36] Another fragment of the law, referred to in n. 35.

[37] But not, it seems, real estate, in view of *CTh* 11. 1. 14.

colonus. It formed, so to speak, a floating charge; the master acted as a running security for the *colonus*' debts as long as the master knew what the debts were. In other words, the colonate was primarily a form of continuing security for an agricultural credit system.

Thus, as noted above, under the Burgundians, Visigoths, and Ostrogoths, the adscripticiate colonate was still alive and practised at least into the first part of the sixth century. But in the Visigothic Codes of 654 and 681 (after the Visigoths had absorbed the Suevic kingdom) we do not see any further trace of the colonate, nor is it found under the Lombards in seventh-century Italy. It may be that references to the colonate were deleted in the revisions of those years and that the colonate existed in the Visigothic kingdom at least until the middle of the seventh century, but it also may have been dropped in the earlier revision of 572.[38] In addition, there equally is no trace of peasants being under the patronage of powerful persons. The only *patrocinium* is that over freeborn persons, who are free to leave their patron and choose another one (*Lex.Vis.* 5. 3. 1–4). This disappearance of practices relating to the colonate from the seventh-century legislation would suggest that there was not a direct transition from the late Roman colonate to the serfdom of the early Middle Ages.[39] But that is another story.

APPENDIX: *Selected Legal Texts*

Ps. Sulpicius Severus, *Epistula ad Salvium*. '. . . ac tibi cur cordi sit terrificare miseros aratores, non plane intellego, et ruricolas meos cur velis exhibitionis urgere formidine, non agnosco; quasi vero illos nesciam consolari, et a pavore retrahere, et docere non tantum esse timoris quantum ipse praetendis. fateor, dum nos campus exciperet, me saepe armis eloquentiae tuae fuisse conterritum,

[38] H. Nehlsen, s.v. *Lex Visigothorum*, *HRG* 2 (1978), 1966–79; Kaser, *Privatrecht*, 2. 44–5; on the Visigothic codes and law in general, see P. D. King, *Law and Society in the Visigothic Kingdom* (Cambridge, 1972).

[39] For a seamless transition, see Kaser, *Privatrecht*, 2. 146, with reference to M. Pallasse, *Orient et Occident à propos du colonat romain du Bas-Empire* (Lyon, 1950). For a warning against such assumptions, see A. Cameron, *The Mediterranean World in Late Antiquity* (New York, 1993), 87–8.

sed frequenter, ut poteram, recidiva vulnera reponebam. tecum sane condidici quo iure coloni quove ordine repetantur, cui conpetat actio, cui non conpetat exitus actionis. Volusianenses ais te velle reduces, ac frequenter iratus ingeminas te rusticos ex mea turricula retracturum; et is qui, ut ego spero adque desidero, mihi antiqua necessitudine sis copulatus, correpturum te homines meos, conventione neglecta, temere minitaris. quaero de insigni prudentia tua utrum ius aliud habeant advocati, aliud ex togatis, an aliud aequum Romae sit, aliud Mactari . . .'

CJ 8. 16. 6: 293. 'Quae praedium in filios a se titulo donationis translatum creditori suo dat pignori, se magis contrario pigneraticio obligavit iudicio, quam quicquam dominis nocet, cum Serviana etiam actio declarat evidenter iure pignoris teneri non posse, nisi quae obligantis in bonis fuerint, et per alium alienam rem invito domino pignori obligari non posse certissimum est.'

CJ 11. 48. 8: 371. 'Omnes profugi in alieno latebras collocantes cum emolumentis tributariis, salva tamen moderatione, revocentur, scilicet ut si, apud quos homines reperiuntur, alienos esse noverant fugitivos et profugis in lucrum suum usi sunt, hoc est sive excoluerunt agros fructibus dominis profuturos sive aliqua ab isdem sibi iniuncta novaverunt nec mercedem laboris debitam consecuti sunt, ab illis tributa quae publicis perierunt functionibus exigantur. ceterum si occultato eo profugi, quod alieni esse videntur, quasi sui arbitrii ac liberi apud aliquem se collocaverunt aut excolentes terras partem fructuum pro solo debitam dominis praestiterunt cetera proprio peculio reservantes, vel quibuscumque operis impensis mercedem placitam consecuti sunt, ab ipsis profugis quaecumque debentur exigantur, nam manifestum est privatum iam esse contractum. si qui vero inter agricolas, ut solet, ex quibuscumque commerciis huiusmodi hominibus inveniuntur esse debitores, coram partibus constitutis iudex ab obnoxiis quod debetur exposcat'

CJ 11. 48. 21: 530. 'Ne diutius dubitetur, si quis ex adscripticia et servi vel adscripticio et ancilla fuisset editus, cuius status sit, vel quae peior fortuna sit, utrumne adscripticia an servilis, sancimus ea quidem, quae in anterioribus legibus cauta sunt pro tali progenie, quae ex mulieribus adscripticiis et viris liberis progenita sit, in suo statu relinqui, et sit adscripticia proles ex tali copulatione procreata. si quis autem vel ex servo et adscripticia, vel ancilla et adscripticio fuerit editus, matris suae ventrem sequatur et talis sit condicionis, qualis et genetrix fuit, sive ancilla sive adscripticia: quod hactenus in liberis tantum et servis observabatur, quae etenim differentia inter servos et adscripticios intellegetur, cum uterque in domini sui positus est potestate, et possit servum cum peculio manumittere et adscripticium cum terra suo dominio expellere?'

CJ 11. 50. 2: 395/403. 'Coloni censibus dumtaxat adscripti, sicuti ab his liberi sunt, quibus eos tributa subiectos non faciunt, ita his, quibus annuis functionibus et debito condicionis obnoxii sunt, paene est ut quadam servitute dediti videantur. (1) quo minus est ferendum, ut eos audeant lite pulsare, a quibus ipsos utpote a dominis una cum possessionibus distrahi posse dubium non est. (2) quam de cetero licentiam submovemus, ne quis audeat domini in iudicio nomen lacessere, et cuius ipsi sunt, eiusdem omnia sua esse cognoscant. (3) cum enim saepissime decretum sit, ne quid de peculio suo cuiquam colonorum ignorante domino praedii aut vendere aut alio modo alienare liceret, quemadmodum contra eius personam aequo poterit consistere iure, quem nec propria quidem leges sui iuris habere voluerunt et adquirendi tantum, non etiam transferendi potestate permissa, domino et adquirere et habere voluerunt? (4) . . .'

CJ 11. 52. 1: 393. 'Per universam diocesim Thraciarum sublato in perpetuum humanae capitationis censu iugatio tantum terrena solvatur. et ne forte colonis tributariae sortis nexibus absolutis vagandi et quo libuerit recedendi facultas permissa videatur, ipsi quidem originario iure teneantur, et licet condicione videantur ingenui, servi tamen terrae ipsius cui nati sunt aestimentur nec recedendi quo velint aut permutandi loca habeant facultatem, sed possessor eorum iure utatur et patroni sollicitudine et domini potestate . . .'

LRB 14. 6. 'Nec servum vel colonum peculium suum posse distrahere, insuper et ementes furti actione tenendus, secundum constitutionem Hermogeniani sub titulo: De eorum contractibus, qui alieno iuri subiecti sunt, vel Theudosiani legem libro V, sub titulo: Nec colonus inscio domino suo alienet peculium vel litem inferat ei civilem, ad Nibridium vicarium Asiae.'

16

Salic Law and Barbarian Diet

Kathy Pearson

One of the most useful sources for the study of diet and food production in late antique society is a legal document, the *Lex Salica*.[1] Its earliest redaction most likely was produced *c*.507–11 during the last years of the reign of Clovis.[2] Several things could have prompted its creation. There perhaps was a desire to emulate written Roman law[3] on the one hand and the legislative activities of other barbarian rulers such as the Visigoth Euric (466–484) and the Burgundian Gundobad (*c*.473–516) on the other.[4] Furthermore, a written version of Frankish traditional oral customary practice might have enhanced Roman perceptions of their new overlord given the long Roman preference for written legislation.

One consideration to which Clovis and his advisers gave particular attention was the regulation of the food supply. Eight of the sixty-five original titles were concerned wholly or partially with foodstuffs, easily making the *Lex Salica* the most substantial body of food-related legislation produced by any Germanic people. Used in conjunction with the findings of archaeological and agricultural research, the *Lex Salica* offers substantial insight into food preferences and production practices among the frontier inhabitants of sixth-century northern Gaul.

[1] K. A. Eckhardt (ed.), *Pactus Legis Salicae, MGH Leg. Germ.* 4. 1 (Hannover, 1962) presents a text and eight variants; for translation see K. Fischer Drew, *The Laws of the Salian Franks* (Philadelphia, 1991).

[2] R. McKitterick, *The Carolingians and the Written Word* (Cambridge, 1989), 40–60; and I. Wood, *The Merovingian Kingdoms 450–751* (London, 1994), 108–14, discuss the complex textual history of *Lex Salica*. Wood's argument for an early date partly rests upon the reference to pagan sacrificial animals in 2. 16; the animal was a *maialem sacriuum*, or sacred gelded boar.

[3] Drew, *Laws*, 28–9; Wood, *Kingdoms*, 41–9.

[4] Drew, *Laws*, 28–9; Wood, *Kingdoms*, 112; McKitterick, *Carolingians*, 61; H. Wolfram, *History of the Goths*, trans. T. J. Dunlap (Berkeley, 1988), 192–7.

The code does have its limitations as a source for the history of diet. For one thing, we have only those laws that were put into written form; any oral law that remained in force is now lost.[5] Furthermore, the compilers of the *Lex Salica* were not concerned with providing a comprehensive body of all laws on foodstuffs, only with establishing certain parameters for dealing with damages to the food supply of a household or community. Written law, constructed from a negative rather than a positive perspective, was more oriented toward the promotion of community harmony by addressing grievances in ways that would prevent blood-feud or the escalation of less serious disputes among neighbours. Nor was Salic law the only legal alternative; even though Clovis intended his code to cover both Franks and Romans, older Roman vulgar law still applied to Romans who occupied lands now under Frankish authority.[6] Finally, the wergilds—the compensations awarded as redress for various offences against property and persons—pose another difficulty. While they may indicate the relative or comparative value of foodstuffs, they cannot be viewed as actual cash fines levied for certain offences.

These limitations do not, however, detract from the sheer volume of laws governing the food supply, which was, of course, the single most important element for survival on a day-to-day basis. This study will ask several questions regarding what the *Lex Salica* can tell us about diet and food history. In particular, two broadly related areas will be addressed: the question of pastoralism versus cultivation of arable land, and the overall nature of sixth-century Frankish agricultural practices.

One of the most important questions that the *Lex Salica* can help illuminate is the long-standing discussion over whether or not Germanic peoples were primarily 'sedentary pastoralists' who relied upon grazing animals, especially cattle, as their primary source of food.[7] The concept of European sedentary pastoralism once was linked to a view that

[5] Wood, *Kingdoms*, 109–10. [6] Drew, *Laws*, 7–8, 29–31.

[7] See R. Hoffmann, 'Medieval Origins of the Common Fields', in W. N. Parker, E. L. Jones (eds.), *European Peasants and their Markets* (Princeton, 1975), 38; A. M. Watson, 'Towards Denser and More Continuous Settlement: New Crops and Farming Techniques in the Early Middle Ages', in J. A. Raftis (ed.), *Pathways to Medieval Peasants* (Toronto, 1981), 65, 69–70; and W. H. TeBrake, *Medieval Frontier: Culture and Ecology in Rijnland* (College Station, Tex., 1985), 24–5.

two fundamental agricultural systems existed in antiquity. The Mediterranean–Middle Eastern pattern concentrated upon wine, cereals, and olive oil, supplemented by secondary foods such as meats, fruits, and fish. A second pattern prevailed north of the Alps and drew upon animals, milk, and cheese as primary food sources while relegating grains, fruits, vegetables, and fish to lesser status.[8] Recent scholarship suggests a more complex picture in which local practices in northern Europe were coloured over time by the degree of Roman–German assimilation in any given region.[9] To this must be added the complications caused by variation in climate, soils, population density, and the relative proportions of different types of landscape, for instance woodlands to marshes.

In general, the provisions of the *Lex Salica* best support the revised picture of a complex mixed agricultural system, in which both stock-raising and cultivation of the arable land played important complementary roles. Minutely detailed regulations governing offences against food animals suggest not a strong preference for 'sedentary pastoralism' featuring cattle, but rather the possibility of a wider animal economy. Titles 2–5 and 7 contain twenty provisions for swine, fourteen for cattle, five for sheep, two for goats, and six for domestic poultry.[10] Titles 2 and 3 focus on larger animals, swine and cattle, and identify a number of categories for each: suckling pigs, weaned pigs, pregnant sows, one- and two-year-old pigs, 'home-fed' pigs, leader sows, and sacrificial gelded boars on the one hand; and nursing calves, yearling calves, two-year-old cows, cows with calves, cows without calves, a yoke-trained cow, oxen, herd bulls, and two-year-old bulls on the other.

The Franks were aware of the relative value of animals according to their age, sex, and reproductive potential, but this does not in itself offer evidence of a marked preference

[8] Hoffmann, 'Medieval Origins', 38; TeBrake, *Frontier*, 24–5.

[9] TeBrake, *Frontier*, 25; A. Verhulst, 'Economic Organization,' in R. McKitterick (ed.), *New Cambridge Medieval History*, ii. (Cambridge, 1995), 486.

[10] *Lex Salica* 2. 1–20; 3. 1–14; 4. 1–5; 5. 1–2; 7. 5–8. Excluded here are laws governing hunting birds and dogs, as well as those for rarely eaten horses, whose primary use was as labour. The relative wergild assessements for sheep versus swine and cattle may indicate that sheep were primarily valued for their wool.

for cattle-based pastoralism at the expense of cultivation of the arable. If anything, the laws suggest a preference for the foraging pig over the grazing cow. Earlier Roman authorities such as Varro likewise concerned themselves with the minute details of animal husbandry, but Roman agricultural practice nevertheless remained cereal-centred.[11] Nor were all animals mentioned in the laws used primarily as foodstuffs. Horses, too, received detailed consideration, being valued primarily as mounts and draught animals, whereas sheep, the most inefficient meat-producer of the major animals, may have been raised primarily for their wool.[12]

Additional evidence also suggests that the Franks did not follow a cattle-based pastoral system. Title 3. 10 addresses the theft of a bull servicing the heifers of a three-village common. There were, and still are, limits on the number of heifers that can be reasonably covered by even the most energetic bull in one breeding season. Varro believed the maximum to be around thirty-five heifers, although he noted that some Romans preferred a ratio of only thirty heifers per bull.[13] Traditional American farming practices before the age of artificial insemination had improved little on Varro's recommendations: farmers in the Carolinas during the 1930s followed a ratio of not more than forty to fifty heifers per bull. The more heifers covered, the greater the reduction in the sperm count, and the greater the risk of breeding failure.[14] A maximum of around forty heifers per Salic bull would seem a reasonable estimate. If a bull was responsible for the heifers of the aforementioned three villages, then any one village

[11] Varro, *Rerum rusticarum* 2–3.

[12] J. P. Pals, 'Observations on the Economy of the Settlement', in W. Groenman-van Waateringe, L. H. van Wijngaarden-Bakker (eds.), *Farm Life in a Carolingian Village* (Maastricht, 1987), 121–2, notes that sheep make heavy demands on grazing for their meat yields. A typical pig carcass averaged 66 per cent total edible, but a typical sheep or goat only 48 per cent. Cattle had the same relative carcass yield as sheep and goats, yet were more efficient in converting fodder to meat. On horses, see *Lex Salica* 38. 1–14.

[13] Varro, *Rerum rusticarum* 2. 5.

[14] Several small farmers who bred livestock in the 1930s, including William R. Roper and Ford Brown (Easley, SC), Carrie Day and John Skelton (Greenville, SC) and Calvin Day (Etoway, NC), agreed that this number was a natural limit on the number of cows that could be effectively serviced by one bull, and that it was constant across breeds.

typically may have possessed between ten and thirteen breeding heifers at any given time. Heifers normally represented between a third and a half of a total herd, as there would be young animals and neutered males in addition to breeding females.[15] Theoretically, then, three villages might have a total population of between sixty to one hundred and seventeen cattle, plus the herd bull, or approximately twenty to forty cattle per village. The lower range of these numbers is consistent with the herd sizes implied in the *Lex Salica*, which refers to 'he who steals twelve head of cattle and no more remain', and to the man 'who steals more [than twelve] up to twenty-five and others remain that were not stolen'. Titles 3. 12–14 suggest that cattle might have been maintained in groups of twelve to twenty-five animals, with an unspecified upper limit somewhat beyond twenty-five.

These small herds represent numbers at the lower limits of breeding strategies, and would be inadequate to support a population heavily dependent upon cattle-rearing as a food source. This is even more so the case given that mediaeval livestock, including cattle, was on the average 40–60 per cent smaller than modern breeds, with correspondingly smaller meat and milk yields.[16] It has been calculated, for example, that the five- to six-person households of third and fourth-century Fedderson Wierde, which relied on animal-based foods, needed a minimum herd of twenty to twenty-five cattle plus a number of swine for their yearly meat, milk, and cheese supplies.[17]

Merovingian village and settlement archaeology suggests that a typical village included six to eight households, although

[15] W. Abel, *Geschichte der deutschen Landwirtschaft vom frühen Mittelalter bis zum 19. Jahrhundert*, ii. *Deutsche Agrargeschichte* (Stuttgart, 1967), 23–4; W. H. TeBrake, 'Ecology and Economy in Early-Medieval Frisia', *Viator*, 9 (1978), 16–23.

[16] For discussion, see K. Pearson, 'Nutrition and the Early-Medieval Diet', *Speculum*, 72–1 (1997), 6 n. 42; 16 n. 144. On milk yields, see F. McCormick, 'Dairying and Beef Production in Early Christian Ireland: The Faunal Evidence', in T. Reeves-Smyth, F. Hamond (eds.), *BAR British Series*, 116 (Oxford, 1983), 254; A. Hagen, *A Handbook of Anglo-Saxon Food Processing and Consumption* (Chippenham, 1992), 17; A. von den Driesch, J. Boessneck, 'Haustierhaltung, Jagd, und Fischfang bei den Bajuwaren', in H. Dannheimer, H. Dopsch (eds.), *Die Bajuwaren von Severin bis Tassilo, 488–788* (Munich, 1988), 198–201.

[17] Abel, *Geschichte*, 23–4. The calculations were in part derived from a study of the remains of stalls found at the site.

some, of course, were larger.[18] Even assuming five- to six-person households, a number that may be too low, a community this size would have required between 120 and 200 cattle and a good number of swine if they were practicing cattle-based pastoralism.[19] Neither breeding parameters nor the *Lex Salica* support these numbers for cattle. Salic communities must, therefore, have employed a more opportunistic form of livestock management, in which swine probably played a dominant role, followed by cattle and other domesticated animals.[20]

Laws protecting arable land likewise indicate that crop-rearing was a significant element in early Frankish food production. Title 9 dealt with potential conflicts caused by animal owners whose livestock wandered into cultivated fields. If a herder's animals damaged another's crop, the animal owner was assessed at 15 *solidi*—the same wergild levied for the theft of an adult heifer or pig.[21] Title 16 treated arson of a granary as an offence identical to burning a sty with pigs or a byre of cattle: in each case, a wergild of 62½ *solidi* plus the value of the grain or the animals was levied against the guilty party.[22] Title 27 noted the value of non-cereal crops: thefts from the pea, lentil, bean, or turnip patches generated a 15 *solidi* wergild, again equivalent to those assessed for full-grown single animals.[23] Men who ploughed and sowed another man's field, or used a cart or horse to carry off a portion of another's harvest, were penalized with the same 45 *solidi* amount appropriate for those who stole a herd bull or a bull responsible for servicing the cows of three communities.[24] Such provisions demonstrate that the Franks were as interested in cereal, legume, and vegetable cultivation as they were in animal husbandry. Such extremely high compensations, however likely, were intended more as preventative measures rather than punitive ones, for it was unlikely that the average Frankish household had access to such amounts.

[18] E. James, *The Franks* (London, 1988), 209–16; R. Hodges, *Dark Ages Economics: The Origins of Towns and Trade, AD 600–1000* (New York, 1982), 132–4.

[19] See D. Herlihy, *Medieval Households* (Cambridge, Mass., 1985), 69; M. Rouche, 'The Early Middle Ages in the West', in P. Veyne (ed.), *A History of Private Life*, i. (Cambridge, Mass., 1987), 465.

[20] Verhulst, 'Economic Organization', 486.

[21] *Lex Salica* 9. 5; 2. 8; 3. 2.

[22] *Lex Salica* 16. 3–4.

[23] *Lex Salica* 27. 7.

[24] *Lex Salica* 27. 32; 3. 8; 3. 10.

Current knowledge of the historical landscape in the lands south of the Rhine suggests a similar complex mixed agricultural system for the early sixth century. The area consisted of deciduous and mixed forest, as well as some marshlands, broken by cultivated fields dating to the pre-Roman period.[25] During Roman times, farms served the needs of the troops stationed along the frontier as well as the farmers themselves. Over time, the lands north and south of the Rhine became home to a substantial mixed population of both Romans and their Germanic neighbours.[26] Various Frankish groups were interacting with the Romans some two centuries before Clovis, as evidenced by the Frankish commanders enrolled in the Roman army of the fourth century.[27]

Romans who settled in northern Gaul of necessity adopted agricultural practices suited to the landscape and climate of the region. The extensive deciduous forests provided excellent foraging for swine, whereas the more demanding cattle and sheep could be reared on a combination of waste- or meadow-grazing and the hay remaining from grain harvests.[28] Deprived of the olive and its omnipresent oil by inhospitable growing conditions, Gallo-Romans in northern Gaul probably resorted to increased meat consumption to compensate for the missing fat in their diets.[29] Indeed, it is tempting to hypothesize that the consumption of a similar diet by both Gallo-Romans and Franks in northern Gaul might account for some of the difficulties in distinguishing members of the two populations from each other. If the Romans did alter their consumption patterns from the Mediterranean regime of high carbohydrate and low animal protein consumption to a diet richer in animal-derived proteins, it is likely that the average height and weight of members of the population would have

[25] N. J. G. Pounds, *An Historical Geography of Europe* (London, 1990), 16–17; TeBrake, *Frontier*, 24–5; and see TeBrake, 'Ecology', for distinctions between Frankish and Frisian lands.

[26] See H. Elton, *Frontiers of the Roman Empire* (Bloomington, 1996), 66–9, 77–83, for the dynamics between Roman armies and the neighbouring communities.

[27] James, *Franks*, 39–44; and R. MacMullen, *Changes in the Roman Empire* (Princeton, 1990), 49–55.

[28] Verhulst, 'Economic Organization', 487; TeBrake, *Frontier*, 24, 35–52; and Pearson, 'Nutrition', 16, 21–3.

[29] See H. H. Lamb, *Climate: Present, Past, and Future*, ii. (London, 1977), 4, 424.

increased by a considerable amount within two generations.[30] The transformation of agricultural practices that was the result both of the environment and interaction between Gallo-Romans and Franks thus may have resulted in a population that no longer reflected the distinctions in size between Romans and barbarians commented on by classical authors such as Tacitus.[31]

Regarding early sixth-century Frankish agricultural practice, the *Lex Salica* makes it clear that the inhabitants of sixth-century northern Gaul systematically exploited many sources of foodstuffs in their efforts to feed their communities.[32] They did so through their attempts to achieve a balanced use of the types of land available to them. In the sixth century, this consisted of the arable land and those adjacent forests, meadows, and wastelands already being exploited in the Roman period.[33]

As already seen, animal-rearing played a significant if not supreme role. Swine were the favoured food animals, followed by cattle and then all the lesser animals. Pigs offered versatility and ease of rearing. They were omnivorous foraging animals capable of producing a higher percentage of meat and edible fats per carcass than any other animal from scarce food supplies. They were also the very image of fecundity: Varro noted that pigs produced two litters a year, and could nurse on average eight piglets per litter.[34] In addition, swine were the easiest animals to pen-raise, for, unlike sheep and cattle, they could be fed on the refuse of the human diet. Reliance on swine as the primary meat animal reduced the need to devote arable land to growing straw, and it is not surprising that, as seen above, the *Lex Salica* devotes more entries to them than to cattle and sheep combined.

[30] See S. Boyd Eaton, M. Shostak, M. Konner, *The Paleolithic Prescription* (New York, 1988), 95–7, who discuss the resultant physiological differences. See also James, *Franks*, 109–11, for the complexities of the Gallic archaeological record, and P. Garnsey, *Famine and Food Supply in the Greco-Roman World* (Cambridge, 1988), 48–58, for the Mediterranean diet and agricultural techniques. For the pastoral system, see Hoffman, 'Medieval Origins', 38.

[31] Tacitus, *Germania* 4; see H. Wolfram, *The Roman Empire and its Germanic Peoples*, trans. T. J. Dunlap (Berkeley, 1997), 7, for discussion of Roman perceptions of barbarian appearance.

[32] TeBrake, *Frontier*, 35–48.

[33] TeBrake, *Frontier*, 35–45.

[34] Varro, *Rerum rusticarum* 2. 4.

Cattle supplied labour and milk products in addition to their meat, but were more difficult to raise than pigs.[35] Cattle required careful management and their populations could be substantially enlarged only through increases in their two sources of feed: grazing lands and harvested hay. Both posed difficulties. Grazing was limited to areas that left animals relatively accessible to their owners, and increased hay supplies had to be produced through expansion of meadowlands or cultivated arable land, both of which increased demands on human labour.[36] Both swine and cattle were occasionally stall-reared, the most labour intensive form of husbandry, for the animals then had to be supplied constantly with fodder foraged or harvested elsewhere.[37] Presumably the benefits outweighed the disadvantages.

Of the remaining large animals, goats and sheep played much lesser roles. Goats were the quintessential mediterranean animal, capable of thriving in the most inhospitable climates.[38] Such qualities would make goats useful in extremely marginal areas where grazing was generally poor, but this was not typical of conditions in northern Gaul. Like sheep, goats had a poor meat-to-carcass ratio when compared with swine and cattle.[39]

Smaller animals of all sorts were eaten as supplemental foodstuffs. The *Lex Salica* mentions roosters, hens, geese, ducks, cranes, and swans among domesticated fowl, and both eggs and flesh could be consumed.[40] Chickens and geese foraged around dwellings and outbuildings, while ducks, cranes, and swans were more suited to households with access to rivers, lakes, and streams. Wild birds such as turtledoves and 'small birds' were netted or trapped.[41] Hunting was another source of meat, although it was probably under-exploited: for reasons that remain mysterious, no barbarian population

[35] *Lex Salica* 3. 6; 3. 8.

[36] Watson, 'Settlement', 68–71; TeBrake, *Frontier*, 28–31; Verhulst, 'Economic Organization', 487.

[37] *Lex Salica* 16. 4.

[38] J. R. Simpson, *The Economics of Livestock Systems in Developing Countries* (Boulder, Colo., 1988), 131–5.

[39] As with cattle, the *Lex Salica* makes no mention of sheep's milk cheese, again suggesting a non-food use of these animals.

[40] *Lex Salica* 7, 5–6, 8.

[41] *Lex Salica* 7. 9–10.

seems to have consumed much game.[42] The high wergilds of hunting dogs and hunting birds thus may reveal a regard for sport among the Franks, given these animals' time-consuming training and their apparently limited utility in supplying the table. Fish and eels were netted from rivers and lakes. Eels evidently were favoured foods, for eel-net theft carried the very high wergild of 45 *solidi*.[43]

The Franks managed these animal resources in several ways. Depending upon conditions, animals could be left to forage in the forests, grazed in herds under the eyes of a herdsman, harvested from the wild, or raised in a variety of enclosures. The value of a specific type of animal was determined by its usefulness or scarcity as a food source, its age, and the labour investment of raising it.[44] The most valuable animals were those kept specifically for breeding purposes, such as herd bulls and herd boars.[45] The high value of leader sows was the result of Frankish awareness that they could make the herdsman's task much easier.[46] By contrast, the low wergilds of all very young animals indicates that mortality was high among newborn livestock of all kinds, and that nursing animals, which required less investment of human labour than weaned animals, were regarded as less valuable because of this.[47] Juvenile animals had higher wergilds than their nursing counterparts because the burden of animal management had passed from the animal mother to human hands.[48] Likewise,

[42] *Lex Salica* 6. 1–3; 7. 1–4; G. G. Astill, S. J. Lobb, 'Excavation of Prehistoric, Roman, and Saxon Deposits at Wraysbury, Berkshire', *Archaeological Journal*, 146 (1989), 113–17; G. F. IJzereef, 'The Animal Remains', in Groenman-van Waateringe, van Wijngaarden-Bakker, *Farm Life*, 39–49; J. Bourdillon, 'Countryside and Town: The Animal Resources of Saxon Southampton', in D. Hooke (ed.), *Anglo-Saxon Settlements* (Oxford, 1988), 180–2; von den Driesch-Boessneck, 'Haustierhaltung', 198–201.

[43] *Lex Salica* 27. 27–28.

[44] For example, *Lex Salica* 2. 3; 2. 5; 2. 15.

[45] *Lex Salica* 2. 14; 3. 8; 3. 10 provide wergilds for a nursing calf (120 denarii), a bull serving cows of a three-village common (1800 denarii), a royal bull (3600 denarii), and a sow with piglets or a breeding boar (700 denarii).

[46] *Lex Salica* 2. 15.

[47] *Lex Salica* 2. 4 provides wergilds for a weaned piglet (40 denarii) and a one-year-old pig (120 denarii); 2. 8 for a two-year-old pig (600 denarii); 3. 1–3 for a nursing calf (120 denarii), a yearling (600 denarii), and a two-year-old cow (600 denarii); 4. 1–2 for a nursing lamb (7 denarii) and a wether of one–two years (120 denarii); and 38. 8–9 for a nursing foal (120 denarii) and a one–two-year-old colt (600 or 1800 denarii).

[48] *Lex Salica* 2. 7; 3. 2; 4. 2.

wergilds for enclosure-reared animals reflected both high human labour costs and the penalty assessment for violating the dwelling spaces of households. Pigs stolen from locked sties—presumably directly adjacent to the dwellings—generated the highest fines, while a suckling piglet taken from the first (or most distant) enclosure only generated one-fifteenth of the fine.[49] Bees were the only source of sugar in the diet and were difficult to manage, given their proclivity for swarming. They, too, were carefully guarded within enclosures and carried extremely high wergilds.[50]

In general, private ownership, at least at the household level, appears to have dominated, for there is no evidence of communal redress for injuries to livestock. However, animals were probably collectively herded. The size of swine herds—*Lex Salica* 2. 20 refers to a herd of over fifty—makes it probable that households pooled these livestock. The same would have held for horses. *Lex Salica* 28. 5 mentions a herd stallion with a harem of seven to twelve mares. Given the expense of feeding a horse, individual Frankish households were unlikely to have maintained a personal herd of this many horses, and communal herding would have been the usual practice. Another strategy would have seen strength in numbers: a herd of more than fifty pigs would have been safer from human or animal predators than a family herd of only five or six animals. In general, then, if a household only possessed a few animals, it would have been logical to pool several small herds belonging to different households under the care of one herdsman rather than allocate several workers to that task.[51] In addition, the herd bull may have been collectively owned by the community, for a bull that serviced the cows of three villages is attested, although it could equally well have been the property of one fortunate landowner who charged a fee for its services.[52]

[49] *Lex Salica* 2. 1–3 offers a sliding scale of proximity-related values: theft from the first or second enclosure required compensation of 120 denarii; from the third enclosure 600 denarii; and from a locked sty 1800 denarii.

[50] *Lex Salica* 8. 1–4: hives kept within locked and roofed structures, as well as hives outside structures, were valued at 1800 denarii; theft of multiple hives that left some remaining required compensation of 600 or 1800 denarii.

[51] See also *Lex Salica* 2. 11; 9. 3; 9. 5.

[52] *Lex Salica* 3. 10.

Management of the grain supply and other plant resources was equally important in this mixed system. The enclosed fields were interspersed with grazing lands and forests, rather than being strictly segregated with each function allocated to its own portion of the community's land.[53] Salic fields and gardens of all sorts were surrounded with enclosures—a reliable sign that these Franks had become a permanently sedentary population.[54] Fences or enclosures served to delineate one household's arable and garden plots from those of other members of the community. There was as yet no open-field system in place, and so presumably no collective cultivation of the arable land. As with livestock, private or household ownership of arable land prevailed.[55] Title 9, with its careful balancing of the rights of the cultivator of arable land versus those of the owner whose animals damaged the field, suggests that tensions often arose over grazing rights (which could be collective)[56] as opposed to the farmer's right to protect his crop (which involved individual or household ownership). However, there was some private ownership of forests and grazing land. Personal control of such lands, normally held collectively, might signify the elite status of that landowner within Salic society, or may indicate the persistence of Roman strategies of ownership.[57]

The high wergilds assigned for damage to or theft from the fields were connected to the difficulties of cereal and legume production. Yields from early medieval fields were typically low, somewhere around 3:1 at best, and the labour required to produce even those yields was arduous.[58] The same yield rates applied to legumes grown in the gardens of the village enclosures, where the penalties for theft were enhanced by the invasion of the household's private space.[59]

Fruit trees and vines were carefully managed. Grafting improved the yields of fruit trees planted within and outside household gardens, with those in closest proximity to the house

[53] Verhulst, 'Economic Organization', 484–6.

[54] *Lex Salica* 2. 1–3; 7. 11–12; 8. 4; 9; 16. 6–7; 27. 7; 27. 9; 27. 11–12; 27. 22; 33.

[55] See Watson, 'Settlement', 65.

[56] Hoffman, 'Medieval Origins', 39; Watson, 'Settlement', 65.

[57] Watson, 'Settlement', 65; *Lex Salica* 27. 17–18; 27. 23–26.

[58] Verhulst, 'Revolution', 21–2.

[59] *Lex Salica* 27. 7; 27. 12.

being more highly valued.[60] Theft from vineyards carried a 15 *solidi* wergild, and the theft of the finished wine one of 45 *solidi*.[61] Again, the recognition both of the value of the foodstuff itself and the labour to produce it were taken into account.

Village communities laboured to maintain the proper balance of their agricultural environment for their personal benefit. That balance could be easily overset by new demands on the lands claimed by the villagers. Title 45, with its provisions restricting the settlement of newcomers or strangers, provides a glimpse into the internal structure of Salic villages. Section 45. 1 allowed a man to move into a village as a replacement for someone else only if no one in the village objected, and 45. 4 permitted a man to remain only if no one raised objections in his first twelve months of residence; 45. 2 outlined the proper procedure for ousting a settler who refused to leave if the inhabitants did object. Such apparent xenophobia may have had less to do with any inherent dislike of outsiders, and more with a village awareness of natural constraints on food production within the community. A stranger or outsider with his own herd of cattle, for instance, might not be seen as a supplier of future foodstuffs, but as a drain upon the resources available to feed the animals of the previously settled members of the community. Competing claims of this nature also occurred on the American frontier, with its rivalries among sheepherders, cattlemen, and farmers in the nineteenth century.

The picture revealed by Salic law suggests that the sixth-century inhabitants of northern Gaul were opportunistic agriculturalists who sought to make the best use of available food resources. Settling in an area that had long been home to a mixed agricultural system, the Franks easily adapted their food production strategies to those of their already-settled neighbours. Both the Franks and the Romans experienced some transformation of their traditional agricultural economies as a result of their interaction in northern Gaul. The Franks of the *Lex Salica* clearly devoted a greater portion of their agricultural energies to non-meat food productions

[60] *Lex Salica* 27. 8–11.

[61] *Lex Salica* 27. 19–20.

than had their more pastoral ancestors. The Romans, denied access to a number of traditional foodstuffs, such as the olive and its oil, by the harsher northern climate, compensated by placing a greater emphasis on stock-rearing than had been the case closer to the Mediterranean.

The legislation of the *Salic Law* attempted to ensure that each community balanced its needs against the available natural and human-managed resources, and sought to protect those resources through the creation of relatively closed agricultural villages. The communities were neither the local components of an imperial food production system nor the relatively unconfined environments of a predominantly pastoral population. They were instead the early medieval solution to the joint problems of food production and protection of the food supply in the countryside of northern Gaul. The creative interaction between the two food production systems, Mediterranean and Germanic, enabled the Salian Franks and their Gallo-Roman neighbours to enjoy a reasonably balanced diet by early-medieval standards, a diet that was probably better on the whole than that available to their Carolingian successors.[62] And the legislation issued to protect and maintain this food production system reflects not only a governmental sensitivity to local needs, but also a policy of fostering stability and continuity that is curiously similar, in intent if not in execution, to the earlier attempts of Roman emperors to do the same with their legislation for the later Roman Empire as a whole.

[62] For the shift to a greater reliance on cereals in the seventh century, see Verhulst, 'Organization', 481, 486–7; and V. Bullough, C. Campbell, 'Female Longevity and Diet in the Middle Ages', *Speculum* 52–2 (1980), 319–25.

Bibliography

Acland, A. F., *Resolving Disputes without Going to Court: A Consumer Guide to Alternative Dispute Resolution* (London, 1995).

Allen, P., *Evagrius Scholasticus, the Church Historian* (Louvain, 1981).

Amelotti, M., (ed.), *Legis Iustiniani imperatoris vocabularium: Subsidia* (Milan, 1972–7).

Amory, A. P., 'The Meaning and Purpose of Ethnic Terminology in the Burgundian Laws', *Early Medieval Europe*, 2 (1993), 1 ff.

Andreau, J., 'La Lettre 7* document sur les métiers bancaires', in *Les Lettres de saint Augustin*, 165–76.

Antonopoulos, P., *Peter the Patrician* (Athens, 1990).

Arjava, A., *Women and Law in Late Antiquity* (Oxford, 1996).

—— 'Paternal Power in Late Antiquity', *JRS* 88 (1998), 147–65.

Arnheim, M. T. W., *The Senatorial Aristocracy in the Later Roman Empire* (Oxford, 1972).

Arvizu, F. de, 'La Femme dans le Code d'Euric', *RHDFE* 62 (1984), 391–405.

Astill, G. G., Lobb, S. J., 'Excavation of Prehistoric, Roman, and Saxon Deposits at Wraysbury, Berkshire', *Archaeological Journal*, 146 (1989), 113–17.

Astuti, G., 'Note critiche sul sistema delle fonti giuridiche nei regni romano-barbarici dell'Occidente', *Atti della Accademia Nazionale dei Lincei. Rendiconti: Classe di scienze sociale*, 25 (1970), 319–48.

Athanassiadi, P., *Julian: An Intellectual Biography*, rev. edn. (London, 1992).

Atkinson, K. M. T., 'The Education of the Lawyer in Ancient Rome', *The South Africa Law Journal*, 87 (1970), 37–40.

Avi-Yonah, M., *The Jews under Roman and Byzantine Rule* (Jerusalem, 1984).

Bachrach, B. S., 'Gildas, Vortigern and Constitutionality in Sub-Roman Britain', *Nottingham Medieval Studies*, 32 (1988), 129–35.

—— 'The Jewish Community in the Later Roman Empire as Seen in the Codex Theodosianus', in J. Neusner, E. S. Frerichs (eds.),

'To See Ourselves as Others See Us': Christians, Jews and 'Others' in Late Antiquity (Chico, Calif., 1985), 399–421.

Bagnall, R. S., *Egypt in Late Antiquity* (Princeton, 1994).

—— Cameron, Al., Schwartz, S., Worp, K. (eds.), *Consuls of the Later Roman Empire* (Atlanta, 1987).

Baldwin, B., *Studies in Lucian* (Toronto, 1973).

—— 'Malchus of Philadelphia', *DOP* 31 (1977), 92.

—— 'Menander Protector', *DOP* 32 (1978), 101 ff.

—— 'Priscus of Panium', *Byzantion*, 50 (1980), 21 ff.

Barnes, T. D., *The Sources of the Historia Augusta* (Brussels, 1978).

—— *Tertullian: A Historical and Literary Study*, rev. edn. (Oxford, 1985).

Beaucamp, J., *Le Statut de la femme à Byzance (4e-7e siècle)*, i: *Le Droit impérial* (Paris, 1990).

—— *Le Statut de la femme à Byzance (4e-7e siècle)*, ii: *Les Pratiques sociales* (Paris, 1992).

—— 'L'Égypte byzantine: biens des parents, bien du couple?', in D. Simon (ed.), *Eherecht und Familiengut in Antike und Mittelalter* (Munich, 1992), 61–76.

Behrends, O., 'Der Assessor zur Zeit der klassischen Rechtswissenschaft', *ZSS RA* 86 (1969), 192–226.

Beloch, J., *Campanien* (2nd ed.; Breslau, 1890).

Berrouard, M.-F., 'Un tournant dans la vie de l'Église d'Afrique: les deux missions d'Alypius en Italie à la lumière des Lettres 10*, 15*, 16*, 22* et 23* A de Saint Augustin', *REA* 31 (1985), 46–70.

Bianchini, M., 'Disparita di culto e matrimonio orientamenti del pensiero cristiano e della legislazione imperiale nel IV. S.', *Serta historica antiqua*, (1986), 233–46.

Binchy, D. A., *Celtic and Anglo-Saxon Kingship* (2 vols.; Oxford, 1970).

Bird, H. W., *The Breviarium of Eutropius* (Liverpool, 1993).

—— *Sextus Aurelius Victor: A Historiographical Study* (Liverpool, 1984).

—— 'Eutropius: His Life and Career', *EMC/CV* 32 (1988), 52 ff.

Birley, A., *The Fasti of Roman Britain* (Oxford: 1981).

Birley, E., *Roman Britain and the Roman Army* (Kendal, 1976).

Blaise, A., *Dictionnaire Latin-Français des auteurs chrétiens* (Paris, 1954; repr. 1993).

Blockley, R. C., (trans.), *The History of Menander the Guardsman* (Liverpool, 1985).

—— *The Fragmentary Classicising Historians of the Later Roman Empire* (2 vols.; Liverpool, 1981–3).

—— 'Doctors as Diplomats in the Sixth Century A. D.', *Florilegium*, 2 (1980), 89–100.

Bourdara, C. A., 'Le Dossier byzantin de Sainte Euphèmie: quelques aspects juridiques', *RHDFE* 66 (1988), 383–9.

Bourdillon, J., 'Countryside and Town: The Animal Resources of Saxon Southampton', in D. Hooke (ed.), *Anglo-Saxon Settlements* (Oxford, 1988).

Boyd, W., 'The Ecclesiastical Edicts of the Theodosian Code', *Columbia Studies in History, Economics and Public Law*, 24 (1905), 1–125.

Bras, G. le, 'Un moment décisif dans l'histoire de l'église et du droit canon: la renaissance gélasienne', *RHDFE* 9 (1930), 506–24.

Brown, P., *Power and Persuasion in Late Antiquity* (Madison, 1992).

—— *Religion and Society in the Age of Saint Augustine* (New York, 1972).

—— 'Religious Coercion in the Later Roman Empire: The Case of North Africa', *Historia*, 47 (1963), 283–305.

Brundage, J. A., *Law, Sex, and Christian Society in Medieval Europe* (Chicago, 1987).

—— *Sex, Law and Marriage in the Middle Ages* (London, 1993).

—— 'Intermarriage between Christians and Jews in Medieval Canon Law', *Jewish History*, 3 (1988), 25–40.

Buckland, W. W., *A Text-Book of Roman Law from Augustus to Justinian* (Cambridge, 1963).

Bullough, V., Campbell, C., 'Female Longevity and Diet in the Middle Ages', *Speculum*, 52/2 (1980), 319–25.

Burgmann, L., 'Latina in der Novellenbearbeitung des Athanasios von Emesa', in A. Salac (ed.), *Novella Constitutio. Studies in Honour of Nicolaas van der Wal* (Groningen, 1990), 57–82.

Busek, V., 'Episcopalis audientia, eine Friedens- und Schiedsgerichtsbarkeit,' *ZSS KA* 28 (1939), 453–92.

Cameron, Al., 'Gratian's Repudiation of the Pontifical Robe', *JRS* 58 (1968), 96–102.

Cameron, Al., 'Polyonomy in the Late Roman Aristocracy: The Case of Petronius Probus', *JRS* 75 (1985), 171–7.

Cameron, Av., *Agathias* (Oxford, 1970).

Cameron, Av., *Christianity and the Roman Empire* (Berkeley, 1991).

Cameron, Av., *The Mediterranean World in Late Antiquity* (New York, 1993).

Cameron, Av., *Procopius and the Sixth Century* (London, 1985).

Cameron, Av., 'History as Text: Coping with Procopius', in C. Holdsworth, T. P. Wiseman (eds.), *The Inheritance of Historiography* (Exeter, 1986), 68 ff.

Cameron, Av., Cameron, Al., 'The Cycle of Agathias', *JHS* 86 (1966), 15 ff.

Carney, T. F., *Bureaucracy in Traditional Society: Romano-Byzantine Bureaucracies Viewed from Within* (Lawrence, Kans., 1971).

Cecconi, G., *Governo imperiale e élites dirigenti nell'Italia tardoantica* (Como, 1994).

Chabot, J. B., (ed.), *Synodicon Orientale* (Paris, 1902).

Chadwick, H., 'New Letters of St. Augustine', *JThS* 34 (1983), 425–52.

Charles-Edwards, T. M., *The Welsh Laws* (Cardiff, 1989).

Chastagnol, A., 'L'administration du diocèse Italien au bas-empire', *Historia*, 12 (1963), 362–6.

Chastagnol, A., 'L'Evolution de l'ordre sénatorial aux IIIe–IVe siècles de notre ère', *Revue historique*, 244 (1970), 305–14.

Christensen, A., *L'Iran sous les Sassanides* (Copenhagen, 1944).

Cimma, M. R., *L'Episcopalis audientia nelle costituzioni imperiali da Costantino a Giustiniano* (Turin, 1989).

Clark, E. A., *Ascetic Piety and Women's Faith* (New York, 1986).

—— *Jerome, Chrysostom, and Friends: Essays and Translations* (New York, 1979).

—— *The Origenist Controversy* (Princeton, 1992).

—— 'John Chrysostom and the *Subintroductae*', in eadem, *Ascetic Piety*, 265–90.

Clark, G., *Women in Late Antiquity: Pagan and Christian Lifestyles* (Oxford, 1993).

Clarke, M. L., *Higher Education in the Ancient World* (London, 1971).

—— *Rhetoric at Rome*, rev. edn. (London, 1996).

Cloke, G., *This Female Man of God: Women and Spiritual Power in the Patristic Age, AD 350–450* (London, 1995).

Collinet, P., *Histoire de l'école de droit de Beyrouth* (Paris, 1925).

Collins, R., *Early Medieval Spain: Unity in Diversity, 400–1000*[2] (London, 1995).

Connolly, R. H. (trans.), *Didascalia apostolorum: The Syriac Version* (Oxford, 1929).

Conti, P. M., *'Devotio' e 'viri devoti' in Italia da Diocleziano ai Carolingi* (Padua, 1971).

Corcoran, S. J. J., *The Empire of the Tetrarchs: Imperial Pronouncements and Government* AD *284–324* (Oxford, 1996).

Cosenza, M. E., *Official Positions after the Time of Constantine* (Lancaster, Penn., 1905).

Costa, C. D. N., 'The "Dialogus"', in T. A. Dorey (ed.), *Tacitus* (London, 1969).

Courtney, E., (ed.), *Musa Lapidaria: A Selection of Latin Verse Inscriptions* (Atlanta, 1995).

Cox Miller, P., *Dreams in Late Antiquity* (Princeton, 1994).

Crone, P., 'Kavad's Heresy and Mazdak's Revolt,' *Iran*, 29 (1991), 21–42.

Crook, J. A., *Legal Advocacy in the Roman World* (London, 1995).

Cuena Boy, F. J., *La 'episcopalis audientia'* (Valladolid, 1985).

D'Arms, J., *Romans on the Bay of Naples* (Cambridge, Mass., 1970).

D'Isanto, G., *Capua romana: ricerche di prosopografia e storia sociale* (Rome, 1993).

—— 'Iscrizioni latine inedite dell'antiquarium di S. Maria Capua Vetere', *Rendiconti dell'Accademia di archeologia lettre e belle arti di Napoli*, 59 (1988), 144–5.

D'Onofrio, M., Pace V., *Campanie Romane*, trans. D. Vaillant (La Pierre-qui-Vire, 1981).

Dagron, G., *Naissance d'une Capitale: Constantinople et ses institutions de 330 à 451* (Paris, 1974).

Dark, K. R., *Civitas to Kingdom* (Leicester, 1994).

Davies, W., *An Early Welsh Microcosm* (London, 1978).

—— *Wales in the Early Middle Ages* (Leicester, 1982).

—— 'The Latin Charter-Tradition in Western Britain, Brittany and Ireland in the Early Medieval Period', in D. Whitelock, R. McKitterick, D. Dumville (eds.), *Ireland in Early Mediaeval Europe* (Cambridge, 1982), 258–80.

—— 'Liber Landavensis: Its Construction and Credibility', *English Historical Review*, 88 (1973), 335–51.

Davies, W., Fouracre, P. (eds.), *The Settlement of Disputes in Early Medieval Europe* (Cambridge, 1986).

de Giovanni, L., *Chiesa e stato nel Codice Teodosiano: Saggio sul libro XVI* (Naples, 1980).

de Wretschko, C., 'De usu Breviarii Alariciani forensi et scholastico per Hispaniam, Galliam, Italiam regionesque vicinas', in Mommsen, *Theodosiani* 1. cccvii–cccxv.

Deane, H. A., *The Political and Social Ideas of St. Augustine* (Columbia, 1963).

Desanti, L., 'Sul matrimonio di donne consacrate a Dio nel diritto romano cristiano', *Studia et documenta historiae iuris*, 53 (1987), 270–96.

Desoto, A., *The Law of Jealousy: Anthropology of Sotah* (Atlanta, 1989).

Dewing, H. B., 'A Dialysis of the Fifth Century in the Princeton Collection of Papyri', *Transactions of the American Philological Association*, 53 (1922), 113–27.

Dinneen, L., *Titles of Address in Christian Greek Epistolography to 527 A.D.* (Washington, DC, 1929).

Dirksen, H. E., *Manuale latinitatis fontium iuris civilis Romanorum* (Berlin, 1837).

Downey, G., 'The Christian Schools of Palestine: A Chapter in Literary History', *Harvard Library Bulletin*, 12 (1958), 297–319.

—— 'Notes on Procopius' *De aedificiis* Book I', in G. Mylonas, D. Raymond (eds.), *Studies presented to D. M. Robinson* (St Louis, 1953), 719–25.

Drew, K. F., 'The Barbarian Kings as Lawgivers and Judges', in R. S. Hoyt (ed.), *Life and Thought in the Early Middle Ages* (Minneapolis, 1967).

—— 'The Germanic Family of the Lex Burgundionum', *Mediaevalia et Humanistica*, 15 (1963), 5–14.

Driesch, A. von den, Boessneck, J., 'Haustierhaltung, Jagd, und Fischfang bei den Bajuwaren', in H. Dannheimer, H. Dopsch (eds.), *Die Bajuwaren von Severin bis Tassilo, 488–788* (Munich, 1988), 198–201.

Dumville, D., 'The Idea of Government in Sub-Roman Britain', in G. Ausenda (ed.), *After Empire: Towards an Ethnology of Europe's Barbarians* (Woodbridge, 1995), 178–80.

Eck, W., 'Der Episcopat im spätantiken Afrika: organisatorische Entwicklung, soziale Herkunft und öffentliche Funktionen', *Historische Zeitschrift*, 236 (1983), 266–95.

Ellis, T. P., *Welsh Tribal Law and Custom in the Middle Ages* (2 vols.; Oxford, 1926).

Elm, S., '*Virgins of God*': *The Making of Asceticism in Late Antiquity* (Oxford, 1994).

Elton, H., *Frontiers of the Roman Empire* (Bloomington, 1996).

Engelbrecht, A., *Das Titelwesen bein den spälateinischen Epistolographen* (Vienna, 1893).

Evans Grubbs, J., *Law and Family in Late Antiquity: The Emperor Constantine's Marriage Legislation* (Oxford, 1995).

—— 'Abduction Marriage in Antiquity: A Law of Constantine and its Social Context', *JRS* 79 (1989), 59–83.

Falchi, G. L., 'La legislazione imperiale circa i matrimoni misti fra Cristiani ed Ebrei nel IV S.', *Atti dell'Accademia Romanistica Constantiniana*, 2 (1988), 203–11.

Festugière, A. J., *Antioche païenne et chrétienne* (Paris, 1959).

Février, P.-A., 'Discours d'église et réalité historique dans les nouvelles Lettres d'Augustin', in *Les Lettres de saint Augustin*, 101–15.

Fink, R., Hoey, A., Snyder, F., 'The *Feriale Duranum*', *Yale Classical Studies*, 7 (1940), 36–7.

Fischer, B., 'Defensor ecclesiae', *Reallexikon für Antike und Christentorn*, iii (Stuttgart, 1957), 656–8.

Fischer Drew, K., *The Laws of the Salian Franks* (Philadelphia, 1991).
Foreville, R., Preface to O. Pontal, *Die Synoden im Merovingerreich* (Paderborn, 1986).
Fornara, C. W., *The Nature of History in Ancient Greece and Rome* (Berkeley, 1983).
Fortina, M., *La legislazione dell'imperatore Costante* (Novara, 1955).
Franciscis, A. de, 'Templum Dianae Tifatinae', *Archivo storico di terra di lavoro*, 1 (1956), 301–58.
Franz, F., 'Das legislative Werk Chilperics I', *ZSS GA* 78 (1961), 1–38.
Frede, M., 'Celsus' attack on the Christians', in J. Barnes, M. Griffin (eds.), *Philosophia Togata II: Plato and Aristotle at Rome* (Oxford, 1997), 234–5.
Frederiksen, M. W., *Campania* N. Purcell (ed.) (Oxford, 1984).
Frend, W. H. C., *The Rise of Christianity* (Philadelphia, 1984).
—— 'Town and Countryside in Early Christianity', in D. Baker (ed.), *The Church in Town and Countryside* (Oxford, 1979), 25–42.
Fridh, A. J., *Terminologie et formules dans les Variae de Cassiodore: etude sur le développement du style administratitif aux derniers siècles de l'antiquité* (Stockholm, 1956).
Frier, B. W., *The Rise of the Roman Jurists* (Princeton, 1985).
Fusco, S.-A., *Pecuniam Commodare. Aspetti economiche e sociale della disciplina giuridica dei rapporti di credito nel V secolo d.C.* (Perugia, 1980).
Garcia Moreno, L. A., 'Legitimate and Illegitimate Violence in Visigothic Law', in G. Halsall (ed.), *Violence and Society in the Early Medieval West* (Rochester, NY, 1998).
Gardner, J., *Women in Roman Law and Society* (London, 1984).
Garnsey, P., *Famine and Food Supply in the Greco-Roman World* (Cambridge, 1988).
Garsoïan, N., 'Le Rôle de l'hiérarchie chrétienne dans les rapports diplomatiques entre Byzance et les Sassanides', *Revue des études armeniennes*, 10 (1973), 119–38.
Gaudemet, J., *Le Bréviaire d'Alaric et les Epitomes*, Ius Romanum Medii Aevi I. 2b aa ß (Milan, 1965).
—— *Le Droit romain dans la littérature chrétienne occidentale du IIIe au Ve siècle* (Varese, 1978).
—— *L'église dans l'empire romain* (Paris, 1958).
—— *La Formation du droit canonique médiéval* (London, 1980).
—— *La Formation du droit séculier et du droit de l'église aux IVe et Ve siècles* (Paris, 1979).

Gaudemet, J., *Les Sources du droit de l'église en occident du IIe au VIe siècle* (Paris, 1985).
—— 'Les Abus des potentes du Bas-Empire', *Irish Jurist*, 1 (1966), 128–35.
—— 'Survivances romaines dans le droit de la monarchie franque du Ve au Xe siècle', *Tijdschrift voor Rechtsgeschiedenis*, 23 (1955), 149–206.
Geary, P. J., *Before France and Germany: The Creation and Transformation of the Merovingian World* (New York, 1988).
Gebbia, C., 'Sant'Agostino e l'episcopalis audientia', *L'Africa romana: Atti del VI convegno di studio, Sassari, 16–18 dicembre 1988* (Sassari, 1989), 683–95.
Gerkan, A. von, Krischen, F., *Thermen und Palaestren* (Berlin, 1928).
Gero, S., 'The See of Peter in Babylon: Western Influences on the Ecclesiology of Early Persian Christianity', in N. Garsoïan, T. Mathews, R. Thomson (eds.), *East of Byzantium: Syria and Armenia in the Formative Period* (Washington, DC, 1982), 45–51.
Giglio, S., *Il tardo impero d'Occidente e il suo senato: privilegi fiscali, patrocinio, giurisdizione penale* (Naples, 1990).
Gil, I. (ed.), *Miscellanea Wisigothica* (Seville, 1972).
Goody, J., *The Oriental, the Ancient, and the Primitive: Systems of Marriage and the Family in the Pre-Industrial Societies of Eurasia* (Cambridge, 1990).
Gordini, G. D., 'Origine e sviluppo del monachesimo a Roma', *Gregorianum*, 37 (1956), 220–60.
Gradenwitz, O., *Heidelberger Index zu Codex Theodosianus* (Berlin, 1931).
Grant, M., *Greek and Roman Historians* (London, 1995).
Grant, R. M., *Miracle and Natural Law in Graeco-Roman and Early Christian Thought* (Amsterdam, 1952).
Greatrex, G., '*Assessores* kaj Historiistoj en la malfrua romia imperio', *Jura Tribuno Internacia*, 2 (1998), 33–50.
Guerout, J., 'Le Testament de sainte Fare: matériaux pour l'étude et l'édition critique de ce document', *Revue d'histoire ecclésiastique*, 60 (1965), 761–821.
Guillaume, J.-M., 'Les Abbayes de femmes en Pays Franc, des origines à la fin du viie siècle', in M. Parisse (ed.), *Rémiremont: L'Abbaye et la ville* (Nancy, 1980), 24–46.
Gulliver, P. H., *Disputes and Negotiations: A Cross-Cultural Perspective* (New York, 1979).
Guyon, J., 'L'architecture religeuse chez Grégoire de Tours', in N. Gauthier, H. Galinié (eds.), *Grégoire de Tours et l'espace gaulois* (Tours, 1997), 197–207.

Hagen, A., *A Handbook of Anglo-Saxon Food Processing and Consumption* (Chippenham, 1992).
Harries, J. D., *Law and Empire in Late Antiquity* (Cambridge, 1998).
—— *Sidonius Apollinaris and the Fall of Rome* (Oxford, 1994).
—— 'Introduction: The Background of the Code', in Harries and Wood (eds.), *Theodosian Code*, 1–18.
—— 'The Roman Imperial Quaestor from Constantine to Theodosius II', *JRS* 78 (1988), 148–72.
—— '"Sacra generalitas": The Administrative Background to the Theodosian Code', in Harries and Wood (eds.), *Theodosian Code*, 31–42.
—— 'Sozomen and Eusebius: The Lawyer as Church Historian in the Fifth Century', in C. Holdman, T. P. Wiseman (eds.), *The Inheritance of Historiography 350–900* (Exeter, 1986), 45 ff.
—— '"Treasure in Heaven": Property and Inheritance among Senators of Late Rome', in E. Craik (ed.), *Marriage and Property* (Aberdeen, 1984).
—— Wood, I. (eds.), *The Theodosian Code: Studies in the Imperial Law of Late Antiquity* (Ithaca, NY, 1993).
Harris, W. V., (ed.), *The Transformations of Urbs Roma in Late Antiquity* (Portsmouth, 1999).
Heather, P. J., 'Literacy and Power in the Migration Period', in A. K. Bowman, G. Woolf (eds.), *Literacy and Power in the Ancient World* (Cambridge, 1994), 183 ff.
—— 'New Men for New Constantines', in P. Magdalino (ed.), *New Constantines* (Aldershot, 1994).
Hefele, C. J., Leclercq, H., *Histoire des conciles d'après les documents originaux* (Paris, 1907).
Heidrich, I., 'Besitz und Besitzverfügung verheirateter und verwitweter freier Frauen im merowingischen Frankenreich', in H.-W. Goetz (ed.), *Weibliche Lebensgestaltung in frühen Mittelalter* (Cologne, 1991), 119–38.
Helmholz, R. H., *Marriage Litigation in Medieval England* (Cambridge, 1974).
—— 'Support Orders, Church Courts, and the Rule of *Filius nullius*: A Reassessment of the Common Law', *Virginia Law Review*, 63 (1977), 431–48.
Herlihy, D., *Medieval Households* (Cambridge, Mass., 1985).
Herzog, R., (ed.), *Nouvelle histoire de la littérature latine* (Paris, 1993).
Heumann, H., Seckel, E. (eds.), *Handlexikon zu den Quellen des romischen Rechts* (Jena, 1907).
Higgit, J., 'The Stone-Cutter and the Scriptorium: Early Medieval Inscription, in Britain and Ireland,' *Epigraphik* (1988), 149–62.

Higham, N., *Rome, Britain, and the Anglo-Saxons* (London: 1992).
Hines, J., 'Britain after Rome: Between Multiculturalism and Monoculturalism', in P. Graves-Brown, S. Jones, C. Gamble (eds.), *Cultural Identity and Archaeology* (London, 1996), 257–9.
Hirschfield, O., 'Die Rangtitel der römischen Kaiserzeit', *Sitzungsberichte der königlichen preussischen Akademie der Wissenschaft*, 25 (1901), 579–610 = idem, *Kleine Schriften* (Berlin, 1913; repr. New York, 1975), 646–81.
Hitzig, H. F., *Die Assessoren der römischen Magistrate und Richter* (Munich, 1893).
Hochstettler, D., *A Conflict of Traditions: Women in Religion in the Early Middle Ages, 500–840* (Lanham, Md., 1992).
—— 'The Meaning of Monastic Cloister for Women according to Caesarius of Arles', in T. F. X. Noble, J. J. Contreni (eds.), *Religion, Culture and Society in the Early Middle Ages* (Kalamazoo, 1987), 27–40.
Hodges, R., *Dark Ages Economics: The Origins of Towns and Trade, AD 600–1000* (New York, 1982).
Hoffmann, R., 'Medieval Origins of the Common Fields', in W. N. Parker, E. L. Jones (eds.), *European Peasants and their Markets* (Princeton, 1975).
Honig, R. M., *Humanitas und Rhetorik in spätrömischen Kaisergesetzen* (Göttingen, 1960), 85–126.
Honoré, T., *Emperors and Lawyers* (London, 1981).
—— *Law in the Crisis of Empire 379–455 AD: The Theodosian Dynasty and its Quaestors* (Oxford, 1998).
—— *Tribonian* (London, 1978).
—— 'Ausonius and Vulgar Law', *Iura*, 35 (1984), 79–82.
—— 'The Making of the Theodosian Code', *ZSS RA* 103 (1986), 172 ff.
Hooke, D., (ed.), *Anglo-Saxon Settlements* (Oxford, 1988).
Humbert, M., 'Enfants à louer ou à vendre: Augustin et l'autorité parentale (*Epist.* 10* et 24*)', in *Les Lettres de saint Augustin*, 189–204.
Hunt, D., 'Christianising the Roman Empire: The Evidence of the Code', in Harries and Wood (eds.), *Theodosian Code*, 143–58.
Jacobsen, W., 'Saints' Tombs in Frankish Church Architecture', *Speculum*, 72 (1977), 1107–43.
Jacques, F., 'Le Défenseur de cité d'après la Lettre 22* de Saint Augustin', *REA* 32 (1986), 56–73.
James, E., *The Franks* (London, 1988).
Jeffreys, E., Croke, B., Scott, R. (eds.), *Studies in John Malalas* (Sydney, 1990).

Jenkins, D., (trans., ed.), *The Law of Hywel Dda* (Llandysul, 1986).

Jerg, E., *Vir venerabilis. Untersuchungen zur Titulatur der Bischöfe in den ausserkirchlichen Texten* (Vienna, 1970).

Joannou, P.-P., *La Législation imperiale et la christianisation de l'empire Romain 311–476* (Rome, 1972).

Joannou, P.-P., (ed.), *Discipline générale antique* (Grottaferrata, 1962).

Jones, A. H. M., *The Later Roman Empire 284–602: A Social, Economic and Administrative Survey* (Norman, Okla., 1964).

Jones, M. E., *The End of Roman Britain* (Ithaca, NY, 1996).

Jonkers, E. J., 'Application of Roman Law by Councils in the Sixth Century', *RHD* 20 (1952), 340–3.

Kajanto, I., *The Latin Cognomina* (Helsinki, 1965).

—— *Supernomina: A Study in Latin Epigraphy* (Helsinki, 1966).

Kaser, M., *Das römische Privatrecht* (2 vols.; Munich, 1971–5).

—— *Das römische Zivilprozessrecht* (Munich, 1966).

Kaster, R. A., *Guardians of Language* (Berkeley, 1988).

Keenan, J. G., 'A Christian Letter from the Michigan Collection', *ZPE* 75 (1988), 267–71.

Kelly, F., *A Guide to Early Irish Law* (Dublin, 1988).

Kelly, J. N. D., *Jerome: His Life, Writings, and Controversies* (New York, 1975).

Kennell, S. A. H., 'Women's Hair and the Law: Two Cases from Late Antiquity', *Klio*, 73 (1991), 526–36.

Kienast, D., *Römische Kaisertabelle: Grundzüge einer römischen Kaiserchronologie* (Darmstadt, 1990).

King, P. D., *Law and Society in the Visigothic Kingdom* (Cambridge, 1972).

—— 'King Chindasvind and the First Territorial Law-Code of the Visigothic Kingdom', in E. James (ed.), *Visigothic Spain: New Approaches* (Oxford, 1980), 131–57.

Klingshirn, W., *Caesarius of Arles: The Making of a Christian Community in Late Antique Gaul* (Cambridge, 1994).

Koch, P., *Die byzantinischen Beamtentitel von 400 bis 700* (Jena, 1903).

Kriegbaum, B., *Kirche der Traditoren oder Kirche der Martyrer?* (Innsbruck, 1986).

Kroeschell, K., 'Söhne und Töchter im germanischen Erbrecht', in G. Landwehr (ed.), *Studien zu den germanischen Volksrechten, Gedächtnisschrift für W. Ebel* (Frankfurt, 1982), 87–107.

Labande-Mailfert, Y., 'Les débuts de Sainte-Croix', in E.-R. Labande (ed.), *Histoire de l'Abbaye Sainte-Croix de Poitiers* (Poitiers, 1986), 21–116.

Ladner, G. B., 'Justinian's Theory of Law and the Renewal Ideology of the "Leges barbarorum"', *Proceedings of the American Philosophical Society*, 119 (1975), 191–200.

Lamb, H. H., *Climate: Present, Past, and Future*, ii (London, 1977).

Lambertini, R., *La codificazione di Alarico II* (Turin, 1990).

—— *Introduzione allo studio esegetico del diritto romano* (Bologna, 1993).

Lambot, C., 'Le prototype des monastères cloîtrés de femmes', *Revue liturgique et monastique*, 23 (1956), 169–74.

—— 'Sermon sur l'aumône à restituer à saint Augustin', *RB* 66 (1956), 149–58.

Lamoreaux, J. C., 'Episcopal Courts in Late Antiquity', *JECS* 3 (1995), 143–67.

Lancel, S., 'L'Affaire d'Antoninus de Fussala: pays, choses et gens de la Numidie d'Hippone saisis dans la durée d'une procédure d'enquète épiscopale (*Epist.* 20*)', in *Les lettres de saint Augustin*, 267–85.

Lancel, S., 'Titres de rang et titres de courtoisie dans les actes de 411', in idem (ed.) *Actes de la conférence de Carthage en 411, i, SCH 194* (Paris, 1972), 328–31.

Lane Fox, R., *Pagans and Christians* (London, 1986).

Lapidge, M., 'Gildas's Education and the Latin Culture of Sub-Roman Britain', in Lapidge and Dumville (eds.), *Gildas*, 28–33.

—— Dumville, D. (eds.), *Gildas: New Approaches* (Woodbridge, 1984), 28–33.

Latte, K., *Römische Religionsgeschichte* (Munich, 1960).

Lear, F. S., 'The Public Law of the Visigothic Code', *Speculum*, 26 (1951), 1–23.

Lécrivain, C., 'Remarques sur l'*Interpretatio* de la "Lex Romana Visigothorum"', *Annales du Midi*, 1 (1889), 145–82.

LeMoine, F. J., 'Jerome's Gift to Women Readers', in Mathisen and Sivan (eds.), *Shifting Frontiers*, 230–41.

Lepelley, C., *Les Cités de l'Afrique romaine au bas-empire*, i. *La Permanence d'une civilisation municipale* (Paris, 1979).

—— 'La crise de l'Afrique romaine au début du Ve siècle, d'après les lettres nouvellement découvertes de Saint Augustin', *CRAI* (1982), 445–63.

—— 'Liberté, colonat et esclavage d'après la lettre 24*: la juridiction épiscopale *de liberali causa*', in *Les lettres de saint Augustin* (Paris, 1983), 329–42.

—— 'Trois documents méconnus retrouvés parmi les spuria de Sulpice Sévère', *Antiquités africaines*, 25 (1989), 235–62.

Les lettres de saint Augustin découvertes par Johannes Divjak: Communications présentées au colloque des 20 et 21 Septembre 1982 (Paris, 1983).

Levy, E., *Gesammelte Schriften* (Cologne, 1963).

Levy, E., *West Roman Vulgar Law: The Law of Property* (Philadelphia, 1951).

—— 'Vulgarization of Roman Law in the Early Middle Ages', *Mediaevalia et Humanistica*, 1 (1943), 14–40.

Liebeschuetz, J. H. W. G., *Antioch* (Oxford, 1972).

Lim, R., 'People as Power: Games, Munificence, and Contested Topography,' in Harris (ed.), *Transformations*, 265–81.

Linder, A., *The Jews in the Legal Sources of the Early Middle Ages* (Detroit, 1997).

—— *The Jews in Roman Imperial Legislation* (Detroit, 1987).

Lintott, A., *Imperium Romanum* (London, 1993).

Löhken, H., *Ordines dignitatum. Untersuchungen zur formalen Konstituierung der spätantiken Führungsschicht* (Cologne, 1982).

Long, J., *Claudian's In Eutropium, or, How, When, and Why to Slander a Eunuch* (Chapel Hill, 1996).

Lotter, F., 'Zu den Anredeformen und ehrenden Epitheta der Bischöfe in Spätantike und frühem Mittelalter', *Deutsches Archiv für Erforschung des Mittelalters*, 27 (1971), 514–17.

Maas, M., *John Lydus and the Roman Past* (London, 1992).

—— 'Roman History and Christian Ideology in Justinianic Reform Legislation', *DOP* 40 (1986), 26 ff.

Maasen, F., *Geschichte der Quellen und der Literatur des canonischen Rechts in Abendlande*, i (Graz, 1870).

MacMullen, R., *Changes in the Roman Empire* (Princeton, 1990).

—— 'Roman Bureaucratese', *Traditio*, 18 (1962), 364–78.

Magioncalda, A., *Lo sviluppo della titolatura imperiale da Augusta a Giustiniano* (Turin, 1991).

Maier, J.-L., (ed.), *Le Dossier du Donatisme*, i (Berlin, 1987).

Marini, F. de, 'Codice Teodosiano e Concilio di Efeso', *Atti dell'Accademia Romanistica Constantiniana*, 5 (1983), 105–22.

Markus, R. A., *Saeculum: History and Society in the Theology of St. Augustine*, rev. edn. (Cambridge, 1988).

—— 'Christianity and Dissent in Roman North Africa: Changing Perspectives in Recent Work', in D. Baker (ed.), *Schism, Heresy and Religious Protest* (Cambridge, 1972), 21–36.

Marquardt, J., *Römische Staatsverwaltung*[2] (Leipzig, 1885).

Marrou, H. I., *A History of Education in Antiquity* (London, 1981).

Martimort, A. G., *Diaconesses: Essai historique* (Rome, 1982); trans. K. D. Whitehead as *Deaconesses: An Historical Study* (San Francisco, 1986).

Martin, R., *Tacitus* (London, 1981).

Martroye, M. F., 'Saint Augustin et la compétence de la juridiction ecclésiastique au Ve siècle', *Mémoires de la Société Nationale des Antiquaires de France* 7th ser., 10 (1911), 1–78.
Mathisen, R. W., *Ecclesiastical Factionalism and Religious Controversy in Fifth-Century Gaul* (Washington, DC, 1989).
—— 'Barbarian Bishops and the Churches "in barbaricis gentibus" during Late Antiquity', *Speculum*, 72 (1997), 664–97.
—— *Roman Aristocrats in Barbarian Gaul: Strategies for Survival in an Age of Transition* (Austin, 1993).
—— 'Emperors, Consuls and Patricians: Some Problems of Personal Preference, Precedence and Protocol', *Byzantinische Forschungen*, 17 (1991), 173–90.
—— '*Et manu papae*: Papal Subscriptions written *sua manu* in Late Antiquity', in G. Schmeling (ed.), *Qui miscuit utile dulci: Festschrift Essays for Paul Lachlan MacKendrick* (Chicago, 1997), 243–51.
—— 'The Late Roman Legal Distribution System as Attested from Subscriptions to Imperial Documents', *Proceedings of the S.C. Historical Association*, (1994), 82–7.
—— 'Leo, Anthemius, Zeno, and Extraordinary Senatorial Status in the Late Fifth Century', *Byzantinische Forschungen*, 17 (1991), 191–222.
—— 'Patricians as Diplomats in Late Antiquity', *Byzantinische Zeitschrift*, 79 (1986), 35–49.
—— 'The "Second Council of Arles" and the Spirit of Compilation and Codification in Late Roman Gaul', *Journal of Early Christian Studies*, 5 (1997), 511–54.
Mathisen, R. W., Sivan, H. (eds.), *Shifting Frontiers in Late Antiquity* (Aldershot, 1996).
Matthews, J. F., *The Roman Empire of Ammianus* (London, 1989).
—— *Western Aristocracies and Imperial Court, A.D. 364–425* (Oxford, 1975, repr. 1998).
—— 'The Making of the Text', in Harries and Wood (eds.), *Theodosian Code*, 19–44.
—— 'The Origin of Ammianus', *CQ* 44 (1994), 268 ff.
Matthews, J., 'A Pious Supporter of Theodosius I: Maternus Cynegius and his Family', *JThS* 18 (1967), 438–46.
Mauro Todini, A. di, *Aspetti della legislazione religiosa del IV secolo* (1990).
Mayer, C., *et al.* (eds.), *Augustinus-Lexikon* (Basle, 1986–94).
Mayo, H., 'The Sources of Female Monasticism in Merovingian Gaul', *Studia Patristica*, 16/2 (1985), 32–7.
Mayr, R., *Vocabularium codicis Justiniani* (Hildesheim, 1965).

McCail, R. C., 'The Education Preliminary to Law', *Byzantion*, 47 (1977), 366–7.

McCormick, F., 'Dairying and Beef Production in Early Christian Ireland: The Faunal Evidence', in T. Reeves-Smyth, F. Hammond (eds.), *BAR British Series*, 116 (Oxford, 1983), 254.

McGinn, T. A. J., '*Ne serva prostituatur*: Restrictive Covenants in the Sale of Slaves', *ZSS RA* 100 (1990), 315–53.

—— 'The Taxation of Roman Prostitutes', *Helios*, 16 (1989), 79–110.

McKitterick, R., *The Carolingians and the Written Word* (Cambridge, 1989).

McLynn, N. B., *Ambrose of Milan* (Berkeley, 1994).

Meer, F. van der, *Augustine the Bishop*, trans. B. Battershaw, G. R. Lamb (London, 1961).

Metz, R., 'Les vierges chrétiennes au IVe siècle', in *Saint Martin et son temps*, *Studia Anselmiana*, 46 (Rome, 1961), 109–32.

Meyer-Marthaler, E., *Römisches Recht in Rätien im frühen und hohen Mittelalter* (Zurich, 1968).

Millar, F., *The Emperor in the Roman World* (London, 1977).

—— *A Study of Cassius Dio* (Oxford, 1964).

—— 'Condemnation to Hard Labour', *Papers of the British School at Rome* (1984), 144 ff.

Mitteis, L., *Reichsrecht und Volksrecht in den ostlichen Provinzen des römischen Kaiserreich* (Leipzig, 1891).

—— *Römisches Staatsrecht*^{2} (Leipzig, 1877).

—— 'Epigraphische Analekten Nr. 8', *Berichte der sächischen Gesellschaft der Wissenschaften*, 2 (1850), 66 ff. = idem, *Gesammelte Schriften*, 8 (Berlin, 1913), 17 ff.

—— 'Interpolationen im Theodosischen Breviar', *Neues Archiv der Gesellschaft für ältere deutsche Geschichtskunde*, 25 (1900), 587–92.

—— 'Sallustius = Salutius und das Signum', *Hermes*, 37 (1902), 443–55.

Mordek, H., *Kirchenrecht und Reform im Frankenreich: Die collectio vetus gallica, die älteste systematische Kanonessammlung des fränkischen Gallien* (Berlin, 1975).

Morony, M., 'Continuity and Change in the Administrative Geography of Late Sasanian and Early Islamic al-Iraq', *Iran*, 20 (1982), 1–49.

Morris, J., *The Age of Arthur* (London: 1973).

Munier, C., 'La Question des appels à Rome d'après la Lettre 20* d'Augustin', in *Les Lettres de saint Augustin*, 287–99.

Murray, A. C., *Germanic Kinship Structure: Studies in Law and Society in Antiquity and the Early Middle Ages* (Toronto, 1983).

Murray, R., *Symbols of Church and Kingdom* (Cambridge, 1975).
Musurillo, H., (ed.), *The Acts of the Christian Martyrs* (Oxford, 1972).
Nash-Williams, V. E., *The Early Christian Monuments of Wales* (Cardiff, 1950).
Neff, S. C., 'Decline and Emergence: Roman Law and the Transition from Antiquity to Feudalism', *Journal of Legal History*, 5 (1984), 91–116.
Nehlsen, H., *Lex Visigothorum, Handwörterbuch zur deutschen Rechtsgeschichte*, ii (Berlin, 1978).
—— 'Alarich II als Gesetzgeber: Zur Geschichte der "Lex romana visigothorum"', *Studien zu den germanischen Volksrechten für Wilhelm Ebel* (Frankfurt, 1982), 143–203.
Newman, L. I., 'Intermarriage between Jews and Christians during the Middle Ages', *Jewish Institute Quarterly*, 2 (1926), 2–8, 21–8.
Nicholas, B., *Introduction to Roman Law* (Oxford, 1962).
Nissen, H., *Italische Landeskunde* (Berlin, 1902).
Nixon, C. E. V., Rodgers, B. S., *In Praise of Later Roman Emperors* (Berkeley, 1994).
Noethlichs, K. L., 'Materialen zum Bischofsbild aus den spätantiken Rechtsquellen', *JAC* 16 (1973), 28–59.
Nonnoi, A., 'Sant' Agostino e il diritto romano', *RISG* 9 (1934), 531–45.
Noordraven, G., *Fiducia in het Romeinse recht* (Arnhem, 1988).
O'Brien, M. B., *Titles of Address in Christian Latin Epistolography to 543 A.D.* (Washington, DC, 1930).
Oost, S. I., 'Galla Placidia and the Law', *CP* 63 (1968), 114–21.
Pakter, W., *Medieval Canon Law and the Jews* (Ebelsbath, 1988).
Pallasse, M., *Orient et Occident à propos du colonat romain du Bas-Empire* (Lyon, 1950).
Pals, J. P., 'Observations on the Economy of the Settlement', in W. Groenman-van-Waateringe, L. H. van Wijngaarden-Baker (eds.), *Farmlife in a Carolingian village* (Maastricht, 1987).
Pardessus, J. M., *Diplomata, chartae, epistolae, leges aliaque instrumenta ad res Gallo-Francicas spectantiam* (2 vols.; Paris, 1843–9).
Pearson, K., 'Nutrition and the Early-Medieval Diet', *Speculum*, 72/1 (1997), 6 ff.
Pedersen, F. S., *Late Roman Public Professionalism* (Odense, 1976).
Penella, R. J., *Greek Philosophers and Sophists of the Fourth Century A.D.* (Liverpool, 1990).
Petit, P., *Libanius et la vie municipale à Antioche au IVe siècle après J.-C.* (Paris, 1955).

Pharr, C., *The Theodosian Code and Novels and the Sirmondian Constitutions* (Princeton, NJ, 1952: repr. New York, 1969).
Pietri, C., *Roma Christiana* (Rome, 1976).
Pietri, L., 'Les Abbés de basilique dans la Gaule de VIe siècle', *RHEF* 69 (1983), 5–28.
—— 'Bâtiments et sanctuaires annexes de la Basilique Saint-Martin de Tours, à la fin du VIe siècle', *RHEF* 62 (1975), 223–34.
Pollock, F., Maitland, F. W., *History of English Law*[2] (Cambridge, 1968).
Pontal, O., *Die Synoden im Merowingerreich* (Paderborn, 1986).
Pounds, N. J. G., *An Historical Geography of Europe* (London, 1990).
Puliatti, S., *Richerche sulle Novelle di Giustino II*, i (Milan, 1984).
Quinn, J. M., 'Anti-Manichean and Other Moral Precisions in *Confessions* 3.7.12–9.17', *Augustinian Studies*, 19 (1988), 165–94.
Rabello, A. M., 'Il problema dei matrimoni fra ebrei e Cristiani nella legislazione imperiale e in quella della chiesa (IV-VI s.)', *Atti dell'Accademia Romanistica Constantiniana*, 2 (1988), 213–24.
Rathbone, D., *Economic Rationalism and Rural Society in Third-Century Egypt: The Heroninos Archive and the Appianus Estate* (Cambridge, 1991).
Rauschen, G., *Jahrbücher der Christlichen Kirche* (Freiburg, 1897).
Rees, B. R., *Pelagius: A Reluctant Heretic* (Woodbridge, 1988).
Richlin, A., 'Invective against Women in Roman Satire', *Arethusa*, 17 (1984), 67–80.
Roberts, S., *Order and Dispute: An Introduction to Legal Anthropology* (London, 1979).
Robinson, O. F., *The Criminal Law of Ancient Rome* (London, 1995).
Rosa Cimma, M., *L'episcopalis audientia nelle costituzioni imperiali da Costantino a Giustiniano* (Turin, 1989).
Rösch, G., *Onoma basileias. Studien zum offiziellen Gebrauch der Kaisertitel in spätantiker und frühbyzantinischer Zeit* (Vienna, 1978).
Rosenwein, B., *Negotiating Space: Power, Restraint, and the Privileges of Immunity in Early Medieval Europe* (Ithaca, 1998).
Rouche, M., 'The Early Middle Ages in the West', in P. Veyne (ed.), *A History of Private Life*, i (Cambridge, Mass., 1987), 465 ff.
Roueché, C., *Performers and Partisans at Aphrodisias in the Roman and Late Roman Periods* (London, 1993).
Rougé, J., 'Escroquerie et brigandage en Afrique romaine au temps de Saint Augustin (*Epist.* 8* et 10*)', in *Les Lettres de saint Augustin*, 177–88.

Rubin, Z., 'Mass Movement in Late Antiquity: Appearances and Realities', in I. Malkin, Z. W. Rubinsohn (eds.), *Leaders and Masses in the Roman World: Studies in Honor of Zvi Yavetz* (Leyden, 1995), 156–68.

Rubin, Z., 'The Reforms of Khusro Anushirwan', in Av. Cameron (ed.), *The Byzantine and Early Islamic Near East,* iii. *States, Resources and Armies* (Princeton, 1995), 227–97.

Rüpke, J., *Kalender und Öffentlichkeit* (Berlin, 1995).

Ryberg, I. S., *The Panel Reliefs of Marcus Aurelius* (New York, 1967).

—— *Rites of the State Religion in Roman Art* (Rome, 1955).

Sachau, E., (ed.), *Syrische Rechtsbücher*, ii (Berlin, 1908).

Saint-Roch, P., *La Pénitence dans les conciles et les lettres des papes des origines à la mort de Grégoire Le Grand* (Rome, 1991).

Saller, R., *Patriarchy, Property, and Death in the Roman Family* (Cambridge, 1994).

Salzman, M., *On Roman Time: The Codex-Calendar of 354 and the Rhythms of Urban Life in Late Antiquity* (Berkeley, 1990).

—— 'The Christianization of Sacred Time and Sacred Space', in Harris (ed.), *Transformations*, 125 ff.

Sargenti, M., Bruno Siola, R. B., *Normativa imperiale e diritto romani negli scritti di S. Ambroggio* (Milan, 1991).

Schaffner, P., 'Britain's *Iudices*', in Lapidge and Dumville (eds.), *Gildas*, 151 ff.

Schott, C., 'Der Stand der Leges-Forschung', *Frühmittelalterliche Studien*, 13 (1979), 29–55.

Schulz, F., *History of Roman Legal Science* (Oxford, 1953).

Schulz, R., *Die Entwicklung des römischen Völkerrechts im vierten und fünften Jahrhundert n. Chr.* (Stuttgart, 1993).

Schürer, E., *The History of the Jewish People in the Age of Jesus Christ*, rev. edn. (2 vols.; Edinburgh, 1979).

Schwartz, E., 'Die Kanonessammlungen der alter Reichskirche', *ZSS KA* 25 (1936), 61 ff.

Seebohm, F., *The Tribal System in Wales* (London, 1895).

Seeck, O., *Geschichte des Untergangs der antiken Welt*, iii (Berlin, 1921).

—— *Regesten der Kaiser und Päpste für die Jahre 311 bis 476 n. Chr.* (Stuttgart, 1919).

Selb, W., 'Episcopalis audientia von der Zeit Konstantins bis zur Nov. XXXV Valentinians III.', *ZSS RA* 84 (1967), 162–217.

Sellew, P., 'Achilles or Christ? Porphyry and Didymus in Debate over Allegorical Interpretation', *Harvard Theological Review*, 82 (1979), 79–100.

Sider, R. D., *Ancient Rhetoric and the Art of Tertullian* (Oxford, 1971).
Sirks, A. J. B., 'La laesio enormis en droit romain et byzantin', *Tijdschrift voor Rechtsgeschiedenis*, 53 (1989), 296–8.
—— 'Reconsidering the Roman Colonate', *ZSS RA* 110 (1993), 331–69.
—— 'Shifting Frontiers in the Law: Romans, Provincials, and Barbarians', in Mathisen and Sivan (eds.), *Shifting Frontiers*, 146–57.
—— 'Sources of the Code', in Harries and Wood (eds.), *Theodosian Code*, 45–67.
Sivan, H. S., 'Rabbinics and Roman Perspectives', *Revue des études juives*, 156 (1997).
—— 'On Hymens and Holiness in Late Antiquity', *JAC* 36 (1993), 81–93.
—— 'Why not Marry a Barbarian? Marital Frontiers in Late Antiquity (The example of *CTh* 3.14.1)', in Mathisen and Sivan (eds.), *Shifting Frontiers*, 136–45.
Stein, E., *Histoire du bas-empire*, trans. J.-R. Palanque (2 vols.; Paris, 1949).
Steinwenter, A., 'Zur Lehre von der episcopalis audientia', *BZ* 30 (1929), 660–8.
Stevens, C. E., 'A Possible Conflict of Laws in Roman Britain', *JRS* 37 (1947), 132–4.
Stickler, A. M., *Historia iuris canonici latina* (Rome, 1974).
Stock, B., *Augustine the Reader: Meditation, Self-Knowledge and the Ethics of Interpretation* (Harvard, 1996).
Strewe, A., *Die Canonessammlung des Dionysius Exiguus in der ersten Redaktion* (Berlin, 1931).
Syme, R., *Ten Studies in Tacitus* (Oxford, 1970).
Szidat, J., 'Zum Sklavenhandel in der Spätantike (Aug. epist. 10*)', *Historia*, 34 (1985), 560–71.
TeBrake, W. H., *Medieval Frontier: Culture and Ecology in Rijnland* (College Station, Tex., 1985).
—— 'Ecology and Economy in Early-Medieval Frisia', *Viator*, 9/1 (1978), 16–23.
Thomas, C., *And Shall these Mute Stones Speak? Post-Roman Inscriptions in Western Britain* (Cardiff, 1994).
—— *Celtic Britain* (London, 1986).
Thompson, E. A., 'Gildas and the History of Britain', *Britannia*, 10 (1979), 303–18.
Tibbetts Schulenberg, J., 'Strict Active Enclosure and Its Effects on the Female Monastic Experience (ca. 500–1100)', in J. Nichols,

L. Thomas Shank (eds.), *Medieval Religious Women*, i. *Distant Echoes* (Kalamazoo, 1984), 51–86.

Tjäder, J.-O., *Die nichtliterarischen Papyri Italiens aus der Zeit 475–700* (2 vols.; Stockholm, 1982).

Treggiari, S., *Roman Marriage: Iusti Coniuges from the Time of Cicero to the Time of Ulpian* (Oxford, 1991).

Ullmann, W., *The Church and the Law in the Earlier Middle Ages: Selected Essays* (London, 1975).

—— 'Public Welfare and Social Legislation in the Early Medieval Councils', in G. J. Cuming, D. Baker (eds.), *Councils and Assemblies* (Cambridge, 1971), 1–35.

Urbainczyk, T., *Socrates of Constantinople* (Ann Arbor, 1997).

Vanzetti, M. Bianchi-Fossati, *Le novelle di Valentiniano III. I Fonti* (Padua, 1988).

Vera, D., 'Simmaco e le sue proprietà: struttura e funzionamento di un patrimonio aristocratico del quarto secolo d.C', in F. Paschoud (ed.), *Symmaque* (Paris, 1986), 231–76.

Vidén, G., *The Roman Chancery Tradition: Studies in the Language of Codex Theodosianus and Cassiodorus' Variae* (Göteborg, 1984).

Vismara, G., *Edictum Theodorici* (Milan, 1967).

—— *Episcopalis audientia* (Milan, 1937).

—— 'Le *causae liberales* nel tribunale di Agostino vescovo di Ippona', *Studia et documenta historiae et iuris*, 61 (1995), 365–72.

Vives, J., (ed.), *Concilios visigóticos e hispanco-romanos* (Barcelona, 1963).

Vogler, C., 'Les Juifs dans le Code Theodosien', *Le Point Theologique*, 33 (1979), 52 ff.

Vööbus, A., *The Canons Ascribed to Maruta of Maipherkat and Related Sources*, *CSCO* vols. 439–40, *Scriptores Syri*, vols. 191–2 (Louvain, 1982).

—— *Celibacy, A Requirement for Admission to Baptism in the Early Syrian Church* (Stockholm, 1951).

—— 'A Calculation of Inheritances', in A. Vööbus (ed.), *The Synodicon in the West Syrian Tradition*, ii (Louvain, 1976), 68–87.

—— 'The Computation of Inheritance of the Arabs', in *The Synodicon in the West Syrian Tradition*, ii (Louvain, 1976), 95–7.

—— 'Les Messalliens et les réformes de Barçauma de Nisibe dans l'église perse', *Contributions of Baltic University*, 34 (1947), 1–27.

—— trans., *Syriac and Arabic Documents Regarding Legislation Relative to Syrian Asceticism* (Stockholm, 1960).

Voss, W. E., *Recht und Rhetorik in den Kaisergesetzen der Spätantike: Eine Untersuchung zum nachklassischen Kauf- und Übereignungsrecht* (Frankfurt-am-Main, 1982).

Wacke, A., 'The Potentiores: Some Relations between Power and Law in the Roman Administration of Justice', *Irish Jurist*, 13 (1978), 372–89.

Wallace-Hadrill, J. M., *The Frankish Church* (Oxford, 1983).

Watson, A. M., *Roman Slave Law* (Baltimore, 1987).

—— 'Towards Denser and More Continuous Settlement: New Crops and Farming Techniques in the Early Middle Ages', in J. A. Raftis (ed.), *Pathways to Medieval Peasants* (Toronto, 1981).

Wemple, S., *Women in Frankish Society: Marriage and the Cloister, 500–900* (Philadelphia, 1981).

Whitby, M., *The Emperor Maurice and his Historian* (Oxford, 1988).

—— 'Greek Historical Writing after Procopius: Variety and Vitality', in Av. Cameron, L. Conrad (eds.), *The Byzantine and Early Islamic Near East,* i. *Problems in the Literary Source Material* (Princeton, 1992).

Wickham, C., *Early Medieval Italy: Central Power and Local Society 400–1000* (London, 1981).

Wieacker, F., 'Lateinische Kommentare im Codex Theodosianus', in *Symbolae Freiburgenses* (Leipzig, 1933), 259 ff.

Wieling, H., 'Iniusta lex Maioriani', *RIDA* 38 (1991), 385–420.

Wild, J. P., 'The Gynaecea', in R. Goodburn, P. Bartholomew (eds.), *Aspects of the Notitia Dignitatum* (*BAR IS*, Supp. 15) (Oxford 1976), 57–98.

—— 'The Gynaeceum at Venta and its Context', *Latomus*, 26 (1967), 648–76.

Wilson, N. G., *Scholars of Byzantium* (London, 1983).

Winterbottom M., trans., *Gildas, The Ruin of Britain and Other Works* (Chichester, 1978).

Wiseman, T. P., 'Practice and Theory in Roman Historiography', *History*, 218 (1981), 375–90.

Wolfram, H., *The Roman Empire and its Germanic Peoples*, T. J. Dunlap trans. (Berkeley, 1997).

—— *History of the Goths*, trans. T. J. Dunlap (Berkeley, 1988).

Wood, I., *The Merovingian Kingdoms 450–751* (London, 1994).

—— 'The Code in Merovingian Gaul', in Harries and Wood (eds.), *Theodosian Code*, 161–77.

Wurm, H., *Studien und Texte zur Dekretalensammlung des Dionysius Exiguus* (Amsterdam, 1964).

Zeumer, K., 'Geschichte der westgotischen Gesetzgebung I-IV', *Neues Archiv der Gesellschaft für ältere deutsche Geschichtskunde*, 23 (1898), 419–516; 24 (1899), 39–122, 571–630; 26 (1901), 91–149.

Zulueta, F. de, (ed.), *The Institutes of Gaius* (Oxford, 1946).

Index